P9-CEH-112

588 Home-Style Recipes—Including Top Award Winners

THIS COOKBOOK, *2002 Taste of Home Annual Recipes*, is destined to become one of the most treasured in your collection because it's chock-full of family-favorite recipes shared by good cooks across North America.

Here you'll find all 552 recipes published during 2001 in *Taste of Home*—the most popular cooking magazine in the country—plus 36 bonus recipes. That's 588 in all!

No matter if you're fixing a weeknight dinner for your family, planning a cozy supper for two or cooking for a holiday crowd, you'll have plenty of great recipes from which to choose. To get you started, here's a look at the winners of our six national recipe contests.

• **Chill-Chasing Chili.** Go ahead and chase away the doldrums, too, with a dozen deliciously different recipes for chili. The aroma of first-place winner Pepperoni Pizza Chili (p. 36) and second-place Creamy White Chili (p. 36) will have you thinking about seconds before you've even had your first spoonful.

• **Tempting Tomatoes.** Get "reddy" to savor fresh-from-the-vine tomatoes. Those late-summer treats star in aptly named Best-of-Show Tomato Quiche (p. 65) and second-place Tomato-Onion Phyllo Pizza (p. 20).

• **Bravo for Brunch.** If you think breakfast isn't all it's cracked up to be, we know eggs-actly how to change your mind: Croissant French Toast (p. 82) and Ham 'n' Cheese Omelet Roll (p. 63).

• **Chip off the Gold Block.** For dessert recipes that are as good as gold, start with morsels of chocolate, vanilla or butterscotch. The top contest honor went to Three-Chip English Toffee (p. 140), and Raspberry Almond Bars (p. 115) came in a delectable second.

• **Marvelous Meat Pies.** If getting to the "meat" of the matter is your priority, try a savory pie as the main event at your next meal. Chicken in Potato Baskets (p. 76) gobbled up first prize, while Spinach-Beef Spaghetti Pie (p. 76) earned a hearty second-place finish.

• **Classic & Classy Cakes.** With more than 9,000 contest entries, this category was a toughie. The winning cakes, however, are tender, tasty and absolutely terrific: Toffee-Mocha Cream Torte (p. 125) and Strawberry Nut Roll (p. 124). As a matter of fact, each runner-up is a slice of heaven, too.

With 588 recipes in this big book, you won't run out of choices any time soon. You can do lots of mixing and matching to create your own family's favorites. You're sure to find something special for everyone and every occasion.

WINNING WAYS. Croissant French Toast (p. 82) won the Grand Prize and Ham 'n' Cheese Omelet Roll (p. 63) took second place in our national brunch recipe contest.

2002 Taste of Home Annual Recipes

Editor: Heidi Reuter Lloyd
Art Director: Kristin Bork
Food Editor: Janaan Cunningham
Associate Editors: Julie Schnittka, Jean Steiner, Susan Uphill, Kristine Krueger
Food Photography Artists: Stephanie Marchese, Vicky Marie Moseley
Art Associates: Linda Dzik, Ellen Lloyd
Production: Catherine Fletcher

Taste of Home®

Executive Editor: Kathy Pohl
Food Editor: Janaan Cunningham
Associate Food Editors: Diane Werner, Coleen Martin
Senior Recipe Editor: Sue A. Jurack
Test Kitchen Director: Karen Johnson
Managing Editor: Ann Kaiser
Assistant Managing Editor: Faithann Stoner
Associate Editors: Kristine Krueger, Sharon Selz
Test Kitchen Home Economists: Pat Schmeling, Sue Draheim, Peggy Fleming, Julie Herzfeldt, Joylyn Jans, Kristin Koepnick, Mark Morgan, Wendy Stenman, Karen Wright
Test Kitchen Assistants: Kris Lehman, Megan Taylor
Editorial Assistants: Barb Czysz, Mary Ann Koebernik
Design Director: Jim Sibilski
Art Director: Emma Acevedo
Food Photography: Rob Hagen, Dan Roberts
Food Photography Artists: Stephanie Marchese, Vicky Marie Moseley
Photo Studio Manager: Anne Schimmel
Production: Ellen Lloyd, Catherine Fletcher
Publisher: Roy Reiman

5400 S. 60th St., Greendale WI 53129

International Standard Book Number: 0-89821-322-3
International Standard Serial Number: 1094-3463

PICTURED AT RIGHT. Clockwise from upper left: Lemon Ice Cream (p. 142); Rosemary Cashew Chicken and Pork Chop Dinner (p. 62); Colorful Fruit Kabobs (p. 28); Honey Garlic Chicken, Citrus Rice Pilaf and Pineapple Angel Dessert (p. 258).

Taste of Home 2002 Annual Recipes

PICTURED ON FRONT COVER. Clockwise from top: Chocolate Chip Pound Cake (p. 126), California Pepper Chili (p. 39) and Buttery Corn Bread (p. 99).

PICTURED ON BACK COVER. Clockwise from top: Butterscotch Delight (p. 145), Pear Melba Dumplings (p. 145), and Coconut Peach Dessert (p. 143).

FOR ADDITIONAL COPIES of this book, write *Taste of Home* Books, P.O. Box 908, Greendale WI 53129.
To order by credit card, call toll-free 1-800/344-2560 or visit our Web site at www.reimanpub.com.

Snacks & Beverages

Turn to this chapter when you want something different and delicious to munch on or when you're looking for a special appetizer or beverage to start a meal.

BEAUTIFUL BEGINNINGS. Clockwise from upper left: Pineapple Iced Tea (p. 8), Smoked Salmon Cherry Tomatoes (p. 7), Soft Giant Pretzels (p. 16), Sweet 'n' Hot Mustard Dip (p. 21), Fancy Berry Beverage (p. 11) and Garden Focaccia (p. 9).

Veggie Party Pizza

(Pictured below)

I originally made this yummy veggie pizza to share with a friend who was watching her cholesterol, but it's so good, I serve it to my family often. Even the kids like to munch on it and ask for it. —*Laura Kadlec*
Maiden Rock, Wisconsin

 Uses less fat, sugar or salt. Includes Nutritional Analysis and Diabetic Exchanges.

2 cups all-purpose flour
2 teaspoons baking powder
1 teaspoon salt
2/3 cup fat-free milk
1/4 cup plus 1 tablespoon canola oil, *divided*

TOPPING:

3 cups 2% cottage cheese
1 envelope ranch salad dressing mix
1/2 cup fat-free mayonnaise *or* salad dressing
1/4 cup fat-free milk
1-1/2 cups chopped broccoli
1-1/2 cups chopped cauliflower
1/2 cup chopped celery
1/3 cup shredded carrot
1/4 cup chopped onion
2 cups (8 ounces) shredded part-skim mozzarella cheese
Sliced ripe *or* stuffed olives, optional

For crust, combine flour, baking powder and salt. Add milk and 1/4 cup oil; mix well. Shape into a ball; knead 10 times. Press onto the bottom and up the sides of an ungreased 15-in. x 10-in. x 1-in. baking pan. Prick with a fork; brush with remaining oil. Bake at 425° for 12-14 minutes or until edges are lightly browned. Cool.

In a mixing bowl, combine cottage cheese, ranch dressing mix, mayonnaise and milk; spread over crust. Sprinkle with vegetables and cheese. Garnish with olives if desired. Refrigerate until serving. **Yield:** 14 servings.

Nutritional Analysis: One serving (calculated without olives) equals 234 calories, 11 g fat (3 g saturated fat), 15 mg cholesterol, 592 mg sodium, 21 g carbohydrate, 1 g fiber, 14 g protein. **Diabetic Exchanges:** 2 vegetable, 1 starch, 1 lean meat, 1 fat.

"DE-LIGHT-FUL" FINGER FOOD for the holidays or other occasions includes Garden Vegetable Spread, Veggie Party Pizza and Seasoned Snack Mix (shown above, clockwise from upper right).

Garden Vegetable Spread

(Pictured below left)

Tempt your guests with this crunchy spread. It's also a delicious dip. —Jan Woodall, Cadiz, Kentucky

☑ Uses less fat, sugar or salt. Includes Nutritional Analysis and Diabetic Exchanges.

1 carton (8 ounces) fat-free spreadable cream cheese
1/2 cup finely chopped green pepper
2 celery ribs, finely chopped
2 medium carrots, finely chopped
6 radishes, finely chopped
4 teaspoons finely chopped onion
1 teaspoon dill weed
Snack toast *and/or* pita bread

In a bowl, combine the first seven ingredients. Serve on snack toast and/or pita bread. Store in the refrigerator. **Yield:** 3 cups.

Nutritional Analysis: One serving (2 tablespoons of spread) equals 14 calories, trace fat (trace saturated fat), 1 mg cholesterol, 59 mg sodium, 2 g carbohydrate, trace fiber, 2 g protein. **Diabetic Exchange:** Free food.

Seasoned Snack Mix

(Pictured at left)

I keep this well-seasoned party mix on hand for whenever "the munchies" strike. It's a light alternative to traditional holiday snack mixes. —Flo Burtnett Gage, Oklahoma

☑ Uses less fat, sugar or salt. Includes Nutritional Analysis and Diabetic Exchanges.

3 cups Rice Chex
3 cups Corn Chex
3 cups Cheerios
3 cups pretzels
2 teaspoons Worcestershire sauce
2 teaspoons butter-flavored sprinkles
1/2 teaspoon garlic powder
1/2 teaspoon seasoned salt
1/2 teaspoon onion powder

In a 15-in. x 10-in. x 1-in. baking pan, combine cereals and pretzels. Lightly coat with nonstick cooking spray; drizzle with Worcestershire sauce. Combine the remaining ingredients and sprinkle over cereal mixture. Bake at 200° for 1-1/2 hours, stirring every 30 minutes. Cool completely. Store in an airtight container. **Yield:** 3 quarts.

Nutritional Analysis: One serving (1 cup) equals 115 calories, 1 g fat (trace saturated fat), 0 cholesterol, 400 mg sodium, 25 g carbohydrate, 1 g fiber, 3 g protein. **Diabetic Exchange:** 1-1/2 starch.

Smoked Salmon Cherry Tomatoes

(Pictured on page 4)

These bright red festive bites are a showstopping finger food during the holiday season. To "lighten" them, simply use reduced-fat or fat-free cream cheese. —Pat Cronin, APO, Paris, France

30 cherry tomatoes
3 ounces smoked salmon, finely chopped
1/3 cup finely chopped onion
1/3 cup finely chopped green pepper
Salt and pepper to taste
1 package (3 ounces) cream cheese, softened
1 teaspoon milk
Fresh dill sprigs

Cut a thin slice off each tomato top; scoop out and discard pulp. Invert tomatoes on paper towels to drain. In a bowl, combine salmon, onion, green pepper, salt and pepper; mix well. Spoon into tomatoes. In a small mixing bowl, beat cream cheese and milk until smooth. Insert a star tip into a pastry or plastic bag. Pipe a small amount of cream cheese mixture onto tomatoes. Garnish with dill. **Yield:** 2-1/2 dozen.

Sausage-Stuffed Mushrooms

These savory mushrooms taste a bit like pizza. They're a flavorful prelude to an Italian dinner or a nice light meal with garlic bread and a salad. —Kathy Andrews Winter Springs, Florida

24 large fresh mushrooms
1 pound bulk Italian sausage
1/2 cup chopped green onions
1 cup spaghetti sauce
1 cup (4 ounces) shredded mozzarella cheese

Remove mushroom stems; set caps aside. Chop stems; set aside. In a skillet, cook sausage over medium heat until no longer pink; remove with a slotted spoon. In the drippings, saute onions and chopped mushroom stems. Stir in spaghetti sauce and sausage. Stuff into mushroom caps. Sprinkle with cheese. Place in a greased 15-in. x 10-in. x 1-in. baking pan. Bake at 350° for 12-15 minutes or until cheese is melted. **Yield:** 2 dozen.

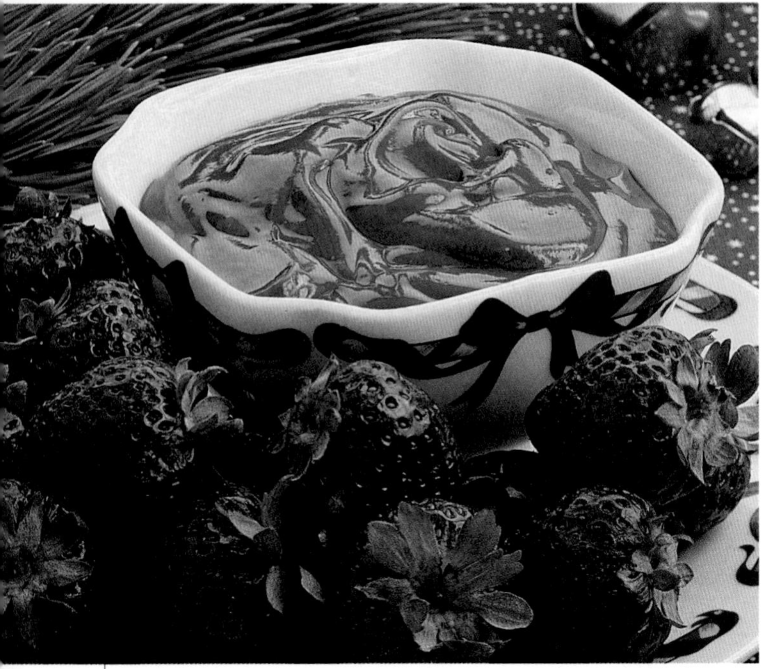

Fudgy Fruit Dip

(Pictured above)

This rich chocolaty dip is especially nice at holiday gatherings or served with fresh strawberries.
—Wilma Knobloch, Steen, Minnesota

✓ Uses less fat, sugar or salt. Includes Nutritional Analysis and Diabetic Exchanges.

1/3 cup fat-free sugar-free hot fudge topping
1/3 cup fat-free vanilla yogurt
1-1/2 teaspoons orange juice concentrate
Fresh strawberries

In a bowl, combine fudge topping, yogurt and orange juice concentrate. Cover and refrigerate for at least 30 minutes. Serve with strawberries. **Yield:** about 1/2 cup.

Nutritional Analysis: One serving (2 tablespoons of dip) equals 67 calories, trace fat (trace saturated fat), trace cholesterol, 32 mg sodium, 15 g carbohydrate, trace fiber, 1 g protein. **Diabetic Exchanges:** 1/2 starch, 1/2 fruit.

Pineapple Iced Tea

(Pictured on page 4)

With five teenagers, we go through lots of beverages. This thirst-quenching tea is easy to mix up and has a sparkling citrus flavor we all enjoy. *—Kathy Kittell Lenexa, Kansas*

✓ Uses less fat, sugar or salt. Includes Nutritional Analysis and Diabetic Exchanges.

1 quart water
7 individual tea bags
1 cup unsweetened pineapple juice
1/3 cup lemon juice
2 tablespoons sugar

In a saucepan, bring water to a boil. Remove from the heat. Add tea bags; cover and steep for 3-5 minutes. Discard tea bags. Stir in the pineapple juice, lemon juice and sugar until sugar is dissolved. Refrigerate overnight for the flavors to blend. Serve over ice. **Yield:** 5 servings.

Nutritional Analysis: One serving (1 cup) equals 51 calories, 0 fat (0 saturated fat), 0 cholesterol, 1 mg sodium, 13 g carbohydrate, 0 fiber, 0 protein. **Diabetic Exchange:** 1 fruit.

Cheese Wedges

These easy cheesy treats are always a hit at evening gatherings. *—Jennifer Eilts, Omaha, Nebraska*

1 package (7 ounces) extra sharp cheddar cheese
1/3 cup seasoned dry bread crumbs
1/2 teaspoon crushed red pepper flakes, optional
1 egg
1 can (8 ounces) pizza sauce, warmed

Cut cheese into 1/2-in. slices; cut each slice in half diagonally. In a shallow bowl, combine bread crumbs and red pepper flakes if desired. In another bowl, beat egg. Dip cheese triangles into egg, then in crumb mixture. Place on a greased baking sheet. Broil 4 in. from heat for 2-3 minutes or until browned and cheese begins to melt. Serve warm with pizza sauce for dipping. **Yield:** 6 servings.

Cayenne Pretzels

These easy-to-coat well-seasoned pretzels were a huge hit at my daughter's graduation party. The longer they sit, the spicier they get! *—Gayle Zebo Warren, Pennsylvania*

1 cup vegetable oil
1 envelope ranch salad dressing mix
1 teaspoon garlic salt
1 teaspoon cayenne pepper
2 packages (10 ounces *each*) pretzel sticks

In a small bowl, combine the oil, dressing mix, garlic salt and cayenne. Divide pretzels between two ungreased 15-in. x 10-in. x 1-in. baking pans. Pour oil mixture over pretzels; stir to coat. Bake at 200°

for 1-1/4 to 1-1/2 hours or until golden brown, stirring occasionally. Cool completely. Store in an airtight container. **Yield:** 3-1/2 quarts.

Garden Focaccia

(Pictured on page 4)

Frozen bread dough is the convenient base for this herb-flavored flat Italian bread. These savory slices are a super appetizer. *—Mary Ann Ludwig Edwardsville, Illinois*

✓ Uses less fat, sugar or salt. Includes Nutritional Analysis and Diabetic Exchanges.

1 loaf (1 pound) frozen bread dough, thawed
1 tablespoon olive *or* vegetable oil
1 tablespoon minced fresh rosemary *or* 1 teaspoon dried rosemary, crushed
1 tablespoon minced fresh thyme *or* 1 teaspoon dried thyme
1 package (8 ounces) cream cheese, softened
1/4 cup finely chopped onion
1 garlic clove, minced
4 large fresh mushrooms, sliced
3 medium tomatoes, sliced
1 small zucchini, thinly sliced
1/4 cup grated Parmesan cheese

On a lightly floured surface, roll dough into a 15-in. x 10-in. rectangle. Place in a greased 15-in. x 10-in. x 1-in. baking pan. Cover and let rise for 30 minutes. Using your fingertips, press indentations into the dough. Brush with oil; sprinkle with rosemary and thyme.

Bake at 400° for 12-15 minutes or until golden brown. Cool slightly. In a mixing bowl, combine cream cheese, onion and garlic. Spread over crust. Top with mushrooms, tomatoes and zucchini; sprinkle with Parmesan cheese. Bake for 12-15 minutes or until lightly browned. Cool for 5 minutes before cutting. **Yield:** 20 slices.

Nutritional Analysis: One slice (prepared with reduced-fat cream cheese) equals 109 calories, 4 g fat (2 g saturated fat), 7 mg cholesterol, 185 mg sodium, 14 g carbohydrate, 1 g fiber, 5 g protein. **Diabetic Exchanges:** 1 vegetable, 1 fat, 1/2 starch.

Homemade Fudge Pops

These creamy, chocolaty pops are requested often by my grandchildren—and their parents! *—Mary Detweiler, West Farmington, Ohio*

1/4 cup cornstarch
1/8 teaspoon salt
3 cups milk
1/2 cup light corn syrup
1 teaspoon vanilla extract
1 cup milk chocolate chips
12 disposable plastic cups (3 ounces)
12 Popsicle sticks

In a heavy saucepan, combine the cornstarch and salt. Gradually stir in milk until smooth. Stir in corn syrup and vanilla. Bring to a boil; cook and stir for 1 minute or until thickened. Reduce heat; stir in chocolate chips until melted. Pour into cups. Cover each cup with heavy-duty foil; insert sticks through foil. Place in a 13-in. x 9-in. x 2-in. pan. Freeze until firm. Remove foil and cups before serving. **Yield:** 1 dozen.

Corny Snack Mix

(Pictured below)

It's hard to stop munching this easy-to-make snack mix! Melted vanilla chips make a delightful coating. *—Sandy Wehring, Fremont, Ohio*

3 quarts popped popcorn
1 package (15 ounces) Corn Pops
1 package (15 ounces) corn chips
2 packages (10 to 12 ounces *each*) vanilla *or* white chips

In several large bowls, combine the popcorn, Corn Pops and corn chips. In a saucepan over medium-low heat, melt chips; stir until smooth. Pour over popcorn mixture and toss to coat. Spread in two 15-in. x 10-in. x 1-in. pans. Cool. Store in airtight containers. **Yield:** 7-1/2 quarts.

Lemon Fondue

(Pictured below)

As pretty as it is luscious, this sunshiny sauce is a lovely complement to angel food or pound cake. It's just right for a special luncheon or as a light-tasting alternative in a holiday dessert buffet. This fondue is a great choice for a fondue buffet. —*Diane Hixon Niceville, Florida*

1 cup sugar
1/2 cup cornstarch
1/2 teaspoon salt
4 cups water
1/2 cup butter *or* margarine
1/2 cup lemon juice
2 tablespoons grated lemon peel
Strawberries, gingerbread *and/or* bite-size meringues

WARM AND WONDERFUL, fondues range from sweet to savory with selections such as Chocolate Mallow Fondue, Cheddar Fondue and Lemon Fondue (shown above, clockwise from upper left).

In a heavy saucepan, combine the sugar, cornstarch and salt. Stir in water until smooth. Bring to a boil over medium heat; cook and stir for 1-2 minutes or until thickened. Remove from the heat; stir in the butter, lemon juice and lemon peel until butter is melted. Transfer to a fondue pot and keep warm. Serve with strawberries, gingerbread and/or meringues. **Yield:** 5 cups.

Cheddar Fondue

(Pictured at left)

This cheesy blend, sparked with mustard and Worcestershire sauce, is so tasty and creamy. Depending on what you serve with it, you've practically got a meal! Choices range from hearty bread cubes to crunchy veggies or savory sausages. —*Norene Wright Manilla, Indiana*

1/4 cup butter *or* margarine
1/4 cup all-purpose flour
1/2 teaspoon salt, optional
1/4 teaspoon pepper
1/4 teaspoon ground mustard
1/4 teaspoon Worcestershire sauce
1-1/2 cups milk
2 cups (8 ounces) shredded cheddar cheese
Bread cubes, ham cubes, bite-size sausage *and/or* broccoli florets

In a saucepan, melt butter; stir in flour, salt if desired, pepper, mustard and Worcestershire sauce until smooth. Gradually add milk. Bring to a boil; cook and stir for 2 minutes or until thickened. Reduce heat. Add cheese; cook and stir until melted. Transfer to a fondue pot or slow cooker; keep warm. Serve with bread, ham, sausage and/or broccoli. **Yield:** 2-1/2 cups.

Chocolate Mallow Fondue

(Pictured at left)

This sweet, velvety chocolate blend makes a wonderful coating for fresh fruit and cake cubes. Don't be surprised if guests scrape the pot clean! —*June Mullins Livonia, Missouri*

2 cups (12 ounces) semisweet chocolate chips
1 can (14 ounces) sweetened condensed milk
1 jar (7 ounces) marshmallow creme
1/2 cup milk
1 teaspoon vanilla extract
Pineapple *or* banana chunks, apple slices, marshmallows, cubed angel food *or* pound cake

In a microwave or heavy saucepan, heat the first five ingredients just until melted; whisk until smooth. Transfer to a fondue pot and keep warm. Serve with fruit and/or cake. **Yield:** 4 cups.

Fancy Berry Beverage

(Pictured on page 4)

We offer this fruity beverage to guests to add a festive touch to holiday gatherings. It pours up frothy, then separates into a dark pink base with a light foamy top. It's wonderful with home-baked cookies.
—*Christine Wilson, Sellersville, Pennsylvania*

2 quarts cranberry juice, chilled
1 quart vanilla ice cream, softened
1 package (10 ounces) frozen sweetened sliced strawberries, thawed and pureed
1-1/4 cups sugar
1 teaspoon vanilla extract
2 cups whipping cream, whipped
1 quart ginger ale, chilled
Fresh strawberries, optional

In a large bowl or container, combine the first five ingredients; stir until smooth and the sugar is dissolved. Fold in whipped cream. Slowly add ginger ale and stir gently to mix. Pour into glasses. Garnish with strawberries if desired. Serve immediately. **Yield:** 5 quarts.

Apple Brickle Dip

I first tasted this quick dip years ago at a friend's Christmas party. I kept going back for more and eventually asked for the recipe. I've been making it for snacks and special occasions ever since.
—*Karen Wydrinski, Woodstock, Georgia*

1 package (8 ounces) cream cheese, softened
1/2 cup packed brown sugar
1/4 cup sugar
1 teaspoon vanilla extract
1 package almond brickle chips (7-1/2 ounces) *or* English toffee bits (10 ounces)
3 medium tart apples, cut into chunks

In a mixing bowl, beat cream cheese, sugars and vanilla. Fold in brickle chips. Serve with apples. Refrigerate any leftovers. **Yield:** 2 cups.

Mini Mexican Quiches

(Pictured above)

This fun finger food is great for a brunch, shower, party or whenever you want to munch a yummy treat. —Linda Hendrix, Moundville, Missouri

1/2 cup butter *or* margarine, softened
1 package (3 ounces) cream cheese, softened
1 cup all-purpose flour
1 cup (4 ounces) shredded Monterey Jack cheese
1 can (4 ounces) chopped green chilies, drained
2 eggs
1/2 cup whipping cream
1/4 teaspoon salt
1/8 teaspoon pepper

In a mixing bowl, cream butter and cream cheese. Add flour; beat until well blended. Shape into 24 balls; cover and refrigerate for 1 hour. Press balls onto the bottom and up the sides of greased miniature muffin cups. Sprinkle a rounded teaspoonful of cheese and 1/2 teaspoon of chilies into each shell. In a bowl, beat eggs, cream, salt and pepper. Spoon into shells. Bake at 350° for 30-35 minutes or until golden brown. Let stand for 5 minutes before serving. Refrigerate leftovers. **Yield:** 2 dozen.

Cranberry Cheese Spread

Here's a creamy sweet and tart spread that's so pretty to put on a holiday buffet. With its jewel-toned cranberry topping, it has a festive look and flavor that truly suits the season. —Nancy Johnson Laverne, Oklahoma

1 package (8 ounces) cream cheese, softened
1/2 cup sour cream
2 tablespoons honey
1/4 teaspoon ground cinnamon
1 can (16 ounces) whole-berry cranberry sauce
1/3 cup slivered almonds, toasted
Assorted crackers

In a small mixing bowl, beat the cream cheese, sour cream, honey and cinnamon until smooth. Spread onto a serving dish or plate. In a bowl, stir cranberry sauce until it reaches spreading consistency; spread over cream cheese mixture. Sprinkle with almonds. Cover and refrigerate for 2-3 hours. Serve with crackers. **Yield:** 12-14 servings.

Sweet Sausage Rolls

It's hard to stop eating these savory sausage rolls in a sweet nutty glaze. —Lori Cabuno, Poland, Ohio

1 tube (8 ounces) refrigerated crescent rolls
24 miniature smoked sausage links
1/2 cup butter *or* margarine, melted
1/2 cup chopped nuts
3 tablespoons honey
3 tablespoons brown sugar

Unroll crescent dough and separate into triangles; cut each lengthwise into three triangles. Place a sausage on the long end and roll up tightly; set aside. Combine the remaining ingredients in an 11-in. x 7-in. x 2-in. baking dish. Arrange sausage rolls, seam side down, in butter mixture. Bake, uncovered, at 400° for 15-20 minutes or until golden brown. **Yield:** 2 dozen.

Nutty Toffee Popcorn

I use pretty holiday tins to deliver this sweetly coated popcorn-nut crunch to family and friends on my Christmas list. It's a different sort of from-the-kitchen treat. —Glenna Hale, Sceptre, Saskatchewan

10 cups popped popcorn
1 cup pecan halves, toasted
1 cup whole unblanched almonds, toasted
1-1/3 cups packed brown sugar
1 cup butter (no substitutes)
1/2 cup light corn syrup
1/2 teaspoon cream of tartar

1/2 teaspoon baking soda
1/2 teaspoon rum extract

In a large bowl, combine the popcorn and nuts. In a heavy saucepan, combine the brown sugar, butter, corn syrup and cream of tartar; stir until sugar is dissolved. Cook, without stirring, over medium heat until a candy thermometer reads 300°-310° (hard-crack stage).

Remove from the heat; stir in baking soda and extract. Immediately pour over popcorn mixture; toss gently. Spread into two greased 15-in. x 10-in. x 1-in. baking pans. Press gently to flatten. Cool completely. Break into pieces. **Yield:** about 2 quarts.

Editor's Note: We recommend that you test your candy thermometer before each use by bringing water to a boil; the thermometer should read 212°. Adjust your recipe temperature up or down based on your test.

Salmon Spread

No one who tastes this creamy spread can believe it's a "lighter" appetizer. It's easy to make and special enough for a holiday party. —*Sandra Chambers, Carthage, Mississippi*

✓ Uses less fat, sugar or salt. Includes Nutritional Analysis and Diabetic Exchanges.

1 carton (8 ounces) fat-free cream cheese spread
2 tablespoons grated onion
1 tablespoon lemon juice
1 teaspoon prepared horseradish
1/2 teaspoon prepared mustard
1 can (14-1/2 ounces) salmon, drained, bones and skin removed
2 tablespoons minced fresh parsley
Crackers *or* bread

In a bowl, combine the cream cheese, onion, lemon juice, horseradish and mustard. Stir in the salmon. Sprinkle with parsley. Serve with crackers or as a sandwich spread. **Yield:** 2 cups.

Nutritional Analysis: One serving (1/4 cup spread) equals 103 calories, 3 g fat (1 g saturated fat), 22 mg cholesterol, 411 mg sodium, 2 g carbohydrate, 0 fiber, 15 g protein. **Diabetic Exchange:** 2 lean meat.

Hot Reuben Dip

If you like a grilled Reuben sandwich, you'll love this warm, cheesy spread. It's wonderful on party rye bread or crackers. You'll find it's hard to stop munching this snack once you start! —*Angela Howell, Prospect Park, Pennsylvania*

1 package (8 ounces) cream cheese, softened
1/2 cup sour cream
2 tablespoons ketchup
1/2 pound deli corned beef, finely chopped
1 cup sauerkraut, chopped, rinsed and drained
1 cup (4 ounces) shredded Swiss cheese
2 tablespoons finely chopped onion
Snack rye bread *or* crackers

In a mixing bowl, beat cream cheese, sour cream and ketchup until smooth. Stir in the corned beef, sauerkraut, Swiss cheese and onion until blended. Transfer to a greased 1-qt. baking dish. Cover and bake at 375° for 30 minutes. Uncover; bake 5 minutes longer or until bubbly. Serve warm with bread or crackers. **Yield:** 3 cups.

Like 'Em Hot Wings

These spicy chicken wings are wonderfully seasoned. They're a crowd-pleasing snack, and they're easy to make. I serve them with ranch dressing for dipping. —*Myra Innes, Auburn, Kansas*

12 whole chicken wings* (about 2-1/2 pounds)
1 bottle (2 ounces) hot pepper sauce (about 1/4 cup)
1 to 2 garlic cloves, minced
1-1/2 teaspoons dried rosemary, crushed
1 teaspoon dried thyme
1/4 teaspoon salt
1/4 teaspoon pepper
Celery and carrot sticks and blue cheese salad dressing, optional

Cut chicken wings into three sections; discard wing tips. In a large resealable plastic bag, combine the hot pepper sauce, garlic and seasonings. Add wings; toss to evenly coat. Transfer to a well-greased 13-in. x 9-in. x 2-in. baking dish. Bake, uncovered, at 425° for 30-40 minutes or until chicken juices run clear, turning every 10 minutes. Serve with celery, carrots and blue cheese dressing if desired. **Yield:** 4-6 servings.

***Editor's Note:** 2 pounds of uncooked chicken wing sections may be substituted for the whole chicken wings. Omit the first step of the recipe.

Taming Sauerkraut

If canned sauerkraut tastes too briny, put it in a sieve and rinse it well under cold water. Drain well before using. If fresh kraut is too salty, soak 15 to 30 minutes in cold water, then drain well.

Hearty Taco Dip

(Pictured below)

I created this dip by accident one day when I wanted to make a taco casserole but I didn't have all the ingredients. Everyone loved it! —*Claudia Jacobsen*
Luverne, North Dakota

1 pound ground beef
1 medium onion, chopped
Dash pepper
1 pound process cheese product, cubed
1 bottle (8 ounces) taco sauce
1/4 cup water
1 medium tomato, chopped
1 medium green pepper, chopped
1 can (2-1/4 ounces) sliced ripe olives, drained
Tortilla chips

In a large saucepan over medium heat, cook the beef, onion and pepper until meat is no longer pink; drain. Add the cheese, taco sauce and water; stir until the cheese is melted. Stir in the tomato, green pepper and olives. Serve warm with tortilla chips. **Yield:** 6 cups.

PUT SOME SIZZLE into snacktime with Cheese Ball Snack Mix, Strawberry-Rhubarb Ice Pops and Hearty Taco Dip (shown above, clockwise from upper right).

Cheese Ball Snack Mix

(Pictured below left)

Folks love the burst of flavor in every bite of this snack mix. —Mary Detweiler, West Farmington, Ohio

1-1/2 cups salted cashews
1 cup crisp cheese ball snacks*
1 cup Corn Chex
1 cup Rice Chex
1 cup miniature pretzels
1 cup chow mein noodles
1/2 cup butter *or* margarine, melted
1 tablespoon soy sauce
1 teaspoon Worcestershire sauce
1/2 teaspoon seasoned salt
1/4 teaspoon chili powder
1/4 teaspoon hot pepper sauce

In a bowl, combine the first six ingredients. In another bowl, combine remaining ingredients. Pour over cereal mixture; toss to coat. Transfer to an ungreased 15-in. x 10-in. x 1-in. baking pan. Bake at 250° for 1 hour, stirring every 15 minutes. **Yield:** about 6 cups.

***Editor's Note:** This recipe was tested with Planter's Cheeze Balls.

Strawberry-Rhubarb Ice Pops

(Pictured at left)

These cool and creamy pops are a deliciously different way to use up the bounty from your rhubarb patch. —Donna Linihan, Moncton, New Brunswick

Uses less fat, sugar or salt. Includes Nutritional Analysis and Diabetic Exchanges.

3 cups chopped fresh *or* frozen rhubarb (1/2-inch pieces)
1/4 cup sugar
3 tablespoons water
1 carton (8 ounces) strawberry yogurt
1/2 cup unsweetened applesauce
1/4 cup finely chopped fresh strawberries
2 drops red food coloring, optional

In a saucepan, bring rhubarb, sugar and water to a boil. Reduce heat; simmer, uncovered, for 10-15 minutes or until mixture is blended and thick. Cool. Set aside 3/4 cup (save remaining rhubarb for another use). In a bowl, combine yogurt, applesauce, strawberries, rhubarb mixture and food coloring if desired. Fill molds or cups with about 1/4 cup fruit mixture; top with holders or insert a wooden stick into each cup. Freeze. **Yield:** 8 pops.

Nutritional Analysis: One ice pop equals 69 calories, 0 fat (0 saturated fat), 3 mg cholesterol, 17 mg sodium, 16 g carbohydrate, 1 g fiber, 2 g protein. **Diabetic Exchange:** 1 fruit.

Guacamole Tortilla Snacks

These zippy wedges always disappear quickly at get-togethers. —Rhonda Black, Salinas, California

Vegetable oil for deep-fat frying
1 dozen corn tortillas (6 inches), quartered
3 ripe avocados, peeled and mashed
3 tablespoons mayonnaise
1 medium onion, diced
1 medium tomato, diced
2 jalapeno peppers, chopped*
2 cups (8 ounces) shredded Monterey Jack, Colby-Jack *or* cheddar cheese

In an electric skillet or deep-fat fryer, heat 1 in. of oil to 375°. Fry tortilla wedges, a few at a time, until golden brown. Drain on paper towels. For guacamole, in a bowl, combine avocados, mayonnaise, onion, tomato and jalapenos. Place tortillas on ungreased baking sheets. Top each with a tablespoonful of guacamole. Sprinkle with cheese. Broil 3-4 in. from heat for 2-3 minutes or until cheese melts. Serve immediately. **Yield:** 4 dozen.

***Editor's Note:** When cutting or seeding hot peppers, use rubber or plastic gloves to protect your hands. Avoid touching your face.

Bird's Nest Snacks

My grandson, Kenny, and I had a great time fixing these sweet snacks for Easter. They look like nests with tiny eggs inside. —Donna Gonda North Canton, Ohio

3 cups miniature marshmallows
3 tablespoons butter *or* margarine
2 tablespoons peanut butter
1 can (5 ounces) chow mein noodles
36 pastel jelly beans *or* peanut M&M's
12 pastel paper cupcake liners

In a heavy saucepan over low heat, cook marshmallows, butter and peanut butter until marshmallows are melted; stir until blended. Remove from the heat; stir in chow mein noodles. Divide into 12 mounds on a waxed paper-lined pan. With lightly buttered hands, quickly shape each mound into a nest; make an indentation in the center. Fill nests with jelly beans. Trim 1/2 in. from each cupcake liner; place nests in liners. Store in an airtight container. **Yield:** 1 dozen.

Soft Giant Pretzels

(Pictured on page 4)

My friends and family love these soft, chewy pretzels. Let your bread machine mix the dough, then all you have to do is shape and bake these fun snacks.
—Sherry Peterson, Fort Collins, Colorado

1 cup plus 2 tablespoons water (70° to 80°)
3 cups all-purpose flour
3 tablespoons brown sugar
1-1/2 teaspoons active dry yeast
2 quarts water
1/2 cup baking soda
Coarse salt

In bread machine pan, place the first four ingredients in order suggested by manufacturer. Select dough setting (check dough after 5 minutes of mixing; add 1 to 2 tablespoons water or flour if needed).

When cycle is completed, turn dough onto lightly floured surface. Divide dough into eight balls. Roll each into a 20-in. rope; form into pretzel shape. In a saucepan, bring water and baking soda to a boil. Drop pretzels into boiling water, two at a time; boil for 10-15 seconds. Remove with a slotted spoon; drain on paper towels.

Place pretzels on greased baking sheets. Bake at 425° for 8-10 minutes or until golden brown. Spritz or lightly brush with water. Sprinkle with salt. **Yield:** 8 pretzels.

Hot Spinach Artichoke Dip

(Pictured at far right)

This tasty appetizer is similar to the version served in restaurants, but it has a fresh homemade flavor that keeps everyone dipping. *—Cathy Carroll Grayson, Louisiana*

1 jar (6-1/2 ounces) marinated artichoke hearts, drained and chopped
2 tablespoons chopped onion
1 tablespoon butter *or* margarine, softened
1 package (10 ounces) frozen chopped spinach, thawed and well drained
1/4 cup grated Parmesan cheese
2 cups (8 ounces) shredded Colby/Monterey Jack cheese
1/2 cup milk
3/4 teaspoon Creole seasoning
Vegetables, tortilla chips *or* crackers

In a skillet, saute artichokes and onion in butter until onion is tender. Stir in spinach and Parmesan cheese; cook over low heat until spinach is heated through. Add Colby/Monterey Jack cheese, milk and Creole seasoning; heat until the cheese is melted. Serve immediately with vegetables, tortilla chips or crackers. **Yield:** 2 cups.

Pork Egg Rolls

(Pictured below right)

I take these hearty egg rolls and their tasty sweet 'n' sour sauce to every family gathering. Everyone seems to enjoy them. —Jody Minke, Forest Lake, Minnesota

1/2 pound ground pork
3/4 cup shredded cabbage
1/2 cup chopped celery
4 green onions, sliced
3 tablespoons vegetable oil
1/2 cup salad shrimp, chopped
1/2 cup water chestnuts, chopped
1/2 cup bean sprouts, chopped
1 garlic clove, minced
2 to 3 tablespoons soy sauce
1 teaspoon sugar
8 refrigerated egg roll wrappers
Vegetable oil for frying
SWEET 'N' SOUR SAUCE:
1 cup sugar
2 tablespoons cornstarch
1 teaspoon seasoned salt
1/2 cup white vinegar
1/2 cup water
1 tablespoon maraschino cherry juice, optional
1 teaspoon Worcestershire sauce

In a large skillet, cook pork over medium heat until no longer pink; drain. Remove pork with a slotted spoon and set aside. In the same skillet, stir-fry cabbage, celery and onions in oil until crisp-tender. Add shrimp, water chestnuts, bean sprouts, garlic, soy sauce, sugar and reserved pork; stir-fry 4 minutes longer or until liquid has evaporated. Remove from heat.

Position egg roll wrappers with a corner facing you. Spoon 1/3 cup pork mixture on bottom third of each wrapper. Fold a bottom corner over filling; fold sides over filling toward center. Moisten top corner with water; roll up tightly to seal. In an electric skillet, heat 1 in. of oil to 375°. Fry egg rolls for 1-2 minutes on each side or until golden brown. Drain on paper towels.

For sauce, combine sugar, cornstarch and seasoned salt in a saucepan; gradually add the remaining ingredients. Bring to a boil; cook and stir for 2 minutes or until thickened. Serve with egg rolls. **Yield:** 8 egg rolls.

Banana Split Shakes

(Pictured below)

These velvety smooth shakes make a special snack. They taste like an ice cream sundae, only you can sip them with a straw. Kids love 'em. —Mary Detweiler West Farmington, Ohio

1/2 cup milk
1 small ripe banana, cut into chunks
10 maraschino cherries
1 tablespoon baking cocoa
1/2 teaspoon coconut extract
3 cups vanilla ice cream, softened

Place milk, banana, maraschino cherries, baking cocoa and coconut extract in a blender; cover and process until smooth. Add ice cream; cover and process until blended. Pour into chilled glasses. Serve immediately. **Yield:** 5 servings.

Sugarcoated Spanish Peanuts

It's just about impossible to stop eating these sweet peanuts. —Judy Jungwirth, Athol, South Dakota

1-1/2 cups sugar
3/4 cup water
1 tablespoon maple flavoring
4-1/2 cups Spanish peanuts with skins
1/2 teaspoon salt

In a large saucepan, combine the first four ingredients. Cook and stir over medium heat for 20 minutes or until almost all of the liquid is absorbed. Spread into a greased 15-in. x 10-in. x 1-in. baking pan; sprinkle with salt. Bake at 350° for 24-26 minutes or until peanuts are well coated, stirring two to three times. Remove to a waxed paper-lined baking sheet to cool completely. Store in an airtight container. **Yield:** 7 cups.

TEMPTING TRIO. It will be difficult to decide what to sample first if you put out Hot Spinach Artichoke Dip, Banana Split Shakes and Pork Egg Rolls (shown above, clockwise from upper left).

Banana Pineapple Slush

(Pictured below)

This sunny, tropical slush refreshes on summer days and is perfect for brunches and showers.
—Beth Myers, Lewisburg, West Virginia

✓ Uses less fat, sugar or salt. Includes Nutritional Analysis and Diabetic Exchanges.

4 cups sugar
2 cups water
1 can (46 ounces) pineapple juice
3 cups orange juice
3/4 cup lemon juice
1/2 cup orange juice concentrate
8 medium ripe bananas, mashed
2 bottles (2 liters *each*) cream soda
3 cans (12 ounces *each*) lemon-lime soda

In a saucepan, bring sugar and water to a boil over medium heat; cool. Pour into a freezer container; add juices, orange juice concentrate and bananas. Cover and freeze. To serve, thaw mixture until slushy; stir in cream soda and lemon-lime soda. **Yield:** about 9-1/2 quarts.

Nutritional Analysis: One 3/4-cup serving (prepared with sugar-free soda) equals 119 calories, 0 fat (0 saturated fat), 0 cholesterol, 23 mg sodium, 30 g carbohydrate, 1 g fiber, 0 protein. **Diabetic Exchange:** 2 fruit.

DAZZLING DRINKS. Add color and flavor to snacktime with Fruity Red Smoothies, Banana Pineapple Slush and Grape Punch (shown above, clockwise from top).

Grape Punch

(Pictured below left)

With its beautiful purple color, fruity flavor and fun fizz, this punch always prompts requests for refills. I like to serve it with Mexican and Italian foods.
—Gayle Lewis, Yucaipa, California

2 cups red grape juice, chilled
2 cups white grape juice, chilled
5 cups lemon-lime soda, chilled

In a large bowl or pitcher, combine both juices; mix well. Stir in the lemon-lime soda just before serving. **Yield:** 18 (1/2-cup) servings.

Fruity Red Smoothies

(Pictured at left)

This thick, tangy drink combines the refreshing flavors of cranberries, raspberries and strawberries. Once you start sipping it, you can't stop!
—Beverly Coyde, Gasport, New York

1 carton (8 ounces) strawberry yogurt
1/2 to 3/4 cup cranberry juice
1-1/2 cups frozen unsweetened strawberries, quartered
1 cup frozen unsweetened raspberries
1 to 1-1/2 teaspoons sugar

In a blender or food processor, combine yogurt and cranberry juice. Add strawberries, raspberries and sugar; cover and process until blended. Pour into glasses; serve immediately. **Yield:** 2 servings.

Cherry Chip Shakes

If you like the flavor of chocolate-covered cherries, you'll love this tempting shake. It's so satisfying.
—Mary Green, Circle Pines, Minnesota

3 cups vanilla ice cream *or* frozen vanilla yogurt

3 tablespoons hot fudge ice cream topping
1/4 cup miniature chocolate chips
4 maraschino cherries
Whipped topping and additional cherries

In a blender, combine the first four ingredients; cover and process until blended. Pour into tall glasses; top with a dollop of whipped topping and a cherry. **Yield:** 2 servings.

Chicken Quesadillas

Tender homemade tortillas make this savory snack extra-special. —Linda Miller, Klamath Falls, Oregon

4 cups all-purpose flour
1-1/2 teaspoons salt
1/2 teaspoon baking powder
1 cup shortening
1-1/4 cups warm water
1 cup *each* shredded cheddar, mozzarella and pepper Jack cheese
2 cups diced cooked chicken
1 cup sliced green onions
1 cup sliced ripe olives
1 can (4 ounces) chopped green chilies, drained
Salsa and sour cream

In a bowl, combine the flour, salt and baking powder. Cut in shortening until crumbly. Add enough warm water, stirring until mixture forms a ball. Let stand for 10 minutes. Divide into 28 portions. On a lightly floured surface, roll each portion into a 7-in. circle. Cook on a lightly greased griddle for 1-1/2 to 2 minutes on each side, breaking any bubbles with a toothpick if necessary. Keep warm.

In a bowl, combine the cheeses. For each quesadilla, place a tortilla on the griddle; sprinkle with about 2 tablespoons cheese mixture, 2 tablespoons chicken, 1 tablespoon onions, 1 tablespoon olives and 1 teaspoon chilies. Top with 1 tablespoon cheese mixture and another tortilla. Cook for 30-60 seconds; turn and cook 30 seconds longer or until cheese is melted. Cut into wedges. Serve with salsa and sour cream. **Yield:** 14 quesadillas.

Lemon Almond Tea

Try this delightful dressed-up version when you want to serve something other than plain iced tea. I've used it for all sorts of events. —Brenda McCaleb Nashville, Tennessee

4 cups water
15 individual tea bags
3/4 cup sugar
3 quarts cold water
1 can (12 ounces) frozen lemonade concentrate
1 to 1-1/2 teaspoons almond extract

In a large saucepan, bring water to a boil. Remove from the heat; add the tea bags. Cover and steep for 5-10 minutes. Discard tea bags. Stir sugar into the tea until dissolved. Stir in the cold water, lemonade concentrate and extract. Serve over ice. **Yield:** about 4 quarts.

Banana Pops

These wholesome treats are as fun to make as they are to eat. My little granddaughter, Taylor, likes to do the scooping and pouring. The hardest part is waiting for the pops to freeze, so she can have one! —Elaine Carver, Portland, Maine

1 cup vanilla yogurt
1/2 cup orange juice
1 medium ripe banana, cut into chunks

In a blender, combine yogurt, orange juice and banana; cover and process until smooth. Pour into ice pop trays, or pour into small plastic disposable cups and insert wooden sticks. Freeze until firm, about 5 hours or overnight. **Yield:** 6 servings.

Dutch Hot Chocolate

When my grandchildren come over, they like to snack on cookies and mugs of this hot chocolate. It has a sweet chocolate flavor with a hint of cinnamon. The flavor of store-bought mixes just can't compare. —Edna Hoffman, Hebron, Indiana

3 quarts milk
6 cups water
1-1/2 cups sugar, *divided*
3 squares (1 ounce *each*) semisweet chocolate
1 cinnamon stick, broken
1/2 cup packed brown sugar

In a saucepan, combine the milk, water, 1 cup sugar, chocolate and cinnamon. Bring to a boil. Reduce heat to low; cook and stir until chocolate is melted. Add brown sugar and remaining sugar; cook and stir until heated through. Discard cinnamon. **Yield:** 18 servings.

Tomato-Onion Phyllo Pizza

(Pictured below)

With a delicate crust and lots of lovely tomatoes on top, this dish is a special one to serve to guests. I make it often when fresh garden tomatoes are in season. It freezes well unbaked, so I can keep one on hand to pop in the oven for a quick dinner. *—Neta Cohen, Bedford, Virginia*

- **5 tablespoons butter *or* margarine, melted**
- **7 sheets phyllo dough (18 inches x 14 inches)**
- **7 tablespoons grated Parmesan cheese, *divided***
- **1 cup (4 ounces) shredded mozzarella cheese**
- **1 cup thinly sliced onion**
- **7 to 9 plum tomatoes (about 1-1/4 pounds), sliced**
- **1-1/2 teaspoons minced fresh oregano *or* 1/2 teaspoon dried oregano**
- **1 teaspoon minced fresh thyme *or* 1/4 teaspoon dried thyme**
- **Salt and pepper to taste**

Brush a 15-in. x 10-in. x 1-in. baking pan with some of the melted butter. Lay a sheet of phyllo in pan, folding edges in to fit (keep remaining dough covered with waxed paper to avoid drying out). Brush dough with butter and sprinkle with 1 tablespoon Parmesan cheese. Repeat layers five times, folding edges for each layer. Top with remaining dough, folding edges to fit pan; brush with remaining butter. Sprinkle with mozzarella cheese; arrange onion and tomatoes over the cheese. Sprinkle with oregano, thyme, salt, pepper and remaining Parmesan. Bake at 375° for 20-25 minutes or until edges are golden brown. **Yield:** 28 slices.

Tangy Fruit Punch

A variety of fruity flavors mingle in this rosy refreshing punch. It's a popular beverage for a brunch, since its versatile sweet-tart taste goes wonderfully with all kinds of foods. *—Ann Cousin, New Braunfels, Texas*

- **1 can (46 ounces) pineapple juice**
- **1 can (12 ounces) frozen orange juice concentrate, thawed**
- **3/4 cup lemonade concentrate**
- **1 cup water, *divided***
- **1/2 cup sugar**
- **2 large ripe bananas**
- **1 package (20 ounces) frozen unsweetened whole strawberries, thawed**
- **2 liters ginger ale, chilled**

In a punch bowl or large container, combine pineapple juice, orange juice concentrate, lemonade concentrate, 1/2 cup water and sugar. Place bananas, strawberries and remaining water in a blender; cover and process until smooth. Stir into the juice mixture. Cover and refrigerate. Just before serving, stir in ginger ale. **Yield:** 25-30 servings (about 5 quarts).

Popcorn Balls

These sweet, chewy snacks are made from one of our state's most popular crops—popcorn! This version has a lovely caramel color and flavor. *—Edna Hoffman, Hebron, Indiana*

- **2 quarts popped popcorn**
- **1 cup packed brown sugar**
- **1/3 cup water**
- **1/3 cup dark corn syrup**
- **1/4 cup butter (no substitutes)**
- **1/2 teaspoon salt**
- **1 teaspoon vanilla extract**

Place popcorn in a large bowl; set aside. In a heavy saucepan, combine the brown sugar, water, corn syrup, butter and salt. Bring to a boil over medium heat, stirring constantly. Continue cooking, without stirring, until a candy thermometer reads 270° (soft-crack stage). Remove from the heat; stir in vanilla. Pour over popcorn; stir until evenly coated. When cool enough to handle, quickly shape into balls. **Yield:** 6 servings.

Editor's Note: We recommend that you test your candy thermometer before each use by bringing water to a boil; the thermometer should read 212°. Adjust your recipe temperature up or down based on your test.

Sweet 'n' Hot Mustard Dip

(Pictured on page 4)

With pretzels, this sweet and spicy mustard is a fun snack. It also sparks the flavor of grilled chicken strips or sausages. —*Rita Reifenstein*
Evans City, Pennsylvania

1-1/2 cups honey
1 cup vinegar
3 eggs
2 containers (1-3/4 ounces *each*) ground mustard
1/2 teaspoon salt
Pretzels, cooked chicken fingers *or* sausage slices

In a blender, combine the first five ingredients; cover and process until blended. Pour into a saucepan; cook and stir over low heat until mixture thickens and reaches 160°. Pour into small jars. Cover and refrigerate for up to 1 week. Serve with pretzels, chicken fingers or sausage. **Yield:** 2-1/3 cups.

Walnut Chicken Spread

It's a breeze to stir together this tasty spread. We enjoy the mild combination of chicken, crunchy walnuts, onion and celery. It's perfect with crackers or as a sandwich filling. —*Joan Whelan*
Green Valley, Arizona

1-3/4 cups finely chopped cooked chicken
1 cup finely chopped walnuts
2/3 cup mayonnaise *or* salad dressing
1 celery rib, finely chopped
1 small onion, finely chopped
1 teaspoon salt
1/2 teaspoon garlic powder
Assorted crackers

In a bowl, combine the chicken, walnuts, mayonnaise, celery, onion, salt and garlic powder. Serve with crackers. Refrigerate any leftovers. **Yield:** 2-1/2 cups.

Haunting Hot Chocolate

(Pictured above)

I serve mugs of this quick-to-fix hot cocoa outside when the kids in our neighborhood go trick-or-treating for Halloween. It's a nice change of pace from traditional candy. —*Suzanne Cleveland*
Lyons, Georgia

✓ Uses less fat, sugar or salt. Includes Nutritional Analysis and Diabetic Exchanges.

1 cup nonfat dry milk powder
5 tablespoons sugar
3 tablespoons baking cocoa
1/8 to 1/4 teaspoon ground cinnamon
Dash salt
3 cups boiling water

In a saucepan, combine the milk powder, sugar, cocoa, cinnamon and salt. Add boiling water; stir until milk powder is dissolved. **Yield:** 5 servings.

Nutritional Analysis: One serving (1 cup) equals 106 calories, trace fat (0 saturated fat), 2 mg cholesterol, 133 mg sodium, 21 g carbohydrate, 1 g fiber, 5 g protein. **Diabetic Exchanges:** 1 fat-free milk, 1/2 fruit.

Salads & Dressings

Folks will happily dish up these satisfying salads—whether they're the first course or the main event. For a special touch, try a tasty homemade dressing.

SALAD SELECTIONS. Clockwise from upper left: Colorful Linguine Salad (p. 25), Colorful Fruit Kabobs (p. 28), Wilted Green Salad (p. 31), Sugar Snap Potato Salad (p. 26), Gran's Granola Parfaits (p. 28) and Veggie Potato Salad (p. 30).

Italian Pasta Salad

(Pictured above)

This zesty recipe combines vegetables and pasta in a creamy dressing. Refreshing and filling, this change-of-pace salad is perfect as a side dish. It's always popular at a potluck. —Tina Dierking, Canaan, Maine

3/4 cup uncooked spiral pasta
1-1/2 cups halved cherry tomatoes
1 cup sliced fresh mushrooms
1/4 cup chopped sweet red pepper
1/4 cup chopped green pepper
3 tablespoons thinly sliced green onions
1-1/2 cups zesty Italian salad dressing
3/4 cup mayonnaise
1/2 cup grated Parmesan cheese
1/3 cup cubed provolone cheese
1 can (2-1/4 ounces) sliced ripe olives, drained
Leaf lettuce, optional

Cook pasta according to package directions; rinse with cold water and drain. Place in a bowl; add tomatoes, mushrooms, peppers, onions and salad dressing. Cover; refrigerate at least 4 hours or overnight; drain. In a bowl, combine mayonnaise and Parmesan cheese; stir in provolone cheese and olives. Gently fold into the pasta mixture. Serve in a lettuce-lined bowl if desired. **Yield:** 6 servings.

Dilly Potato Salad

When my sister-in-law shared the recipe for this savory potato salad one summer, it became an instant favorite with my family. The dill pickle relish and fresh dill perk up the flavor. —Tiffany Twait, Meridian, Idaho

8 medium potatoes, cubed
4 hard-cooked eggs, sliced
1 cup mayonnaise
1/2 cup sour cream
1/2 cup dill pickle relish
1 can (2-1/4 ounces) sliced ripe olives, drained
2 teaspoons prepared mustard
2 garlic cloves, minced
2 tablespoons snipped fresh dill *or* 2 teaspoons dill weed
3/4 teaspoon celery seed
1/2 teaspoon salt
1/4 teaspoon paprika

Place potatoes in a saucepan and cover with water. Cover; bring to a boil. Reduce heat; cook for 20-30 minutes or until tender. Drain and cool. Place potatoes in a large bowl; add eggs. In a small bowl, combine remaining ingredients. Pour over potatoes and toss to coat. Cover and refrigerate for several hours before serving. **Yield:** 8 servings.

Cucumber Tomato Salad

My mother shared the recipe with me after falling in love with this fresh-tasting dish at a family reunion. —Leslie Monroe, Camp Lejeune, North Carolina

✓ Uses less fat, sugar or salt. Includes Nutritional Analysis and Diabetic Exchanges.

2 large cucumbers, peeled and diced
2 large tomatoes, diced
1 medium green pepper, diced
1 medium onion, diced
1 bottle (8 ounces) fat-free Italian salad dressing
Sugar substitute equivalent to 2 teaspoons sugar

In a bowl, combine the cucumbers, tomatoes, green pepper and onion. Combine salad dressing and sugar substitute; pour over vegetables. Refrigerate for at least 1 hour. Serve with a slotted spoon. **Yield:** 14 servings.

Nutritional Analysis: One serving (1/2 cup) equals 29 calories, 0 fat (0 saturated fat), 0 cholesterol, 230 mg sodium, 6 g carbohydrate, 1 g fiber, 1 g protein. **Diabetic Exchange:** 1 vegetable.

Colorful Linguine Salad

(Pictured on page 22)

This light, satisfying dish is great after a fun day in the summer sun. —Lee Ann Berijan, Blaine, Minnesota

✓ Uses less fat, sugar or salt. Includes Nutritional Analysis and Diabetic Exchanges.

1 medium zucchini, thinly sliced
1/2 cup julienned carrots
1/2 cup fresh *or* frozen pea pods
3 cups cooked linguine
3/4 cup julienned sweet red pepper

DRESSING:

3 tablespoons white wine vinegar *or* cider vinegar
2 tablespoons olive *or* canola oil
2 teaspoons Dijon mustard
1 garlic clove, minced
1 teaspoon sugar
1 teaspoon dried thyme, optional
1/2 teaspoon salt
1/4 teaspoon white pepper

Place zucchini and carrots in a steamer basket; place in a saucepan over 1 in. of water. Bring to a boil; cover and steam for 2-3 minutes. Add pea pods; steam for 1 minute. Transfer vegetables to a large bowl; add linguine and red pepper. In a small bowl, whisk together the dressing ingredients. Pour over linguine mixture and toss to coat. Cover and refrigerate for 1 hour or until serving. **Yield:** 4 servings.

Nutritional Analysis: One serving (1-1/2 cups) equals 252 calories, 8 g fat (1 g saturated fat), 0 cholesterol, 466 mg sodium, 39 g carbohydrate, 4 g fiber, 7 g protein. **Diabetic Exchanges:** 2 starch, 1-1/2 fat, 1 vegetable.

Pea Pod Primer

Pea pods come in two main varieties: snow peas and sugar snap peas. Snow peas are thin and crisp with bright green, nearly translucent pods. Sugar snaps are plumper with more-prominent

Citrus Shrimp Salad

(Pictured below)

I tasted this refreshing salad at a gathering I attended with my sister. I pestered her until she got me a copy of the recipe. —Nancy Rollag, Kewaskum, Wisconsin

✓ Uses less fat, sugar or salt. Includes Nutritional Analysis and Diabetic Exchanges.

2 tablespoons reduced-fat plain yogurt
4-1/2 teaspoons Dijon mustard
1 tablespoon honey
2 tablespoons orange juice
2 tablespoons white wine vinegar *or* cider vinegar
1/4 cup fat-free Italian salad dressing
1/8 teaspoon pepper
3 tablespoons finely chopped green onions
2 pounds cooked medium shrimp, peeled and deveined
8 cups torn romaine
2 cups pink grapefruit sections (about 2 large)
2 cups navel orange sections (3 to 4 large)

In a large bowl, whisk together the first eight ingredients in the order listed. Add shrimp; toss to coat. Let stand for 15-30 minutes. Drain, reserving the marinade. Arrange romaine on a serving platter or individual plates; top with shrimp, grapefruit and oranges. Drizzle with reserved marinade. **Yield:** 8 servings.

Nutritional Analysis: One serving (1 cup) equals 136 calories, 1 g fat (0 saturated fat), 135 mg cholesterol, 341 mg sodium, 15 g carbohydrate, 3 g fiber, 17 g protein. **Diabetic Exchanges:** 2 very lean meat, 1 fruit.

Curly Endive Salad

(Pictured below)

My wife grows herbs in our tiny city garden. I use oregano and mint to season this refreshingly different salad, which I created. With its slightly bitter flavor, the endive goes well with spicy or plain foods since it contrasts with both. *—Roger Burch*
Staten Island, New York

4 cups torn curly endive *or* escarole
1/4 cup chopped red onion
24 whole stuffed olives
2 tablespoons olive *or* vegetable oil
1 tablespoon red wine vinegar *or* cider vinegar
3 tablespoons minced fresh oregano *or* 3 teaspoons dried oregano
1 tablespoon minced fresh mint *or* 1 teaspoon dried mint flakes
1/4 teaspoon salt
1/8 teaspoon pepper
2 ounces crumbled feta cheese

In a salad bowl, toss the endive, onion and olives. In a jar with a tight-fitting lid, combine the oil, vinegar, oregano, mint, salt and pepper; shake well. Drizzle over salad and toss to coat. Top with cheese. **Yield:** 4 servings.

Sugar Snap Potato Salad

(Pictured on page 23)

We use our harvest of fresh Wisconsin sugar snap peas to make this tangy salad. It's pretty and refreshing, plus it's easy to fix and fun to serve. *—Gerri Okray*
Plover, Wisconsin

✓ Uses less fat, sugar or salt. Includes Nutritional Analysis and Diabetic Exchanges.

1-1/2 pounds small red potatoes, quartered
1/2 pound fresh sugar snap peas
1/2 cup finely chopped red onion
1/3 cup mayonnaise
1/3 cup plain yogurt
1 garlic clove, minced
3 tablespoons Dijon mustard
2 teaspoons dill weed
1/2 teaspoon salt

Cook potatoes in boiling water until tender, about 12 minutes. Rinse with cold water and drain. Place the potatoes in a large bowl; add peas and onion. In a small bowl, combine the remaining ingredients. Pour over potato mixture and gently toss to coat. Cover and refrigerate for at least 1 hour. **Yield:** 12 servings.

Nutritional Analysis: One 3/4-cup serving (prepared with reduced-fat mayonnaise and reduced-fat yogurt) equals 84 calories, 3 g fat (0 saturated fat), 3 mg cholesterol, 253 mg sodium, 13 g carbohydrate, 2 g fiber, 2 g protein. **Diabetic Exchanges:** 1 starch, 1/2 fat.

Creamy Fruit Salad

Lots of refreshing fruits combine with a creamy sauce in this salad that I created for my diabetic husband. I've never served it to anyone who didn't like it. It always generates recipe requests.
—Joan Logan Lindley, Brackettville, Texas

✓ Uses less fat, sugar or salt. Includes Nutritional Analysis and Diabetic Exchanges.

1 can (20 ounces) unsweetened pineapple chunks, drained
1 can (15 ounces) sliced peaches in juice, drained
1 can (11 ounces) mandarin oranges, drained
4 medium tart apples, peeled and diced
1-1/2 cups cold fat-free milk
1/3 cup orange juice concentrate
1 package (1 ounce) sugar-free instant vanilla pudding mix
3/4 cup fat-free sour cream

In a large bowl, combine the fruit; set aside. In another bowl, whisk milk, orange juice concentrate and pudding mix for 2 minutes or until smooth. Add sour cream; mix well. Fold into fruit. Cover and refrigerate until serving. **Yield:** 16 servings.

Nutritional Analysis: One serving (1/2 cup) equals 96 calories, 0 fat (0 saturated fat), 0 cholesterol, 100 mg sodium, 22 g carbohydrate, 2 g fiber, 2 g protein. **Diabetic Exchange:** 1-1/2 fruit.

Creamy Dijon Dressing

Even those who don't like low-fat dressings will love this smooth, tangy salad topper. A blend of honey, orange juice and mustard gives it wonderful flavor.
—Genise Krause, Sturgeon Bay, Wisconsin

 Uses less fat, sugar or salt. Includes Nutritional Analysis and Diabetic Exchanges.

1/2 cup Dijon mustard
1/2 cup fat-free mayonnaise
1/2 cup orange juice
1/4 cup honey
2 tablespoons cider vinegar
1/4 teaspoon celery salt
Salad greens and vegetables of your choice

In a blender or food processor, combine the first six ingredients; cover and process until smooth. Serve over greens and vegetables. Store in the refrigerator. Shake before serving. **Yield:** 1-2/3 cups.

Nutritional Analysis: One serving (2 tablespoons dressing) equals 40 calories, 1 g fat (0 saturated fat), 1 mg cholesterol, 223 mg sodium, 8 g carbohydrate, 0 fiber, 1 g protein. **Diabetic Exchange:** 1 fat.

Paprika Salad Dressing

Fresh greens really perk up with this zesty homemade dressing. —Sharon Nichols, Brookings, South Dakota

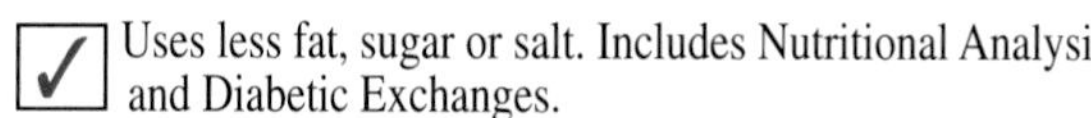
Uses less fat, sugar or salt. Includes Nutritional Analysis and Diabetic Exchanges.

1/2 cup sour cream
1/4 cup mayonnaise
2 tablespoons steak sauce
1/4 teaspoon salt
1/2 teaspoon paprika
1/4 teaspoon celery seed
1/8 teaspoon hot pepper sauce
Torn salad greens

In a small bowl, combine the first seven ingredients with a wire whisk. Serve over salad greens. Refrigerate leftovers. **Yield:** 1 cup.

Nutritional Analysis: One 2-tablespoon serving (prepared with fat-free sour cream and reduced-fat mayonnaise) equals 43 calories, 3 g fat (1 g saturated fat), 4 mg cholesterol, 204 mg sodium, 4 g carbohydrate, trace fiber, 1 g protein. **Diabetic Exchange:** 1/2 starch.

Tropical Slaw

(Pictured above)

This refreshing dish is an excellent accompaniment to any meal on a hot day. I also enjoy it during the cold months—the blend of crunchy cabbage, sweet fruit and chewy coconut seems to mentally transport me to a warm tropical island. It goes over well at potlucks.
—Anna Marie Nichols, Americus, Georgia

1 can (20 ounces) pineapple tidbits
1 tablespoon lemon juice
1 medium firm banana, sliced
3 cups shredded cabbage
1 can (11 ounces) mandarin oranges, drained
1 cup miniature marshmallows
1 cup flaked coconut
1 cup chopped walnuts
1 cup raisins
1/2 teaspoon salt
1 carton (8 ounces) pineapple yogurt

Drain pineapple, reserving 2 tablespoons juice; set pineapple aside. Stir lemon juice and banana into reserved pineapple juice. In a large salad bowl, combine the cabbage, oranges, marshmallows, coconut, walnuts, raisins, salt, pineapple and banana mixture. Add yogurt; toss to coat. Cover and refrigerate until serving. **Yield:** 10 servings.

Colorful Fruit Kabobs

(Pictured above and on page 23)

These luscious fruit kabobs are perfect as a summer salad, appetizer or snack. The citrus glaze clings well and keeps the fruit looking fresh. —Ruth Ann Stelfox Raymond, Alberta

Assorted fruit—strawberries, seedless red grapes, cubed cantaloupe, honeydew and pineapple, and sliced kiwifruit and star fruit
1/3 cup sugar
2 tablespoons cornstarch
1 cup orange juice
2 teaspoons lemon juice

Alternately thread fruit onto skewers; set aside. In a saucepan, combine sugar and cornstarch. Stir in orange juice and lemon juice until smooth. Bring to a boil; cook and stir for 1-2 minutes or until thickened. Brush over fruit. Refrigerate until serving. **Yield:** 1 cup sauce.

Hash Brown Potato Salad

I've used this recipe for 20 years, and it's still a family favorite. It stirs up and cooks in a jiffy—and it tastes as good as a German potato salad that takes all day. —Joan Hallford, North Richland Hills, Texas

5 bacon strips, diced
6 green onions, sliced
1 package (1 pound) frozen cubed hash brown potatoes
1/4 cup white wine vinegar *or* cider vinegar
1/2 teaspoon celery salt

Place bacon in a 1-1/2-qt. microwave-safe bowl. Cover and microwave on high for 5-6 minutes or until bacon is crisp. Remove with a slotted spoon to paper towels to drain. Add onions to the drippings; cover and microwave on high for 1 minute. Add the potatoes; cover and cook on high for 10 minutes, stirring several times. Add vinegar, celery salt and bacon; toss. **Yield:** 4 servings.

Editor's Note: This recipe was tested in an 850-watt microwave.

Salad with Mustard Dressing

This unique salad uses my favorite from-scratch dressing. The mustard adds a little zip to the dressing. —Bernice Morris, Marshfield, Missouri

1 cup vegetable oil
1/2 cup white wine vinegar *or* cider vinegar
1/3 cup sugar
1/4 cup finely chopped onion
4 teaspoons ground mustard
1 teaspoon celery seed
1 teaspoon salt
1 package (3 ounces) cream cheese, optional
8 to 10 cups torn salad greens
1 package (6 ounces) cashews

In a jar with a tight-fitting lid, combine first seven ingredients; shake well. If desired, roll cream cheese into 3/4-in. balls. In a salad bowl, combine greens, cashews and cream cheese balls. Drizzle with dressing; toss to coat. Refrigerate leftover dressing. **Yield:** 8 servings (1-3/4 cups dressing).

Gran's Granola Parfaits

(Pictured on page 22)

When my mother-in-law (Gran to our kids) had us over for brunch, I especially enjoyed her yogurt parfaits. They were refreshing, light and wholesome. —Angela Keller, Newburgh, Indiana

2 cups old-fashioned oats
1 cup Wheaties
1 cup whole almonds
1 cup pecan halves
1 cup flaked coconut
4-1/2 teaspoons wheat germ
1 tablespoon sesame seeds, toasted
1 teaspoon ground cinnamon
1/4 cup butter *or* margarine, melted

2 tablespoons maple syrup
2 tablespoons honey
1 can (20 ounces) pineapple tidbits, drained
1 can (15 ounces) mandarin oranges, drained
1 cup halved green grapes
2 to 3 medium firm bananas, sliced
1 cup sliced fresh strawberries
1 carton (32 ounces) vanilla yogurt

In a bowl, combine first eight ingredients. Combine butter, syrup and honey; drizzle over oat mixture and stir until well coated. Pour into greased 13-in. x 9-in. x 2-in. baking pan. Bake, uncovered, at 350° for 30 minutes, stirring every 10 minutes. Cool on a wire rack; crumble into pieces.

Combine fruits in a large bowl. For each parfait, layer 2 tablespoons yogurt, 2 tablespoons granola and 3 rounded tablespoons fruit in a parfait glass or dessert bowl. Repeat layers. Sprinkle with remaining granola. Serve immediately. **Yield:** 16 servings.

Frosted Gelatin Salad

I often take this fruity salad to potlucks and other gatherings. With its fluffy topping, it's always popular.
—Sherry Hulsman, Louisville, Kentucky

✓ Uses less fat, sugar or salt. Includes Nutritional Analysis and Diabetic Exchanges.

1 can (15 ounces) blueberries
1 can (8 ounces) unsweetened pineapple tidbits
1 package (.6 ounce) sugar-free raspberry gelatin
2 cups boiling water
1 package (8 ounces) fat-free cream cheese, softened
1/2 cup fat-free sour cream
1/3 cup sugar
1/2 teaspoon vanilla extract

Drain blueberries and pineapple, reserving juice; set fruit aside. In a bowl, dissolve gelatin in boiling water. Add enough water to reserved fruit juices to measure 1-1/4 cups; stir into gelatin. Chill until partially set. Stir in reserved fruit. Pour into an 8-in. square dish. Refrigerate until firm. In a mixing bowl, combine cream cheese and sour cream. Beat in sugar and vanilla. Carefully spread over the gelatin. Refrigerate until serving. **Yield:** 9 servings.

Nutritional Analysis: One serving equals 125 calories, 1 g fat (trace saturated fat), 3 mg cholesterol, 191 mg sodium, 25 g carbohydrate, 1 g fiber, 6 g protein. **Diabetic Exchanges:** 1 starch, 1 fruit.

Dilled Crab Salad

(Pictured below)

I love dill, and when it's in season in my garden, I use as much as possible. The tangy flavor of dill accents this cool and crunchy seafood salad. —Mary Steine
West Bend, Wisconsin

✓ Uses less fat, sugar or salt. Includes Nutritional Analysis and Diabetic Exchanges.

2 packages (8 ounces *each*) flaked imitation crabmeat
3 cups fresh sugar snap peas, halved widthwise
2 medium cucumbers, sliced
1 medium sweet red pepper, julienned
1/2 cup thinly sliced red onion
1/2 cup snipped fresh dill
1/3 cup prepared ranch dressing
1/3 cup sour cream
1 teaspoon lemon juice
Boston lettuce

In a bowl, combine the crab, peas, cucumbers, red pepper, onion and dill. Combine the dressing, sour cream and lemon juice; mix well. Pour over crab mixture and toss to coat. Cover and refrigerate for 4 hours or overnight. Serve on a bed of lettuce. **Yield:** 10 servings.

Nutritional Analysis: One 1-cup serving (prepared with fat-free ranch dressing and reduced-fat sour cream) equals 94 calories, 1 g fat (0 saturated fat), 12 mg cholesterol, 481 mg sodium, 13 g carbohydrate, 2 g fiber, 7 g protein. **Diabetic Exchanges:** 1 lean meat, 1/2 starch.

Veggie Potato Salad

(Pictured below and on page 22)

You must try this recipe! It's a savory salad that's great for any kind of party. I've even made it with fat-free Caesar dressing and my friends and family liked it just as much. —*Michaela Greenberg Johnston, Rhode Island*

✓ Uses less fat, sugar or salt. Includes Nutritional Analysis and Diabetic Exchanges.

1 pound small red potatoes, cooked and cubed
1-1/2 cups chopped fresh broccoli
1/2 cup sliced celery
1/4 cup chopped red onion
1/4 cup sliced radishes
2 tablespoons chopped green pepper
1/3 cup fat-free Italian salad dressing
1/2 teaspoon salt-free seasoning blend
1/4 teaspoon dill weed

In a large salad bowl, toss the potatoes and vegetables. In a small bowl, blend the salad dressing and seasonings; add to potato mixture and toss to coat. Cover and refrigerate for 1 hour or until serving. **Yield:** 5 servings.

Nutritional Analysis: One serving (3/4 cup) equals 79 calories, trace fat (trace saturated fat), 0 cholesterol, 177 mg sodium, 16 g carbohydrate, 3 g fiber, 3 g protein. **Diabetic Exchange:** 1 starch.

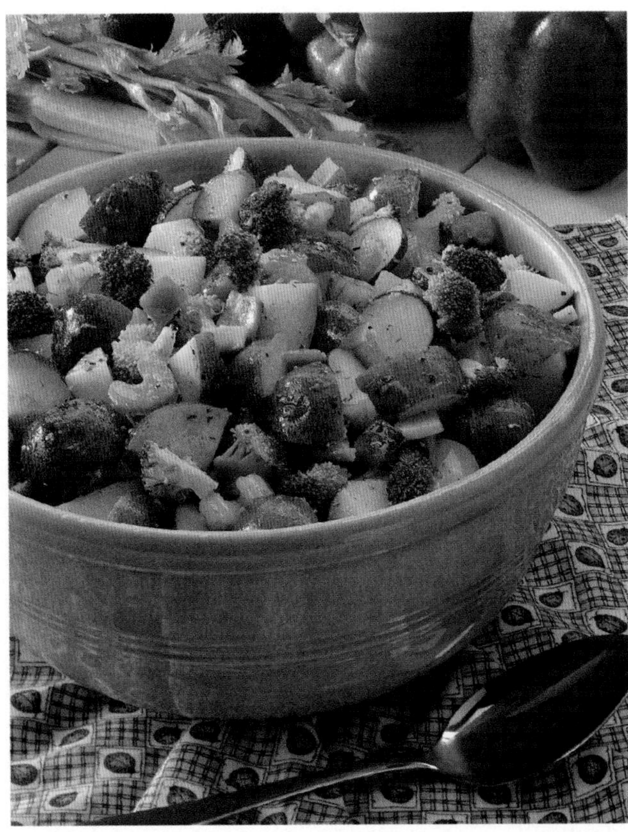

Cottage Cheese Gelatin Mold

My husband is diabetic, so finding dishes for him is quite a challenge. One day I dreamed up this cool treat and he loved it. It works great as a salad or dessert. —*Vera Ambroselli, Lehigh Acres, Florida*

✓ Uses less fat, sugar or salt. Includes Nutritional Analysis and Diabetic Exchanges.

1 package (.3 ounce) sugar-free gelatin flavor of your choice
1-1/2 cups boiling water
1-3/4 cups fat-free cottage cheese
1-1/2 cups reduced-fat whipped topping

In a bowl, dissolve gelatin in boiling water. In a blender or food processor, process the cottage cheese until smooth. Stir into gelatin. Refrigerate until partially set. Fold in whipped topping. Pour into a 3-cup mold coated with nonstick cooking spray. Refrigerate until set. **Yield:** 6 servings.

Nutritional Analysis: One serving (1/2 cup) equals 92 calories, 2 g fat (2 g saturated fat), 6 mg cholesterol, 256 mg sodium, 6 g carbohydrate, 0 fiber, 9 g protein. **Diabetic Exchanges:** 1 lean meat, 1/2 starch.

Snow Peas with Sesame Dressing

I've had the recipe for this salad for years. It goes well with any meat and is terrific for family or company. —*Sue Braunschweig, Delafield, Wisconsin*

3 cups fresh snow peas
2 cups cauliflowerets
1 can (8 ounces) sliced water chestnuts, drained
1 tablespoon chopped sweet red pepper
1/3 cup vegetable oil
2 to 3 tablespoons white wine vinegar *or* cider vinegar
2 tablespoons sesame seeds, toasted
2 to 3 garlic cloves, minced
1 tablespoon sugar
1 tablespoon lemon juice
3/4 to 1 teaspoon salt
1/8 to 1/4 teaspoon lemon-pepper seasoning

Cook peas in boiling salted water until crisp-tender, about 1-1/2 minutes. Drain and rinse in cold water. Cook cauliflower in boiling salted water until crisp-tender, about 3 minutes. Drain and rinse in cold water. In a bowl, combine peas, cauliflower, water chestnuts and red pepper. Cover and refrigerate for at least 1 hour. In a jar with a tight-fitting lid, combine the remaining ingredients; shake well.

Cover and refrigerate for at least 1 hour. Just before serving, shake dressing and pour half over the pea mixture; toss to coat. Refrigerate remaining dressing. **Yield:** 8 servings.

Crunchy Fruit Salad

Bursting with lightly dressed fresh fruit and crunchy sunflower kernels, this deliciously different salad is fun and refreshing. —*Karen Barefield Minneapolis, Kansas*

✓ Uses less fat, sugar or salt. Includes Nutritional Analysis and Diabetic Exchanges.

2 medium apples, chopped
1 medium firm banana, sliced
1/3 cup sunflower kernels
1/4 cup green grapes, halved
1/4 cup chopped celery
1/4 cup reduced-fat plain yogurt

In a bowl, combine the first five ingredients. Add yogurt; stir to coat. Refrigerate until serving. **Yield:** 4 servings.

Nutritional Analysis: One serving (3/4 cup) equals 151 calories, 7 g fat (1 g saturated fat), 1 mg cholesterol, 85 mg sodium, 22 g carbohydrate, 4 g fiber, 3 g protein. **Diabetic Exchanges:** 1-1/2 starch, 1/2 fruit.

Wilted Green Salad

(Pictured on page 23)

My husband refused to eat wilted lettuce until I tried this recipe suggested by a friend. He likes this milder dressing with just a subtle hint of vinegar. —*LaVonne Hegland, St. Michael, Minnesota*

✓ Uses less fat, sugar or salt. Includes Nutritional Analysis and Diabetic Exchanges.

10 cups torn leaf lettuce
6 cups torn fresh spinach
2 green onions, sliced
1/4 cup cider vinegar
2 tablespoons water
2 tablespoons canola oil
Sugar substitute equivalent to 2 teaspoons sugar
4 turkey bacon strips, cooked and crumbled

In a large salad bowl, toss the lettuce, spinach and onions; set aside. In a small saucepan, combine the vinegar, water, oil and sugar substitute; bring to a boil. Pour over lettuce and toss; sprinkle with bacon. Serve immediately. **Yield:** 8 servings.

Nutritional Analysis: One serving (2 cups) equals 71 calories, 5 g fat (1 g saturated fat), 6 mg cholesterol, 132 mg sodium, 5 g carbohydrate, 1 g fiber, 3 g protein. **Diabetic Exchanges:** 1 vegetable, 1 fat.

Fruity Rice Salad

(Pictured above)

This cool refreshing salad is perfect to serve on hot summer days. Rice blends with peaches, grapes, celery, raisins, pecans and a dressing that's just lightly sweet. It's a pretty dish to take to any table. —*Gitta Hoffman, Mesa, Arizona*

1 package (3 ounces) cream cheese, softened
1/2 cup plain yogurt
1/4 cup honey
2 tablespoons lemon juice
1 teaspoon grated lemon peel
2 cups cooked long grain rice, cooled
3 fresh peaches or nectarines, pitted and chopped *or* 1-1/2 cups frozen sliced peaches, thawed and chopped
1 cup halved green grapes
1/2 cup sliced celery
1/2 cup raisins
1/2 cup chopped pecans

In a mixing bowl, combine the first five ingredients; beat until smooth. Add the rice, peaches, grapes, celery and raisins; stir well. Cover and refrigerate for at least 6 hours. Just before serving, stir in the pecans. **Yield:** 6 servings.

Soups & Sandwiches

A steaming pot of soup or chili on the stove chases away chills in a hurry. Add a platter piled high with tasty sandwiches and you have a satisfying lunch or dinner.

SAVORY ASSORTMENT. Clockwise from upper left: Cowpoke Chili (p. 38), Venison Stromboli (p. 43), Wisconsin Split Pea Soup (p. 47), Sunday Gumbo (p. 44) and Grilled Beef Gyros (p. 38).

Kielbasa Bundles

(Pictured above)

My family really enjoys these flavorful sausage sandwiches. —Robin Touhey, San Angelo, Texas

1/2 pound fully cooked kielbasa *or* Polish sausage, chopped
1 small onion, chopped
1/4 cup chopped green pepper
1 garlic clove, minced
1 tablespoon butter *or* margarine
1/3 cup barbecue sauce
2 tubes (8 ounces *each*) refrigerated crescent rolls
4 slices process American cheese, halved
1 egg white
1 tablespoon water
Sesame seeds

In a large skillet, cook sausage for 5-8 minutes; drain. Add onion, green pepper, garlic and butter; cook until vegetables are tender. Stir in barbecue sauce; heat through. Unroll crescent roll dough and separate into eight rectangles; seal perforations. Place a cheese slice on half of each rectangle; top with 2 tablespoons sausage mixture. Fold dough over filling and pinch edges to seal; fold seam under. Beat egg white and water; brush over dough. Sprinkle with sesame seeds.

Place bundles seam side down on greased baking sheets. Bake at 350° for 15-18 minutes or until golden brown. **Yield:** 8 servings.

Pork and Beef Barbecue

I love to try new recipes, and this zesty sandwich filling is one of my favorites. I think every man should have cooking experience, if for no other reason than to appreciate what his wife and mother have done for him all his life! —Corbin Detgen, Buchanan, Michigan

✓ Uses less fat, sugar or salt. Includes Nutritional Analysis and Diabetic Exchanges.

1 can (6 ounces) tomato paste
1/2 cup packed brown sugar
1/4 cup chili powder
1/4 cup cider vinegar
2 teaspoons Worcestershire sauce
1 teaspoon salt
1-1/2 pounds beef stew meat, cut into 3/4-inch cubes
1-1/2 pounds pork chop suey meat *or* pork tenderloin, cut into 3/4-inch cubes
3 medium green peppers, chopped
2 large onions, chopped
14 sandwich rolls, split
Lettuce and tomatoes, optional

In a slow cooker, combine the first six ingredients. Stir in beef, pork, green peppers and onions. Cover and cook on high for 6-8 hours or until meat is tender. Shred meat with two forks. Serve on rolls with lettuce and chopped tomatoes if desired. **Yield:** 14 servings.

Nutritional Analysis: One serving (prepared with lean beef stew meat and pork tenderloin) equals 315 calories, 7 g fat (2 g saturated fat), 59 mg cholesterol, 596 mg sodium, 40 g carbohydrate, 3 g fiber, 25 g protein. **Diabetic Exchanges:** 2-1/2 starch, 2 lean meat, 1 vegetable.

Meaty Mushroom Chili

Since our two daughters did not like beans in their chili, I adapted a recipe to suit our whole family's tastes. We all agree that mushrooms are an appealing alternative and go very well with the ground beef and sausage. —Marjol Burr, Catawba, Ohio

1 pound bulk Italian sausage
1 pound ground beef
1 cup chopped onion
1 pound fresh mushrooms, sliced
1 can (46 ounces) V8 juice
1 can (6 ounces) tomato paste
1 teaspoon sugar
1 teaspoon salt
1 teaspoon garlic powder
1 teaspoon dried oregano
1 teaspoon Worcestershire sauce

1/2 teaspoon dried basil
1/2 teaspoon pepper
Sour cream, optional

In a large saucepan, cook the sausage, beef and onion over medium heat until the meat is no longer pink; drain. Stir in the mushrooms, V8 juice, tomato paste and seasonings. Bring to a boil. Reduce heat; cover and simmer for 1 hour. Garnish with sour cream if desired. **Yield:** 8 servings.

Beef Barley Soup

Curling is a favorite winter sport around here. Our Farmers' Curling Bonspiel features hearty food like this. —Joanne Shewchuk, St. Benedict, Saskatchewan

3 meaty beef soup bones (beef shanks *or* short ribs)
2-1/2 quarts water
1 medium onion, chopped
5 teaspoons beef bouillon granules
1 tablespoon cider vinegar
1/2 to 1 teaspoon salt
1/4 teaspoon pepper
2 bay leaves
1-1/2 cups chopped carrots
1-1/2 cups chopped celery
2 medium potatoes, peeled and cubed
1/2 cup medium pearl barley
1/2 teaspoon dried thyme
1/4 to 1/2 teaspoon dill weed

In a Dutch oven or soup kettle, place soup bones, water, onion, bouillon, vinegar, salt, pepper and bay leaves. Slowly bring to a boil; skim foam with a slotted spoon. Reduce heat; cover and simmer for 3-4 hours. Discard bay leaves. Set bones aside to cool; remove meat from bones and dice. Skim fat from the broth surface. Add meat, carrots, celery, potatoes, barley, thyme and dill. Cover and cook for 1 hour or until barley and vegetables are tender. **Yield:** 9 servings (about 2 quarts).

Rosy Potato Soup

Chives, parsley and paprika delicately season this distinctive soup. —Holly Youngers, Cunningham, Kansas

1 large onion, chopped
3/4 cup chopped celery
3 tablespoons butter *or* margarine
1 tablespoon all-purpose flour
1/2 to 3/4 teaspoon salt
3 cups milk
3 medium potatoes, peeled, cooked and sliced (2-1/2 cups)
1 tablespoon minced fresh parsley
1 tablespoon paprika

In a large saucepan, saute the onion and celery in butter until tender. Stir in flour and salt until blended. Gradually add milk. Bring to a boil; cook and stir for 2 minutes or until thickened and bubbly. Reduce heat. Add potatoes, parsley and paprika; heat through. **Yield:** 5 servings.

Elk Meat Chili

(Pictured below)

The longer this hearty chili simmers, the better it tastes! It's great cold-weather fare at our ranch.
—Jo Maasberg, Farson, Wyoming

2 pounds ground elk *or* buffalo meat
1/2 cup chopped onion
3 garlic cloves, minced
2 cans (14-1/2 ounces *each*) diced tomatoes, undrained
1 can (28 ounces) pork and beans, undrained
3 tablespoons salsa
1 tablespoon brown sugar
1 tablespoon chili powder
1/2 teaspoon garlic salt
1/2 teaspoon pepper

In a Dutch oven, cook elk, onion and garlic over medium heat until meat is no longer pink; drain. Stir in the remaining ingredients; bring to a boil. Reduce heat; cover and simmer for 2 hours. **Yield:** 6-8 servings.

Creamy White Chili

(Pictured below)

I got this wonderful recipe from my sister-in-law, who made a big batch and served a crowd one night. It was a hit. Plus, it's easy and quick, which is helpful since I'm a college student. —*Laura Brewer, Lafayette, Indiana*

1 pound boneless skinless chicken breasts, cut into 1/2-inch cubes
1 medium onion, chopped
1-1/2 teaspoons garlic powder
1 tablespoon vegetable oil
2 cans (15-1/2 ounces *each*) great northern beans, rinsed and drained
1 can (14-1/2 ounces) chicken broth
2 cans (4 ounces *each*) chopped green chilies
1 teaspoon salt
1 teaspoon ground cumin
1 teaspoon dried oregano
1/2 teaspoon pepper
1/4 teaspoon cayenne pepper
1 cup (8 ounces) sour cream
1/2 cup whipping cream

In a large saucepan, saute chicken, onion and garlic powder in oil until chicken is no longer pink. Add beans, broth, chilies and seasonings. Bring to a boil. Reduce heat; simmer, uncovered, for 30 minutes. Remove from the heat; stir in sour cream and cream. Serve immediately. **Yield:** 7 servings.

CHILI CONCOCTIONS like Creamy White Chili and Pepperoni Pizza Chili (shown above, top to bottom) offer a mouth-watering variety of flavors.

Pepperoni Pizza Chili

(Pictured below left)

I first made this recipe one day when I decided I just didn't enjoy making pizza crust—I simply put the pizza in a bowl instead! —*Marilouise Wyatt, Cowen, West Virginia*

1 pound ground beef
1 can (16 ounces) kidney beans, rinsed and drained
1 can (15 ounces) pizza sauce
1 can (14-1/2 ounces) Italian stewed tomatoes
1 can (8 ounces) tomato sauce
1-1/2 cups water
1 package (3-1/2 ounces) sliced pepperoni
1/2 cup chopped green pepper
1 teaspoon pizza seasoning *or* Italian seasoning
1 teaspoon salt
Shredded mozzarella cheese, optional

In a large saucepan, cook beef over medium heat until no longer pink; drain. Stir in the beans, pizza sauce, tomatoes, tomato sauce, water, pepperoni, green pepper, pizza seasoning and salt. Bring to a boil. Reduce heat; simmer, uncovered, for 30 minutes or until chili reaches desired thickness. Garnish with cheese if desired. **Yield:** 8 servings.

Cabbage Sausage Soup

My partner and I grow 300 acres of cabbage twice a year, then we harvest it by hand. This hearty soup showcases cabbage in a savory tomato broth. —*Bill Brim, Tifton, Georgia*

1 pound bulk Italian sausage
1 large onion, chopped
2 garlic cloves, minced
7 cups chopped cabbage (about 1-1/2 pounds)
4 cans (28 ounces *each*) diced tomatoes, undrained

2 teaspoons dried basil
2 teaspoons brown sugar
1 teaspoon dried oregano
3/4 teaspoon minced fresh rosemary *or* 1/4 teaspoon dried rosemary, crushed
1 bay leaf
1/2 teaspoon salt
1/8 teaspoon pepper

In a Dutch oven or soup kettle, cook sausage, onion and garlic over medium heat until meat is browned. Add cabbage; cook and stir for 3-5 minutes or until cabbage is crisp-tender. Stir in the remaining ingredients. Bring to a boil. Reduce heat; cover and simmer for 30-35 minutes or until cabbage is tender. Discard bay leaf before serving. **Yield:** 16 servings (4 quarts).

Sloppy Joes with Lentils

This is a great dish when friends are coming over. With both ground beef and lentils, these sandwiches are extra hearty. —*Paul Noetzel, Grafton, Wisconsin*

1 pound ground beef
1/2 cup chopped onion
1 garlic clove, minced
2 cups water
1 can (8 ounces) tomato sauce
1/2 cup dry lentils, rinsed
1/2 cup ketchup
1 teaspoon cider vinegar
1/2 teaspoon ground mustard
1/4 teaspoon pepper
6 to 8 hamburger buns, split

In a skillet, cook beef, onion and garlic over medium heat until meat is no longer pink; drain. Add the water, tomato sauce, lentils, ketchup, vinegar, mustard and pepper. Bring to a boil. Reduce heat; cover and simmer for 60-70 minutes or until lentils are tender. Serve on buns. **Yield:** 6-8 servings.

Yellow Split Pea Soup

This is a great new twist on traditional pea soup. It tastes wonderful and has a sunny yellow color.
—*Lynn Jurss, Thousand Oaks, California*

✓ Uses less fat, sugar or salt. Includes Nutritional Analysis and Diabetic Exchanges.

1 large onion, coarsely chopped
1 large celery rib with leaves, chopped
1 tablespoon olive *or* canola oil
1 tablespoon stick margarine
6 cups chicken broth
1 pound dry yellow split peas
2 tablespoons lemon juice
1/2 teaspoon ground cumin
1/2 teaspoon pepper
2 tablespoons minced fresh parsley
1/4 cup pistachios

In a large saucepan, saute onion and celery in oil and margarine until tender. Add broth; bring to a boil. Add peas; return to a boil. Reduce heat; cover and simmer for 1 hour or until peas are tender. Stir in lemon juice, cumin and pepper; simmer for 5 minutes. In small batches, puree soup in a blender; return to pan. Heat for 4-5 minutes. Garnish with parsley and pistachios. **Yield:** 6 servings.

Nutritional Analysis: One serving (1 cup) equals 374 calories, 7 g fat (1 g saturated fat), 0 cholesterol, 959 mg sodium, 57 g carbohydrate, 1 g fiber, 24 g protein. **Diabetic Exchanges:** 3 starch, 2 lean meat, 1 vegetable.

Bold Bean and Pork Chili

Sometimes I'll start making this chili on a Sunday—up to where it's time to add the beans. Then the next day, I'll take it out of the fridge and finish it off in just a few minutes. —*Natercia Yailaian*
Somerville, Massachusetts

1 pork shoulder *or* butt roast (4 to 5 pounds), trimmed and cut into 3/4-inch cubes
3 tablespoons olive *or* vegetable oil
2 large onions, chopped
8 garlic cloves, minced
4 cans (14-1/2 ounces *each*) chicken broth
1 can (28 ounces) crushed tomatoes
1/2 to 2/3 cup chili powder
3 tablespoons dried oregano
2 to 3 tablespoons ground cumin
4-1/2 teaspoons salt
2 teaspoons cayenne pepper
4 cans (15 ounces *each*) black beans, rinsed and drained
Minced fresh cilantro, optional

In a Dutch oven, saute pork in oil until no longer pink; drain. Add onions; cook and stir for 3 minutes. Add garlic; cook 2 minutes longer. Stir in the broth, tomatoes and seasonings. Bring to a boil. Reduce heat; simmer, uncovered, for 1 hour, stirring several times. Skim fat; stir in beans. Simmer 15-30 minutes longer or until chili reaches desired thickness. Garnish with cilantro if desired. **Yield:** 15 servings.

Grilled Beef Gyros

(Pictured below and on page 32)

A spicy marinade adds zip to these grilled beef slices tucked inside pita bread. Friends from Greece gave us their recipe for the cucumber sauce, which provides a cool contrast to the hot beef. I never have to worry about leftovers when I serve these sandwiches.
—Lee Rademaker, Hayfork, California

1 medium onion, cut into chunks
2 garlic cloves
2 tablespoons sugar
1 tablespoon ground mustard
1/2 teaspoon ground ginger *or* 2 teaspoons minced fresh gingerroot
1-1/2 teaspoons pepper
1/2 teaspoon cayenne pepper
1/2 cup soy sauce
1/4 cup water
1 boneless beef sirloin tip roast (2 to 3 pounds), cut into 1/4-inch-thick slices

CUCUMBER SAUCE:
1 medium cucumber, peeled, seeded and cut into chunks
4 garlic cloves
1/2 teaspoon salt
1/3 cup cider vinegar
1/3 cup olive *or* vegetable oil
2 cups (16 ounces) sour cream

8 to 10 pita breads, warmed and halved
Thinly sliced onion
Chopped tomato

In a blender or food processor, place the onion, garlic, sugar, mustard, ginger, pepper and cayenne; cover and process until onion is finely chopped. Add soy sauce and water; process until blended. Place the beef in a large resealable plastic bag. Add marinade. Seal bag and turn to coat; refrigerate for 1-2 hours. For sauce, combine the cucumber, garlic and salt in a blender or food processor; cover and process until cucumber is chopped. Add vinegar and oil; process until blended. Transfer to a bowl; stir in sour cream. Refrigerate until serving. Drain and discard marinade.

Grill beef, covered, over medium-hot heat until meat reaches desired doneness. Place beef in pita halves. Top with cucumber sauce, sliced onion and chopped tomato. Refrigerate any remaining sauce. **Yield:** 8-10 sandwiches.

Cowpoke Chili

(Pictured on page 32)

Many friends and relatives have requested my chili recipe, which I've been using for 25 years. It won first place in a local contest, chosen from among 10 other entries. *—Ramona Nelson, Fairbanks, Alaska*

1 pound ground beef
1 small onion, chopped
1 garlic clove, minced
1 can (10-1/2 ounces) condensed beef broth, undiluted
1 can (8 ounces) tomato sauce
1 can (6 ounces) tomato paste
1 can (15-1/2 ounces) hot chili beans
1 can (15 ounces) black beans, rinsed and drained
2 tablespoons sugar
1 tablespoon butter *or* margarine
1 teaspoon chili powder
1/4 teaspoon salt
1/4 teaspoon dried oregano
1/8 teaspoon ground cumin
1/8 teaspoon crushed red pepper flakes
Dash cayenne pepper
2 cups frozen lima beans, thawed
Cherry tomatoes, fresh oregano and small chili peppers, optional

In a large saucepan, cook beef, onion and garlic over medium heat until meat is no longer pink; drain. Stir in the broth, tomato sauce and paste until blended. Add the next 10 ingredients. Bring to a boil. Reduce heat; cover and simmer for 30 minutes. Add lima beans; cook 5-10 minutes longer or until beans are tender. Garnish with tomatoes, oregano and peppers if desired. **Yield:** 7 servings.

California Pepper Chili

(Pictured on front cover)

In my opinion, this is the world's best chili! It features three meats in a peppery eye-opening broth.
—Robyn Thompson, Los Angeles, California

1/2 pound bacon, diced
2-1/2 pounds beef stew meat, cut into 3/4-inch cubes
1-1/2 pounds pork stew meat, cut into 3/4-inch cubes
2 medium onions, chopped
6 to 8 garlic cloves, minced
1 to 2 tablespoons chopped seeded fresh serrano chili peppers
1 to 2 tablespoons chopped seeded fresh poblano chili peppers
1 to 2 tablespoons chopped seeded fresh jalapeno peppers
2 to 3 teaspoons cayenne pepper
1-1/2 teaspoons dried oregano
1 teaspoon salt
1 teaspoon ground cumin
1 can (15 ounces) tomato puree
1 can (14-1/2 ounces) beef broth
7 plum tomatoes, chopped
Shredded cheddar cheese, optional

In a large saucepan, cook bacon over medium heat until crisp. Remove to paper towels to drain, reserving 3 tablespoons drippings. In the drippings, cook the beef, pork and onions until meat is browned; drain. Add the garlic, peppers and seasonings; cook and stir for 1-2 minutes. Stir in the tomato puree, broth and tomatoes. Bring to a boil. Reduce heat; cover and simmer for 1 to 1-1/2 hours or until meat is tender. Garnish with reserved bacon and cheese if desired. **Yield:** 8 servings.

Editor's Note: When cutting or seeding hot peppers, use rubber or plastic gloves to protect your hands. Avoid touching your face.

Zippy Pork Chili

(Pictured above right)

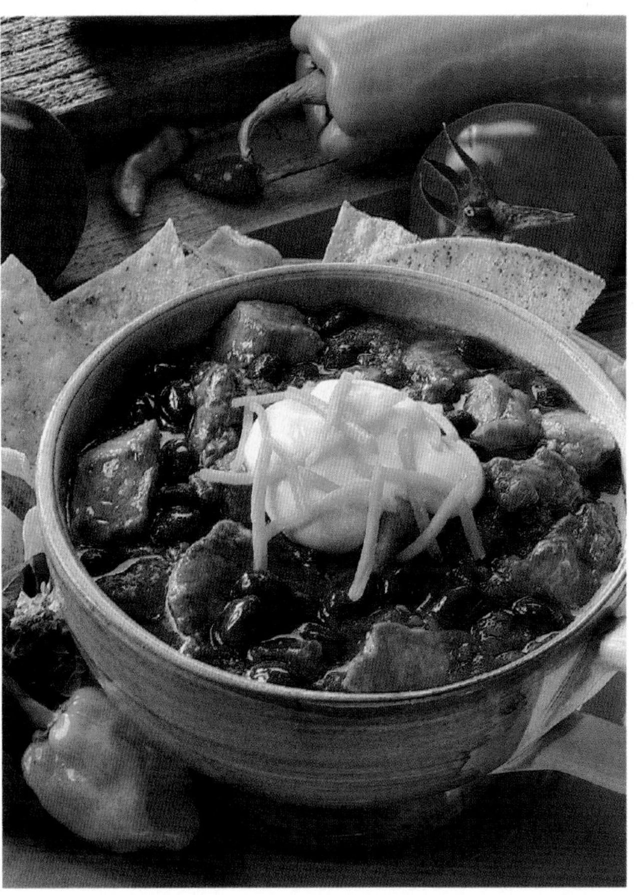

In addition to eating this chili the traditional way (with a spoon!), my family likes to scoop bites onto tortilla chips. The leftovers are great rolled in tortillas and reheated, too. It's so comforting to have a pot simmering when cold Kansas winds are blowing.
—Michelle Beran, Claflin, Kansas

1 boneless pork roast (3 to 4 pounds), cut into 1-inch cubes
1 medium onion, chopped
1 garlic clove, minced
2 tablespoons vegetable oil
2 cans (15-1/2 ounces *each*) chili beans
2 cans (10 ounces *each*) diced tomatoes and green chilies, undrained
1 can (14-1/2 ounces) diced tomatoes, undrained
1 cup water
1 teaspoon beef bouillon granules
Chili powder, pepper and cayenne pepper to taste
Sour cream, tortilla chips and shredded cheddar cheese, optional

In a Dutch oven, cook pork, onion and garlic in oil over medium heat until meat is browned. Add the beans, tomatoes, water, bouillon and seasonings. Bring to a boil. Reduce heat; cover and simmer for 2 hours or until meat is tender. If desired, serve with sour cream, tortilla chips and cheese. **Yield:** 10 servings.

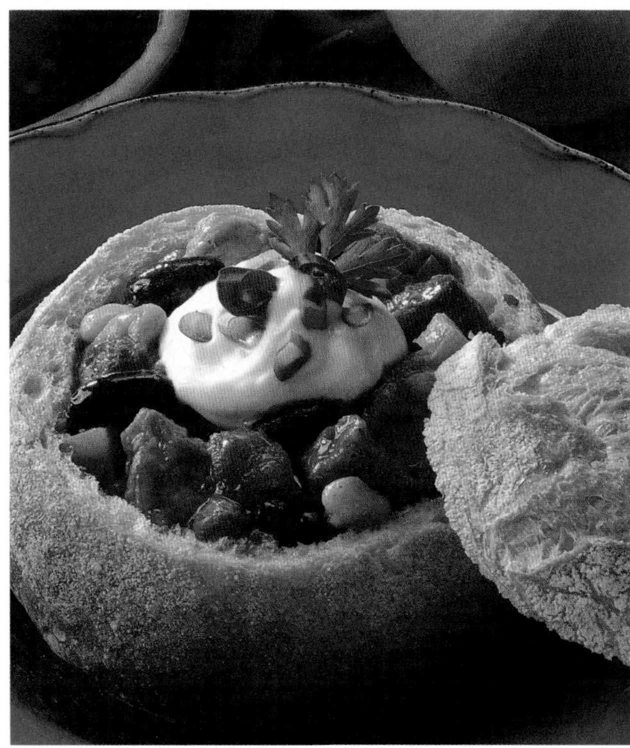

Chili in Bread Bowls

(Pictured above)

Some say you can have your cake and eat it, too...I say eat your chili and the bowl, too! I work the graveyard shift at a post office. During those hours, there is no place to buy meals, so I often bring in this chili to share. —*Nancy Clancy, Standish, Maine*

1 tablespoon all-purpose flour
1/4 teaspoon salt
1/8 teaspoon pepper
1/2 pound *each* lean beef stew meat, boneless skinless chicken breast and boneless pork, cut into cubes
1 tablespoon vegetable oil
1 medium onion, chopped
1 medium green pepper, chopped
1 jalapeno pepper, seeded and chopped*
1 can (28 ounces) diced tomatoes, drained
1 can (16 ounces) kidney beans, rinsed and drained
1 can (15-1/2 ounces) navy beans *or* great northern beans, rinsed and drained
1 can (8 ounces) tomato sauce
1 tablespoon chili powder
1 garlic clove, minced
1-1/2 teaspoons ground cumin
1/2 teaspoon dried basil
1/4 to 1/2 teaspoon cayenne pepper
9 large hard rolls
Sour cream, chopped green onions and sweet red pepper, optional

In a large resealable plastic bag, combine the flour, salt and pepper. Add meat in batches; toss to coat. In a large skillet, brown meat in oil in batches. Transfer to a 5-qt. slow cooker with a slotted spoon. Stir in onion, peppers, tomatoes, beans, tomato sauce and seasonings. Cover and cook on low for 7-8 hours or until the meat is tender. Cut tops off rolls; carefully hollow out bottom halves. Spoon about 1 cup of chili into each roll. Garnish with sour cream, onions and red pepper if desired. **Yield:** 9 servings.

***Editor's Note:** When cutting or seeding hot peppers, use rubber or plastic gloves to protect your hands. Avoid touching your face.

Potato and Cabbage Soup

I traced this hearty soup recipe to my great-grandmother, whose parents were potato farmers in Ireland. My mom served many a bowlful of this soup while I was growing up, and I've done the same for my family. —*Pat Rimmel, Ford City, Pennsylvania*

1 large onion, chopped
2 tablespoons butter *or* margarine
10 cups water
6 cups chopped cabbage
4 cups diced peeled potatoes
3 tablespoons chicken bouillon granules
1/2 teaspoon coarsely ground pepper
1/2 teaspoon dried minced garlic
4 cups cubed fully cooked ham

In a large saucepan or Dutch oven, saute onion in butter until tender. Add the water, cabbage, potatoes, bouillon, pepper and garlic. Cover and simmer for 20-25 minutes or until potatoes are tender. Stir in ham; heat through. **Yield:** 12-14 servings (about 3-1/2 quarts).

Dandy Corn Dogs

These homemade corn dogs are a real treat. The coating is tender and has the tangy taste of mustard.
—*Lauren Heyn, Oak Creek, Wisconsin*

1 cup all-purpose flour
2 tablespoons cornmeal
4 teaspoons ground mustard
2 teaspoons baking powder
1/4 teaspoon salt
1 egg, beaten
3/4 cup milk
10 wooden skewers

10 hot dogs
Oil for deep-fat frying

In a bowl, combine the dry ingredients. Stir in the egg and milk just until moistened. Insert skewers into hot dogs; dip into batter. In a skillet, heat 2 in. of oil to 375°. Fry corn dogs for 5-8 minutes or until golden brown. Drain on paper towels. **Yield:** 10 servings.

Barbecued Beef Chili

Served with bread and a side salad, this slow-cooker chili makes a hearty meal. The recipe was inspired by two friends when we were talking about food at a potluck barbecue. —Phyllis Shyan, Elgin, Illinois

7 teaspoons chili powder
1 tablespoon garlic powder
2 teaspoons celery seed
1 teaspoon coarsely ground pepper
1/4 to 1/2 teaspoon cayenne pepper
1 fresh beef brisket* (3 to 4 pounds)
1 medium green pepper, chopped
1 small onion, chopped
1 bottle (12 ounces) chili sauce
1 cup ketchup
1/2 cup barbecue sauce
1/3 cup packed brown sugar
1/4 cup cider vinegar
1/4 cup Worcestershire sauce
1 teaspoon ground mustard
1 can (15-1/2 ounces) hot chili beans
1 can (15-1/2 ounces) great northern beans, rinsed and drained

Combine the first five ingredients; rub over brisket. Cut into eight pieces; place in a slow cooker. Combine the green pepper, onion, chili sauce, ketchup, barbecue sauce, brown sugar, vinegar, Worcestershire sauce and mustard; pour over meat. Cover and cook on high for 5-6 hours or until meat is tender. Remove meat; cool slightly. Meanwhile, skim fat from cooking juices. Shred meat with two forks; return to slow cooker. Reduce heat to low. Stir in the beans. Cover and cook for 1 hour or until heated through. **Yield:** 12 servings.

***Editor's Note:** This is a fresh beef brisket, not corned beef.

Thyme for Meatball Soup

(Pictured at right)

Thyme is one of my favorite herbs to grow. It adds a fresh spark to this hearty soup. —Jennie Freeman Long Creek, Oregon

✓ Uses less fat, sugar or salt. Includes Nutritional Analysis and Diabetic Exchanges.

1 egg
1/4 cup dry bread crumbs
2 tablespoons minced fresh thyme *or* 2 teaspoons dried thyme, *divided*
1/2 teaspoon salt
1-1/2 pounds ground beef
1 small onion, chopped
2 medium carrots, chopped
3/4 pound fresh mushrooms, sliced
1 tablespoon olive *or* vegetable oil
1-1/4 pounds red potatoes, cubed
2 cans (14-1/2 ounces *each*) beef broth
1 can (14-1/2 ounces) stewed tomatoes

In a bowl, combine egg, bread crumbs, half of the thyme and salt. Crumble beef over mixture and mix well. Shape into 1-in. balls. In a Dutch oven or soup kettle, brown meatballs; drain and set aside. In the same pan, saute onion, carrots and mushrooms in oil until onion is tender. Stir in the potatoes, broth, tomatoes, meatballs and remaining thyme. Bring to a boil. Reduce heat; cover and simmer for 25-30 minutes or until potatoes are tender. **Yield:** 12 servings.

Nutritional Analysis: One serving (prepared with lean ground beef) equals 190 calories, 8 g fat (2 g saturated fat), 39 mg cholesterol, 775 mg sodium, 14 g carbohydrate, 2 g fiber, 17 g protein. **Diabetic Exchanges:** 2 lean meat, 1 starch.

Baked Potato Soup

(Pictured below)

My husband and I enjoyed a delicious potato soup at a restaurant while on vacation, and I came home determined to duplicate it. It took me 5 years to get the taste right, but the wait was worth it! —Joann Goetz Genoa, Ohio

4 large baking potatoes (about 2-3/4 pounds)
2/3 cup butter *or* margarine
2/3 cup all-purpose flour
3/4 teaspoon salt
1/4 teaspoon white pepper
6 cups milk
1 cup (8 ounces) sour cream
1/4 cup thinly sliced green onions
10 bacon strips, cooked and crumbled
1 cup (4 ounces) shredded cheddar cheese

Bake potatoes at 350° for 65-75 minutes or until tender; cool completely. Peel and cube potatoes. In a large saucepan, melt butter; stir in flour, salt and pepper until smooth. Gradually add milk. Bring to a boil; cook and stir for 2 minutes or until thickened. Remove from the heat; whisk in sour cream. Add potatoes and green onions. Garnish with bacon and cheese. **Yield:** 10 servings.

NOTHING warms up a cool day in a more satisfying way than steaming soups like Classic Chicken Noodle Soup, Baked Potato Soup and French Onion Tomato Soup (shown above, top to bottom).

French Onion Tomato Soup

(Pictured at left)

Tomato juice gives extra flavor to this wonderful soup that's so quick and easy to prepare. I found the recipe many years ago in a recipe book of my mother's and have shared it with many people.
—Clara Honeyager, Mukwonago, Wisconsin

4 cups thinly sliced onions
1 garlic clove, minced
2 tablespoons butter *or* margarine
1 can (46 ounces) tomato juice
2 teaspoons beef bouillon granules
3 tablespoons lemon juice
2 teaspoons dried parsley flakes
2 teaspoons brown sugar
6 slices French bread, toasted
2 cups (8 ounces) shredded mozzarella cheese

In a large saucepan, saute onions and garlic in butter until tender. Add the tomato juice, bouillon, lemon juice, parsley and brown sugar. Bring to a boil. Reduce heat; simmer, uncovered, for 10 minutes, stirring occasionally. Ladle soup into 10-oz. ovenproof soup bowls or ramekins. Top with French bread; sprinkle with cheese. Broil 4-6 in. from the heat for 2-3 minutes or until cheese is bubbly. **Yield:** 6 servings.

Classic Chicken Noodle Soup

(Pictured at left)

After working all day, my husband, Todd, and I enjoy this hearty soup along with crusty rolls and a salad. It's real comfort food. —Nila Grahl Des Plaines, Illinois

1 broiler/fryer chicken (3 to 4 pounds), cut up
10 cups water
1 large carrot, sliced
1 large onion, sliced
1 celery rib, sliced
1 garlic clove, minced
1 bay leaf
1 teaspoon dried thyme
1 teaspoon salt
1/4 teaspoon pepper
SOUP INGREDIENTS:
2 large carrots, sliced
2 celery ribs, sliced
1 medium onion, chopped
2 cups uncooked fine egg noodles
1 cup frozen peas
1/2 cup frozen cut green beans

In a large soup kettle or Dutch oven, combine the first 10 ingredients. Bring to a boil. Reduce heat; cover and simmer for 1-1/2 to 2 hours or until meat is tender. Remove chicken; cool. Remove and discard skin and bones. Chop chicken; set aside. Strain broth, discarding vegetables and bay leaf. Return broth to pan; add carrots, celery and onion. Bring to a boil. Reduce heat; cover and simmer for 10 minutes or until vegetables are tender.

Add noodles and chicken. Bring to a boil. Reduce heat; cover and simmer for 6 minutes. Stir in peas and beans. Cook for 2-4 minutes or until the beans and noodles are tender. **Yield:** 6-8 servings.

Venison Stromboli

(Pictured on page 32)

The first time I served this dish to my deer-hunting family, everyone thought I had ordered from an Italian restaurant. My brother-in-law even asked me to make this for his birthday dinner. *—Dianna Croskey Gibsonia, Pennsylvania*

2 loaves (1 pound *each*) frozen bread dough, thawed
1 pound ground venison
1 medium onion, chopped
1/2 medium green pepper, chopped
1 can (4 ounces) mushroom stems and pieces, drained
2 tablespoons olive *or* vegetable oil
1 teaspoon Italian seasoning
3 tablespoons prepared Italian salad dressing, *divided*
1 cup (4 ounces) shredded cheddar cheese
1 cup (4 ounces) shredded mozzarella cheese
2 packages (3 ounces *each*) sliced pepperoni
1/4 cup grated Parmesan cheese
Spaghetti sauce, warmed, optional

Let dough rise in a warm place until doubled. Meanwhile, in a skillet over medium heat, cook venison, onion, green pepper and mushrooms in oil until meat is no longer pink. Drain. Stir in Italian seasoning; set aside. On a lightly floured surface, punch dough down. Roll out each loaf into a 16-in. x 8-in. rectangle; cut in half widthwise. Brush 1/2 tablespoon Italian dressing over each square to within 1 in. of edges. On half of each square, mound a fourth of the venison mixture, cheddar cheese, mozzarella and pepperoni. Fold dough over filling and seal edges well.

Place on a greased baking sheet. Brush with remaining dressing; sprinkle with Parmesan cheese. Bake at 350° for 30-35 minutes or until golden brown. Slice; serve with spaghetti sauce if desired. **Yield:** 4 loaves (1-2 servings each).

Ham 'n' Veggie Soup

When I add some ham to this flavorful broth, which is already chock-full of vegetables, the colorful dish becomes a complete meal. The recipe makes a nice size batch for the family. *—Barbara Thompson Lansdale, Pennsylvania*

1 medium onion, thinly sliced and separated into rings
1 medium zucchini, cubed
1 tablespoon olive *or* vegetable oil
1 pound fresh mushrooms, sliced
3 cups fresh *or* frozen corn
3 cups cubed fully cooked ham
6 medium tomatoes, peeled, seeded and chopped
1/2 cup chicken broth
1-1/2 teaspoons salt
1/2 teaspoon pepper
1/2 teaspoon garlic powder
Shredded mozzarella cheese

In a large saucepan, saute the onion and zucchini in oil for 5 minutes or until the onion is tender. Add the mushrooms, corn and ham; cook and stir for 5 minutes. Stir in the tomatoes, broth and seasonings. Bring to a boil. Reduce heat; cover and simmer for 5 minutes. Uncover; simmer for 5-8 minutes longer. Garnish with mozzarella cheese. **Yield:** 8-10 servings.

Microwave Minestrone

(Pictured above)

This hearty soup is packed with vegetables and pasta and couldn't be any easier to prepare. By the time I set the table, it's ready. —*Emma Magielda, Amsterdam, New York*

- **1 cup *each* sliced carrots, celery and zucchini**
- **1/2 cup diced sweet yellow pepper**
- **1 small onion, chopped**
- **1 tablespoon olive *or* vegetable oil**
- **1 can (15 ounces) cannellini *or* white kidney beans, rinsed and drained**
- **1 can (14-1/2 ounces) beef broth**
- **1 can (14-1/2 ounces) diced tomatoes, undrained**
- **1 cup medium pasta shells, cooked and drained**
- **1/2 to 1 teaspoon dried basil**
- **1/2 teaspoon salt**
- **1/4 teaspoon pepper**

In a 2-qt. microwave-safe bowl, combine the carrots, celery, zucchini, yellow pepper and onion. Drizzle with oil; toss to coat. Cover and microwave on high for 5 minutes. Stir in the remaining ingredients. Cover and cook on high for 15 minutes. **Yield:** 5 servings.

Editor's Note: This recipe was tested in an 850-watt microwave.

Vegetarian Chili

My husband and I try to have at least one vegetarian meal each week, and this is one of our favorites. The recipe makes a large pot of chili that's chock-full of color and flavor. —*Marilyn Barilleaux, Bothell, Washington*

✓ Uses less fat, sugar or salt. Includes Nutritional Analysis and Diabetic Exchanges.

- **4 medium zucchini, chopped**
- **2 medium onions, chopped**
- **1 medium green pepper, chopped**
- **1 medium sweet red pepper, chopped**
- **4 garlic cloves, minced**
- **1/4 cup olive *or* canola oil**
- **2 cans (28 ounces *each*) Italian stewed tomatoes, cut up**
- **1 can (15 ounces) tomato sauce**
- **1 can (15 ounces) pinto beans, rinsed and drained**
- **1 can (15 ounces) black beans, rinsed and drained**
- **1 jalapeno pepper, seeded and chopped***
- **1/4 cup *each* minced fresh cilantro and parsley**
- **2 tablespoons chili powder**
- **1 tablespoon sugar**
- **1 teaspoon salt**
- **1 teaspoon ground cumin**

In a Dutch oven, saute zucchini, onions, peppers and garlic in oil until tender. Stir in the tomatoes, tomato sauce, beans, jalapeno and seasonings. Bring to a boil over medium heat. Reduce heat; cover and simmer for 30 minutes, stirring occasionally. **Yield:** 16 servings.

Nutritional Analysis: One serving (1 cup) equals 131 calories, 4 g fat (trace saturated fat), 0 cholesterol, 622 mg sodium, 18 g carbohydrate, 6 g fiber, 5 g protein. **Diabetic Exchanges:** 1 starch, 1 vegetable, 1 fat.

***Editor's Note:** When cutting or seeding hot peppers, use rubber or plastic gloves to protect your hands. Avoid touching your face.

Sunday Gumbo

(Pictured on page 32)

With sausage, chicken and shrimp plus rice, a medley of vegetables and the "heat" of cayenne, this warming soup is one my husband and I enjoy for dinner many Sunday evenings. It's wonderful with crusty bread. —*Debbie Burchette, Summitville, Indiana*

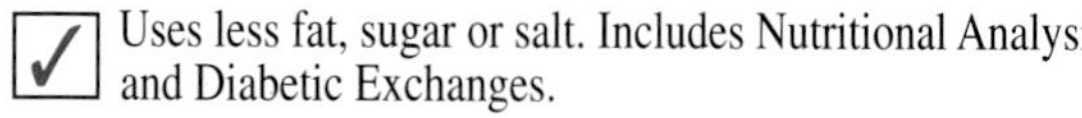

1 pound Italian sausage links, sliced
1 pound boneless skinless chicken breasts, cubed
3 tablespoons vegetable oil
1 medium sweet red pepper, chopped
1 medium onion, chopped
3 celery ribs, chopped
1 teaspoon dried marjoram
1 teaspoon dried thyme
1/2 teaspoon garlic powder
1/2 teaspoon cayenne pepper
3 cans (14-1/2 ounces *each*) chicken broth
2/3 cup uncooked brown rice
1 can (14-1/2 ounces) diced tomatoes, undrained
1 pound uncooked medium shrimp, peeled and deveined
2 cups frozen sliced okra

In a Dutch oven, brown sausage and chicken in oil. Remove with a slotted spoon and keep warm. In the drippings, saute red pepper, onion and celery until tender. Stir in the seasonings; cook for 5 minutes. Stir in the broth, rice and sausage mixture; bring to a boil. Reduce heat; cover and simmer for 20-25 minutes or until rice is tender. Stir in tomatoes, shrimp and okra; cook for 10 minutes or until shrimp turn pink, stirring occasionally. **Yield:** 16 servings (about 4 quarts).

Nutritional Analysis: One 1-cup serving (prepared with reduced-fat turkey Italian sausage) equals 187 calories, 7 g fat (1 g saturated fat), 87 mg cholesterol, 633 mg sodium, 11 g carbohydrate, 2 g fiber, 19 g protein. **Diabetic Exchanges:** 2 lean meat, 1 vegetable, 1/2 starch.

Cream of Asparagus Soup

I associate asparagus with springtime...and its beautiful green color with new life. That's why this delightful soup is the perfect starter to our family's Easter dinner each year. —*Lynn Vogel*
Pittsburgh, Pennsylvania

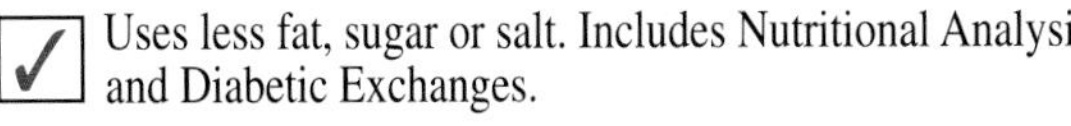
Uses less fat, sugar or salt. Includes Nutritional Analysis and Diabetic Exchanges.

3 medium leeks (white portion only), chopped
3 tablespoons butter *or* stick margarine
4 cups chicken broth
1-1/2 pounds fresh asparagus, trimmed and cut into 1-inch pieces
2 cups diced peeled potatoes
1/8 to 1/4 teaspoon white pepper
1/2 cup 2% milk
1 tablespoon minced fresh parsley

In a large saucepan, saute the leeks in butter. Add broth, asparagus, potatoes and pepper. Bring to a boil. Reduce heat; cover and simmer for 10 minutes or until vegetables are tender. In a blender, process soup in batches until smooth; return to the pan. Add milk; cook over low heat until heated through. Sprinkle with parsley. **Yield:** 6 servings.

Nutritional Analysis: One serving (1 cup) equals 178 calories, 8 g fat (4 g saturated fat), 17 mg cholesterol, 748 mg sodium, 22 g carbohydrate, 4 g fiber, 6 g protein. **Diabetic Exchanges:** 1-1/2 fat, 1 starch, 1 vegetable.

Rock'n and Roast'n Chili

I got the basics of this recipe from a friend at a Super Bowl party and tweaked it from there. People who like spicy food really go for it. But I do have to tone it down a bit for my wife and my mom. —*Rob Via*
Charlotte, North Carolina

2 pounds beef stew meat, cut into 3/4-inch cubes
1 medium onion, chopped
2 to 3 garlic cloves, minced
2 tablespoons vegetable oil
1 jar (16 ounces) hot banana peppers
2 cans (14-1/2 ounces *each*) diced tomatoes, undrained
1 can (10 ounces) diced tomatoes and green chilies, undrained
1 can (6 ounces) tomato paste
1 can (16 ounces) kidney beans, rinsed and drained
1 can (4 ounces) chopped green chilies
1 fresh jalapeno *or* banana pepper, seeded and chopped
2 tablespoons chili powder
1 to 2 tablespoons hot pepper sauce
1 teaspoon salt
1/8 teaspoon ground cumin
Additional banana peppers, optional

In a large saucepan, cook beef, onion and garlic in oil over medium heat until meat is no longer pink; drain. Remove stems and seeds of 10 hot banana peppers; chop (refrigerate remaining peppers for another use). Add peppers, tomatoes, tomato paste, beans, chilies, jalapeno and seasonings to beef mixture. Bring to a boil. Reduce heat; cover and simmer for 2 hours or until meat is tender. Uncover; simmer until chili reaches desired thickness. Garnish with peppers if desired. **Yield:** 8 servings.

Editor's Note: When cutting or seeding hot peppers, use rubber or plastic gloves to protect your hands. Avoid touching your face.

Southwestern Tomato Soup

(Pictured below)

This smooth flavorful tomato soup is unbeatable when the season's ripest tomatoes are available and the weather starts to cool. Each delicious fresh-tasting bowlful will warm you from the inside out.
—Sherri Jackson, Chillicothe, Ohio

10 plum tomatoes, halved lengthwise
1 to 2 Anaheim peppers, halved and seeded
1/2 cup chopped onion
2 garlic cloves, minced
1 tablespoon olive *or* vegetable oil
2 cans (14-1/2 ounces *each*) chicken broth
1 tablespoon minced fresh cilantro *or* parsley
2 teaspoons ground cumin
1/2 teaspoon sugar
1/2 teaspoon salt
1/4 teaspoon pepper
Vegetable oil for frying
8 corn tortillas (6 inches), cut into 1/4-inch strips
Sour cream, optional

Place tomatoes cut side down on a broiler pan; broil 3-4 in. from the heat for 15-20 minutes. Peel and discard skins. Repeat with peppers, broiling for 5-10 minutes. In a skillet, saute onion and garlic in oil until tender. Transfer to a blender or food processor; add the tomatoes and peppers. Cover and process until smooth. Pour into a large saucepan; cook and stir over medium heat for 2 minutes.

Press mixture through a strainer with a spoon; discard seeds. Return tomato mixture to the pan. Add broth, cilantro, cumin, sugar, salt and pepper. Cover and cook on low for 15-20 minutes or until heated through. Meanwhile, heat 1/2 in. of oil in a skillet to 375°. Fry tortilla strips, in batches, for 3-5 minutes or until golden brown; drain on paper towels. Garnish bowls of soup with tortilla strips. Serve with sour cream if desired. **Yield:** 6 servings.

Russian Borscht

I immigrated to the United States from western Russia in 1998. When I made friends, I found that many people had heard of Borscht, a traditional soup made with fresh beets, but few knew how to cook it. So I prepared this recipe from my grandmother, and everyone seemed to like it.
—Svetlana Chriscaden, Falconer, New York

8 cups water
1 pound beef shanks
5 whole peppercorns
2 bay leaves
1 teaspoon salt
1/2 teaspoon dill weed
3 medium uncooked beets, peeled and shredded
2 tablespoons vegetable oil, *divided*
2 teaspoons white vinegar
2 medium potatoes, peeled and cubed
2 medium carrots, sliced
1 cup shredded cabbage
2 tablespoons minced fresh parsley
1 medium onion, chopped
1 tablespoon all-purpose flour
2 medium tomatoes, chopped
1/2 cup sour cream

Place the first six ingredients in a large soup kettle or Dutch oven; bring to a boil. Reduce heat; cover and simmer for 1-1/2 hours or until beef is tender. Meanwhile, in a skillet, saute beets in 1 tablespoon oil for 3 minutes. Stir in vinegar; set aside. Remove beef with a slotted spoon; cool. Remove meat from bones; discard bones. Cut meat into chunks; set aside. Strain broth, discarding peppercorns and bay leaves. Skim fat. Add enough water to broth to measure 6 cups; return to kettle. Add potatoes, carrots, cabbage, parsley and beets. Bring to a boil.

In a skillet, saute onion in remaining oil for 5-7 minutes or until tender. Sprinkle with flour; stir until blended. Whisk into soup. Reduce heat; cover and simmer for 30 minutes or until vegetables are tender. Add tomatoes. Process soup in small batches in a blender or food processor; pour into a large saucepan. Add beef; heat through. Garnish with sour cream. **Yield:** 8 servings.

Wisconsin Split Pea Soup

(Pictured on page 32)

Marjoram, garlic, potatoes and carrots blend nicely with split peas in this hearty yet economical soup. I also plant peas in my garden. They grow so well that I pick enough to freeze and enjoy all winter.
—Linda Rock, Stratford, Wisconsin

1 pound dry split peas
2-1/2 quarts water
1 meaty ham bone
1-1/2 cups chopped onion
1 cup *each* diced celery, carrots and potatoes
1 teaspoon dried parsley flakes
1/2 teaspoon pepper
1/4 teaspoon garlic salt
1/4 teaspoon dried marjoram
Salt to taste

In a Dutch oven or soup kettle, place the peas, water and ham bone; bring to a boil. Reduce heat; cover and simmer for 2 hours, stirring occasionally. Stir in the remaining ingredients. Bring to a boil. Reduce heat; cover and simmer for 30 minutes or until vegetables are tender. Remove ham bone; when cool enough to handle, remove meat from the bone. Chop ham and return to the soup; heat through. **Yield:** 12 servings (3 quarts).

Ground Beef Chili

(Pictured above right)

Everyone who tastes my chili comments that it is restaurant-quality. It's especially good with homemade corn bread. I enjoy developing original recipes like this.
—Shannon Wright, Erie, Pennsylvania

3 pounds ground beef
1 large onion, chopped
1 medium green pepper, chopped
2 celery ribs, chopped

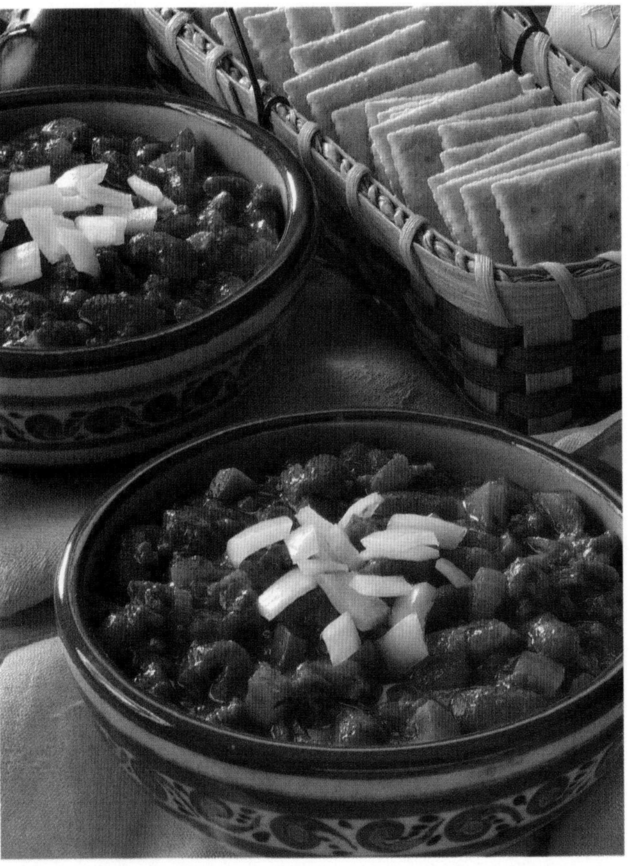

2 cans (16 ounces each) kidney beans, rinsed and drained
1 can (29 ounces) tomato puree
1 jar (16 ounces) salsa
1 can (14-1/2 ounces) diced tomatoes, undrained
1 can (10-1/2 ounces) condensed beef broth, undiluted
1 to 2 cups water
1/4 cup chili powder
2 tablespoons Worcestershire sauce
1 tablespoon dried basil
2 teaspoons ground cumin
2 teaspoons steak sauce
1 teaspoon garlic powder
1 teaspoon salt
1 teaspoon coarsely ground pepper
1-1/2 teaspoons browning sauce, optional
Additional chopped onion, optional

In a Dutch oven, cook the beef, onion, green pepper and celery over medium heat until meat is no longer pink and vegetables are tender; drain. Stir in the beans, tomato puree, salsa, tomatoes, broth, water, seasonings and browning sauce if desired. Bring to a boil. Reduce heat; simmer, uncovered, for 30 minutes or until chili reaches desired thickness. Garnish with chopped onion if desired. **Yield:** 16 servings.

Side Dishes & Condiments

When you need an accompaniment to a main dish or a tasty topping for a favorite food, turn to this chapter. You'll find plenty of pleasing choices.

WINNING SIDES. Clockwise from upper left: Asparagus Nut Stir-Fry (p. 52), Spicy Sweet Potatoes (p. 52), Chunky Ketchup (p. 54), Romaine Roasted Corn (p. 55) and Hot Pepper Jelly (p. 55).

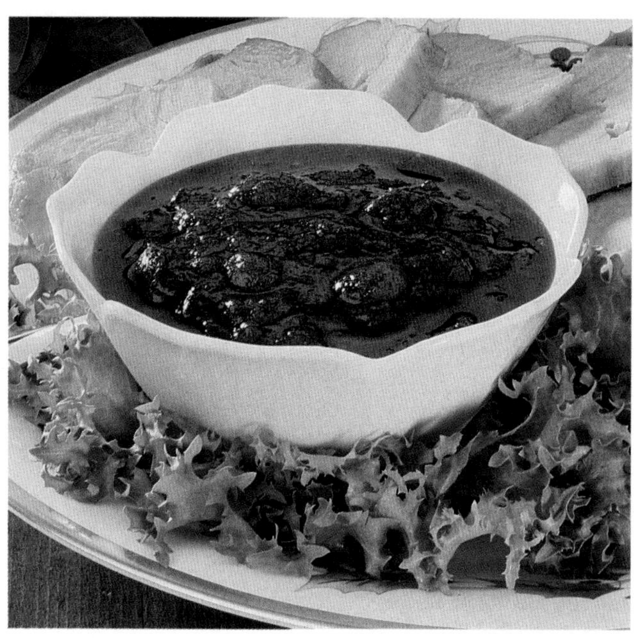

Pear Cranberry Sauce

(Pictured above)

We don't care for regular cranberry sauce, so I usually perk it up with other fruit. This pear version is a family favorite. —Joyce Bowman, Lady Lake, Florida

2-1/2 cups cubed peeled ripe pears (about 3 medium)
1 cup water
1/2 teaspoon ground ginger *or* 1 to 2 teaspoons minced fresh gingerroot
1 cinnamon stick (3 inches), broken in half
1 package (12 ounces) fresh *or* frozen cranberries
1 to 1-1/4 cups sugar

In a saucepan, combine the pears, water, ginger and cinnamon. Bring to a boil. Reduce heat; simmer, uncovered, for 5 minutes. Stir in cranberries and sugar. Return to a boil. Reduce heat; simmer, uncovered, for 10-12 minutes or until the cranberries have popped and sauce is slightly thickened, stirring several times. Discard cinnamon sticks. Mash sauce if desired. Cool. Cover and refrigerate. **Yield:** about 2 cups.

Latkes

I inherited my mother's love of cooking. I serve these crispy potato pancakes for Hanukkah and other celebrations. —Rachel Delano, Toppahannock, Virginia

2 cups shredded peeled potatoes (about 2 medium)
1/2 cup finely chopped onion
2 green onions, chopped
1 egg, lightly beaten
Salt and pepper to taste
Oil for frying

Place potatoes in a clean linen towel; squeeze, reserving liquid in a measuring cup. Set aside until potato starch settles. Drain off top liquid; set potato starch aside. In a bowl, combine potatoes, onions, egg, salt, pepper and reserved potato starch.

Heat 2 tablespoons oil in a large skillet. Shape potato mixture by 2 tablespoonfuls into patties; place in hot oil, pressing lightly to flatten. Fry until golden brown, about 1-1/2 minutes on each side. Drain on paper towels. Serve immediately or place in a warm oven until ready to serve. **Yield:** 1-1/2 dozen.

Gingered Squash and Pears

Butternut squash and pears are a delightful duo delicately seasoned with ginger, honey and nutmeg. —Jane Rossi, Charlotte, North Carolina

✓ Uses less fat, sugar or salt. Includes Nutritional Analysis and Diabetic Exchanges.

1 medium butternut squash, peeled, seeded and cubed (about 6-1/2 cups)
1 medium pear, peeled and cubed
1/4 teaspoon ground ginger *or* 1-1/2 teaspoons grated fresh gingerroot
1 tablespoon honey
1/8 teaspoon ground nutmeg

Place squash in a large skillet; cover with water. Bring to a boil. Reduce heat; cover and simmer for 10 minutes or until tender. Drain. Stir in pear and ginger. Cover and cook for 5-7 minutes or until pear is tender. Stir in honey and heat through. Sprinkle with nutmeg. **Yield:** 8 servings.

Nutritional Analysis: One serving (3/4 cup) equals 72 calories, trace fat (trace saturated fat), 0 cholesterol, 5 mg sodium, 19 g carbohydrate, 4 g fiber, 1 g protein. **Diabetic Exchange:** 1 starch.

White Sauce for Pasta

My husband, Jimmy, and I created the recipe for this versatile sauce. —Ruth Marie Lyons, Boulder, Colorado

✓ Uses less fat, sugar or salt. Includes Nutritional Analysis and Diabetic Exchanges.

2 tablespoons stick margarine
3 tablespoons all-purpose flour
2 tablespoons butter-flavored granules*
1 tablespoon reduced-sodium chicken bouillon granules

1-1/2 cups boiling water
1 cup fat-free milk
Pepper to taste

In a saucepan, melt margarine. Stir in flour, butter-flavored granules and bouillon until blended. Gradually add water and milk. Bring to a boil; cook and stir for 2 minutes or until thickened. Season with pepper. **Yield:** 2 cups.

Nutritional Analysis: One serving (1/4 cup) equals 46 calories, 3 g fat (trace saturated fat), 1 mg cholesterol, 476 mg sodium, 4 g carbohydrate, 0 fiber, 2 g protein. **Diabetic Exchange:** 1 fat.

***Editor's Note:** This recipe was tested with Butter Buds Butter Flavor Mix.

Lemon Curd

I use homegrown lemons to make this special spread, which tastefully tops muffins and bread.
—Mary Thompson, Weslaco, Texas

4 eggs
2 cups sugar
1 cup butter (no substitutes), melted
2/3 cup lemon juice
3 tablespoons grated lemon peel
1/8 teaspoon salt

In the top of a double boiler, beat eggs and sugar. Stir in butter, lemon juice, peel and salt. Cook over simmering water for 15 minutes or until mixture is thickened and reaches 160°. Cover and store in the refrigerator for up to 1 week. Serve chilled. **Yield:** 3-1/2 cups.

Greenbrier's Potatoes

These popular potatoes are served at The Greenbrier resort in White Sulphur Springs, West Virginia. The old-fashioned scalloped potatoes set up firmly and cut into individual servings.

5 pounds potatoes, peeled and sliced
2 cups whipping cream
2 garlic cloves, minced
1/2 teaspoon salt
1/2 teaspoon pepper
6 eggs, lightly beaten
3-1/2 cups shredded Parmesan cheese, *divided*

Rinse potatoes with cold water; place in a large saucepan. Add the cream, garlic, salt and pepper; bring to a boil. Reduce heat; cover and simmer for 30 minutes or until potatoes are crisp-tender. Remove from the heat; stir in eggs and 2-3/4 cups of cheese. Pour into a greased 13-in. x 9-in. x 2-in. baking dish. Sprinkle with the remaining cheese. Bake, uncovered, at 400° for 25-30 minutes or until potatoes are tender. **Yield:** 12-16 servings.

Breaded Eggplant Slices

These crisp golden rounds are a fun and different way to serve eggplant.
—Phyllis Schmalz
Kansas City, Kansas

✓ Uses less fat, sugar or salt. Includes Nutritional Analysis and Diabetic Exchanges.

1 medium eggplant (about 1 pound)
1/2 cup dry bread crumbs
1/4 cup grated Parmesan cheese
1 bottle (8 ounces) fat-free Italian salad dressing

Cut eggplant into 1/2-in. slices. In a shallow bowl, combine bread crumbs and cheese. Place salad dressing in another bowl. Dip eggplant into dressing, then coat with crumb mixture. Arrange in a single layer on baking sheets coated with nonstick cooking spray. Bake at 450° for 12-15 minutes or until golden brown, turning once. **Yield:** 4 servings.

Nutritional Analysis: One serving equals 153 calories, 3 g fat (2 g saturated fat), 7 mg cholesterol, 975 mg sodium, 25 g carbohydrate, 4 g fiber, 6 g protein. **Diabetic Exchanges:** 2 vegetable, 1 starch.

Gingered Peas and Water Chestnuts

This recipe from a friend has a nice combination of flavors and textures. —Joan Solberg, Ashland, Wisconsin

1 can (14-1/2 ounces) chicken broth
2 packages (10 ounces *each*) frozen peas
1 can (8 ounces) sliced water chestnuts, drained and halved
1 jar (4 ounces) whole mushrooms, drained
5 green onions, cut into 1/2-inch slices
2 tablespoons butter *or* margarine
1/2 to 1 teaspoon salt
1/2 to 3/4 teaspoon ground ginger
1/8 teaspoon garlic salt
1/8 teaspoon pepper
1/8 teaspoon ground nutmeg
2 tablespoons cornstarch

Set aside 1/4 cup broth. In a saucepan, combine vegetables, butter, seasonings and remaining broth. Bring to a boil. Reduce heat; cover and simmer for 4-5 minutes. Combine cornstarch and reserved broth until smooth; stir into pea mixture. Bring to a boil; cook and stir for 2 minutes or until thickened and bubbly. **Yield:** 6 servings.

Asparagus Nut Stir-Fry

(Pictured on page 48)

This pretty side dish is an excellent way to serve one of the first springtime vegetables from our garden.
—Margaret Souders, Elizabethtown, Pennsylvania

1-1/2 pounds fresh asparagus spears, trimmed
2 tablespoons vegetable oil
1/4 cup thinly sliced sweet red pepper
1/4 cup coarsely chopped walnuts
1/4 teaspoon ground ginger *or* 1 teaspoon minced fresh gingerroot
1 garlic clove, minced
1/8 teaspoon crushed red pepper flakes
2 tablespoons chicken broth
2 tablespoons soy sauce
1/2 teaspoon sugar
1/2 teaspoon salt

In a skillet or wok, stir-fry asparagus in oil until crisp-tender, about 10 minutes. Remove and keep warm. In the same skillet, stir-fry red pepper, walnuts, ginger, garlic and pepper flakes for 2 minutes or until red pepper is crisp-tender. Stir in the broth, soy sauce, sugar and salt; heat through. Add asparagus; stir to coat. **Yield:** 6 servings.

Broiled Tomatoes with Dill Sauce

One summer, we had lots of garden tomatoes and used them in every kind of recipe. This was a favorite.
—Lavonne Hartel, Williston, North Dakota

1/2 cup sour cream
1/4 cup mayonnaise *or* salad dressing
2 tablespoons finely chopped onion
4 teaspoons snipped fresh dill *or* 1-1/4 teaspoons dill weed, *divided*
4 large ripe tomatoes
4 teaspoons butter *or* margarine, softened
Salt and pepper to taste

In a bowl, combine the sour cream, mayonnaise, onion and 3 teaspoons dill or 1 teaspoon dill weed; mix well. Refrigerate for 1 hour. Cut the tomatoes in half horizontally. Spread each with 1/2 teaspoon butter; sprinkle with salt, pepper and remaining dill. Place on a baking sheet or broiler pan. Broil 3 in. from the heat for 5-7 minutes or until heated through. Serve with dill sauce. **Yield:** 8 servings.

Caraway Red Cabbage

My family just loves this fresh-tasting cabbage dish. It's low in fat, sugar and salt—and quick to prepare.
—Rosemarie Kondrk, Old Bridge, New Jersey

✓ Uses less fat, sugar or salt. Includes Nutritional Analysis and Diabetic Exchanges.

1/2 cup chopped onion
1 tablespoon butter *or* stick margarine
1/2 cup water
4 teaspoons white vinegar
3/4 teaspoon caraway seeds
1/2 teaspoon salt
9 cups shredded red cabbage
Sugar substitute equivalent to 4 teaspoons sugar

In a large saucepan, saute onion in butter until tender. Add water, vinegar, caraway seeds, salt and cabbage. Cover; simmer for 30 minutes, stirring occasionally. Stir in sugar substitute. **Yield:** 10 servings.

Nutritional Analysis: One serving (1/2 cup) equals 31 calories, 1 g fat (1 g saturated fat), 3 mg cholesterol, 141 mg sodium, 5 g carbohydrate, 2 g fiber, 1 g protein. **Diabetic Exchange:** 1 vegetable.

Spicy Sweet Potatoes

(Pictured on page 48)

My family fell in love with the combination of sweet and spicy in this pretty potato side dish the very first time they tried it. *—Lynn Thomas, London, Ontario*

✓ Uses less fat, sugar or salt. Includes Nutritional Analysis and Diabetic Exchanges.

3 large sweet potatoes, peeled and cut into 1-inch cubes (about 6 cups)
2 tablespoons olive *or* canola oil
2 tablespoons brown sugar
1 teaspoon chili powder
1/2 teaspoon salt
1/4 teaspoon cayenne pepper

In a resealable plastic bag, toss potatoes and oil. Add rest of ingredients; toss to coat. Transfer to a greased 11-in. x 7-in. x 2-in. baking dish. Bake, uncovered, at 400° for 40-45 minutes or until potatoes are tender, stirring every 15 minutes. **Yield:** 8 servings.

Nutritional Analysis: One serving (3/4 cup) equals 149 calories, 4 g fat (1 g saturated fat), 0 cholesterol, 164 mg sodium, 28 g carbohydrate, 3 g fiber, 2 g protein. **Diabetic Exchanges:** 1-1/2 starch, 1/2 fat.

Baked Zucchini Squares

This zucchini bake is perfect for summer get-togethers. It goes a long way at a group gathering.
—Anna Tarlini, Philadelphia, Pennsylvania

1 cup biscuit/baking mix
1/2 cup grated Parmesan cheese

1 tablespoon minced fresh parsley
1-1/2 teaspoons dried oregano
1-1/2 teaspoons dried basil
1/2 teaspoon salt
4 eggs
1/2 cup vegetable oil
1 small onion, chopped
3 medium zucchini, thinly sliced

In a bowl, combine the biscuit mix, Parmesan cheese, parsley, oregano, basil and salt. Combine eggs, oil and onion; stir into dry ingredients just until combined. Stir in zucchini. Transfer to a greased 13-in. x 9-in. x 2-in. baking dish. Bake at 350° for 30-35 minutes or until golden brown and set. Cut into squares. **Yield:** 16-20 servings.

Spinach Rice Bake

This is one of my best, most requested spinach recipes. It's tasty. —Kathy Kittell, Lexena, Kansas

1 package (10 ounces) frozen chopped spinach
1 cup cooked long grain rice
1 cup (4 ounces) shredded cheddar cheese
2 eggs, lightly beaten
1/3 cup milk
3 tablespoons finely chopped onion
2 tablespoons minced fresh parsley
2 tablespoons butter *or* margarine, softened
1/2 teaspoon salt
1/2 teaspoon Worcestershire sauce
1/4 teaspoon dried thyme
1/8 to 1/4 teaspoon ground nutmeg

Cook spinach according to package directions; drain well. Add remaining ingredients; mix well. Transfer to a greased 1-qt. baking dish. Cover and bake at 350° for 20 minutes. Uncover; bake 20-25 minutes longer or until a knife inserted near center comes out clean. **Yield:** 4 servings.

Cranberry Orange Salsa

This tart tangy blend is wonderful with carved turkey, on turkey sandwiches or with pork. —Joan Flowers Hickory Hills, Illinois

1 package (12 ounces) fresh *or* frozen cranberries (3 cups), thawed and coarsely chopped
1/2 cup honey
2 medium navel oranges, peeled, sectioned and cut into 1/2-inch chunks
1 small red onion, finely chopped

1/2 cup dried apricots, cut into thin strips
1/4 to 1/2 cup minced fresh cilantro *or* parsley
1 to 2 jalapeno peppers, seeded and minced
2 tablespoons lime juice

In a bowl, combine cranberries and honey. Stir in the oranges, onion, apricots, cilantro, jalapenos and lime juice. Cover and refrigerate for at least 2 hours. Serve over turkey. **Yield:** 3 cups.

Sweet 'n' Tangy Freezer Pickles

(Pictured above)

A batch of these puckery slices can keep in the freezer for up to 6 weeks—if they last that long. Mine never do. —Jean Vance, Charlotte, North Carolina

10 to 12 medium pickling cucumbers (about 2 pounds), thinly sliced
3 medium onions, thinly sliced
1 large green pepper, chopped
3 tablespoons salt, *divided*
2 cups sugar
1 cup white vinegar
1 tablespoon celery seed

In a large container, combine cucumbers, onions, green pepper and 2 tablespoons salt. Cover with crushed ice; mix well. Refrigerate for 8 hours. Drain; rinse and drain again. In a saucepan, combine the sugar, vinegar, celery seed and remaining salt. Bring to a boil; cook and stir for 1 minute. Spoon over cucumber mixture. Pour into jars or freezer containers. Cool. Top with lids. Cover and freeze for up to 6 weeks. Thaw at room temperature for 4 hours before serving. **Yield:** 4 pints.

Four-Tomato Salsa

(Pictured above)

A variety of tomatoes, onions and peppers make this chunky salsa so good. It's super with tortilla chips or meat. —*Connie Siese, Wayne, Michigan*

✓ Uses less fat, sugar or salt. Includes Nutritional Analysis and Diabetic Exchanges.

7 plum tomatoes, chopped
7 medium tomatoes, chopped
3 medium yellow tomatoes, chopped
3 medium orange tomatoes, chopped
1 teaspoon salt
2 tablespoons lime juice
2 tablespoons olive *or* vegetable oil
1 medium white onion, chopped
2/3 cup chopped red onion
2 green onions, chopped
1/2 cup *each* chopped sweet red, orange, yellow and green pepper
3 pepperoncinis, chopped
3 pickled sweet banana wax peppers, chopped
1/2 cup minced fresh parsley
2 tablespoons minced fresh cilantro *or* additional parsley
1 tablespoon dried chervil

In a colander, combine the tomatoes and salt. Let drain for 10 minutes. Transfer to a large bowl. Stir in the lime juice, oil, onions, peppers, parsley, cilantro and chervil. Refrigerate or freeze leftovers. **Yield:** 14 cups.

Nutritional Analysis: One serving (1/4 cup salsa) equals 16 calories, 1 g fat (0 saturated fat), 0 cholesterol, 63 mg sodium, 3 g carbohydrate, 1 g fiber, 1 g protein. **Diabetic Exchange:** Free food.

Editor's Note: Look for pepperoncinis (pickled peppers) and pickled banana peppers in the pickle and olive aisle of your grocery store.

Cheddar Cabbage Casserole

Even those who don't generally care for cooked cabbage seem to like it this way. —*Mildred Fowler, Thomaston, Georgia*

1 large head cabbage, shredded
10 tablespoons butter *or* margarine, softened, *divided*
1/4 cup all-purpose flour
1/2 teaspoon salt
1/8 teaspoon pepper
4 cups milk
2 cups (8 ounces) shredded cheddar cheese
1 cup soft bread crumbs

In a large kettle or Dutch oven, cook cabbage in boiling salted water for 2-3 minutes or until crisp-tender; drain well. Add 2 tablespoons butter; set aside. In a small saucepan, melt 6 tablespoons butter; stir in flour, salt and pepper until smooth. Gradually add milk. Bring to a boil; cook and stir for 2 minutes or until thickened.

Place half of the cabbage in a greased 13-in. x 9-in. x 2-in. baking dish. Pour half of the sauce over cabbage. Repeat layers. Sprinkle with cheese. Melt remaining butter; toss with bread crumbs. Sprinkle over cheese. Bake, uncovered, at 350° for 18-22 minutes or until cheese is melted. **Yield:** 12 servings.

Chunky Ketchup

(Pictured on page 49)

I came up with this chunky ketchup to jazz up chopped steak sandwiches and hot sausage sandwiches. —*Susan Stahr, Driftwood, Pennsylvania*

8 cups chopped seeded peeled tomatoes
2 medium onions, chopped
2 medium green peppers, chopped
2 cups sugar
2 cans (6 ounces *each*) tomato paste
2 tablespoons salt
1/2 cup white vinegar

In a large saucepan, combine first six ingredients; bring to a boil. Reduce heat; simmer, uncovered, for 1-1/2 hours or until slightly thickened. Stir in vinegar; heat through. Ladle hot mixture into hot jars, leaving 1/4-in. headspace. Adjust caps. Process for 20 minutes in a boiling-water bath. **Yield:** 3-1/2 pints.

Romaine Roasted Corn

(Pictured on page 48)

Wrapped in lettuce and baked, this corn is tender and delicious. —Margaret Wagner Allen, Abingdon, Virginia

6 tablespoons butter *or* margarine, softened
1 teaspoon dried rosemary, crushed
1/2 teaspoon dried marjoram
6 ears corn on the cob, husks removed
1 bunch romaine
Salt and pepper to taste

In a mixing bowl, combine the butter, rosemary and marjoram; spread over corn. Wrap each ear in two to three romaine leaves. Place in a 13-in. x 9-in. x 2-in. baking dish. Cover and bake at 450° for 30-35 minutes or until corn is tender. Discard romaine before serving. Sprinkle corn with salt and pepper. **Yield:** 6 servings.

Hot Pepper Jelly

(Pictured on page 48)

We enjoy this fiery pepper spread on crackers with cream cheese. It also makes a terrific holiday gift. —Richard Harris, Kingston, Tennessee

1-1/2 cups white vinegar
1 medium sweet red pepper, cut into wedges
2/3 cup chopped habanero peppers
6 cups sugar, *divided*
2 pouches (3 ounces *each*) liquid fruit pectin
1 teaspoon red food coloring, optional
Cream cheese and crackers

Place vinegar and peppers in a blender; cover and puree. Add 2 cups sugar; blend well. Pour into a saucepan. Stir in the remaining sugar; bring to a boil. Strain mixture and return to pan. Stir in pectin and food coloring if desired. Return to a rolling boil over high heat. Boil for 2 minutes, stirring constantly. Remove from the heat; skim off foam. Pour hot liquid into hot jars, leaving 1/2-in. headspace. Adjust caps. Process for 5 minutes in a boiling-water bath. Serve with cream cheese on crackers. **Yield:** 5 half-pints.

Roasted Corn Salsa

This colorful salsa goes well with barbecued meats, but it's also tasty served with chips. It's one of those recipes that fits in just about anywhere, anytime. —Nancy Horsburgh, Everett, Ontario

2 medium ears sweet corn in husks
2 medium tomatoes, chopped
1 small onion, chopped
2 tablespoons minced fresh cilantro *or* parsley
1 tablespoon lime juice
1 tablespoon finely chopped green pepper
1 tablespoon finely chopped sweet red pepper
1 teaspoon minced seeded jalapeno pepper
1/4 teaspoon salt
Dash pepper

Peel back husks of corn but don't remove; remove silk. Replace husks and tie with kitchen string. Place corn in a bowl and cover with water; soak for 20 minutes. Drain. Grill corn, covered, over medium-high heat for 20-25 minutes or until husks are blackened and corn is tender, turning several times. Cool. Remove corn from cobs and place in a bowl. Add remaining ingredients. **Yield:** about 2-1/2 cups.

Nutritional Analysis: One serving (1/4 cup salsa) equals 24 calories, 0 fat (0 saturated fat), 0 cholesterol, 64 mg sodium, 5 g carbohydrate, 1 g fiber, 1 g protein. **Diabetic Exchange:** 1 vegetable.

Tomato Eggplant Salsa

Eggplant and a zesty combination of peppers, herbs and seasonings make this unique salsa a real crowd-pleaser. —Anna Free, Plymouth, Ohio

3/4 cup water
1 small sweet red pepper, chopped
1 celery rib, chopped
2 jalapeno peppers, seeded and minced
2 garlic cloves, minced
1 bay leaf
2 teaspoons minced fresh thyme *or* 1/2 teaspoon dried thyme, *divided*
1 teaspoon hot pepper sauce
1-1/2 cups cubed eggplant
1/4 cup plus 1 tablespoon olive *or* vegetable oil, *divided*
5 plum tomatoes, chopped
3 green onions, cut into 1-inch strips
1/2 teaspoon salt

In a saucepan, combine the water, red pepper, celery, jalapenos, garlic, bay leaf, half of the thyme and hot pepper sauce. Bring to a boil. Reduce heat; simmer, uncovered, for 15 minutes or until liquid is evaporated. Remove from the heat; discard bay leaf. In a skillet, saute eggplant in 1/4 cup oil until tender. Transfer to a bowl. Add red pepper mixture, tomatoes, onions, salt and remaining thyme and oil; mix well. Cover and refrigerate until serving. **Yield:** about 2-1/2 cups.

✓ Uses less fat, sugar or salt. Includes Nutritional Analysis and Diabetic Exchanges.

Main Dishes

You'll find a variety of tantalizing choices for meat, fish, fowl and pasta dishes in this handy chapter.

FANTASTIC FARE. Clockwise from upper left: Lemon Cream Chicken (p. 88), Spinach-Beef Spaghetti Pie (p. 76), Salmon Asparagus Tart (p. 84), Meal on a Stick (p. 89) and Hungarian Goulash (p. 86).

YOU WON'T MISS the meat in Black Bean Tart and Spinach Cheese Manicotti (shown above, top to bottom).

Black Bean Tart

(Pictured above)

This colorful tart was a hit with friends. I served it with a green salad and crusty bread, plus sour cream on the side. —*Ellen Papa, Miami, Florida*

1-1/2 cups all-purpose flour
1 teaspoon ground cumin
1 teaspoon chili powder
1 teaspoon paprika
1/2 teaspoon salt
6 tablespoons cold butter *or* margarine
4 to 6 tablespoons cold water

FILLING:
2 cans (15 ounces each) black beans, rinsed and drained, *divided*
2 tablespoons sour cream
1 teaspoon salt, *divided*
1 package (10 ounces) frozen corn, thawed
1 tablespoon vegetable oil
1 cup chopped sweet red pepper
1/2 cup chopped green onions
1/4 to 1/2 cup minced fresh cilantro *or* parsley
1 to 2 jalapeno peppers, seeded and chopped*
1/4 teaspoon pepper
1-1/2 cups (6 ounces) shredded Monterey Jack cheese
Sour cream, optional

In a bowl, combine the first five ingredients. Cut in butter until mixture resembles coarse crumbs. Stir in enough water to form a ball. Press dough onto the bottom and up the sides of an ungreased 9-in. fluted tart pan with a removable bottom. Chill for 15 minutes. Line unpricked crust with a double thickness of heavy-duty foil. Bake at 350° for 10 minutes. Remove foil; bake 8-10 minutes longer or until golden. Cool on a wire rack.

In a blender, combine 1 cup beans, sour cream and 1/2 teaspoon salt; cover and process until smooth. Spread over crust. In a skillet, saute corn in oil until tender. Remove from the heat; add red pepper, onions, cilantro, jalapenos, pepper and remaining salt. Add cheese and remaining beans. Mound over the pureed beans. Bake at 350° for 20-25 minutes or until cheese is melted. Serve with sour cream if desired. **Yield:** 6-8 servings.

***Editor's Note:** When cutting or seeding hot peppers, use rubber or plastic gloves to protect your hands. Avoid touching your face.

Spinach Cheese Manicotti

(Pictured above left)

The creamy cheese filling in these savory stuffed shells has pretty flecks of spinach. —*Margaret Truxton, Pinehurst, North Carolina*

1 medium onion, finely chopped
3 garlic cloves, minced
1 tablespoon vegetable oil
1-1/2 cups ricotta cheese
1 cup (4 ounces) shredded mozzarella cheese, *divided*
4 ounces cream cheese, softened
6 tablespoons grated Parmesan cheese, *divided*
1 teaspoon Italian seasoning
1/2 teaspoon pepper
1 package (10 ounces) frozen chopped spinach, thawed and squeezed dry
8 manicotti shells, cooked and drained
1 jar (26 ounces) spaghetti sauce

In a small skillet, saute onion and garlic in oil for 3 minutes; set aside. In a mixing bowl, combine the ricotta, 1/2 cup mozzarella, cream cheese, 4 tablespoons Parmesan, Italian seasoning and pepper; beat until smooth. Stir in the onion mixture and spinach. Spoon or pipe into the manicotti shells. Pour half of the spaghetti sauce into a greased 13-

in. x 9-in. x 2-in. baking dish. Arrange shells over sauce; top with rest of sauce. Cover; bake at 350° for 25 minutes. Uncover; sprinkle with remaining mozzarella and Parmesan. Bake 5-10 minutes longer or until cheese is melted. **Yield:** 4 servings.

Almond Salmon Patties

Folks tell me this is one of my specialties. Almonds give these light patties a crisp coating and sour cream adds richness. They're flavorful and special enough for company. —DeWhitt Sizemore, Woodlawn, Virginia

2 eggs, *separated*
1 cup (8 ounces) sour cream
1-1/2 cups soft bread crumbs
2 tablespoons minced chives
1/2 teaspoon seafood seasoning
1/4 teaspoon salt
Dash pepper
1 can (14-3/4 ounces) salmon, drained, bones and skin removed
1-1/4 cups finely chopped almonds
1 tablespoon vegetable oil
Lemon wedges, optional

In a bowl, combine the egg yolks and sour cream. Add bread crumbs and seasonings. Stir in salmon. In a mixing bowl, beat egg whites until stiff; fold into the salmon mixture. Shape into 12 patties; coat with almonds. Heat oil in a large skillet; fry patties over medium heat for 4-5 minutes on each side or until golden brown. Serve with lemon if desired. **Yield:** 6 servings.

Fisherman's Specialty

A friend at work shared some of his fresh catch prepared in this simple way. After one bite, I knew it was the best fried fish I'd ever tasted. The fillets come out moist and not fishy-tasting. —Bruce Headley, Greenwood, Missouri

2 eggs
1 to 2 teaspoons lemon-pepper seasoning, *divided*
6 bluegill *or* perch fillets (2 to 3 ounces *each*)
1 cup crushed saltines (about 30 crackers)
Vegetable oil

In a shallow bowl, beat the eggs and 1 teaspoon lemon-pepper. Dip fillets in egg mixture, then coat with cracker crumbs. Sprinkle with remaining lemon-pepper. In a skillet, heat 1/4 in. of oil. Fry fillets for 3-4 minutes on each side or until fish flakes easily with a fork. **Yield:** 3 servings.

Cheesy Pasta Pea Bake

This is a nice change from plain macaroni and cheese —it's comfort food at its best. —Ruth Rigoni, Hurley, Wisconsin

✓ Uses less fat, sugar or salt. Includes Nutritional Analysis and Diabetic Exchanges.

12 ounces uncooked medium shell pasta
1/2 pound fresh mushrooms, quartered
1/2 cup chopped green onions
1 garlic clove, minced
2 tablespoons butter *or* margarine
3 tablespoons all-purpose flour
1 tablespoon cornstarch
3 cups milk
1/2 cup chicken broth
1 cup frozen peas
1 teaspoon chopped seeded jalapeno pepper*
1/2 to 1 teaspoon salt
1/4 teaspoon pepper
Dash hot pepper sauce
2 cups (8 ounces) shredded cheddar cheese, *divided*
1-1/2 cups (6 ounces) shredded Monterey Jack cheese
1/4 cup dry bread crumbs

Cook pasta according to package directions. In a skillet, saute mushrooms, onions and garlic in butter for 5 minutes. Stir in flour and cornstarch until blended. Gradually add milk and broth. Bring to a boil; cook and stir for 2 minutes or until thickened. Reduce heat. Add peas, jalapeno, salt, pepper and pepper sauce; simmer for 1 minute. Stir in 1-1/2 cups cheddar cheese and Monterey Jack cheese until melted. Remove from the heat.

Drain pasta and place in a greased 13-in. x 9-in. x 2-in. baking dish. Add cheese sauce and mix well. Sprinkle with bread crumbs and remaining cheddar cheese. Bake, uncovered, at 375° for 35-40 minutes or until golden brown and bubbly. **Yield:** 12 servings.

Nutritional Analysis: One serving (prepared with fat-free milk, 1/2 teaspoon salt and reduced-fat cheeses) equals 284 calories, 9 g fat (6 g saturated fat), 29 mg cholesterol, 337 mg sodium, 33 g carbohydrate, 2 g fiber, 18 g protein. **Diabetic Exchanges:** 2 starch, 2 meat.

***Editor's Note:** When cutting or seeding hot peppers, use rubber or plastic gloves to protect your hands. Avoid touching your face.

Chicken Cordon Bleu Calzones

(Pictured below)

These puffs are an elegant alternative to a traditional chicken pie. They combine the delicate flavor of chicken cordon bleu with the impressive look of beef Wellington. —Kathy Gounaud, Warwick, Rhode Island

4 boneless skinless chicken breasts (1 pound)
1 cup sliced fresh mushrooms
1/2 medium onion, chopped
2 tablespoons butter *or* margarine
3 tablespoons cornstarch
1-1/4 cups milk
1 tablespoon minced fresh basil *or* 1 teaspoon dried basil
1 teaspoon salt
1/4 teaspoon pepper
1 package (17-1/4 ounces) frozen puff pastry, thawed
8 thin slices deli ham
4 slices provolone cheese
Additional milk, optional

Place chicken in a greased 2-qt. baking dish; cover with water. Cover and bake at 350° for 30 minutes or until juices run clear. Meanwhile, in a skillet, saute mushrooms and onion in butter until tender. Combine cornstarch and milk until smooth; stir into skillet. Add seasonings. Bring to a boil; cook and stir for 2 minutes or until thickened.

Drain chicken. Cut pastry sheets in half widthwise. On one side of each half, place a chicken breast, 1/4 cup mushroom mixture, two ham slices and one cheese slice. Fold pastry over filling; seal edges. Place on a greased baking sheet. Brush tops with milk if desired. Bake at 400° for 15-20 minutes or until puffed and golden. **Yield:** 4 servings.

Baked Halibut

I got this easy delicious recipe from Sandy Schroth of the Puffin Bed & Breakfast in Gustavus, Alaska. —Mrs. Edward Mahnke, Houston, Texas

3 pounds halibut steaks (1 inch thick)
1 cup (8 ounces) sour cream
1/2 cup grated Parmesan cheese
1/4 cup butter *or* margarine, softened
1/2 teaspoon dill weed
1/2 teaspoon salt
1/4 teaspoon pepper
Paprika

Place halibut in a greased 13-in. x 9-in. x 2-in. baking dish. Combine sour cream, cheese, butter, dill, salt and pepper; spoon over halibut. Cover and bake at 375° for 20 minutes. Uncover; sprinkle with paprika. Bake 10-15 minutes longer or until fish flakes easily with a fork. **Yield:** 4-6 servings.

Cajun Corned Beef Hash

Neither the flavor nor the texture is "mushy" when you whip up a skillet of this tongue-tingling hash. This is an all-time favorite of mine. I created it after eating a similar variation in Texas. —Del Mason, Martensville, Saskatchewan

6 cups frozen shredded hash brown potatoes, thawed
1/4 cup butter *or* margarine
1/2 cup *each* finely chopped green onions, sweet red pepper and green pepper
1 teaspoon seasoned salt
3/4 teaspoon Cajun seasoning
3/4 teaspoon chili powder
1/2 teaspoon pepper
1-1/2 cups chopped cooked corned beef
1 tablespoon white vinegar
8 eggs
Additional Cajun seasoning and hot pepper sauce, optional

In a large skillet, cook hash browns in butter until almost tender. Stir in onions, peppers and seasonings. Cook until hash browns are lightly browned and peppers are tender. Add corned beef; heat through. Meanwhile, in a skillet with high sides, bring vinegar and 2 to 3 in. of water to a boil. Reduce heat; simmer gently. Break cold eggs, one at a time, into a custard cup or saucer.

Holding the cup close to the surface of the water, slip eggs, one at a time, into simmering water. Cook, uncovered, until whites are completely set and yolks begin to thicken, about 3-4 minutes. With a slotted spoon, lift poached eggs out of the water. Serve over hash mixture. Sprinkle with additional Cajun seasoning and serve with hot pepper sauce if desired. **Yield:** 4 servings.

Tropical Sausage Kabobs

I've prepared these yummy kabobs for family and friends for years. They're a favorite to serve on the patio on summer evenings. —*Joan Hallford*
North Richland Hills, Texas

1 tablespoon cornstarch
3 tablespoons Dijon mustard
3/4 cup ginger ale
1/3 cup honey
1 pound fully cooked kielbasa *or* Polish sausage, cut into 1-inch chunks
4 medium firm bananas, cut into 1-inch slices
2 fresh pineapples, peeled and cut into 1-inch chunks *or* 2 cans (20 ounces *each*) pineapple chunks, drained

In a small saucepan, combine the cornstarch and mustard until smooth. Gradually stir in ginger ale and honey until well blended. Bring to a boil; cook and stir for 2 minutes or until thickened and bubbly. Alternately thread sausage and fruit onto metal or soaked wooden skewers. Brush with mustard sauce. Grill, uncovered, over medium-hot heat for 4 minutes or until evenly browned, basting and turning several times. **Yield:** 4-6 servings.

Beef Stew Pie

(Pictured above right)

My daughter and I often serve this pie to our families, and it's always a hit. It's especially good made the day before, so the flavors can blend. I sometimes double the recipe so we're sure to have leftovers.
—*Karol Sprague, Gobles, Michigan*

6 tablespoons all-purpose flour, *divided*
1-1/2 teaspoons salt
1/2 teaspoon pepper
1 pound boneless beef round steak, cut into 1-inch pieces
2 tablespoons vegetable oil
1/2 cup chopped onion
2 garlic cloves, minced
2-1/4 cups water, *divided*
1 tablespoon tomato paste

1/2 teaspoon Italian seasoning
1/2 teaspoon dried basil
1 bay leaf
2 cups cubed cooked potatoes
1-1/2 cups sliced cooked carrots
2 tablespoons minced fresh parsley
Pastry for single-crust pie (9 inches)

In a large resealable plastic bag, combine 3 tablespoons flour, salt and pepper. Add beef in batches and shake to coat. In a large skillet, saute beef in oil until browned. Add onion and garlic; cook and stir until onion is tender. Add 1/4 cup water, stirring to scrape browned bits from skillet.

Combine 1-1/2 cups water, tomato paste, Italian seasoning and basil; gradually stir into skillet. Add bay leaf. Bring to a boil. Reduce heat; cover and simmer for 1-1/4 to 1-1/2 hours or until meat is tender. Combine the remaining flour and water until smooth; gradually stir into skillet. Bring to a boil; cook and stir for 2 minutes or until thickened and bubbly. Discard bay leaf. Stir in potatoes, carrots and parsley. Transfer to a greased 2-qt. baking dish.

On a floured surface, roll out pastry to fit dish. Place over filling; flute edges and cut slits in top. Bake at 425° for 25-30 minutes or until crust is golden brown. Let stand for 10 minutes before serving. **Yield:** 4-6 servings.

COME HOME to savory Rosemary Cashew Chicken or Pork Chop Dinner (shown above, top to bottom) when you save time and fuss by using your slow cooker.

Pork Chop Dinner

(Pictured above)

Family and friends call me the "Crock-Pot Queen". Of my many slow-cooked specialties, this tender dinner is my husband's favorite. —*Janet Phillips Meadville, Pennsylvania*

✓ Uses less fat, sugar or salt. Includes Nutritional Analysis and Diabetic Exchanges.

6 pork loin chops (3/4 inch thick)
1 tablespoon vegetable oil
1 large onion, sliced
1 medium green pepper, chopped
1 can (4 ounces) mushroom stems and pieces, drained
1 can (8 ounces) tomato sauce
1 tablespoon brown sugar
2 teaspoons Worcestershire sauce
1-1/2 teaspoons cider vinegar
1/2 teaspoon salt
Hot cooked rice, optional

In a skillet, brown chops on both sides in oil; drain. Place in a slow cooker. Add the onion, green pepper and mushrooms. In a bowl, combine the tomato sauce, brown sugar, Worcestershire sauce, vinegar and salt. Pour over meat and vegetables. Cover and cook on low for 4-5 hours or until meat is tender. Serve with rice if desired. **Yield:** 6 servings.

Nutritional Analysis: One serving (calculated without rice) equals 199 calories, 8 g fat (2 g saturated fat), 59 mg cholesterol, 507 mg sodium, 10 g carbohydrate, 1 g fiber, 22 g protein. **Diabetic Exchanges:** 3 lean meat, 1-1/2 vegetable.

Rosemary Cashew Chicken

(Pictured at left)

This elegant entree with fresh herb flavor is absolutely mouth-watering. —*Ruth Andrewson, Peck, Idaho*

1 broiler/fryer chicken (3 to 4 pounds), cut up and skin removed
1 medium onion, thinly sliced
1/3 cup orange juice concentrate
1 teaspoon dried rosemary, crushed
1 teaspoon salt
1/4 teaspoon cayenne pepper
2 tablespoons all-purpose flour
3 tablespoons water
1/4 to 1/2 cup chopped cashews
Hot cooked pasta

Place chicken in a slow cooker. Combine the onion, orange juice concentrate, rosemary, salt and cayenne; pour over chicken. Cover and cook on low for 4-5 hours or until chicken juices run clear. Remove chicken and keep warm. In a saucepan, combine flour and water until smooth. Stir in cooking juices. Bring to a boil; cook and stir for 2 minutes or until thickened. Stir in cashews. Pour over chicken. Serve with pasta. **Yield:** 4-6 servings.

Lots-a-Veggies Stew

When I needed a no-fuss meal, I created this catchall dish. —*Judy Page, Edenville, Michigan*

✓ Uses less fat, sugar or salt. Includes Nutritional Analysis and Diabetic Exchanges.

1 pound ground beef
1 medium onion, diced
2 garlic cloves, minced
1 can (16 ounces) baked beans, undrained
1 can (16 ounces) kidney beans, rinsed and drained
1 can (15 ounces) butter beans, rinsed and drained
1 can (14-1/2 ounces) beef broth
1 can (11 ounces) whole kernel corn, undrained
1 can (10-1/2 ounces) condensed vegetable soup, undiluted
1 can (6 ounces) tomato paste
1 medium green pepper, diced
1 cup sliced carrots

1 cup sliced celery
2 tablespoons chili powder
1 teaspoon dried oregano
1 teaspoon dried thyme
1 teaspoon salt, optional
1/2 teaspoon dried marjoram
1/2 teaspoon pepper

In a skillet, cook beef, onion and garlic over medium heat until meat is no longer pink; drain. Transfer to a 5-qt. slow cooker. Add remaining ingredients; mix well. Cover; cook on low for 5 hours or until vegetables are tender. **Yield:** 10 servings.

Nutritional Analysis: One 1-cup serving (prepared with lean ground beef and without salt) equals 272 calories, 6 g fat (2 g saturated fat), 21 mg cholesterol, 1,088 mg sodium, 40 g carbohydrate, 9 g fiber, 20 g protein. **Diabetic Exchanges:** 2 starch, 2 vegetable, 1 lean meat.

Curried Chicken 'n' Broccoli

You can't beat this dish, since it's easy, nutritious and delicious. I've received many compliments on it.
—Esther Shank, Harrisonburg, Virginia

1 package (14 ounces) frozen broccoli florets, thawed
2 cups cooked chicken strips
1 can (10-3/4 ounces) condensed cream of chicken soup, undiluted
1/2 cup mayonnaise
1 tablespoon lemon juice
1/4 to 1/2 teaspoon curry powder
1/4 teaspoon salt
1/2 cup shredded cheddar cheese
Hot cooked rice

Place the broccoli in a 1-1/2-qt. microwave-safe dish. Top with the chicken. In a bowl, combine the soup, mayonnaise, lemon juice, curry powder and salt. Spoon over chicken. Sprinkle with cheese. Cover and microwave at 70% power for 8-10 minutes. Serve over rice. **Yield:** 4 servings.

Editor's Note: This recipe was tested in an 850-watt microwave.

Crock-Pot Pizza

Always a hit at our church dinners, this hearty casserole keeps folks coming back for more.
—Julie Sterchi, Harrisburg, Illinois

1 package (12 ounces) wide egg noodles
1-1/2 pounds ground beef *or* turkey
1/4 cup chopped onion
1 jar (28 ounces) spaghetti sauce
1 jar (4-1/2 ounces) sliced mushrooms, drained
1-1/2 teaspoons Italian seasoning
1 package (3-1/2 ounces) sliced pepperoni, halved
3 cups (12 ounces) shredded mozzarella cheese
3 cups (12 ounces) shredded cheddar cheese

Cook noodles according to package directions. Meanwhile, in a large skillet, cook beef and onion over medium heat until meat is no longer pink; drain. Stir in spaghetti sauce, mushrooms and Italian seasoning. Drain noodles. In a 5-qt. slow cooker coated with nonstick cooking spray, spread a third of the meat sauce. Cover with a third of the noodles and pepperoni. Sprinkle with a third of the cheeses. Repeat layers twice. Cover and cook on low for 3-4 hours or until heated through and cheese is melted. **Yield:** 6-8 servings.

Ham 'n' Cheese Omelet Roll

(Pictured on page 1)

This brunch dish has wonderful ingredients and an impressive look all rolled into one! —Nancy Daugherty
Cortland, Ohio

4 ounces cream cheese, softened
3/4 cup milk
2 tablespoons all-purpose flour
1/4 teaspoon salt
12 eggs
2 tablespoons Dijon mustard
2-1/4 cups shredded cheddar *or* Swiss cheese, *divided*
2 cups finely chopped fully cooked ham
1/2 cup thinly sliced green onions

Line the bottom and sides of a greased 15-in. x 10-in. x 1-in. baking pan with parchment paper; grease the paper and set aside. In a small mixing bowl, beat cream cheese and milk until smooth. Add flour and salt; mix until combined. In a large mixing bowl, beat the eggs until blended. Add cream cheese mixture; mix well. Pour into prepared pan. Bake at 375° for 30-35 minutes or until eggs are puffed and set. Remove from the oven. Immediately spread with mustard and sprinkle with 1 cup cheese. Sprinkle with ham, onions and 1 cup cheese. Roll up from a short side, peeling parchment paper away while rolling. Sprinkle top of roll with the remaining cheese; bake 3-4 minutes longer or until cheese is melted. **Yield:** 12 servings.

Peasant Pasta Stew

(Pictured below)

When I was trying to duplicate a favorite restaurant recipe, I came up with this hearty stew. Pork, pasta, vegetables and beans in a thick tomato broth make it a warm and satisfying supper. My husband and I love the savory Italian flavor. —*Eileen Snider*
Cincinnati, Ohio

1-1/2 cups beef broth
2 celery ribs, chopped
2 large carrots, cut into 1/4-inch slices
1 medium onion, chopped
1 can (46 ounces) V8 juice
1 can (14-1/2 ounces) Italian diced tomatoes, undrained
2 cans (6 ounces *each*) Italian tomato paste
1 tablespoon dried oregano
1-1/2 teaspoons pepper
1/4 teaspoon garlic powder
3/4 pound ground pork
3/4 cup canned kidney beans, rinsed and drained
3/4 cup canned great northern beans, rinsed and drained
1 cup medium shell pasta, cooked and drained
Shredded Parmesan cheese

In a large saucepan, combine the broth, celery, carrots and onion. Bring to a boil. Reduce heat; cover and simmer for 5-7 minutes or until vegetables are crisp-tender. Stir in the V8 juice, tomatoes, tomato paste, oregano, pepper and garlic powder. Cover and simmer for 40-45 minutes.

Meanwhile, in a skillet, cook pork over medium heat until no longer pink; drain. Add meat and beans to soup; cover and simmer 30-45 minutes longer or until heated through. Stir in pasta just before serving. Garnish with cheese. **Yield:** 8 servings.

Lamb with Apricots

When I was a new bride, I decided to prepare a special Hanukkah dinner for my husband, David, and me to share. The star was this lamb entree, which had been one of my favorites when I was growing up. Dried apricots add a touch of sweetness to the tender lamb, which is gently spiced. —*Rachel Delano*
Tappahannock, Virginia

1 large onion, chopped
2 tablespoons olive *or* vegetable oil
1 boneless lamb shoulder roast (2-1/2 to 3 pounds), cubed
1 teaspoon *each* ground cumin, cinnamon and coriander
Salt and pepper to taste
1/2 cup dried apricots, halved
1/4 cup orange juice
1 tablespoon ground almonds
1/2 teaspoon grated orange peel
1-1/4 cups chicken broth
1 tablespoon sesame seeds, toasted

In a large skillet, saute the onion in oil until tender. Add the lamb, cumin, cinnamon, coriander, salt and pepper. Cook and stir for 5 minutes or until the meat is browned. Add apricots, orange juice, almonds and orange peel. Transfer to a 2-1/2-qt. baking dish. Stir in broth. Cover and bake at 350° for 1-1/2 hours or until meat is tender. Sprinkle with sesame seeds. **Yield:** 8-10 servings.

Louisiana Jambalaya

My husband helped add a little spice to my life. He grew up on Cajun cooking, while I ate mostly meat-and-potatoes meals. —*Sandi Pichon*
Slidell, Louisiana

1/2 pound fully cooked smoked sausage, halved and sliced

2 cups cubed fully cooked ham
1/4 cup vegetable oil
2 celery ribs, chopped
1 large onion, chopped
1 medium green pepper, chopped
5 green onions, thinly sliced
2 garlic cloves, minced
1 can (14-1/2 ounces) diced tomatoes, undrained
1 teaspoon dried thyme
1 teaspoon salt
1/2 teaspoon pepper
1/4 teaspoon cayenne pepper
2 cans (14-1/2 ounces *each*) chicken broth
1 cup uncooked long grain rice
1/3 cup water
4-1/2 teaspoons Worcestershire sauce
2 pounds cooked shrimp, peeled and deveined

In a Dutch oven, saute sausage and ham in oil until lightly browned. Remove and keep warm. In the drippings, saute the celery, onion, green pepper, green onions and garlic until tender. Add tomatoes, thyme, salt, pepper and cayenne; cook 5 minutes longer. Stir in broth, rice, water and Worcestershire sauce. Bring to a boil. Reduce heat; cover and simmer for 20 minutes or until rice is tender. Stir in sausage mixture and shrimp; heat through. Serve immediately. **Yield:** 10-12 servings.

Bacon-Wrapped Venison

My husband, Ron, and I both like to hunt. We created this dish, which is special enough for company.
—Phyllis Abrams, Alton, New York

1-1/2 to 2 pounds venison tenderloin
2 tablespoons olive *or* vegetable oil, *divided*
1 garlic clove, minced
1/2 cup all-purpose flour
3/4 teaspoon salt
1/2 teaspoon pepper
1/2 pound fresh mushrooms, sliced
4 bacon strips
1 tablespoon cornstarch
1-1/4 cups beef broth
2 tablespoons minced fresh parsley, optional

Rub tenderloin with 1-2 teaspoons of oil and the garlic. Combine the flour, salt and pepper; sprinkle over tenderloin and shake off excess. In a skillet, brown tenderloin on all sides in remaining oil. Remove and keep warm. In the same skillet, saute mushrooms until tender; remove and set aside. Wrap bacon around tenderloin, securing the ends with toothpicks. Return to the skillet. Cook over medium heat until bacon is crisp and a thermometer inserted into tenderloin reads 160°, turning frequently. Remove and keep warm.

In a small bowl, combine the cornstarch and broth until smooth; add to skillet. Bring to a boil; cook and stir for 2 minutes or until thickened. Add the parsley and reserved mushrooms; cook and stir until heated through. Discard the toothpicks from the tenderloin; serve with mushroom sauce. **Yield:** 6-8 servings.

Best-of-Show Tomato Quiche

I knew this delicious recipe was a "keeper" when I first tried it in the 1970s as a new bride—it impressed my in-laws when I made it for them! Now I sometimes substitute Mexican or Cajun seasoning for the basil. No matter how it's seasoned, it's wonderful.
—Dorothy Swanson, Affton, Missouri

3/4 cup all-purpose flour
1/2 cup cornmeal
1/2 teaspoon salt
1/8 teaspoon pepper
1/3 cup shortening
4 to 5 tablespoons cold water

FILLING:

2 cups chopped plum tomatoes
1 teaspoon salt
1/2 teaspoon dried basil
1/8 teaspoon pepper
1/2 cup chopped green onions
1/2 cup shredded cheddar cheese
1/2 cup shredded Swiss cheese
2 tablespoons all-purpose flour
1 cup evaporated milk
2 eggs

In a bowl, combine the flour, cornmeal, salt and pepper. Cut in the shortening until crumbly. Add water, tossing with a fork until dough forms a ball. Refrigerate for 30 minutes. On a lightly floured surface, roll out the dough to fit a 9-in. pie plate; transfer pastry to plate. Trim to 1/2 in. beyond edge of plate; flute edges. Bake at 375° for 10 minutes. Cool completely.

Place tomatoes in the crust; sprinkle with salt, basil, pepper, onions and cheeses. In a bowl, whisk the flour, milk and eggs until smooth. Pour over the filling. Bake at 375° for 40-45 minutes or until a knife inserted near the center comes out clean. Let stand for 10 minutes before cutting. **Yield:** 6-8 servings.

Oregano Turkey Casserole

This comforting casserole is a great way to use up left-over turkey—the oregano really enhances its flavor.
—Edie DeSpain, Logan, Utah

4 ounces uncooked spaghetti
2 cups sliced fresh mushrooms
1/2 cup julienned green pepper
1/4 cup butter *or* margarine
2 tablespoons all-purpose flour
2 tablespoons minced fresh oregano *or* 2 teaspoons dried oregano
1/2 teaspoon salt
1/4 teaspoon pepper
1 teaspoon chicken bouillon granules
1/4 cup boiling water
1-1/3 cups evaporated milk
2-1/2 cups cubed cooked turkey
2 tablespoons chopped pimientos
2 tablespoons grated Parmesan cheese

Cook spaghetti according to package directions. Meanwhile, in a skillet, saute mushrooms and green pepper in butter until tender. Stir in flour, oregano, salt and pepper. Dissolve bouillon in water; gradually add to skillet. Stir in milk. Bring to a boil; cook and stir for 2 minutes or until thickened. Add turkey and pimientos.

Drain spaghetti; toss with turkey mixture. Pour into a greased 11-in. x 7-in. x 2-in. baking dish. Sprinkle with Parmesan cheese. Bake, uncovered, at 350° for 18-22 minutes or until heated through. **Yield:** 6-8 servings.

Slow-Cooked Goose

My husband, Willard, and I own a hunting lodge and host about 16 hunters a week. The slow cooker makes easy work of fixing this flavorful goose dish, which is a favorite of our guests. The recipe makes lots of savory gravy to serve over mashed potatoes.
—Edna Ylioja, Lucky Lake, Saskatchewan

1/2 cup soy sauce
4 teaspoons vegetable oil
4 teaspoons lemon juice
2 teaspoons Worcestershire sauce
1 teaspoon garlic powder
2 pounds cubed goose breast
3/4 to 1 cup all-purpose flour
1/4 cup butter *or* margarine
1 can (10-3/4 ounces) condensed golden mushroom soup, undiluted
1-1/3 cups water
1 envelope onion soup mix
Hot cooked mashed potatoes, noodles *or* rice

In a large resealable plastic bag, combine the first five ingredients; add goose. Seal and turn to coat. Refrigerate 4 hours or overnight. Drain and discard marinade. Place flour in another large resealable plastic bag; add goose in batches and shake to coat. In a large skillet over medium heat, melt butter. Brown goose on all sides. Transfer to a slow cooker. Add soup, water and soup mix. Cover and cook on high 4-5 hours or until meat is tender. Serve over mashed potatoes, noodles or rice. **Yield:** 4 servings.

Stuffing-Topped Venison Chops

A moist stuffing with apples and golden raisins is great with pork chops, so I decided to test it with venison chops. My husband, Todd, keeps our freezer full of venison. These chops are tasty, tender and special enough for company.
—Sue Gronholz
Beaver Dam, Wisconsin

4 venison loin chops (1-1/4 inches thick)
2 tablespoons vegetable oil
1 to 1-1/2 cups beef broth

APPLE STUFFING:

2 cups cubed day-old bread
1 cup chopped peeled tart apple
1/4 cup sugar
1/4 cup raisins
1/4 cup chopped onion
1/4 cup butter *or* margarine, melted
1/4 cup hot water
1 teaspoon salt
1/2 teaspoon pepper
1/8 teaspoon rubbed sage

In a skillet, brown chops in oil on both sides. Transfer to a greased 11-in. x 7-in. x 2-in. baking dish; add enough broth to reach the top of chops. In a bowl, combine stuffing ingredients; mix well. Spoon over chops. Cover; bake at 350° for 30 minutes. Uncover; bake 20-30 minutes longer or until a meat thermometer reads 160°. **Yield:** 4 servings.

Cheesy Veal Pie

This special pie tastes just like veal Parmesan in a savory pastry crust. My daughter used to ask for it often on her birthday. I've also made it with chicken, and it's just as tasty!
—Grace Epperson
Richmond, Michigan

1/2 cup all-purpose flour
1 pound veal *or* boneless skinless chicken breasts, cubed

1/4 cup butter *or* margarine
1 can (14-1/2 ounces) diced tomatoes, undrained
1 can (8 ounces) tomato sauce
1/4 cup chopped onion
1 teaspoon dried basil
1/2 teaspoon garlic salt
1/2 teaspoon dried oregano
1/8 teaspoon pepper
3 tablespoons grated Parmesan cheese

HERB-CHEESE CRUST:

1-1/2 cups all-purpose flour
1/4 cup grated Parmesan cheese
1 teaspoon garlic salt
1 teaspoon dried oregano
1/2 cup cold butter *or* margarine
4 to 6 tablespoons cold water
1/2 cup shredded cheddar cheese

Place flour in a large resealable bag; add veal, a few pieces at a time, and shake to coat. In a skillet, cook veal in butter until no longer pink. Add tomatoes, tomato sauce, onion and seasonings. Bring to a boil. Reduce heat; cover and simmer for 30 minutes or until meat is tender. Stir in Parmesan cheese.

In a bowl, combine the first four crust ingredients. Cut in butter until crumbly. Gradually add water, tossing with a fork until dough forms a ball. Divide dough in half. Roll out one portion to fit a 9-in. pie plate; place in plate. Trim pastry to 1/2 in. beyond edge of plate; flute edges. Spoon meat filling into crust. Sprinkle with cheddar cheese. Roll out remaining pastry to 1/8-in. thickness. With a 2-in. biscuit cutter, cut out circles; place over cheese, overlapping slightly. Bake at 400° for 35-40 minutes or until golden brown. **Yield:** 6-8 servings.

Creamed Chicken in a Basket

(Pictured at right)

Chunks of tender chicken in a creamy sauce are spooned into puff pastry shells in this delicious dish, which has long been one of our family's favorites. I served it to my husband and our five children for years, and now it's a "must" for our Easter brunch.

—Sue Bolsinger, Anchorage, Alaska

6 bone-in chicken breast halves (about 4 pounds)
1 small onion, quartered
2 celery ribs with leaves, cut into chunks
2-1/2 cups water
2 teaspoons salt, *divided*
6 whole peppercorns
8 to 10 frozen puff pastry shells
1/2 cup butter *or* margarine
1/2 cup all-purpose flour
1/4 teaspoon ground nutmeg
1/8 teaspoon pepper
1/2 pound fresh mushrooms, sliced
1 can (5 ounces) sliced water chestnuts, drained
1 jar (2 ounces) diced pimientos, drained
1 tablespoon lemon juice
2 cups whipping cream

Place the chicken, onion, celery, water, 1 teaspoon salt and peppercorns in a large saucepan. Bring to a boil; skim foam. Reduce heat; cover and simmer 35-40 minutes or until juices run clear. Remove chicken with a slotted spoon; set aside until cool enough to handle. Bake pastry shells according to package directions. Remove chicken from bones; cut into cubes and set aside. Discard skin and bones. Strain broth, discarding vegetables and peppercorns. Set aside 2 cups broth (save remaining broth for another use).

In a saucepan, melt butter. Stir in flour until smooth. Gradually add reserved broth, nutmeg, pepper and remaining salt. Bring to a boil; cook and stir 2 minutes. Remove from the heat; stir in the mushrooms, water chestnuts, pimientos, lemon juice and chicken. Return to the heat. Gradually stir in the cream and heat through (do not boil). Spoon into pastry shells. **Yield:** 8-10 servings.

Pumpkin Pancakes

(Pictured below)

The flavors of autumn star in these delightful pumpkin pancakes topped with a sweet apple cider sauce.
—Brenda Parker, Portage, Michigan

HOT CIDER SYRUP:
3/4 cup apple cider *or* juice
1/2 cup packed brown sugar
1/2 cup corn syrup
2 tablespoons butter *or* margarine
1/2 teaspoon lemon juice
1/8 teaspoon ground cinnamon
1/8 teaspoon ground nutmeg
PANCAKES:
1 cup all-purpose flour
1 tablespoon sugar
2 teaspoons baking powder
1/2 teaspoon salt
1/2 teaspoon ground cinnamon
2 eggs, *separated*
1 cup milk
1/2 cup cooked *or* canned pumpkin
2 tablespoons vegetable oil

In a saucepan, combine the syrup ingredients. Bring to a boil over medium heat, stirring occasionally. Reduce heat; simmer, uncovered, for 20-25 minutes or until slightly thickened. Let stand for 30 minutes before serving.

For pancakes, combine the dry ingredients in a bowl. In another bowl, whisk the egg yolks, milk, pumpkin and oil. Stir into dry ingredients just until moistened. In a mixing bowl, beat the egg whites until soft peaks form; fold into batter.

Pour batter by 1/4 cupfuls onto a hot greased griddle. Turn when bubbles form on top of pancakes. Cook until second side is golden. Serve with syrup. **Yield:** 15 pancakes (1 cup syrup).

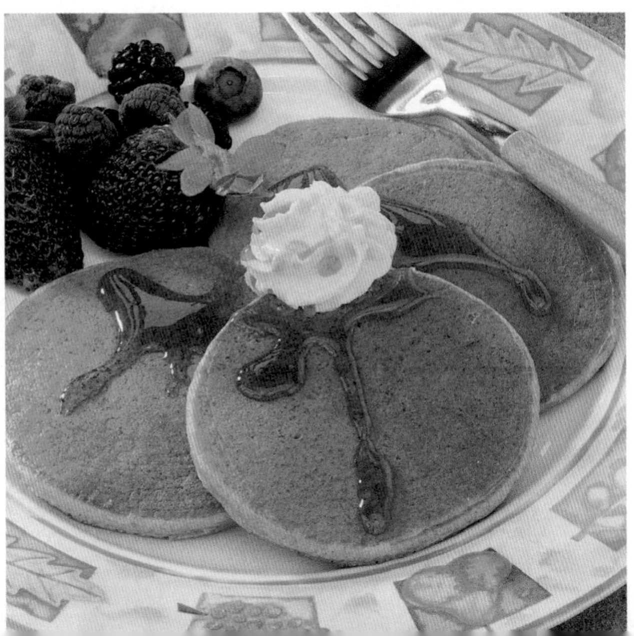

Dijon Thyme Chicken

Mustard and thyme give breaded chicken a tasty new twist. The meat always comes out so moist and tender.
—Galen Stanley, St. Charles, Missouri

1/2 cup butter *or* margarine, melted
3 to 4 tablespoons Dijon mustard
1 small onion, chopped
2 garlic cloves, minced
1 tablespoon minced fresh thyme *or* 1 teaspoon dried thyme
1/2 teaspoon crushed red pepper flakes
4 boneless skinless chicken breast halves
1 cup dry bread crumbs

In a bowl, combine the butter, mustard, onion, garlic, thyme and pepper flakes. Dip chicken in butter mixture, then coat with bread crumbs. Place in a greased 11-in. x 7-in. x 2-in. baking dish. Bake, uncovered, at 350° for 30-35 minutes or until chicken juices run clear. **Yield:** 4 servings.

BLT Brunch Pie

My boys can't wait to pick the first ripe tomatoes in our garden to be used in this terrific pie. The crust is so easy to make. *—Shara Walvoort, Oostburg, Wisconsin*

1-1/4 cups all-purpose flour
2 teaspoons baking powder
1/2 teaspoon salt
1/2 teaspoon dried basil
1/2 cup shortening
1/2 cup sour cream
FILLING:
3/4 cup mayonnaise
1 cup (4 ounces) shredded cheddar cheese
1 can (4-1/2 ounces) mushroom stems and pieces, drained
8 bacon strips, cooked and crumbled
1 tablespoon chopped green pepper
1 tablespoon chopped onion
3 medium tomatoes, peeled and sliced

In a bowl, combine the first four ingredients. Cut in shortening until crumbly. Stir in sour cream. Cover; refrigerate 30 minutes. Press pastry into a 9-in. pie plate. Bake at 375° for 10 minutes. Cool completely. In a bowl, combine the mayonnaise, cheddar cheese, mushrooms, bacon, green pepper and onion. Layer half of the tomatoes in crust; top with half of the mayonnaise mixture. Repeat layers. Bake at 350° for 30-35 minutes or until golden brown. Refrigerate leftovers. **Yield:** 6-8 servings.

Editor's Note: Reduced-fat or fat-free sour cream and mayonnaise may not be substituted for regular sour cream and mayonnaise.

Beef Cabbage Stir-Fry

Cabbage, which is grown extensively in this area, is a favorite of my family. I've had this recipe for years, and my husband and kids still request it often.
—Colette Jaworski, Buford, Georgia

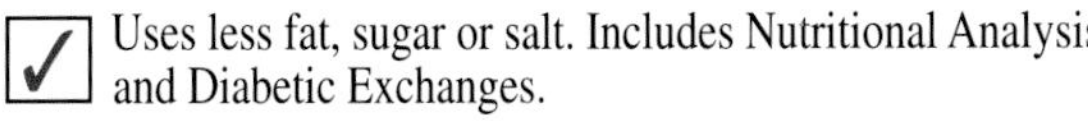
✓ Uses less fat, sugar or salt. Includes Nutritional Analysis and Diabetic Exchanges.

3 cups shredded cabbage
2 tablespoons canola oil
1 pound beef sirloin steak, cut into 1/4-inch strips
2 large onions, thinly sliced and separated into rings
3 celery ribs, sliced
1 can (14 ounces) bean sprouts, drained
1 can (8 ounces) bamboo shoots, drained
1 can (8 ounces) sliced water chestnuts, drained
2 tablespoons sugar
1 tablespoon cornstarch
1/2 cup beef broth
1/2 cup soy sauce
Hot cooked rice

In a large skillet or wok, stir-fry cabbage in oil until cabbage begins to soften. Add beef; cook and stir for 3 minutes. Add the onions and celery; stir-fry for 2-3 minutes or until vegetables are crisp-tender. Add bean sprouts, bamboo shoots and water chestnuts. In a small bowl, combine the cornstarch, broth and soy sauce until smooth; stir into beef mixture. Bring to a boil; cook and stir for 2 minutes or until thickened and vegetables are tender. Serve over rice. **Yield:** 8 servings.

Nutritional Analysis: One 1-cup serving (prepared with reduced-sodium soy sauce; calculated without rice) equals 242 calories, 13 g fat (4 g saturated fat), 37 mg cholesterol, 682 mg sodium, 18 g carbohydrate, 4 g fiber, 15 g protein. **Diabetic Exchanges:** 1-1/2 meat, 1 starch, 1 vegetable, 1 fat.

Bruschetta Chicken

(Pictured above right)

My husband and I enjoy serving this tasty chicken to company as well as family. It looks like we fussed, but it's really fast and easy to fix.
—Carolin Cattoi-Demkiw, Lethbridge, Alberta

✓ Uses less fat, sugar or salt. Includes Nutritional Analysis and Diabetic Exchanges.

1/2 cup all-purpose flour
2 eggs, lightly beaten

4 boneless skinless chicken breast halves (1 pound)
1/4 cup grated Parmesan cheese
1/4 cup dry bread crumbs
1 tablespoon butter *or* margarine, melted
2 large tomatoes, seeded and chopped
3 tablespoons minced fresh basil
2 garlic cloves, minced
1 tablespoon olive *or* vegetable oil
1/2 teaspoon salt
1/4 teaspoon pepper

Place flour and eggs in separate shallow bowls. Dip chicken in flour, then in eggs; place in a greased 13-in. x 9-in. x 2-in. baking dish. Combine the Parmesan cheese, bread crumbs and butter; sprinkle over chicken. Loosely cover baking dish with foil. Bake at 375° for 20 minutes. Uncover; bake 5-10 minutes longer or until top is browned. Meanwhile, in a bowl, combine the remaining ingredients. Spoon over the chicken. Return to the oven for 3-5 minutes or until tomato mixture is heated through. **Yield:** 4 servings.

Nutritional Analysis: One serving (prepared with 1/2 cup egg substitute) equals 358 calories, 13 g fat (5 g saturated fat), 86 mg cholesterol, 623 mg sodium, 22 g carbohydrate, 2 g fiber, 36 g protein. **Diabetic Exchanges:** 4-1/2 lean meat, 1 starch, 1 vegetable.

Taco Chili Pie

(Pictured above)

This zesty pie combines ground beef, stewed tomatoes, kidney beans and pinto beans with zippy seasonings, all tucked into a flaky golden crust. It's a great dish to take to a potluck because it slices so nicely, you can easily dish it up for a crowd. —*Liza Taylor Seattle, Washington*

1 pound ground beef
2 cups sliced fresh mushrooms
1 cup chopped onion
4 cups torn fresh spinach
1 can (16 ounces) kidney beans, rinsed and drained
1 can (15 ounces) pinto beans, rinsed and drained
1 can (15 ounces) tomato sauce
1 can (14-1/2 ounces) stewed tomatoes, undrained
2 tablespoons taco seasoning
1 tablespoon sugar
1 tablespoon molasses

CRUST:
4-1/2 cups all-purpose flour
4 teaspoons sugar
2 teaspoons salt
2 cups cold butter *or* margarine
12 to 14 tablespoons cold water

In a skillet, cook the beef, mushrooms and onion over medium heat until meat is no longer pink; drain. Stir in the spinach, beans, tomato sauce, stewed tomatoes, taco seasoning, sugar and molasses. Bring to a boil. Reduce heat; simmer, uncovered, for 20-30 minutes. Meanwhile, for crust, combine the flour, sugar and salt. Cut in butter until mixture resembles coarse crumbs. Gradually add water, tossing with a fork until dough forms a ball. Divide dough into fourths; flatten each portion into a circle and cover with plastic wrap. Refrigerate for 30 minutes.

Line two 9-in. pie plates with pastry. Divide beef mixture between crusts. Roll out remaining pastry to fit tops of pies; place over filling. Trim, seal and flute edges. Cut slits in top. Bake at 400° for 20 minutes. Reduce heat to 375°; bake 30-35 minutes longer or until golden. Let stand for 10-15 minutes before cutting. **Yield:** 2 pies (6-8 servings each).

Venison Meatballs

I learned to cook game while my husband was a forestry student. We lived off the land as much as possible. I still enjoy these savory meatballs in a slightly sweet barbecue sauce. I make a big batch for an annual pool party and there are never any left.
—*Sheila Reed, Fredericton, New Brunswick*

1 medium onion, finely chopped
1/2 cup uncooked instant rice
1 teaspoon salt
1/4 teaspoon pepper
1 pound ground venison
3/4 cup water
1/3 packed brown sugar
1/3 cup ketchup
1/3 cup condensed tomato soup, undiluted
1 tablespoon ground mustard
2 teaspoons paprika

In a bowl, combine the first four ingredients. Crumble venison over mixture and mix well. Shape into 1-1/2-in. balls. Place in a greased 8-in. square baking dish. Combine the remaining ingredients; pour over meatballs. Bake, uncovered, at 375° for 35-45 minutes or until meat is no longer pink. **Yield:** 4 servings.

Marinated Beef Fondue

Guests will enjoy cooking this boldly seasoned meat, then dipping it in their choice of two tasty sauces.
—DeEtta Rasmussen, Fort Madison, Iowa

3/4 cup soy sauce
1/4 cup Worcestershire sauce
2 garlic cloves, minced
2-1/2 pounds beef tenderloin, cut into 1-inch cubes
2-1/2 pounds pork tenderloin, cut into 1-inch cubes
HORSERADISH SAUCE:
1 cup (8 ounces) sour cream
3 tablespoons prepared horseradish
1 tablespoon chopped onion
1 teaspoon vinegar
1/2 teaspoon salt
1/4 teaspoon pepper
BARBECUE SAUCE:
1 can (8 ounces) tomato sauce
1/3 cup steak sauce
2 tablespoons brown sugar
6 to 9 cups peanut *or* vegetable oil

In a large resealable plastic bag, combine soy sauce, Worcestershire sauce and garlic. Add meat. Seal and turn to coat; refrigerate for 4 hours, turning occasionally. Meanwhile, in a small bowl, combine horseradish sauce ingredients; cover and refrigerate. In another bowl, combine the tomato sauce, steak sauce and brown sugar; cover and refrigerate. Drain and discard marinade. Pat meat dry with paper towels.

Using one fondue pot for every six people, heat 2-3 cups oil in each pot to 375°. Use fondue forks to cook meat in oil until it reaches desired doneness. Serve with the horseradish and barbecue sauces. **Yield:** 12-16 servings.

Zippy Seafood Stew

Garden-fresh leeks and peppers add punch to this deliciously spiced stew. The flavors blend together well, showcasing the shrimp and scallops. I'd have to say this is one of my favorites.
—Paul Noetzel, Grafton, Wisconsin

3 to 4 medium leeks (white portion only), sliced
1 jalapeno pepper, seeded and chopped*
3 garlic cloves, minced
2 tablespoons olive *or* vegetable oil
1-1/2 cups tomato puree
1 cup water
1 cup chicken *or* vegetable broth
1 teaspoon salt
3/4 teaspoon ground cumin
1/4 teaspoon ground cinnamon
1/8 teaspoon cayenne pepper
3/4 pound uncooked medium shrimp, peeled and deveined
3/4 pound sea scallops

In a Dutch oven or large kettle, saute the leeks, jalapeno and garlic in oil until tender. Add the tomato puree, water, broth and seasonings; bring to a boil. Reduce heat; simmer, uncovered, for 10-15 minutes. Add shrimp and scallops; simmer 5 minutes longer or until shrimp turn pink and scallops are opaque. **Yield:** 6-8 servings.

***Editor's Note:** When cutting or seeding hot peppers, use rubber or plastic gloves to protect your hands. Avoid touching your face.

Sausage Spinach Turnovers

One Christmas, I gave these tasty meat pies to our neighbors as gifts instead of sweets, and they loved them! The hand-held pies make a handy take-along lunch for munching as you go. I freeze the leftovers and reheat them later in the microwave when I need a meal in a hurry.
—Vicky Henry, Aurora, Colorado

1 pound bulk pork sausage
1/3 cup chopped onion
1 package (10 ounces) frozen chopped spinach, thawed and squeezed dry
1-1/2 cups (6 ounces) shredded sharp cheddar cheese
2 teaspoons prepared mustard
1 teaspoon dried marjoram
Salt and pepper to taste
1 loaf (16 ounces) frozen bread dough, thawed
1 egg white, beaten

In a skillet, cook sausage and onion over medium heat until meat is no longer pink; drain. Stir in the spinach, cheese, mustard, marjoram, salt and pepper. Cook and stir until cheese is melted. Remove from the heat; cool slightly.

Divide dough into eight portions; roll each into a 6-in. circle. Spoon about 1/2 cup meat mixture on half of each circle. Brush edges with egg white; fold dough over filling and press edges with a fork to seal. Place on greased baking sheets. Cover and let rise in a warm place for 20 minutes. Brush tops with egg white; cut slits in the top of each. Bake at 350° for 20 minutes or until golden brown. **Yield:** 8 turnovers.

Salmon Fettuccine

(Pictured below)

My husband, Chet, and I both love sport fishing—in fact, we even went fishing on our honeymoon! This tasty recipe is a favorite when we have leftover cooked salmon to use up. It's also great with canned salmon.
—Lisa Royston, Wasilla, Alaska

- **8 ounces uncooked fettuccine**
- **1-1/2 cups sliced fresh mushrooms**
- **1 small zucchini, sliced**
- **2 tablespoons chopped onion**
- **2 tablespoons butter *or* margarine**
- **1 tablespoon all-purpose flour**
- **3/4 cup milk**
- **3/4 cup canned *or* fully cooked salmon chunks**
- **1/2 cup frozen peas, thawed**
- **1/2 cup diced fresh tomato**
- **1 tablespoon minced fresh parsley**
- **1/4 teaspoon salt**
- **1/8 to 1/4 teaspoon pepper**
- **1/8 teaspoon dried basil**
- **1/8 teaspoon dried oregano**

Cook fettuccine according to package directions. Meanwhile, in a large skillet, saute the mushrooms, zucchini and onion in butter until crisp-tender. Stir in flour until blended. Gradually add milk. Bring to a boil; cook and stir for 1 minute or until thickened. Add the salmon, peas, tomato, parsley and seasonings; heat through. Drain fettuccine; top with salmon mixture. **Yield:** 4 servings.

Grilled Herbed Salmon

(Pictured below)

Fishing for salmon is how we make our livelihood, so we eat it four or more times a week. This recipe is quick, has tasty seasonings and lets the goodness of grilled salmon come through. *—Jenny Roth, Homer, Alaska*

"REEL-Y" DELICIOUS DINNERS start with recipes such as Grilled Herbed Salmon, Salmon Cups and Salmon Fettuccine (shown above, clockwise from top).

1/2 cup butter (no substitutes)
1/3 cup lemon juice
2 tablespoons minced parsley
1-1/2 teaspoons soy sauce
1-1/2 teaspoons Worcestershire sauce
1 teaspoon dried oregano
1/2 teaspoon garlic powder
1/4 teaspoon salt
1/8 teaspoon pepper
1 salmon fillet (2-1/2 to 3 pounds and 3/4 inch thick)

In a saucepan, combine the first nine ingredients. Cook and stir over low heat until butter is melted; set aside. Coat grill rack with nonstick cooking spray before starting grill. Place salmon skin side down on grill. Grill, covered, over medium-hot heat for 5 minutes. Baste with butter sauce. Grill 10-15 minutes longer or until fish flakes easily with a fork, basting frequently. **Yield:** 6-8 servings.

Salmon and Shrimp with Garlic Rice

Sometimes I think that everyone in Alaska catches salmon. I've cooked it so many ways. This impressive dish pairs salmon and shrimp with a mild sauce.
—Darlene Sullivan, Wasilla, Alaska

5 tablespoons butter *or* margarine, *divided*
3 tablespoons all-purpose flour
1-1/2 cups half-and-half cream
1-1/2 cups (6 ounces) shredded cheddar cheese, *divided*
1 teaspoon salt
1/2 teaspoon ground mustard
1/4 teaspoon dill weed
Dash cayenne pepper
1/2 pound medium uncooked shrimp, peeled and deveined
1-1/2 pounds salmon fillets
3 garlic cloves, minced
1 cup uncooked long grain rice
2 cups chicken broth

In a large saucepan, melt 3 tablespoons butter. Stir in flour until smooth; gradually add cream. Bring to a boil; cook and stir for 2 minutes or until thickened. Add 1 cup cheese, salt, mustard, dill and cayenne; stir until cheese is melted. Remove from the heat; stir in shrimp. Pat salmon dry; place in a greased 13-in. x 9-in. x 2-in. baking dish. Pour shrimp mixture over salmon. Top with remaining cheese. Bake, uncovered, at 400° for 25-30 minutes or until fish flakes easily with a fork and shrimp turn pink.

Meanwhile, in a saucepan, saute garlic in remaining butter until tender. Add rice; cook and stir for 2 minutes. Stir in broth; bring to a boil. Reduce heat; cover and cook for 15 minutes or until rice is tender. Serve with the salmon and shrimp mixture. **Yield:** 6 servings.

Salmon Cups

(Pictured below left)

My family likes this dish because it's a different way to enjoy the bounty of fish we have here. Two sauces—one rich, warm and cheesy, and the other light, cool and refreshing—complement the salmon nicely.
—Sue Bolsinger, Anchorage, Alaska

3/4 cup crushed cornflakes
1/2 cup milk
2 eggs, lightly beaten
3 tablespoons butter *or* margarine, melted
2 tablespoons grated onion
1/2 teaspoon garlic salt
1/8 teaspoon pepper
2 cups canned *or* fully cooked salmon chunks
CHEESE SAUCE:
2 tablespoons butter *or* margarine
2 tablespoons all-purpose flour
1-1/4 cups milk
1/2 cup shredded cheddar cheese
1 jar (2 ounces) diced pimientos, drained
1/2 teaspoon salt
1 garlic clove, minced
Dash pepper and hot pepper sauce
CUCUMBER SAUCE:
1/2 cup diced cucumber
1/2 cup plain yogurt
1/2 teaspoon dill weed
1/2 teaspoon dried minced onion
1/4 teaspoon prepared horseradish
1/8 teaspoon salt

In a bowl, combine the first eight ingredients. Place four greased 8-oz. custard cups in an 11-in. x 7-in. x 2-in. baking dish. Fill cups with salmon mixture; gently press down with a spoon until flattened. Fill dish with boiling water to a depth of 1 in. Bake, uncovered, at 375° for 25-30 minutes or until a meat thermometer reads 160°.

In a saucepan, melt butter. Stir in flour until smooth; gradually add milk. Bring to a boil; cook and stir for 1 minute or until thickened. Add cheese, pimientos, salt, garlic, pepper and hot pepper sauce; cook and stir until cheese is melted. In a bowl, combine cucumber sauce ingredients. Unmold salmon cups; serve with sauces. **Yield:** 4 servings.

Lemon Dill Walleye

In our area, walleye is popular and abundant. In this light entree, the fish is moist and nicely flavored with dill and lemon. —Dawn Piasta, Dauphin, Manitoba

✓ Uses less fat, sugar or salt. Includes Nutritional Analysis and Diabetic Exchanges.

1 large onion, halved and thinly sliced
1 tablespoon butter *or* stick margarine
4 cups water
1 tablespoon snipped fresh dill *or* 1 teaspoon dill weed
3/4 cup fat-free milk
2 medium lemons, thinly sliced
1/8 teaspoon pepper
2 pounds walleye, cod, halibut *or* orange roughy fillets

In a large skillet, saute onion in butter until tender. Add water and dill; bring to a boil. Reduce heat; simmer, uncovered, for 4-5 minutes. Add milk; stir in lemons and pepper. Top with fillets. Cover and simmer for 12-15 minutes or until fish flakes easily with a fork. Transfer fish to a serving platter and keep warm. Strain cooking liquid, reserving lemons, onion and dill; serve with fish. **Yield:** 8 servings.

Nutritional Analysis: One serving (calculated with walleye and butter) equals 116 calories, 2 g fat (trace saturated fat), 70 mg cholesterol, 113 mg sodium, 5 g carbohydrate, 1 g fiber, 18 g protein. **Diabetic Exchanges:** 2-1/2 very lean meat, 1 vegetable.

Spiced Pork Potpie

Full of apples, cranberries, sweet potatoes, cinnamon and cloves, this scrumptious meat pie smells just like autumn as it bakes! The original recipe called for a pastry crust, but I prefer the fuss-free batter crust. —Kay Krause, Sioux Falls, South Dakota

1-1/2 pounds cubed pork shoulder roast
1/2 cup butter *or* margarine, *divided*
2 cups apple cider *or* juice
1 cup water
1 cup chopped peeled tart apple
1/2 cup dried cranberries
1/2 cup dried pitted prunes, chopped
2 teaspoons ground cinnamon
1-1/2 teaspoons ground ginger
2 whole cloves
6 tablespoons all-purpose flour
1 can (15 ounces) sweet potatoes, drained and cubed

CRUST:
1 cup all-purpose flour
1-1/2 teaspoons baking powder
1/2 teaspoon salt
3/4 cup milk
1/2 cup butter *or* margarine, melted

In a Dutch oven, cook pork in 2 tablespoons butter until no longer pink. Add the cider and water; bring to a boil. Reduce heat; simmer for 10 minutes. Stir in the fruit and seasonings; simmer 10 minutes longer. Melt remaining butter; stir in flour until smooth. Slowly add to meat mixture. Bring to a boil; cook for 1-2 minutes or until thickened. Discard cloves. Stir in sweet potatoes. Pour into a greased 3-qt. baking dish.

For crust, combine the flour, baking powder and salt in a bowl. Combine the milk and butter; stir into dry ingredients until smooth. Spread over filling. Bake at 400° for 28-32 minutes or until crust is browned. **Yield:** 6 servings.

Pasta Frittata

This well-seasoned frittata, starring ham, eggs, cheese and pasta, is always popular on a buffet. It bakes up a lovely golden brown and slices like a dream. Folks can bring their appetites when this dish is served and walk away satisfied! —Penny McBride, Decatur, Illinois

1 large onion, chopped
1 tablespoon vegetable oil
12 ounces sliced deli ham, finely chopped
4 garlic cloves, minced
6 eggs
3 egg whites
1/2 cup shredded mozzarella cheese
1/2 cup shredded Colby cheese
2 tablespoons minced fresh parsley
1 to 1-1/2 teaspoons Italian seasoning
1/2 teaspoon salt
1/2 teaspoon pepper
Dash cayenne pepper
2 cups cooked angel hair pasta

In an ovenproof skillet, saute onion in oil. Add ham and garlic; saute 1 minute longer. Remove and set aside. In a bowl, whisk the eggs and egg whites. Add cheeses, parsley and seasonings. Add the ham mixture and pasta. Coat the same skillet with cooking spray if necessary. Add pasta mixture. Cover and cook over medium heat for 3 minutes. Uncover. Bake at 400° for 13 minutes or until set. Let stand for 5 minutes before cutting. **Yield:** 6 servings.

Herbed Pork Chops

Pork chops and other meats really perk up when they're seasoned with this homemade herb blend. Watching your salt? Leave it out and you'll still get plenty of flavor. —*Jean Morgan, Roscoe, Illinois*

✓ Uses less fat, sugar or salt. Includes Nutritional Analysis and Diabetic Exchanges.

1/3 cup dried parsley flakes
1/4 cup dried marjoram
1/4 cup dried thyme
3 tablespoons rubbed sage
2 tablespoons garlic powder
2 tablespoons onion powder
1 teaspoon salt
1 teaspoon ground cinnamon
4 boneless pork loin chops (1 pound)
1 tablespoon canola oil

In a bowl, combine the first eight ingredients. Rub 1/2 teaspoon herb mixture over each pork chop. In a nonstick skillet, brown chops in oil for 4-5 minutes on each side or until a meat thermometer reaches 160°. Store remaining rub in a covered container. **Yield:** 4 servings (1-1/4 cups rub).

Nutritional Analysis: One serving equals 190 calories, 9 g fat (2 g saturated fat), 62 mg cholesterol, 51 mg sodium, 0 carbohydrate, 0 fiber, 25 g protein. **Diabetic Exchanges:** 3 lean meat, 1/2 fat.

Wild Rice Mushroom Omelet

(Pictured above right)

Since wild rice is plentiful here, I love to create recipes starring that crunchy staple. Pork sausage helps spice up the rice flavor in this hearty omelet, which is draped with a silky-smooth cheese sauce. You can easily serve it to guests with little last-minute fuss.
—*Bonnie Bourdeau, Akeley, Minnesota*

1/2 pound bulk pork sausage
1 medium onion, chopped
1 celery rib, finely chopped
2 tablespoons butter *or* margarine
1 can (4 ounces) mushroom stems and pieces, drained
1-1/2 cups cooked wild rice
1 teaspoon dried parsley flakes
14 eggs
1/2 cup water
1/4 teaspoon salt
1/8 teaspoon pepper

CHEESE SAUCE:

2 tablespoons butter *or* margarine
1 teaspoon chicken bouillon granules
2 tablespoons all-purpose flour
1 cup milk
1/4 cup cubed process cheese product
Minced fresh parsley, optional

In a skillet, cook sausage over medium heat until no longer pink; drain. Remove and set aside. In the skillet, saute onion and celery in butter until tender. Add mushrooms; heat through. Stir in sausage, rice and parsley.

In a bowl, whisk eggs, water, salt and pepper. Heat an 8-in. nonstick skillet coated with nonstick cooking spray over medium heat. Add 1/2 cup egg mixture. As eggs set, lift edges, letting uncooked portion flow underneath. When nearly set, spoon 1/2 cup of sausage-rice mixture over one side of eggs; fold in half and press down lightly for about 30 seconds. Remove and keep warm. Repeat to make six more omelets.

For cheese sauce, melt butter in a saucepan over medium heat. Stir in bouillon until dissolved. Stir in flour until smooth. Gradually add milk. Bring to a boil; cook and stir for 2 minutes or until thickened. Reduce heat to low; stir in cheese until melted. Drizzle over omelets. Sprinkle with parsley if desired. **Yield:** 7 omelets.

Chicken in Potato Baskets

(Pictured below)

These petite pies with their hash brown crusts are so pretty that I like to serve them for special luncheons. Chock-full of meat and veggies in a creamy sauce, they're a meal-in-one and a great way to use up left-over chicken or turkey. —*Helen Lamison Carnegie, Pennsylvania*

4-1/2 cups frozen shredded hash brown potatoes, thawed
6 tablespoons butter *or* margarine, melted
1-1/2 teaspoons salt
1/4 teaspoon pepper
FILLING:
1/2 cup chopped onion
1/4 cup butter *or* margarine
1/4 cup all-purpose flour
2 teaspoons chicken bouillon granules
1 teaspoon Worcestershire sauce
1/2 teaspoon dried basil
2 cups milk
3 cups cubed cooked chicken
1 cup frozen peas, thawed

In a bowl, combine the potatoes, butter, salt and pepper. Press into six greased 10-oz. custard cups; set aside. In a saucepan, saute onion in butter. Add the flour, bouillon, Worcestershire sauce and basil. Stir in the milk. Bring to a boil; cook and stir for 2 minutes or until thickened. Add chicken and peas. Spoon into prepared crusts. Bake, uncovered, at 375° for 30-35 minutes or until crust is golden brown. **Yield:** 6 servings.

Spinach-Beef Spaghetti Pie

(Pictured on page 56)

With its angel hair pasta crust, this cheesy ground beef, tomato and spinach pie is always a hit. —*Carol Hicks, Pensacola, Florida*

6 ounces uncooked angel hair pasta
2 eggs, lightly beaten
1/3 cup grated Parmesan cheese
1 pound ground beef
1/2 cup chopped onion
1/4 cup chopped green pepper
1 jar (14 ounces) meatless spaghetti sauce
1 teaspoon Creole seasoning
3/4 teaspoon garlic powder
1/2 teaspoon dried basil
1/2 teaspoon dried oregano
1 package (8 ounces) cream cheese, softened
1 package (10 ounces) frozen chopped spinach, thawed and squeezed dry
1/2 cup shredded mozzarella cheese

Cook pasta according to package directions; drain. Add eggs and Parmesan cheese. Press onto the bottom and up the sides of a greased 9-in. deep-dish pie plate. Bake at 350° for 10 minutes. Meanwhile, in a skillet, cook the beef, onion and green pepper over medium heat until meat is no longer pink; drain. Stir in the spaghetti sauce and seasonings. Bring to a boil. Reduce heat; cover and simmer for 10 minutes.

Between two pieces of waxed paper, roll out cream cheese into a 7-in. circle. Place in the crust. Top with spinach and meat sauce. Sprinkle with mozzarella cheese. Bake at 350° for 20-30 minutes or until set. **Yield:** 6-8 servings.

Baked Pheasant in Gravy

Pheasant is moist, tender and flavorful when it's prepared this way. —*Lou Bishop, Phillips, Wisconsin*

1/2 cup all-purpose flour
1/2 cup packed brown sugar
6 pheasant *or* grouse breast halves
3 tablespoons butter *or* margarine
1 can (10-3/4 ounces) condensed cream of celery soup, undiluted
1 to 1-1/3 cups water
1 cup chicken broth
1 can (2.8 ounces) french-fried onions
Mashed potatoes *or* hot cooked rice

In a large resealable plastic bag, combine flour and brown sugar; add pheasant pieces, one at a time, and shake to coat. In a large skillet over medium heat, brown pheasant on both sides in butter. Transfer to a greased 13-in. x 9-in. x 2-in. baking dish. Combine soup, water and broth until blended; pour over pheasant. Bake, uncovered, at 350° for 40 minutes. Sprinkle with onions. Bake 5-10 minutes longer or until juices run clear. Serve with potatoes or rice. **Yield:** 6 servings.

South Dakota Meat Loaf

I've made other meat loaves, but I always come back to this one, which is based on my mom's recipe.
—Lauree Buus, Rapid City, South Dakota

✓ Uses less fat, sugar or salt. Includes Nutritional Analysis and Diabetic Exchanges.

1 egg
1/3 cup evaporated milk
3/4 cup quick-cooking oats
1/4 cup chopped onion
2 tablespoons Worcestershire sauce
1 teaspoon salt
1/2 teaspoon rubbed sage
1/8 teaspoon pepper
1-1/2 pounds ground beef
1/4 cup ketchup

In a large bowl, combine the first eight ingredients. Crumble beef over mixture and mix well. Press into an ungreased 8-in. x 4-in. x 2-in. loaf pan. Bake, uncovered, at 350° for 1-1/4 hours; drain. Drizzle with ketchup; bake 10 minutes longer or until meat is no longer pink and a meat thermometer reads 160°. **Yield:** 6 servings.

Nutritional Analysis: One serving (prepared with fat-free evaporated milk and lean ground beef) equals 272 calories, 12 g fat (4 g saturated fat), 77 mg cholesterol, 683 mg sodium, 13 g carbohydrate, 1 g fiber, 27 g protein. **Diabetic Exchanges:** 3 lean meat, 1-1/2 fat, 1/2 starch.

Quail with Mushroom Sauce

This golden quail is so moist and tender. The rich cream sauce, dotted with onions and mushrooms, complements the bird nicely.
—Joelann Sygo, Gaylord, Michigan

2 cups sliced fresh mushrooms
1 small onion, sliced
4 tablespoons butter *or* margarine, *divided*
1 pound boneless quail breasts *or* boneless skinless chicken breast halves
1 package (3 ounces) cream cheese, softened
1/4 to 1/2 cup milk
1/2 cup dry bread crumbs, toasted

In a skillet, saute mushrooms and onion in 2 tablespoons butter. Remove and set aside. In the same skillet, melt remaining butter; saute quail over medium heat for 8 minutes on each side. Meanwhile, in a small saucepan, heat and stir cream cheese and milk over low heat until smooth. Stir in sauteed mushrooms and onion. Sprinkle bread crumbs over both sides of quail; serve with mushroom sauce. **Yield:** 4 servings.

Greek Shepherd's Pie

It's so hard to resist a big scoop of this comforting casserole with its fluffy mashed potato topping.
—Sharon Ann McCray, San Francisco, California

4 large potatoes, peeled and cubed
1/2 cup sour cream
1/4 cup butter *or* margarine
5-1/2 cups cubed eggplant (about 1 large)
2 teaspoons salt
2 tablespoons all-purpose flour
1/4 cup vegetable oil
1 pound ground lamb
1/2 pound ground turkey
1 jar (26 ounces) meatless spaghetti sauce
2 tablespoons dried minced onion
2 tablespoons minced fresh parsley
1 teaspoon garlic powder
1/2 teaspoon dried rosemary, crushed
1/2 teaspoon dried basil
1/2 teaspoon pepper
1 cup (4 ounces) crumbled feta cheese

In a saucepan, cook potatoes in boiling water until tender; drain. Mash potatoes with sour cream and butter; set aside. In a bowl, combine eggplant and salt. Let stand for 10 minutes; drain. Add flour and toss to coat. In a skillet, cook eggplant in oil over medium heat until browned and oil is absorbed. Transfer to a greased 3-qt. baking dish.

In the same skillet, cook lamb and turkey over medium heat until no longer pink; drain. Stir in the spaghetti sauce, onion, parsley and seasonings. Cook until heated through, about 5 minutes. Pour meat mixture over eggplant; sprinkle with feta cheese. Spread mashed potatoes over the top. Bake, uncovered, at 350° for 35-45 minutes or until top begins to brown. Let stand for 10-15 minutes before serving. **Yield:** 6 servings.

Farmer's Market Sausage Pie

(Pictured above)

Our son, Lukas, named this savory pie for the Saturday morning market held near our state capitol. Most of the fresh ingredients called for in the recipe can be found there. —Teri Schuman, Oregon, Wisconsin

4 Italian sausage links, casings removed, halved and cut into 1/2-inch pieces
1 medium tomato, cut into chunks
1 small yellow tomato, cut into chunks
1 cup thinly sliced zucchini
1 cup thinly sliced yellow summer squash
1/2 cup julienned green pepper
1/2 cup julienned sweet red pepper
1 tablespoon Italian salad dressing mix
1/2 teaspoon garlic powder
1/4 to 1/2 teaspoon fennel seed, crushed
Pastry for double-crust pie (9 inches)
1 cup (4 ounces) shredded cheddar cheese
1 cup (4 ounces) shredded mozzarella cheese

In a large skillet, cook sausage over medium heat until no longer pink; drain. Stir in tomato, squash, peppers, salad dressing mix, garlic powder and fennel seed. Cook and stir for 10 minutes; drain. Cool for 10 minutes. Line a 9-in. pie plate with bottom pastry; trim even with edge. Fill with sausage mixture. Sprinkle with cheeses. Roll out remaining pastry to fit top of pie; place over filling. Trim, seal and flute edges. Cut slits in top.

Bake at 375° for 35-40 minutes or until filling is bubbly and crust is golden brown. Let stand for 10 minutes before cutting. **Yield:** 8 servings.

Wild Rice Venison Stew

With three hunters in the family and plenty of wild rice on hand, this hearty stew is a "must" at our house. —Darla Haseltine, Wyoming, Minnesota

✓ Uses less fat, sugar or salt. Includes Nutritional Analysis and Diabetic Exchanges.

1/3 cup all-purpose flour
1/2 teaspoon pepper
1-1/2 pounds venison, cut into 1-inch cubes
2 tablespoons canola oil
2-3/4 cups water
1 can (14-1/2 ounces) beef broth
1/2 teaspoon beef bouillon granules
2 medium potatoes, peeled and cubed
1 medium onion, cut into wedges
2 medium carrots, cut into 3/4-inch pieces
1/3 cup uncooked wild rice

In a large resealable plastic bag, combine flour and pepper. Add venison; shake to coat. In a Dutch oven, brown meat in oil. Add water, broth and bouillon; bring to a boil. Reduce heat; cover and simmer for 1-1/4 hours. Stir in the potatoes, onion, carrots and rice; return to a boil. Reduce heat; cover and simmer for 30-40 minutes or until vegetables and rice are tender. **Yield:** 6 servings.

Nutritional Analysis: One serving (1 cup) equals 301 calories, 8 g fat (2 g saturated fat), 103 mg cholesterol, 362 mg sodium, 24 g carbohydrate, 2 g fiber, 32 g protein. **Diabetic Exchanges:** 3-1/2 lean meat, 1-1/2 starch, 1 vegetable.

Spicy Chicken

I serve this zippy chicken with plenty of sour cream and full glasses of milk to calm the bite. It's a super way to stay toasty on blustery autumn days. —Donna Michaelis, Madison, Wisconsin

1 medium onion, chopped
6 garlic cloves, minced
5 tablespoons butter *or* margarine, *divided*
3 cups chicken broth
2 cans (15 ounces *each*) tomato sauce
2 cups chopped green onions
2 tablespoons Worcestershire sauce
2 teaspoons dried thyme
1-1/2 teaspoons cayenne pepper
1/2 teaspoon hot pepper sauce
1 tablespoon salt
1-1/2 teaspoons garlic powder
1-1/2 teaspoons pepper
1 teaspoon dried basil
1/4 teaspoon ground cumin

2 pounds boneless skinless chicken breasts, cubed
16 ounces angel hair pasta
1/2 cup sour cream

In a large saucepan or Dutch oven, saute the onion and garlic in 2 tablespoons butter until tender. Stir in the broth, tomato sauce, green onions, Worcestershire sauce, thyme, cayenne and hot pepper sauce. Bring to a boil. Reduce heat; simmer, uncovered, for 10 minutes. Meanwhile, in a large resealable plastic bag, combine the salt, garlic powder, pepper, basil and cumin; mix well. Add chicken and toss to coat.

In a skillet, saute chicken in remaining butter until juices run clear. Add chicken to tomato sauce; simmer for 10 minutes. Cook pasta according to package directions; drain. Top with chicken mixture. Garnish with sour cream. **Yield:** 8 servings.

BLT Egg Bake

BLTs are a favorite at my house, so I created this recipe to combine those flavors in a "dressier" dish. It was such a hit, I served it to my church ladies' group at a brunch I hosted. I received lots of compliments and wrote out the recipe many times that day.
—Priscilla Detrick, Catoosa, Oklahoma

1/4 cup mayonnaise
5 slices bread, toasted
4 slices process American cheese
12 bacon strips, cooked and crumbled
4 eggs
1 medium tomato, halved and sliced
2 tablespoons butter *or* margarine
2 tablespoons all-purpose flour
1/4 teaspoon salt
1/8 teaspoon pepper
1 cup milk
1/2 cup shredded cheddar cheese
2 green onions, thinly sliced
Shredded lettuce

Spread mayonnaise on one side of each slice of toast and cut into small pieces. Arrange toast, mayonnaise side up, in a greased 8-in. square baking dish. Top with cheese slices and bacon. In a skillet, fry eggs over medium heat until completely set; place over bacon. Top with tomato slices; set aside.

In a saucepan, melt butter. Stir in flour, salt and pepper until smooth. Gradually add milk. Bring to a boil; cook and stir for 2 minutes or until thickened. Pour over tomato. Sprinkle with cheddar cheese and onions. Bake, uncovered, at 325° for 10 minutes. Cut into squares; serve with lettuce. **Yield:** 4 servings.

Cranberry Turkey Stir-Fry

(Pictured below)

Soy sauce and cranberry sauce team up to give this pretty turkey stir-fry a sweet and savory flavor.
—Gwendolyn Roux, Oceanside, California

✓ Uses less fat, sugar or salt. Includes Nutritional Analysis and Diabetic Exchanges.

2 garlic cloves, minced
1 tablespoon canola oil
2 cups julienned carrots
2 cups uncooked turkey breast strips
2 cups julienned zucchini
1 cup canned bean sprouts
1 can (8 ounces) jellied cranberry sauce
1/3 cup apple juice
1/4 cup reduced-sodium soy sauce
1/4 cup cider vinegar
1 tablespoon cornstarch
1/4 cup cold water
4 cups hot cooked rice

In a nonstick skillet or wok, stir-fry garlic in oil for 30 seconds. Add carrots; stir-fry for 2 minutes. Add turkey, zucchini and bean sprouts; stir-fry 3 minutes longer. Combine cranberry sauce, apple juice, soy sauce and vinegar; stir into skillet. Bring to a boil. Combine cornstarch and cold water until smooth; gradually stir into skillet. Bring to a boil; cook and stir for 1-2 minutes or until thickened and bubbly and turkey juices run clear. Serve over rice. **Yield:** 4 servings.

Nutritional Analysis: One serving (1 cup turkey mixture with 1 cup rice) equals 530 calories, 10 g fat (2 g saturated fat), 55 mg cholesterol, 696 mg sodium, 83 g carbohydrate, 5 g fiber, 26 g protein. **Diabetic Exchanges:** 3 starch, 2 lean meat, 2 fruit, 1 vegetable.

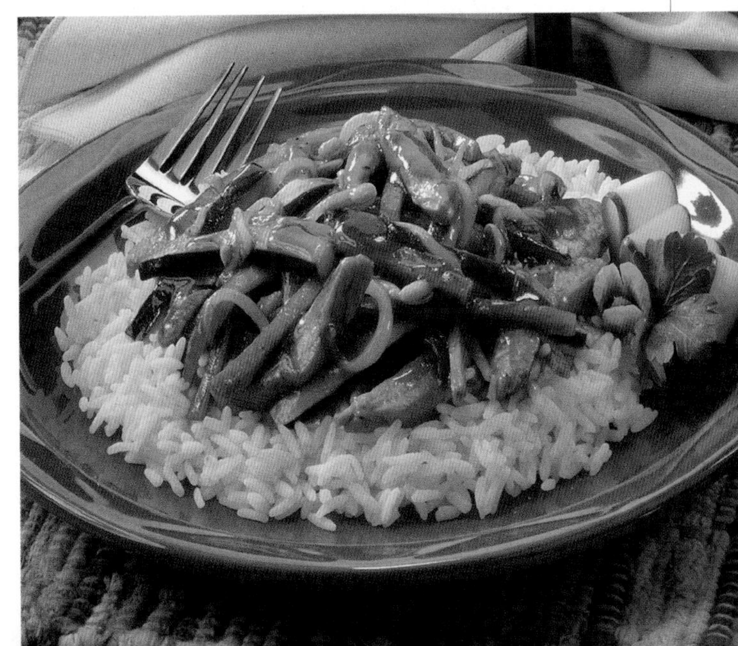

Pineapple Chicken

Pineapple and soy sauce pair nicely for marinating chicken breasts. The meat comes out of the oven moist and tasty. —Emma Magielda, Amsterdam, New York

✓ Uses less fat, sugar or salt. Includes Nutritional Analysis and Diabetic Exchanges.

1 can (8 ounces) unsweetened crushed pineapple, undrained
2 tablespoons cider vinegar
2 tablespoons reduced-sodium soy sauce
1 garlic clove, minced
1/8 teaspoon pepper
6 boneless skinless chicken breast halves (1-1/2 pounds)

In a large resealable plastic bag, combine the first five ingredients. Add chicken. Seal bag and turn to coat; refrigerate for 30 minutes. Place the chicken and marinade in an 11-in. x 7-in. x 2-in. baking dish coated with nonstick cooking spray. Cover and bake at 350° for 25 minutes or until chicken juices run clear. **Yield:** 6 servings.

Nutritional Analysis: One serving (1 chicken breast half with 2 tablespoons sauce) equals 149 calories, 1 g fat (trace saturated fat), 66 mg cholesterol, 276 mg sodium, 5 g carbohydrate, 1 g fiber, 27 g protein. **Diabetic Exchanges:** 2 lean meat, 1 fruit.

Beef-Stuffed Sopaipillas

This recipe reminds me of good times at a local restaurant when I was a kid. —Lara Pennell, Irving, Texas

2 cups all-purpose flour
1 teaspoon salt
1 teaspoon baking powder
1/2 cup water
1/4 cup evaporated milk
1-1/2 teaspoons vegetable oil
Additional oil for frying

FILLING:
1 pound ground beef
3/4 cup chopped onion
1/2 teaspoon salt
1/2 teaspoon garlic powder
1/4 teaspoon pepper

SAUCE:
1 can (10-3/4 ounces) condensed cream of chicken soup, undiluted
1/2 cup chicken broth
1 can (4 ounces) chopped green chilies
1/2 teaspoon onion powder
2 cups (8 ounces) shredded cheddar cheese

In a bowl, combine the flour, salt and baking powder. Stir in water, milk and oil with a fork until a ball forms. On a lightly floured surface, knead dough gently for 2-3 minutes. Cover and let stand for 15 minutes. Divide into four portions; roll each into a 6-1/2-in. circle. In an electric skillet or deep-fat fryer, heat oil to 375°. Fry circles, one at a time, for 2-3 minutes on each side or until golden brown. Drain on paper towels.

In a skillet, cook beef and onion over medium heat until meat is no longer pink; drain. Stir in the salt, garlic powder and pepper. In a saucepan, combine the soup, broth, chilies and onion powder. Cook for 10 minutes or until heated through. To assemble, cut a slit on one side of each sopaipilla; fill with 1/2 cup meat mixture. Sprinkle with cheese. Serve with sauce. **Yield:** 4 servings.

Mushroom Shrimp Creole

We especially enjoy this hearty main dish on chilly or stormy days. The tomatoes, mushrooms, onions, green peppers and shrimp are nicely spiced with seasonings. —Shirlee Vader, Hensley, Arkansas

6 bacon strips, diced
2 large onions, chopped
1-1/2 cups chopped green peppers
1 garlic clove, minced
1 can (29 ounces) diced tomatoes, undrained
1 can (6 ounces) tomato paste
4-1/2 teaspoons brown sugar
1 tablespoon Worcestershire sauce
1 teaspoon salt
1/2 teaspoon pepper
1/2 teaspoon dried basil
1 bay leaf
1-1/2 pounds cooked medium shrimp, peeled and deveined
1 jar (4-1/2 ounces) whole mushrooms, drained
2 tablespoons butter *or* margarine
1 tablespoon lemon juice
1/4 teaspoon dried savory
Hot cooked rice

In a large skillet, cook bacon over medium heat until crisp. Remove to paper towels to drain. In the drippings, saute onions, green peppers and garlic. Add the next eight ingredients. Bring to a boil. Reduce heat; cover and simmer for 30-45 minutes. Add the shrimp, mushrooms, butter, lemon juice and savory. Cook 5-10 minutes longer or until heated through. Discard bay leaf. Stir in bacon. Serve over rice. **Yield:** 6-8 servings.

Venison Cabbage Rolls

For a good-looking hearty venison entree without a strong game flavor, I recommend these cabbage rolls.
—Marcy Cella, L'Anse, Michigan

8 large cabbage leaves
1 pound ground venison
1 medium onion, chopped
1 teaspoon salt
1/4 teaspoon ground nutmeg
1 can (15 ounces) tomato sauce, *divided*
2 cups uncooked instant brown rice
1 cup (4 ounces) shredded cheddar cheese

In a large pot of boiling water, cook cabbage leaves for 3 minutes; drain and set aside. In a skillet over medium heat, cook venison, onion, salt and nutmeg until meat is no longer pink; drain. Stir in 1 cup tomato sauce. Place 1/3 cup meat mixture on each cabbage leaf; fold in sides. Starting at an unfolded edge, roll up completely to enclose filling.

Cook rice according to package directions; stir in remaining tomato sauce. Transfer to a large skillet; add cabbage rolls. Cover and simmer for 20 minutes. Sprinkle with cheese; heat until cheese begins to melt. **Yield:** 4 servings.

Peach Salsa with Pork

My husband and I had a dish similar to this in a restaurant, so we were determined to re-create it. It's so refreshing. *—Lisa St. Pierre, Pleasanton, California*

1 pork tenderloin (3/4 pound)
2 teaspoons olive *or* vegetable oil
1/2 teaspoon dried oregano
1/2 teaspoon ground cumin
SALSA:
2 cups fresh *or* frozen sliced peaches, chopped
1 tablespoon lime juice
1 to 3 tablespoons honey
1 tablespoon minced fresh cilantro *or* parsley
1 to 2 jalapeno peppers, seeded and minced*
Salt and pepper

Place pork in a greased 11-in. x 7-in. x 2-in. baking dish; rub meat with oil. Sprinkle with oregano and cumin. Bake, uncovered, at 400° for 25 minutes or until a meat thermometer reads 160°. Let stand for 10 minutes; slice. In a bowl, combine the salsa ingredients. Serve with pork. **Yield:** 2-3 servings.

***Editor's Note:** When cutting or seeding hot peppers, use rubber or plastic gloves to protect your hands. Avoid touching your face.

French Canadian Meat Pie

(Pictured below)

This hearty pie recipe was passed on for four generations by my mother's family in Quebec.
—Diane Davies, Indian Trail, North Carolina

1 pound ground beef
3/4 pound ground pork
3/4 cup chopped onion
2 celery ribs, chopped
2 garlic cloves, minced
6 cups hot mashed potatoes (prepared without milk and butter)
1/4 cup chicken broth
1/2 teaspoon dried rosemary, crushed
1/2 teaspoon rubbed sage
1/2 teaspoon dried thyme
1/4 teaspoon dried marjoram
Salt and pepper to taste
Pastry for two double-crust pies (9 inches)
Milk, optional

In a large skillet, cook the first five ingredients over medium heat until meat is no longer pink and vegetables are tender; drain. Remove from heat. Stir in potatoes, broth and seasonings. Line two 9-in. pie plates with pastry. Divide meat mixture between crusts. Top with remaining pastry; trim, seal and flute edges. Cut slits in top. Brush with milk if desired. Bake at 375° for 30-35 minutes or until crust is golden brown. **Yield:** 2 pies (6-8 servings each).

Grilled Salmon Fillet

Growing up on a family-owned resort, I was expected to help around the kitchen. Grilling salmon became my specialty. —Paul Noetzel, Grafton, Wisconsin

1 salmon fillet (about 1 pound)
2 tablespoons lemon juice
2 tablespoons red wine vinegar
2 teaspoons grated lemon peel
1-1/2 teaspoons dried basil
1 teaspoon garlic powder
1 teaspoon soy sauce
4-1/2 teaspoons grated Parmesan cheese
Dash pepper

Place fish, skin side down, in a disposable foil pan. Combine the lemon juice, vinegar, lemon peel, basil, garlic powder and soy sauce; pour over fish. Sprinkle with Parmesan cheese and pepper. Place pan on grill. Cover grill and cook over medium heat for 15-20 minutes or until fish flakes easily with a fork. **Yield:** 4 servings.

Creamy Garden Spaghetti

(Pictured below)

This cheesy dish is a favorite I make often for family and friends. —Karrie Fimbres, Sparks, Nevada

1/2 pound fresh broccoli, broken into florets
1-1/2 cups sliced zucchini
1-1/2 cups sliced fresh mushrooms
1 large carrot, sliced
1 tablespoon olive *or* vegetable oil
8 ounces uncooked spaghetti
1/4 cup chopped onion

3 garlic cloves, minced
2 tablespoons butter *or* margarine
2 tablespoons all-purpose flour
2 teaspoons chicken bouillon granules
1 teaspoon dried thyme
2 cups milk
1/2 cup shredded Swiss cheese
1/2 cup shredded mozzarella cheese

In a large skillet, saute the broccoli, zucchini, mushrooms and carrot in oil until crisp-tender. Remove from the heat and set aside. Cook spaghetti according to package directions. In another saucepan, saute onion and garlic in butter until tender. Stir in the flour, bouillon and thyme until blended. Gradually add milk. Bring to a boil; cook and stir for 2 minutes or until thickened. Reduce heat to low; stir in cheeses until melted. Add the vegetables; heat through. Drain spaghetti; toss with vegetable mixture. **Yield:** 4 servings.

My Mom's Meat Loaf Wellington

Ever since the Taste of Home Restaurant opened its doors in downtown Greendale, Wisconsin, diners have been asking us to share this recipe, so here it is.

3 eggs
1/2 cup ketchup
2-1/2 teaspoons seasoned salt
2 teaspoons Worcestershire sauce
1/4 teaspoon ground mustard
1/8 teaspoon pepper
3/4 pound lean ground beef
3/4 pound *each* ground veal and pork
1/3 cup chopped onion
3/4 cup dry bread crumbs
1 package (17-1/4 ounces) frozen puff pastry, thawed

MADEIRA SAUCE:

1/4 cup butter *or* margarine
5 tablespoons all-purpose flour
2 cups beef consomme
1 tablespoon tomato paste
1/4 teaspoon dried thyme
1/4 teaspoon dried rosemary, crushed
1/4 teaspoon browning sauce, optional
Dash cloves
1/2 cup Madeira wine *or* beef broth
2 cups sliced fresh mushrooms
2 tablespoons olive *or* vegetable oil

In a bowl, beat 2 eggs, ketchup, seasoned salt, Worcestershire sauce, mustard and pepper. Crumble meat over mixture and mix well. Sprinkle with onion and bread crumbs; mix gently. Shape into two loaves, about 9 in. x 3 in. On a lightly floured surface, roll out each pastry sheet into an 18-in. x 16-in. rectangle. Invert meat loaves and place in center of each pastry; fold short sides of pastry over loaf. Fold long sides over loaf and pastry; seal seams. Place seam side down on a rack in a 15-in. x 10-in. x 1-in. baking pan. Beat remaining egg; brush over pastry. Bake at 350° for 60-70 minutes or until a meat thermometer reads 160°-170°. Meanwhile, for sauce, melt butter in a saucepan. Whisk in flour until smooth. Stir in the consomme, tomato paste, thyme, rosemary, browning sauce if desired and cloves. Bring to a boil; cook and stir for 2 minutes or until thickened. Stir in wine or broth. In a skillet, saute mushrooms in oil until tender. Serve the mushrooms and sauce over meat loaf slices. **Yield:** 2 meat loaves (5-6 servings each) and about 2-1/2 cups sauce.

Croissant French Toast

(Pictured on page 1)

More like a dessert than a breakfast main dish, this rich French toast is topped with two delicious sauces.
—June Dickenson, Philippi, West Virginia

VANILLA SAUCE:
- **1 tablespoon all-purpose flour**
- **4 egg yolks**
- **1 tablespoon vanilla extract**
- **2 cups whipping cream**
- **1/2 cup sugar**
- **2 scoops vanilla ice cream**

BERRY SAUCE:
- **2 cups unsweetened raspberries**
- **2 tablespoons sugar**

FRENCH TOAST:
- **3 eggs**
- **4 croissants, split**
- **2 tablespoons butter *or* margarine**

In a bowl, combine flour, egg yolks and vanilla; set aside. In a saucepan over medium-high heat, bring the whipping cream and sugar to a boil; remove from the heat. Stir a small amount of hot cream into egg yolk mixture; return all to the pan, stirring constantly. Bring to a gentle boil; cook and stir for 2 minutes. Remove from the heat; stir in ice cream until melted. Set aside.

For berry sauce, combine raspberries and sugar in a saucepan. Simmer, uncovered, for 2-3 minutes. Remove from heat; set aside. In a bowl, beat eggs. Dip both sides of croissants in egg mixture. On a griddle, brown croissants on both sides in butter. Serve with vanilla and berry sauces. **Yield:** 4 servings.

Savory Pork Chops

I love these tender pork chops smothered in a mouth-watering sauce. *—Debbie Terenzini Wilkerson*
Lusby, Maryland

- **2 tablespoons all-purpose flour**
- **1 tablespoon ground mustard**
- **1 teaspoon seasoned salt**
- **1/8 teaspoon pepper**
- **4 pork chops (3/4 inch thick)**
- **2 tablespoons vegetable oil**

MUSTARD SAUCE:
- **2 teaspoons ground mustard**
- **1 cup water**
- **1/2 cup chopped onion**
- **2 tablespoons ketchup**
- **2 tablespoons orange marmalade**
- **1 tablespoon soy sauce**
- **1 tablespoon Dijon mustard**

In a bowl, combine the first four ingredients. Dredge pork chops in flour mixture. In a skillet over medium heat, brown chops in oil on both sides, about 8 minutes. Combine the sauce ingredients; pour over chops. Cover and simmer until meat is tender, about 20 minutes. Spoon sauce over chops when serving. **Yield:** 4 servings.

Almond Bacon Chicken

We enjoyed this flavorful dish at a friend's house years ago, and I had to have the recipe. she assembled it quickly, and it cooked in no time. *—Ruth Peterson*
Jenison, Michigan

- **4 bacon strips**
- **4 boneless skinless chicken breast halves**
- **1/4 teaspoon pepper**
- **1 can (10-3/4 ounces) condensed cream of onion soup, undiluted**
- **1/4 cup chicken broth**
- **1/4 cup sliced almonds, toasted**

In a microwave, cook bacon on paper towels on high for 1-3 minutes or until partially cooked. Wrap a strip around each chicken breast. Sprinkle with pepper. Arrange in an 8-in. square microwave-safe dish. Cover and microwave on high for 7 minutes; drain. In a bowl, combine soup and broth; cover and microwave 2 minutes. Spoon around chicken. Cook, uncovered, 5-7 minutes longer or until juices run clear. Let stand 5 minutes before serving. Sprinkle with nuts. **Yield:** 4 servings.

Editor's Note: This recipe was tested in an 850-watt microwave.

Shrimp Creole

Since I retired from the Air Force, I've made dinner for myself and my wife, Alice, who's a busy nurse. We tend a vegetable and herb garden together, and many of our veggies end up in delicious dishes like this one.
—DeWhitt Sizemore, Woodlawn, Virginia

1 cup chopped onion
1/2 cup chopped green pepper
1/2 cup chopped celery
1/4 cup butter *or* margarine
1 can (28 ounces) crushed tomatoes, undrained
6 garlic cloves, minced
2 bay leaves
1 teaspoon salt
1/2 teaspoon cayenne pepper
2 tablespoons all-purpose flour
3 tablespoons water
1 pound uncooked medium shrimp, peeled and deveined
1 tablespoon Worcestershire sauce
1/4 to 1/2 teaspoon hot pepper sauce
1/2 cup thinly sliced green onions
2 tablespoons minced fresh parsley
Hot cooked rice

In a Dutch oven, saute onion, green pepper and celery in butter until tender. Add the tomatoes, garlic, bay leaves, salt and cayenne. Bring to a boil. Reduce heat; simmer, uncovered, for 35 minutes, stirring occasionally. Discard the bay leaves. In a small bowl, whisk together flour and water until smooth; add to tomato mixture. Bring to a boil, stirring constantly. Stir in shrimp, Worcestershire and hot pepper sauce. Simmer, uncovered, for 5 minutes or until shrimp turn pink. Stir in green onions and parsley. Serve over rice. **Yield:** 4-6 servings.

Zesty Beef Brisket

I cook often for church functions. This tender, well-seasoned beef is really very little fuss to make for a crowd.
—Al Latimer, Bentonville, Arkansas

2 tablespoons ground mustard
1 tablespoon dried oregano
2 teaspoons chili powder
1 teaspoon garlic powder
1 teaspoon salt
1 teaspoon pepper
1 fresh beef brisket* (3 pounds)
Barbecue *or* horseradish sauce

In a small bowl, combine the first six ingredients. Rub over brisket. Place in a greased roasting pan. Cover and bake at 325° for 2-1/2 to 3 hours or until tender. Thinly slice meat across the grain. Serve with barbecue or horseradish sauce or cooking juices. **Yield:** 8-10 servings.

***Editor's Note:** This is a fresh beef brisket, not corned beef.

Vegetable Ham Stew

I created this savory stew while trying to use up leftover ham. My husband loved it and told me to write down the recipe. —Shannon Smith, Mt. Horeb, Wisconsin

✓ Uses less fat, sugar or salt. Includes Nutritional Analysis and Diabetic Exchanges.

4 cups water
2 cans (14-1/2 ounces *each*) diced tomatoes, undrained
3 cups shredded cabbage
2 cups diced fully cooked lean ham
3 large carrots, cut into 1-inch pieces
1-1/2 cups chopped celery
3/4 cup chopped onion
1/2 cup chopped green pepper
1 tablespoon sugar
2 teaspoons dried basil
1/2 teaspoon pepper
1/4 teaspoon garlic powder
2 bay leaves
1/4 cup cornstarch
1/4 cup cold water

In a Dutch oven, combine the first 13 ingredients; bring to a boil. Reduce heat; cover and simmer for 1-1/4 hours or until cabbage is tender, stirring occasionally. Combine cornstarch and cold water until smooth; stir into stew. Bring to a boil; cook and stir for 2 minutes or until thickened. Discard bay leaves. **Yield:** 11 servings (2-3/4 quarts).

Nutritional Analysis: One serving (1 cup) equals 90 calories, 1 g fat (0 saturated fat), 12 mg cholesterol, 511 mg sodium, 13 g carbohydrate, 3 g fiber, 6 g protein. **Diabetic Exchanges:** 1 starch, 1/2 very lean meat.

Salmon Asparagus Tart

(Pictured on page 56)

This is a fresh way to use canned salmon. What a super springtime treat! —Abby Crawford, Corvallis, Oregon

1 pound asparagus, trimmed and cut into 2-inch pieces
1/4 cup finely chopped onion
1/4 cup chopped sweet red *or* yellow pepper
2 tablespoons butter *or* margarine
4 ounces cream cheese, softened

1/2 cup mayonnaise*
2 tablespoons all-purpose flour
2 eggs, lightly beaten
1/2 cup half-and-half cream
1 teaspoon dill weed
1/2 teaspoon dried basil
1/4 teaspoon pepper
1 can (15 ounces) salmon, drained, bones and skin removed
2 cups (8 ounces) shredded Swiss cheese
2 tablespoons grated Parmesan cheese

In a saucepan, bring 1 in. of water to a boil. Place asparagus in a steamer basket over water; cover and steam for 4-5 minutes or until crisp-tender. Drain and set aside. In a skillet, saute onion and red pepper in butter until tender; set aside. In a mixing bowl, combine the cream cheese, mayonnaise, flour, eggs, cream, dill, basil and pepper. Fold in the salmon, asparagus, onion mixture and Swiss cheese. Transfer to a greased 9-in. pie plate. Sprinkle with Parmesan cheese. Bake at 350° for 35 minutes or until a knife inserted near the center comes out clean. **Yield:** 6 servings.

***Editor's Note:** Reduced-fat or fat-free mayonnaise may not be substituted for regular mayonnaise.

Turkey Meat Loaf

My family loves this meat loaf served with carrots and new potatoes. —Tamie Foley, San Dimas, California

✓ Uses less fat, sugar or salt. Includes Nutritional Analysis and Diabetic Exchanges.

2 egg whites
1/3 cup ketchup
1 tablespoon Worcestershire sauce
1 teaspoon dried basil
1/2 teaspoon salt
1/2 teaspoon pepper
1 small onion, grated
1 small potato, finely shredded
1 small sweet red pepper, finely chopped
2 pounds lean ground turkey

In a large bowl, whisk together the first six ingredients. Stir in onion, potato and red pepper. Crumble turkey over mixture and mix well. Shape into a 12-in. x 4-in. loaf in a foil-lined 13-in. x 9-in. x 2-in. baking pan. Bake, uncovered, at 350° for 60-70 minutes or until meat is no longer pink and a meat thermometer reads 165°. **Yield:** 8 servings.

Nutritional Analysis: One serving equals 200 calories, 9 g fat (3 g saturated fat), 90 mg cholesterol, 409 mg sodium, 7 g carbohydrate, 1 g fiber, 21 g protein. **Diabetic Exchanges:** 3 lean meat, 1 fat.

Slow-Cooked Lamb Chops

(Pictured below)

This recipe for lamb chops is great for people who are trying lamb for the first time, since the meat turns out extra tender and tasty. —Sandra McKenzie Braham, Minnesota

4 bacon strips
4 lamb shoulder blade chops, trimmed
2-1/4 cups thinly sliced peeled potatoes
1 cup thinly sliced carrots
1/2 teaspoon dried rosemary, crushed
1/4 teaspoon garlic powder
1/4 teaspoon salt
1/4 teaspoon pepper
1/4 cup chopped onion
2 garlic cloves, minced
1 can (10-3/4 ounces) condensed cream of mushroom soup, undiluted
1/3 cup milk
1 jar (4-1/2 ounces) sliced mushrooms, drained

Wrap bacon around lamb chops; secure with toothpicks. Place in slow cooker. Cover and cook on high for 1-1/2 hours. Remove chops; discard toothpicks and bacon. Drain liquid. Add potatoes and carrots; top with lamb chops. Sprinkle with rosemary, garlic powder, salt, pepper, onion and garlic. In a bowl, combine soup and milk; mix well. Add mushrooms. Pour over the chops. Cover and cook on low for 4-6 hours or until meat and vegetables are tender. **Yield:** 4 servings.

Pizza Carbonara

(Pictured above)

Convenient refrigerated pizza crust is dressed up with a creamy Parmesan sauce and a topping of Monterey Jack cheese, bacon and green onions in this tasty recipe. It's a deliciously different addition to a pizza party. —Sherry Keethler, Lake St. Louis, Missouri

1 tube (10 ounces) refrigerated pizza crust
1/3 cup finely chopped onion
2 garlic cloves, minced
1 tablespoon butter *or* margarine
1 tablespoon all-purpose flour
1/8 teaspoon white pepper
1 cup milk
1/4 teaspoon chicken bouillon granules
1/4 cup grated Parmesan cheese
1/2 pound sliced bacon, cooked and crumbled
1-1/2 cups (6 ounces) shredded Monterey Jack cheese
3 green onions, thinly sliced

Unroll pizza crust. Press onto a greased 12-in. pizza pan; build up edges slightly. Prick dough thoroughly with a fork. Bake at 425° for 7-10 minutes or until lightly browned. Meanwhile, in a saucepan, saute onion and garlic in butter until tender. Stir in flour and pepper until blended. Gradually add milk and bouillon. Bring to a boil; cook and stir for 2 minutes or until thickened. Reduce heat; stir in Parmesan cheese. Spread over hot crust. Sprinkle with bacon, Monterey Jack cheese and green onions. Bake at 425° for 8-12 minutes or until cheese is melted. Let stand for 5 minutes before cutting. **Yield:** 4-6 servings.

Hungarian Goulash

(Pictured on page 56)

With tender beef and a rich flavorful sauce, this entree is an old favorite with my family. —Joan Rose, Langley, British Columbia

1 pound beef stew meat, cut into 1-inch cubes
1 pound lean boneless pork, cut into 1-inch cubes
2 large onions, thinly sliced
2 tablespoons vegetable oil
2 cups water
2 tablespoons paprika
1/2 teaspoon salt
1/2 teaspoon dried marjoram
1 tablespoon all-purpose flour
1 cup (8 ounces) sour cream
Hot cooked noodles

In a large skillet over medium heat, brown beef, pork and onions in oil; drain. Add the water, paprika, salt and marjoram; bring to a boil. Reduce heat; cover and simmer for 1-1/2 hours or until meat is tender. Just before serving, combine flour and sour cream until smooth; stir into meat mixture. Bring to a boil over medium heat; cook and stir for 1-2 minutes or until thickened and bubbly. Serve over noodles. **Yield:** 6-8 servings.

Spanish Rice with Turkey

Not everyone in the family cared for Spanish rice until they tried this hearty version. Now, instead of complaints, I hear, "More, please." —Sylvia Wallace, Adams, New York

☑ Uses less fat, sugar or salt. Includes Nutritional Analysis and Diabetic Exchanges.

1 pound ground turkey breast
1/2 cup chopped onion
1/2 cup chopped green pepper
1/2 teaspoon garlic powder
2 cans (14-1/2 ounces *each*) diced tomatoes, undrained
2 cups cooked long grain brown rice
1 teaspoon sugar
1 teaspoon chili powder
1/4 teaspoon pepper
1/8 teaspoon hot pepper sauce
1/2 cup shredded reduced-fat cheddar cheese

In a skillet, cook the turkey, onion, green pepper and garlic powder over medium heat until meat is no longer pink; drain. Stir in the next six ingredients. Bring to a boil. Reduce heat; cover and simmer for 15-20 minutes or until heated through.

Sprinkle with cheese. **Yield:** 5 servings.

Nutritional Analysis: One serving (1 cup) equals 308 calories, 11 g fat (4 g saturated fat), 78 mg cholesterol, 384 mg sodium, 30 g carbohydrate, 4 g fiber, 24 g protein. **Diabetic Exchanges:** 2 starch, 2 lean meat, 1-1/2 vegetable.

Black Beans 'n' Rice

A co-worker who was born in Cuba helped me perfect the recipe for this hearty dish. It's also a great way to use up leftover ham. —Helen Simms, Lyons, Michigan

✓ Uses less fat, sugar or salt. Includes Nutritional Analysis and Diabetic Exchanges.

1 pound dry black beans, rinsed
7 cups water
1 cup diced fully cooked lean ham
5 garlic cloves, minced
1-1/4 teaspoons pepper
1-1/4 teaspoons ground cumin
1 teaspoon salt
1 bay leaf
1/2 teaspoon liquid smoke, optional
4 cups chicken broth
2 cups uncooked long grain rice
1 tablespoon red wine vinegar *or* cider vinegar
2 teaspoons olive *or* canola oil
3/4 cup shredded reduced-fat cheddar cheese
3/4 cup chopped sweet red pepper
2 tablespoons chopped jalapeno peppers*

Place beans in a Dutch oven; add water to cover by 2 in. Bring to a boil; boil for 2 minutes. Remove from the heat; cover and let stand for 1 hour. Drain and rinse beans, discarding liquid. Return beans to the pan. Add 7 cups water, ham, garlic, pepper, cumin, salt, bay leaf and liquid smoke if desired. Bring to a boil. Reduce heat; cover and simmer for 1-1/2 hours or until beans are tender.

Meanwhile, in a saucepan, bring broth and rice to a boil. Reduce heat; cover and simmer for 20 minutes or until rice is tender. Just before serving, discard bay leaf from bean mixture; add vinegar and oil. Serve over rice. Sprinkle each serving with 1 tablespoon cheese, 1 tablespoon red pepper and 1 teaspoon jalapenos. **Yield:** 12 servings.

Nutritional Analysis: One serving (1 cup bean mixture with 1/2 cup rice) equals 324 calories, 5 g fat (2 g saturated fat), 12 mg cholesterol, 843 mg sodium, 53 g carbohydrate, 7 g fiber, 17 g protein. **Diabetic Exchanges:** 3 starch, 1 meat, 1 vegetable.

***Editor's Note:** When cutting or seeding hot peppers, use rubber or plastic gloves to protect your hands. Avoid touching your face.

Lemon Chicken Skewers

(Pictured below and on page 56)

This easy-to-assemble recipe, is always a hit when we have a party. —Margaret Wagner Allen, Abingdon, Virginia

✓ Uses less fat, sugar or salt. Includes Nutritional Analysis and Diabetic Exchanges.

1/4 cup olive *or* vegetable oil
3 tablespoons lemon juice
1 tablespoon white wine vinegar *or* cider vinegar
2 garlic cloves, minced
2 teaspoons grated lemon peel
1 teaspoon salt
1/2 teaspoon sugar
1/4 teaspoon dried oregano
1/4 teaspoon pepper
1-1/2 pounds boneless skinless chicken breasts, cut into 1-1/2-inch pieces
3 medium zucchini, halved lengthwise and cut into 1-1/2-inch slices
3 medium onions, cut into wedges
12 cherry tomatoes

In a bowl, combine the first nine ingredients; set aside 1/4 cup for basting. Place chicken and vegetables in a resealable plastic bag; add remaining marinade. Seal bag and turn to coat; refrigerate for 4 hours or overnight. Drain and discard marinade. Alternately thread chicken and vegetables onto metal or soaked wooden skewers. Grill, covered, over medium heat for 6 minutes. Turn and baste with the reserved marinade. Cook 6 minutes longer or until chicken juices run clear. **Yield:** 6 servings.

Nutritional Analysis: One serving equals 219 calories, 6 g fat (1 g saturated fat), 66 mg cholesterol, 278 mg sodium, 12 g carbohydrate, 3 g fiber, 29 g protein. **Diabetic Exchanges:** 3 lean meat, 2 vegetable.

Basic Crepes

This is one of my favorite recipes. It's best to make the batter at least 30 minutes ahead so the flavor can absorb all the moisture before you start cooking the crepes. —Janaan Cunningham, Food Editor

4 eggs
1-1/2 cups milk
1-1/2 teaspoons sugar
1/8 teaspoon salt
1 cup all-purpose flour
Butter *or* stick margarine, softened

In a bowl, whisk eggs, milk, sugar and salt. Add flour; beat until smooth. Let stand for 30 minutes. Melt 1 teaspoon butter in an 8-in. skillet. Pour 2 tablespoons batter into center of skillet; lift and turn pan to cover bottom. Cook until lightly browned; turn and brown the other side. Remove to a wire rack; cover with paper towel. Repeat with remaining batter, adding butter to skillet as needed. When cool, stack crepes with waxed paper or paper towels in between. **Yield:** 16 crepes.

Apple Pecan Crepes

(Pictured below)

This is a very easy, quick and delicious brunch item. Prepare a big batch—people tend to go back for seconds or thirds. —Carolyn Hayes, Marion, Illinois

1 can (21 ounces) apple pie filling
1/2 cup coarsely chopped pecans
1/2 teaspoon ground cinnamon
12 prepared crepes (7 inches *each*)*
1 egg, beaten
3/4 cup half-and-half cream
2 tablespoons sugar
1/2 teaspoon vanilla extract
1/4 teaspoon almond extract

In a bowl, combine the pie filling, pecans and cinnamon; mix well. Spread 2 rounded tablespoonfuls down the center of each crepe; roll up tightly. Place in a greased 13-in. x 9-in. x 2-in. baking dish. Bake, uncovered, at 375° for 10-14 minutes or until heated through. Meanwhile, in a microwave-safe bowl, combine the egg, cream, sugar and extracts. Cover; microwave at 50% power 5-6 minutes or until thickened, stirring every 2 minutes. Cool. Serve over crepes. **Yield:** 6 servings.

***Editor's Note:** The Basic Crepes recipe to the left, can be used in Apple Pecan Crepes. This recipe was tested in an 850-watt microwave.

Maple Barbecued Ribs

February and March tempt us with the first taste of spring and the start of maple syrup season. What a great flavor for ribs! —Linda Russell, Exeter, Ontario

3 pounds pork spareribs
1 cup maple syrup
1 small onion, chopped
1 tablespoon sesame seeds
1 tablespoon white vinegar
1 tablespoon Worcestershire sauce
1 tablespoon chili sauce
2 garlic cloves, minced
1/2 teaspoon salt
1/2 teaspoon ground ginger
1/4 teaspoon ground mustard
1/8 teaspoon pepper

Place ribs meat side down on a rack in a shallow baking pan. Bake at 350° for 40 minutes. Drain and cool slightly. Meanwhile, combine the remaining ingredients in a saucepan; cook and stir over medium heat until mixture comes to a boil. Cut ribs into serving-size pieces; return to pan, meat side up. Pour sauce over ribs. Bake, uncovered, at 350° for 1 hour or until tender, basting occasionally. **Yield:** 3 servings.

Lemon Cream Chicken

(Pictured on page 56)

My neighbors are wonderful about sharing the bounty of their lemon trees. If you want an entree that's quick, easy and elegant, you can't beat this one. —Mary Anne McWhirter, Pearland, Texas

1/2 cup plus 1 tablespoon all-purpose flour, *divided*
1/2 teaspoon salt
1/2 teaspoon pepper
6 boneless skinless chicken breast halves

1/4 cup butter *or* margarine
1 cup chicken broth
1 cup whipping cream, *divided*
3 tablespoons lemon juice
1/2 pound fresh mushrooms, sliced

In a resealable plastic bag, combine 1/2 cup flour, salt and pepper. Add chicken and shake to coat. In a large skillet, cook chicken in butter for 8-9 minutes on each side or until juices run clear. Remove chicken and keep warm. Add broth to the drippings. Bring to a boil over medium heat; stir to loosen browned bits from pan. Simmer, uncovered, for 10 minutes or until broth is reduced to 1/3 cup.

Stir in 3/4 cup cream, lemon juice and mushrooms. Cook over medium-low heat for 5 minutes. Combine remaining flour and cream until smooth; stir into skillet. Bring to a boil; cook and stir for 2 minutes or until thickened. Return chicken to skillet and heat through. **Yield:** 6 servings.

Brunch Berry Pizza

This beautiful berry-topped pizza tastes just as good as it looks! —Maria Schuster, Wolf Point, Montana

1 cup all-purpose flour
1/4 cup confectioners' sugar
1/2 cup cold butter *or* margarine
1/2 cup chopped pecans
1 package (8 ounces) cream cheese, softened
1 egg
1/3 cup sugar
TOPPING:
1-3/4 cups frozen mixed berries, thawed
1/2 cup sugar
2 tablespoons cornstarch
1/4 cup water
2-1/2 cups fresh strawberries, sliced
2 cups fresh blackberries
2 cups fresh raspberries
1 cup fresh blueberries

In a bowl, combine flour and confectioners' sugar. Cut in butter until crumbly. Stir in pecans. Press into an ungreased 12-in. pizza pan. Bake at 350° for 12-14 minutes or until crust is set and edges are lightly browned. Meanwhile, in a mixing bowl, beat cream cheese, egg and sugar until smooth. Spread over crust. Bake 8-10 minutes longer or until set. Cool to room temperature.

For topping, process mixed berries and sugar in a blender or food processor until blended. In a saucepan, combine cornstarch and water until smooth. Add berry mixture. Bring to a boil; cook and stir 2 minutes or until thickened. Set saucepan in ice water for 15 minutes, stirring several times. Spread berry mixture over cream cheese layer. Arrange fresh fruit on top. Refrigerate for at least 2 hours before slicing. **Yield:** 10-12 servings.

Meal on a Stick

(Pictured on page 56)

My husband and I love to grill these kabobs. The curry adds flavor. —Sundra Hauck, Bogalusa, Louisiana

2 eggs, lightly beaten
2 teaspoons Worcestershire sauce
1-1/4 cups seasoned bread crumbs
1 teaspoon curry powder
1-1/2 pounds ground beef
24 stuffed olives
8 plum tomatoes, halved
2 medium green peppers, cut into quarters
8 small red potatoes, partially cooked
8 large fresh mushrooms
1/4 cup barbecue sauce

In a bowl, combine the first four ingredients. Crumble beef over mixture; mix. Divide into 24 portions; shape each around an olive. Alternately thread meatballs and vegetables onto metal or soaked wooden skewers. Grill kabobs, covered, over medium-hot heat for 5 minutes. Turn; brush with barbecue sauce. Cook 5 minutes more or until meatballs are no longer pink, basting once. **Yield:** 6-8 servings.

Baked Parmesan Perch

Let compliments be your catch of the day when you serve this crispy fish. —Carol Gaus, Itasca, Illinois

✓ Uses less fat, sugar or salt. Includes Nutritional Analysis and Diabetic Exchanges.

2 tablespoons dry bread crumbs
1 tablespoon grated Parmesan cheese
1 tablespoon paprika
1 teaspoon dried basil
1 pound perch *or* fish fillets of your choice
1 tablespoon butter *or* margarine, melted

In a shallow bowl, combine the bread crumbs, Parmesan cheese, paprika and basil. Brush fish fillets with butter, then dip into the crumb mixture. Place in a greased baking pan. Bake, uncovered, at 500° for 10 minutes or until fish flakes easily with a fork. **Yield:** 4 servings.

Nutritional Analysis: One serving (prepared with stick margarine) equals 158 calories, 6 g fat (2 g saturated fat), 52 mg cholesterol, 176 mg sodium, 4 g carbohydrate, 1 g fiber, 23 g protein. **Diabetic Exchanges:** 2-1/2 lean meat, 1/2 fat.

Breads, Rolls & Muffins

Fresh-from-the-oven breads, rolls and muffins are a welcome accompaniment to any meal or a tasty snack on their own.

HOME-BAKED GOODNESS. Clockwise from upper left: Caramel-Pecan Sticky Buns (p. 98), Sesame Wheat Bread (p. 103), Banana Wheat Muffins (p. 92), Cherry Pecan Coffee Cake (p. 95), Sunflower Oat Bread (p. 103) and Lemon Nut Crescents (p. 101).

Cranberry Nut Bagels

After 3 years of trial and error, I came up with a simple and delicious bagel recipe for the bread machine.
—John Russell, Greentown, Indiana

1 cup plus 2 tablespoons water (70° to 80°)
2 tablespoons sugar
1 teaspoon salt
1-1/4 teaspoons ground cinnamon
1/4 cup quick-cooking oats
3 cups bread flour
2-1/2 teaspoons active dry yeast
3/4 cup dried cranberries
1/4 cup chopped pecans
TOPPING:
2 tablespoons brown sugar
1 teaspoon ground cinnamon

In bread machine pan, place the first seven ingredients in order suggested by manufacturer. Select dough setting (check dough after 5 minutes of mixing; add 1 to 2 tablespoons of water or flour if needed). Just before the final kneading (your machine may audibly signal this), add the cranberries and pecans. When cycle is completed, turn dough onto a lightly floured surface; cover and let rest for 5 minutes. Divide into eight balls. Push thumb through the center of each ball to form a 1-in. hole. Place on a lightly floured surface. Cover and let rest for 5 minutes.

In a large saucepan, bring 2 qts. water to a boil. Drop bagels, one at a time, into boiling water. Cook for 45 seconds; turn and cook 45 seconds longer. Remove with a slotted spoon; drain well on paper towels. Combine brown sugar and cinnamon; sprinkle over bagels. Place 2 in. apart on greased baking sheets. Bake at 375° for 20-25 minutes or until golden brown. **Yield:** 8 bagels.

Oatmeal Raisin Muffins

Whenever I share these spiced muffins, they're snapped up in a hurry. —Clyde Blount, Pearl, Mississippi

1 cup quick-cooking oats
1-1/4 cups buttermilk
1 egg, lightly beaten
1/2 cup packed brown sugar
1/3 cup vegetable oil
1-3/4 cups all-purpose flour
1 teaspoon baking powder
1 teaspoon baking soda
1/2 teaspoon salt
1/4 teaspoon ground cinnamon
1/4 teaspoon ground cloves
1/2 cup raisins

In a small bowl, combine oats and buttermilk. In a small mixing bowl, combine the egg, brown sugar and oil; stir in oat mixture. Combine the dry ingredients; stir into batter just until moistened. Fold in raisins. Fill greased or paper-lined muffin cups three-fourths full. Bake at 400° for 15-18 minutes or until a toothpick comes out clean. Cool for 5 minutes before removing from pan to a wire rack. **Yield:** 1 dozen.

Banana Wheat Muffins

(Pictured on page 90)

I use locally ground flour when making these moist and mouth-watering muffins. They have a slight crunch that's delightful.
—Donna Brockett
Kingfisher, Oklahoma

1-1/3 cups all-purpose flour
2/3 cup whole wheat flour
1 teaspoon baking soda
1/2 teaspoon salt
1 cup mayonnaise*
3/4 cup sugar
1 cup mashed ripe bananas (2 to 3 medium)

In a bowl, combine the flours, baking soda and salt. In another bowl, combine mayonnaise, sugar and bananas; stir into dry ingredients just until moistened. Fill greased or paper-lined muffin cups two-thirds full. Bake at 350° for 20-25 minutes or until a toothpick comes out clean. Cool for 5 minutes before removing from pans to wire racks. Serve warm. **Yield:** 1 dozen.

***Editor's Note:** Reduced-fat or fat-free mayonnaise may not be substituted for regular mayonnaise.

Braided Egg Bread

My grandmother inspired me to try cooking. Homemade bread is my passion. I've always loved it, and in order to satisfy my appetite for it, I decided I'd have to learn to make my own bread. Nothing tastes better than a warm slice topped with butter.
—Al Latimer, Bentonville, Arkansas

8 to 9 cups bread flour
2 packages (1/4 ounce *each*) quick-rise yeast
2 tablespoons sugar
1 tablespoon salt
2-1/2 cups water
1/4 cup butter *or* margarine
1/4 cup honey

4 eggs
Cornmeal
2 teaspoons cold water
Sesame *or* poppy seeds

In a mixing bowl, combine 5 cups flour, yeast, sugar and salt. Heat water, butter and honey to 120°-130°. Add to dry ingredients; beat on medium speed. Separate one egg; refrigerate the egg white. Add egg yolk and remaining eggs to yeast mixture; beat until smooth. Add enough remaining flour to form a stiff dough. Turn onto a floured surface; knead until smooth and elastic, about 6-8 minutes. Place in a greased bowl, turning once to grease top. Cover and let rise in a warm place until doubled, about 1 hour.

Punch dough down and divide in half. Divide each portion into thirds; shape each into a rope about 18 in. long. Sprinkle two greased baking sheets with cornmeal; place three ropes on each baking sheet and braid. Pinch ends firmly and tuck under. Cover and let rise until nearly doubled, about 45 minutes.

Beat cold water and reserved egg white; brush over dough. Sprinkle with sesame or poppy seeds. Bake at 375° for 18-20 minutes or until lightly browned. Remove from pans to wire racks. **Yield:** 2 loaves.

Golden Bread

My son, Kendall, likes working right by my side in the kitchen. For this recipe, he helps me measure and add all the ingredients. Then we let the machine do the work. Kendall likes watching it knead the dough. He's happy to share the tasty loaf with his older sister.
—Sheri Hatten, Devils Lake, North Dakota

1/2 cup water (70° to 80°)
1 cup small-curd cottage cheese
2 tablespoons butter *or* margarine, softened
1 egg
1 tablespoon sugar
1/2 teaspoon salt
3 cups bread flour
1 teaspoon active dry yeast

In bread machine pan, place all ingredients in order suggested by manufacturer. Select basic bread setting. Choose crust color and loaf size if available. Bake according to bread machine directions (check dough after 5 minutes of mixing; add 1 to 2 tablespoons of water or flour if needed). **Yield:** 1 loaf (about 1-1/2 pounds).

Editor's Note: If your bread machine has a time-delay feature, we recommend you do not use it for this recipe.

Cinnamon Swirl Bread

(Pictured below)

My aunt gave me the recipe for these pretty, rich-tasting loaves many years ago. I use my bread machine for the first step in the recipe. *—Peggy Burdick*
Burlington, Michigan

1 cup warm milk (70° to 80°)
1/4 cup water (70° to 80°)
2 eggs
1/4 cup butter *or* margarine, softened
1 teaspoon salt
1/4 cup sugar
5 cups bread flour
2-1/4 teaspoons active dry yeast
FILLING:
2 tablespoons butter *or* margarine, melted
1/3 cup sugar
1 tablespoon ground cinnamon
GLAZE:
1 cup confectioners' sugar
4 to 5 teaspoons milk
1/2 teaspoon vanilla extract

In bread machine pan, place the first eight ingredients in order suggested by manufacturer. Select dough setting (check dough after 5 minutes of mixing; add 1 to 2 tablespoons water or flour if needed). When cycle is completed, turn dough onto a lightly floured surface; divide in half. Roll each portion into a 10-in. x 8-in. rectangle. Brush with butter. Combine sugar and cinnamon; sprinkle over dough. Roll up tightly jelly-roll style, starting with a short side. Pinch seams and ends to seal. Place seam side down in two greased 9-in. x 5-in. x 3-in. loaf pans. Cover and let rise in a warm place until doubled, about 1 hour.

Bake at 350° for 25 minutes. Cover with foil; bake 5-10 minutes longer or until golden brown. Remove from pans to wire racks to cool completely. Combine glaze ingredients; spoon over loaves. **Yield:** 2 loaves.

Cinnamon Focaccia

(Pictured above)

A cinnamon-sugar and nut topping and a drizzle of glaze add sweetness to this lovely bread.
—Page Alexander, Baldwin City, Kansas

6 to 6-1/2 cups all-purpose flour
2 packages (1/4 ounce *each*) active dry yeast
1 teaspoon salt
2 cups warm water (120° to 130°)
1/4 cup vegetable oil
1/4 cup butter *or* margarine, melted
1/3 cup sugar
1 teaspoon ground cinnamon
1/2 to 1 cup chopped nuts
1-1/2 cups confectioners' sugar
3 to 4 tablespoons half-and-half cream

In a mixing bowl, combine 2 cups flour, yeast and salt. Add water and oil; beat until smooth. Stir in enough remaining flour to form a soft dough. Turn onto a floured surface; knead until smooth and elastic, about 6-8 minutes. Place in a greased bowl, turning once to grease top. Cover and let rise in a warm place until doubled, about 1 hour.

Punch dough down. Turn onto a lightly floured surface; divide in half. Pat each portion flat. Cover and let stand for 10 minutes. Press dough into two greased 12-in. pizza pans. Prick top of dough with a fork. Brush with butter. Combine sugar and cinnamon; sprinkle over dough. Top with nuts. Let stand 10-15 minutes. Bake at 350° for 25-30 minutes or until lightly browned. Remove from pans to wire racks. Combine confectioners' sugar and enough cream to achieve a glaze consistency; drizzle over warm bread. **Yield:** 2 round loaves.

Strawberry Muffins

I was pleased to find these low-fat treats are moist and tasty. *—Amanda Denton, Barre, Vermont*

✓ Uses less fat, sugar or salt. Includes Nutritional Analysis and Diabetic Exchanges.

1-3/4 cups all-purpose flour
3/4 cup sugar
1 teaspoon baking soda
1/4 teaspoon ground nutmeg
2 eggs, lightly beaten
1/2 cup fat-free plain yogurt
1/4 cup butter *or* stick margarine, melted and cooled
1 teaspoon vanilla extract
1-1/4 cups coarsely chopped fresh *or* frozen unsweetened strawberries

In a bowl, combine the first four ingredients. In another bowl, combine the eggs, yogurt, butter and vanilla; mix well. Stir into the dry ingredients just until moistened. Fold in strawberries. Fill muffin cups coated with nonstick cooking spray or lined with paper liners two-thirds full. Bake at 375° for 15-18 minutes or until a toothpick comes out clean. Cool for 5 minutes before removing from pan to a wire rack. Serve warm. **Yield:** 1 dozen.

Nutritional Analysis: One muffin equals 173 calories, 5 g fat (3 g saturated fat), 46 mg cholesterol, 163 mg sodium, 29 g carbohydrate, 1 g fiber, 4 g protein. **Diabetic Exchanges:** 1 starch, 1 fruit, 1 fat.

Favorite Buttermilk Bread

Honey helps this bread's crust bake up golden brown, and wheat germ adds extra nutrition.
—Michele Surgeon, Medford, Oregon

✓ Uses less fat, sugar or salt. Includes Nutritional Analysis and Diabetic Exchanges.

6 teaspoons active dry yeast
3/4 cup warm water (110° to 115°)
3 cups warm 1% buttermilk* (110° to 115°)
3/4 cup butter *or* stick margarine, melted and cooled
1/4 cup honey
3 teaspoons salt
1/2 teaspoon baking soda
3/4 cup toasted wheat germ
9 to 10 cups all-purpose flour

In a large mixing bowl, dissolve yeast in warm water. Add the buttermilk, butter, honey, salt, baking soda, wheat germ and 4 cups flour; mix well. Gradually stir in enough remaining flour to form a soft dough. Turn onto a heavily floured surface; knead until smooth and elastic, about 6-8 minutes. Place in a greased bowl, turning once to grease top. Cover and let rise in a warm place until doubled, about 1 hour.

Punch dough down. Turn onto a floured surface;

divide into thirds. Divide each portion into thirds; shape each into a 12-in. rope. Braid three ropes; pinch ends to seal and tuck under. Place in a greased 9-in. x 5-in. x 3-in. loaf pan. Repeat with remaining dough. Cover and let rise in a warm place until doubled, about 45 minutes. Bake at 350° for 40-45 minutes or until golden brown. Remove from pans to wire racks. **Yield:** 3 loaves (12 slices each).

Nutritional Analysis: One slice equals 183 calories, 4 g fat (3 g saturated fat), 11 mg cholesterol, 275 mg sodium, 31 g carbohydrate, 1 g fiber, 5 g protein. **Diabetic Exchanges:** 2 starch, 1/2 fat.

***Editor's Note:** Warmed buttermilk will appear curdled.

Cherry Pecan Coffee Cake

(Pictured on page 90)

This impressive heart-shaped coffee cake is filled with fruits and nuts. —Linda Pauls, Buhler, Kansas

4-3/4 to 5-1/4 cups all-purpose flour
1/2 cup sugar
1-1/2 teaspoons salt
2 packages (1/4 ounce *each*) active dry yeast
1 cup (8 ounces) sour cream
1/3 cup water
5 tablespoons butter *or* margarine, *divided*
2 eggs
FILLING:
1 cup finely chopped dried apricots
1 cup chopped maraschino cherries
3/4 cup chopped pecans
1/4 cup sugar
Confectioners' sugar icing

In a mixing bowl, combine 2 cups flour, sugar, salt and yeast. In a saucepan, heat sour cream, water and 4 tablespoons butter to 120°-130°; add to dry ingredients. Beat on medium for 2 minutes. Add eggs and 1/2 cup flour; beat 2 minutes. Stir in enough remaining flour to form a soft dough. Turn onto a floured surface; knead until smooth and elastic, about 6-8 minutes. Place in a greased bowl, turning once to grease top. Cover and let rise in a warm place until doubled, about 1-1/4 hours.

Punch dough down; divide in half. Roll each portion into a 24-in. x 7-in. rectangle. Melt remaining butter; brush over dough. Combine filling ingredients; sprinkle over dough. Roll up jelly-roll style, starting with a long side; pinch seam to seal. Carefully shape each roll into a 26-in. rope. Place each rope seam side down on a greased baking sheet. Pinch ends together to form a ring. Shape into a heart if desired. With scissors, cut from outside edge two-thirds of the way toward center of heart or ring at 1-in. intervals. Separate pieces; slightly twist to show filling.

Cover and let rise in a warm place until doubled, about 45 minutes. Bake at 350° for 25-27 minutes or until lightly browned. Remove from pans to wire racks to cool. Drizzle with icing. **Yield:** 2 coffee cakes (12 servings each).

Herbed Bubble Bread

It takes just four ingredients to dress up a purchased package of frozen rolls to make this buttery, crusty loaf. —Anita Whorton, Powder Springs, Georgia

1/4 cup butter *or* margarine, melted
1 teaspoon garlic powder
1 teaspoon dried oregano
1/2 teaspoon dried thyme
1 package (16 ounces) frozen dinner roll dough, thawed

In a small bowl, combine the butter, garlic powder, oregano and thyme. Cut each roll in half; dip into butter mixture. Arrange in a greased 12-cup fluted tube pan. Pour remaining herb mixture over top. Cover and let rise in a warm place for 1 hour or until doubled. Bake at 350° for 15-20 minutes or until golden brown. **Yield:** 12 servings.

Good Ol' Banana Muffins

These golden old-fashioned muffins are a great treat anytime. —Clyde Blount, Pearl, Mississippi

1/2 cup butter *or* margarine, softened
1 cup sugar
2 eggs
3 medium ripe bananas, mashed
2 cups self-rising flour*
1 teaspoon baking soda
1/2 cup chopped pecans

In a mixing bowl, cream butter and sugar. Add eggs, one at a time, beating well after each addition. Beat in bananas. Combine flour and baking soda; add to creamed mixture just until moistened. Stir in pecans. Fill greased or paper-lined muffin cups three-fourths full. Bake at 350° for 20-25 minutes or until a toothpick comes out clean. Cool for 5 minutes before removing from pans to wire racks. **Yield:** 14 muffins.

***Editor's Note:** As a substitute for *each* cup of self-rising flour, place 1-1/2 teaspoons baking powder and 1/2 teaspoon salt in a measuring cup. Add all-purpose flour to measure 1 cup.

Cinnamon Crumb Coffee Cake

This scrumptious coffee cake is served at Sunday brunch in The Wisconsin Room of The American Club, a luxurious resort hotel in Kohler, Wisconsin.

1/3 cup packed almond paste
1/4 cup butter *or* margarine, softened
1 cup plus 5 tablespoons sugar, *divided*
1/3 cup shortening
6 egg yolks
1/2 cup milk
2 cups cake flour
1 teaspoon baking powder
2 egg whites
STREUSEL:
1/4 cup all-purpose flour
1/4 cup sugar
1 tablespoon ground cinnamon
1/4 cup cold butter *or* margarine

In a mixing bowl, cream almond paste, butter and 1 cup plus 2 tablespoons sugar. Add shortening; beat for 2 minutes. Add egg yolks; mix well. Gradually beat in milk. Combine flour and baking powder; gradually add to creamed mixture and mix well. In another mixing bowl, beat egg whites until frothy. Beat in remaining sugar, 1 tablespoon at a time, until stiff peaks form. Fold into batter. Transfer to two greased and floured 8-in. round baking pans.

For streusel, combine the flour, sugar and cinnamon in a bowl. Cut in butter until crumbly; sprinkle over batter. Bake at 350° for 30-35 minutes or until a toothpick inserted near the center comes out clean. Cool for 10 minutes before removing from pans to wire racks. **Yield:** 2 coffee cakes.

Pear Fritters

My husband and I enjoy these fritters with our morning coffee. —Kelly Cox, Fayetteville, North Carolina

2-1/4 cups all-purpose flour
1 package (1/4 ounce) active dry yeast
1 teaspoon ground cinnamon
1/2 teaspoon salt
1/4 teaspoon ground nutmeg
1/2 cup milk
1/4 cup vegetable oil
2 tablespoons honey
2 eggs
1 medium ripe pear, peeled and chopped
Oil for deep-fat frying
Sugar *or* confectioners' sugar

In a mixing bowl, combine the flour, yeast, cinnamon, salt and nutmeg. In a saucepan, heat the milk, oil and honey to 120°-130°. Add to dry ingredients; beat until moistened. Add eggs; beat on medium speed for 3 minutes. Stir in pear. Cover and let rise in a warm place until doubled, about 1 hour. In an electric skillet or deep-fat fryer, heat oil to 375°. Drop batter by tablespoonfuls, a few at a time, into hot oil. Fry until golden brown on both sides. Drain on paper towels. Roll in sugar while warm. Serve warm. **Yield:** about 3 dozen.

Sky-High Biscuits

My recipe for high and flaky biscuits never fails to win a ribbon. —Ruth Burrus, Zionsville, Indiana

2 cups all-purpose flour
1 cup whole wheat flour
2 tablespoons sugar
4-1/2 teaspoons baking powder
3/4 teaspoon cream of tartar
1/2 teaspoon salt
3/4 cup cold butter *or* margarine
1 egg
1 cup milk

In a bowl, combine the first six ingredients. Cut in butter until crumbly. Combine egg and milk; stir into crumb mixture just until moistened. Turn onto a floured surface; knead 10-15 times. Roll out to 1-in. thickness; cut with a 2-1/2-in. biscuit cutter. Place on a greased baking sheet. Bake at 450° for 10-15 minutes or until golden brown. **Yield:** 1 dozen.

Bran Yeast Bread

The chewy slices of this bread get a little crunch from the grain. —Corbin Detgen, Buchanan, Michigan

✓ Uses less fat, sugar or salt. Includes Nutritional Analysis and Diabetic Exchanges.

1 package (1/4 ounce) active dry yeast
1/4 cup warm water (110° to 115°)
1/3 cup boiling water
2 tablespoons vegetable oil
1/3 cup plus 1 teaspoon sugar
1 teaspoon salt
1/3 cup cold water
1/3 cup wheat bran
1 cup whole wheat flour
1-3/4 to 2 cups all-purpose flour

In a mixing bowl, dissolve yeast in warm water; set aside. In another bowl, combine boiling water, oil, sugar and salt; stir until sugar is dissolved. Stir in cold water and bran. Stir into yeast mixture. Add whole wheat flour and 1-1/2 cups all-purpose flour. Beat on medium speed for 2-3 minutes. Stir in enough remaining all-purpose flour to form a stiff dough.Turn onto a floured surface; knead until smooth and elastic, about 8 minutes. Place in a greased bowl, turning once to grease top. Cover and let rise in a warm place until doubled, about 1 hour.

Punch the dough down; cover and let rest for 8 minutes. Shape into a loaf. Place in a greased 9-in. x 5-in. x 3-in. loaf pan. Cover and let rise until doubled, about 45 minutes. Bake at 350° for 35-45 minutes or until golden brown. Remove from pan to cool on a wire rack. **Yield:** 1 loaf (16 slices).

Nutritional Analysis: One slice equals 113 calories, 2 g fat (0 saturated fat), 0 cholesterol, 146 mg sodium, 22 g carbohydrate, 2 g fiber, 3 g protein. **Diabetic Exchange:** 1-1/2 starch.

Oatmeal Cinnamon Bread

We grow a couple hundred acres of certified oat seed each year, so I use oats in lots of my recipes.
—Shirley Brockmueller, Freeman, South Dakota

2 packages (1/4 ounce *each*) active dry yeast
1/2 cup warm water (110° to 115°)
1-1/2 cups quick-cooking oats
1-1/2 cups warm milk (110° to 115°)
2/3 cup shortening
1 cup sugar, *divided*
2 eggs, lightly beaten
2 teaspoons salt
5 to 5-1/2 cups all-purpose flour
2 tablespoons butter *or* margarine, melted
2 teaspoons ground cinnamon

In a mixing bowl, dissolve yeast in warm water. Add oats, milk, shortening, 1/2 cup sugar, eggs, salt and 2 cups flour; beat until smooth. Add enough remaining flour to form a soft dough. Turn onto a floured surface; knead until smooth and elastic, about 6-8 minutes. Place in a greased bowl, turning once to grease top. Cover and let rise in a warm place until doubled, about 1 hour. Punch dough down; cover and let rest for 10 minutes. Divide in half; roll each portion into a 16-in. x 8-in. rectangle. Brush with butter.

Combine cinnamon and remaining sugar; sprinkle over dough to within 1/2 in. of edges. Roll up jelly-roll style, starting with a short side; pinch seams to seal. Place loaves seam side down in two greased 9-in. x 5-in. x 3-in. loaf pans. Cover and let rise in a warm place until doubled, about 25 minutes. Bake at 375° for 40-45 minutes or until golden brown. Cover loosely with foil if bread browns too quickly. Remove from pans to cool on wire racks. **Yield:** 2 loaves.

Honey Cloverleaf Rolls

(Pictured below)

These lovely rolls get their great taste from honey and thyme. The combination of sweet and savory is something special.—Eleanor Davis, Pittsburgh, Pennsylvania

1 tablespoon active dry yeast
1/4 cup warm water (110° to 115°)
3 tablespoons honey
1/2 cup mashed potatoes (prepared with milk)
1/2 cup buttermilk
1/4 cup butter *or* margarine, melted
3 tablespoons minced fresh thyme *or* 1 tablespoon dried thyme
1 teaspoon salt
1 egg
1 cup whole wheat flour
2 to 2-1/2 cups all-purpose flour

GLAZE:

1 egg
1 teaspoon milk

In a mixing bowl, dissolve yeast in water. Stir in honey; let stand for 5 minutes. Add the potatoes, buttermilk, butter, thyme and salt. Add the egg, whole wheat flour and 1 cup of all-purpose flour; beat on medium speed to form a soft dough. Stir in enough remaining all-purpose flour to from a stiff dough. Turn onto a floured surface; knead until smooth and elastic, about 6-8 minutes. Place in a greased bowl, turning once to grease top. Cover and let rise in a warm place until doubled, about 1 hour.

Punch dough down. Turn onto a lightly floured surface. Divide into three portions; divide each into 18 pieces. Shape each into a ball; place three balls each in greased muffin cups. Cover and let rise until doubled, about 25 minutes. For the glaze, combine egg and milk; brush over rolls. Bake at 400° for 15-18 minutes or until golden brown. Remove from pans to wire racks to cool. **Yield:** 1-1/2 dozen.

Caramel-Pecan Sticky Buns

(Pictured above and on page 90)

My mother used to make these delicious cinnamon rolls when I was a child. Later, she taught my sister and me how to make them. —Judy Powell, Star, Idaho

1 package (1/4 ounce) active dry yeast
3/4 cup warm water (110° to 115°)
3/4 cup warm milk (110° to 115°)
1/4 cup sugar
3 tablespoons vegetable oil
2 teaspoons salt
3-3/4 to 4-1/4 cups all-purpose flour

FILLING:

1/4 cup butter *or* margarine, softened
1/4 cup sugar
3 teaspoons ground cinnamon
3/4 cup packed brown sugar
1/2 cup whipping cream
1 cup coarsely chopped pecans

In a mixing bowl, dissolve yeast in warm water. Add the milk, sugar, oil, salt and 1-1/4 cups flour. Beat on medium speed for 2-3 minutes or until smooth. Stir in enough remaining flour to form a soft dough. Turn onto a floured surface; knead until smooth and elastic, about 6-8 minutes. Place in a greased bowl, turning once to grease top. Cover and let rise in a warm place until doubled, about 1 hour. Punch dough down. Turn onto a lightly floured surface. Roll into an 18-in. x 12-in. rectangle. Spread butter to within 1/2 in. of edges. Combine sugar and cinnamon; sprinkle over butter.

Roll up jelly-roll style, starting with a long side; pinch seam to seal. Cut into 12 slices. Combine brown sugar and cream; pour into a greased 13-in. x 9-in. x 2-in. baking pan. Sprinkle with pecans. Place rolls cut side down over pecans. Cover and let rise until doubled, about 1 hour. Bake at 350° for 30-35 minutes or until well browned. Cool for 1 minute before inverting onto a serving platter. **Yield:** 1 dozen.

Cranberry Nut Muffins

This is one of my favorite recipes to make with my granddaughter. —Claire Olson, Saginaw, Michigan

2 cups all-purpose flour
1 cup sugar
3 teaspoons baking powder
3/4 teaspoon salt
1/2 cup orange juice
1/2 cup milk
1/3 cup butter *or* margarine, melted
1 egg, beaten
1-1/2 cups fresh *or* frozen cranberries, halved
1/2 cup chopped pecans
2 tablespoons grated orange peel

In a mixing bowl, combine the flour, sugar, baking powder and salt. In another bowl, combine the orange juice, milk, butter and egg; stir into dry ingredients just until moistened. Fold in cranberries, pecans and orange peel. Fill greased or paper-lined muffin cups three-fourths full. Bake at 400° for 18-20 minutes or until a toothpick comes out clean. Cool for 5 minutes before removing from pans to wire racks. **Yield:** about 1 dozen.

Low-Fat Pumpkin Bread

I modified a recipe to come up with this low-fat yet moist and tasty pumpkin bread. I make it for the holidays and to give as hostess gifts. —Rita Horton Lincoln, Illinois

✓ Uses less fat, sugar or salt. Includes Nutritional Analysis and Diabetic Exchanges.

2 cups sugar
1 can (15 ounces) solid-pack pumpkin
1 cup unsweetened applesauce
1/2 cup egg substitute
3-1/3 cups all-purpose flour
2 teaspoons ground cinnamon
2 teaspoons baking soda
1 teaspoon baking powder
1/2 teaspoon salt
1/2 teaspoon ground nutmeg *or* allspice
1 cup chopped nuts *or* raisins, optional

In a mixing bowl, combine the sugar, pumpkin, applesauce and egg substitute; mix well. Combine the flour, cinnamon, baking soda, baking powder, salt and nutmeg; gradually add to pumpkin mixture and mix well. Stir in nuts or raisins if desired. Pour into two 8-in. x 4-in. x 2-in. loaf pans coated with nonstick cooking spray. Bake at 350° for 50-60 minutes or until a toothpick inserted near the center comes out clean. Cool for 10 minutes before removing from pans to wire racks. **Yield:** 2 loaves (14 slices per loaf).

Nutritional Analysis: One slice (calculated without nuts or raisins) equals 122 calories, trace fat (trace saturated fat), 0 cholesterol, 149 mg sodium, 28 g carbohydrate, 1 g fiber, 2 g protein. **Diabetic Exchange:** 1-1/2 starch.

Stuffing Bread

I decided to add traditional seasonings into bread, so I wouldn't have to start with plain bread cubes when making stuffing. —Marion Lowery, Medford, Oregon

3-1/2 to 4 cups all-purpose flour
2 tablespoons active dry yeast
2 tablespoons sugar
1 tablespoon rubbed sage
2 teaspoons poultry seasoning
1 teaspoon salt
1 teaspoon dried basil
1 teaspoon dried thyme
1/2 teaspoon ground mustard
1/2 teaspoon dried rosemary, crushed
1/2 teaspoon pepper
1/2 teaspoon paprika
1-1/2 cups warm water (120° to 130°)
2 tablespoons vegetable oil
1 egg

STUFFING:
3 eggs, lightly beaten*
1/4 cup butter *or* margarine, melted
3 to 4 cups chicken broth *or* water

In a mixing bowl, combine 2 cups flour, yeast, sugar and seasonings. Add water and oil; beat just until moistened. Add egg and beat until smooth. Stir in enough remaining flour to form a soft dough. Turn onto a floured surface; knead until smooth and elastic, about 6-8 minutes. Place in a greased bowl, turning once to grease top. Cover and let rise in a warm place until doubled, about 1 hour. Punch dough down. Shape into a large round loaf. Place on a greased baking sheet. Cover and let rise until doubled, about 45 minutes. Bake at 375° for 25-35 minutes or until golden brown. Remove to wire rack to cool.

To make stuffing, cut cooled bread into 1-in. slices, then into cubes. Let stand 24 hours to dry. In a large bowl, combine bread cubes, eggs, butter and enough broth to achieve desired moistness. Stir to blend. Transfer to a greased 2-qt. baking dish. Cover and bake at 350° for 60 minutes. Uncover; bake 10 minutes longer or until lightly browned. **Yield:** 8 servings.

***Editor's Note:** Stuffing may be used to stuff a turkey, chicken or pork roast by substituting 3/4 cup egg substitute for eggs.

Buttery Corn Bread

(Pictured below and on front cover)

I got this recipe from a longtime friend several years ago. I love to serve this melt-in-your-mouth corn bread hot from the oven with butter and syrup. —Nicole Callen, Auburn, California

2/3 cup butter *or* margarine, softened
1 cup sugar
3 eggs
1-2/3 cups milk
2-1/3 cups all-purpose flour
1 cup cornmeal
4-1/2 teaspoons baking powder
1 teaspoon salt

In a mixing bowl, cream butter and sugar. Combine the eggs and milk. Combine flour, cornmeal, baking powder and salt; add to creamed mixture alternately with egg mixture. Pour into a greased 13-in. x 9-in. x 2-in. baking pan. Bake at 400° for 22-27 minutes or until a toothpick inserted near the center comes out clean. Cut into squares; serve warm. **Yield:** 12-15 servings.

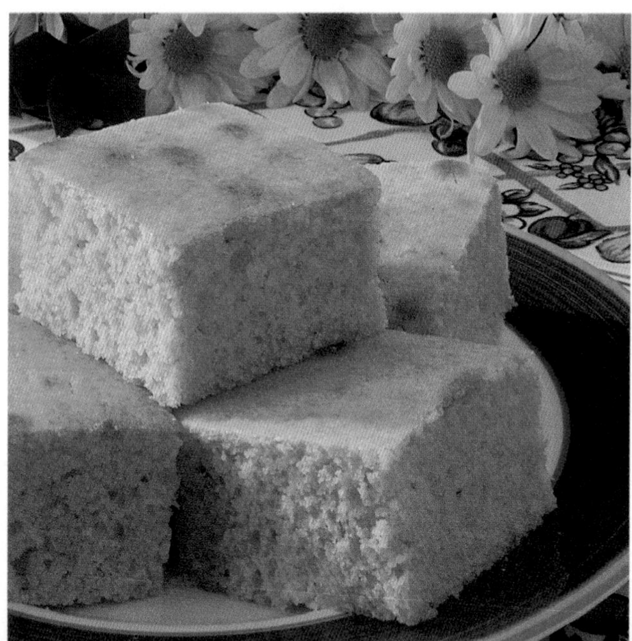

Moist Bran Muffins

My husband requests these hearty bran muffins for breakfast, but they're also a super snack.
—Elizabeth Probelski, Port Washington, Wisconsin

✓ Uses less fat, sugar or salt. Includes Nutritional Analysis and Diabetic Exchanges.

2 cups All-Bran
1 cup plain fat-free yogurt
2/3 cup unsweetened applesauce
1/2 cup fat-free milk
1/2 cup egg substitute
1/3 cup packed brown sugar
2 tablespoons molasses
1 tablespoon canola oil
1 teaspoon vanilla extract
1-1/2 cups all-purpose flour
1 teaspoon baking powder
1 teaspoon baking soda
1 teaspoon ground cinnamon
1/4 teaspoon salt

In a bowl, combine the bran, yogurt, applesauce and milk; let stand for 5 minutes. Add egg substitute, brown sugar, molasses, oil and vanilla; mix well. In another bowl, combine the dry ingredients. Stir in bran mixture just until moistened. Fill muffin cups coated with nonstick cooking spray two-thirds full. Bake at 400° for 15-20 minutes or until a toothpick comes out clean. Cool for 5 minutes before removing from pans to wire racks. **Yield:** about 1-1/2 dozen.

Nutritional Analysis: One muffin equals 105 calories, 1 g fat (trace saturated fat), trace cholesterol, 158 mg sodium, 21 g carbohydrate, 3 g fiber, 4 g protein. **Diabetic Exchange:** 1-1/2 starch.

Walnut Banana Bread

Between Thanksgiving and Christmas I bake 200 loaves of bread. —Douglas Jenkins, Ottawa, Kansas

1/2 cup shortening
1 cup sugar
2 eggs
1 cup mashed ripe bananas (2 to 3 medium)
1 tablespoon milk
2 cups all-purpose flour
1 teaspoon baking soda
1/4 teaspoon salt
1/2 cup chopped walnuts

In a mixing bowl, cream shortening and sugar. Add eggs, one at a time, beating well after each addition. Beat in bananas and milk. Combine the flour, baking soda and salt; gradually add to creamed mixture and mix well. Stir in nuts. Pour into a greased 9-in. x 5-in. x 3-in. loaf pan. Bake at 325° for 65-70 minutes or until a toothpick comes out clean. Cool for 10 minutes before removing from pan to a wire rack. **Yield:** 1 loaf.

Mini Corn Muffins

When my great-grandson was a teenager, he and his friends could hardly wait for these muffins to come out of the oven. —Ruby Williams, Bogalusa, Louisiana

✓ Uses less fat, sugar or salt. Includes Nutritional Analysis and Diabetic Exchanges.

1/2 cup all-purpose flour
1/2 cup cornmeal
1 tablespoon sugar
2 teaspoons baking powder
1/4 teaspoon salt
1/4 cup egg substitute
1/2 cup fat-free evaporated milk
2 tablespoons canola oil

In a bowl, combine the flour, cornmeal, sugar, baking powder and salt. Add egg substitute, milk and oil; stir just until moistened. Fill miniature muffin cups coated with nonstick cooking spray three-fourths full. Bake at 400° for 10-12 minutes or until a toothpick comes out clean. Cool for 5 minutes before removing from pans to wire racks. **Yield:** 16 muffins.

Nutritional Analysis: One muffin equals 58 calories, 2 g fat (0 saturated fat), 0 cholesterol, 82 mg sodium, 8 g carbohydrate, 0 fiber, 2 g protein. **Diabetic Exchange:** 1/2 starch.

Brown Sugar Muffins

Most of what I bake, I give away as a thank-you for a favor of kindness. These muffins are tasty at breakfast or as a quick snack. —Corbin Detgen, Buchanan, Michigan

1/3 cup butter *or* margarine, softened
1/2 cup packed brown sugar
2 eggs
1 cup Wheaties
1/2 cup milk
1 teaspoon vanilla extract
1-1/4 cups all-purpose flour
1-1/2 teaspoons baking powder
1/2 teaspoon salt

In a mixing bowl, cream butter and brown sugar. Add eggs, one at a time, beating well after each addition. Stir in cereal. Combine milk and vanilla. Combine flour, baking powder and salt; add to creamed mixture alternately with milk mixture, beating just until moistened. Fill paper-lined muffin cups two-thirds full. Bake at 400° for 13-15 minutes or until a toothpick comes out clean. Cool for 5 minutes before removing from pan to a wire rack. **Yield:** about 1 dozen.

Cheddar Sausage Muffins

Folks say breakfast is my specialty, and these hearty muffins fit right in with a good country breakfast.
—Clyde Blount, Pearl, Mississippi

- **2 cups all-purpose flour**
- **2 tablespoons sugar**
- **3 teaspoons baking powder**
- **1/2 teaspoon salt**
- **1 egg**
- **1 cup milk**
- **1/4 cup butter *or* margarine, melted**
- **1/2 pound bulk pork sausage, cooked and drained**
- **1/2 cup shredded cheddar cheese**

In a bowl, combine the dry ingredients. Combine egg, milk and butter; stir into dry ingredients just until moistened. Fold in sausage and cheese. Fill greased or paper-lined muffin cups two-thirds full. Bake at 375° for 18-22 minutes or until a toothpick comes out clean. Cool for 5 minutes before removing from pans. Serve warm. Refrigerate leftovers. **Yield:** 1 dozen.

Lemon Nut Crescents

(Pictured on page 90)

For an evening snack or even for breakfast, these nutty pastries are terrific.
—Carolyn Kyzer Alexander, Arkansas

- **1 tube (8 ounces) refrigerated crescent rolls**
- **3 tablespoons butter *or* margarine, softened, *divided***
- **1/3 cup chopped nuts**
- **1 tablespoon grated lemon peel**
- **1/4 cup sugar**
- **1/4 cup sour cream**
- **1 tablespoon lemonade concentrate**

Unroll crescent roll dough and separate into eight triangles. Spread with 1 tablespoon butter. Combine nuts and lemon peel; sprinkle over dough. Roll into crescents. Place on an ungreased baking sheet. Bake at 375° for 10-12 minutes or until golden brown. Meanwhile, combine the sugar, sour cream, lemonade concentrate and remaining butter in a saucepan. Bring to a boil, stirring occasionally. Brush over warm rolls. **Yield:** 8 rolls.

Sugared Rhubarb Muffins

(Pictured below)

These lightly sweet muffins make a memorable breakfast treat and are also great with a soup or salad.
—Corrie Davidson, Rainier, Alberta

✓ Uses less fat, sugar or salt. Includes Nutritional Analysis and Diabetic Exchanges.

- **2 cups all-purpose flour**
- **1-1/4 cups sugar, *divided***
- **2 teaspoons baking powder**
- **1/2 teaspoon salt**
- **1 egg**
- **1 cup fat-free milk**
- **1/3 cup canola oil**
- **1 cup chopped fresh *or* frozen rhubarb**

In a bowl, combine flour, 1 cup sugar, baking powder and salt. In another bowl, beat egg, milk and oil. Stir into dry ingredients just until moistened. Fold in rhubarb. Fill paper-lined muffin cups three-fourths full. Sprinkle with remaining sugar. Bake at 350° for 25-30 minutes or until a toothpick comes out clean. Cool 5 minutes before removing from pan to a wire rack. **Yield:** 1 dozen.

Nutritional Analysis: One muffin equals 226 calories, 7 g fat (1 g saturated fat), 18 mg cholesterol, 153 mg sodium, 38 g carbohydrate, 1 g fiber, 4 g protein. **Diabetic Exchanges:** 2 starch, 1-1/2 fat.

Chocolate Chip Coffee Cake

(Pictured above)

When I was a teacher, this recipe was recommended by one of my student's parents. It's delicious!
—Michelle Krzmarzick, Redondo Beach, California

- **1 cup butter *or* margarine, softened**
- **1 package (8 ounces) cream cheese, softened**
- **1-1/2 cups sugar, *divided***
- **2 eggs**
- **1 teaspoon vanilla extract**
- **2 cups all-purpose flour**
- **1 teaspoon baking powder**
- **1/2 teaspoon baking soda**
- **1/4 teaspoon salt**
- **1/4 cup milk**
- **1 cup (6 ounces) semisweet chocolate chips**
- **1/4 cup chopped pecans**
- **1 teaspoon ground cinnamon**

In a mixing bowl, cream the butter, cream cheese and 1-1/4 cups sugar. Beat in eggs and vanilla. Combine the flour, baking powder, baking soda and salt; add to creamed mixture alternately with milk. Stir in chocolate chips. Pour into a greased 9-in. springform pan. Combine the pecans, cinnamon and remaining sugar; sprinkle over batter.

Bake at 350° for 50-55 minutes or until a toothpick inserted near the center comes out clean. Cool for 15 minutes. Carefully run a knife around edge of pan to loosen. Remove sides of pan. Cool completely before cutting. **Yield:** 10-12 servings.

Zu-Key-Ni Dill Muffins

These light muffins are a favorite menu item at the historic Baldpate Inn, where I'm innkeeper and cook.
—Lois Smith, Estes Park, Colorado

- **3-1/2 cups all-purpose flour**
- **1/3 cup sugar**
- **2 tablespoons baking powder**
- **1 tablespoon dill weed**
- **2 teaspoons salt**
- **2 cups grated unpeeled zucchini**
- **2 eggs**
- **1-1/2 cups milk**
- **1/2 cup vegetable oil**
- **1/2 cup grated Parmesan cheese**

In a large bowl, combine first five ingredients. Add zucchini; stir until coated. Combine eggs, milk and oil; stir into zucchini mixture just until moistened. Fill greased or paper-lined muffin cups two-thirds full. Sprinkle with cheese. Bake at 400° for 18-20 minutes or until a toothpick comes out clean. Cool for 5 minutes before removing from pans to wire racks. **Yield:** about 2 dozen.

Whole Wheat Oatmeal Bread

This hearty bread has a pretty golden crust and great flavor. *—Wendy Masters, Grand Valley, Ontario*

- **1-1/4 cups water (70° to 80°)**
- **2 tablespoons honey**
- **2 tablespoons butter *or* margarine, softened**
- **1-1/4 teaspoons salt**
- **2 tablespoons nonfat dry milk powder**
- **1-3/4 cups bread flour**
- **1 cup whole wheat flour**
- **1/3 cup quick-cooking oats**
- **1-1/4 teaspoons active dry yeast**

In bread machine pan, place all ingredients in order suggested by manufacturer. Select basic bread setting. Choose crust color and loaf size if available. Bake according to bread machine directions (check dough after 5 minutes of mixing; add 1 to 2 tablespoons of water or flour if needed). **Yield:** 1 loaf (1-1/2 pounds).

Pecan Pumpkin Loaf

This is a moist, golden bread that's chock-full of nuts. We love it. *—Douglas Jenkins, Ottawa, Kansas*

- **1/3 cup shortening**
- **1-1/3 cups sugar**
- **1 cup canned *or* cooked pumpkin**
- **2 eggs**
- **1/2 teaspoon vanilla extract**
- **1-2/3 cups all-purpose flour**
- **1 teaspoon baking soda**

3/4 teaspoon salt
1/2 teaspoon ground cinnamon
1/2 teaspoon ground nutmeg
1/4 teaspoon baking powder
1/3 cup water
1 cup chopped pecans *or* walnuts

In a mixing bowl, cream shortening and sugar. Add pumpkin; beat well. Add the eggs, one at a time, beating well after each addition. Beat in vanilla. Combine the dry ingredients; add to pumpkin mixture alternately with water. Stir in nuts. Pour into a greased 9-in. x 5-in. x 3-in. loaf pan. Bake at 350° for 55-65 minutes or until a toothpick comes out clean. Cool for 10 minutes before removing from pan to a wire rack. **Yield:** 1 loaf.

Sunflower Oat Bread

(Pictured on page 90)

This golden bread incorporates grains that my sons, Tim and Jon, wouldn't normally touch. —*Kay Krause Sioux Falls, South Dakota*

3 to 4 cups all-purpose flour
1 cup old-fashioned oats, *divided*
1/4 cup sugar
3 tablespoons chopped walnuts
2 tablespoons sunflower kernels
2 teaspoons active dry yeast
3/4 teaspoon salt
3/4 cup water
1/3 cup vegetable oil
1/4 cup buttermilk
1/4 cup honey
2 eggs
3/4 cup whole wheat flour
1 tablespoon cold water

In a mixing bowl, combine 2 cups all-purpose flour, 3/4 cup oats, sugar, walnuts, sunflower kernels, yeast and salt. In a saucepan, heat the water, oil, buttermilk and honey to 120°-130°. Add to dry ingredients; beat until well blended. Beat in 1 egg until smooth. Stir in whole wheat flour and enough remaining all-purpose flour to form a soft dough. Turn onto a floured surface; knead until smooth and elastic, about 6-8 minutes. Place in a greased bowl, turning once to grease top. Cover and let rise in a warm place until doubled, about 1 hour.

Punch dough down; turn onto a lightly floured surface. Divide in half; shape into round loaves. Sprinkle 2 tablespoons oats on a greased baking sheet; place loaves over oats. Cover and let rise until doubled, about 45 minutes. Beat remaining egg and cold water; brush over loaves. Sprinkle with remaining oats. Bake at 350° for 20-25 minutes or until golden brown. Cool on wire racks. **Yield:** 2 loaves.

Sesame Wheat Bread

(Pictured below and on page 90)

Unlike many whole wheat breads that are dense and heavy, this makes a light tender loaf. —*Rene Ralph, Broken Arrow, Oklahoma*

2 packages (1/4 ounce *each*) active dry yeast
1 cup warm water (110° to 115°)
1 cup warm milk (110° to 115°)
1/2 cup honey
3 tablespoons shortening
1 tablespoon salt
1 egg
1/4 cup sesame seeds, toasted
2-1/2 cups whole wheat flour
3 to 3-1/2 cups all-purpose flour
2 tablespoons butter *or* margarine, melted
Additional sesame seeds, optional

In a mixing bowl, dissolve yeast in water. Add milk, honey, shortening, salt, egg, sesame seeds, whole wheat flour and 1-1/2 cups all-purpose flour. Beat until smooth. Stir in enough remaining all-purpose flour to form a stiff dough. Turn onto a floured surface; knead until smooth and elastic, about 6-8 minutes. Place in a greased bowl, turning once to grease top. Cover and let rise in a warm place until doubled, about 1 hour.

Punch dough down. Turn onto a lightly floured surface; divide in half. Shape into loaves. Place in two greased 9-in. x 5-in. x 3-in. loaf pans. Brush with butter; sprinkle with sesame seeds if desired. Cover; let rise until doubled, about 45 minutes. Bake at 350° for 35-40 minutes or until golden. Remove from pans to wire racks to cool. **Yield:** 2 loaves.

Cookies & Bars

These tempting treats are so good, they'll have everyone in your family asking for "just one more".

GREAT CHOICES, BAR NONE. Clockwise from upper left: Cappuccino Cake Brownies (p. 113), Butterscotch Cashew Bars (p. 114), Almond Kiss Cookies (p. 112), Two-Tone Fudge Brownies (p. 112), Vanilla Chip Maple Cookies (p. 109) and Pear Crescent Cookies (p. 114).

Whole Wheat Cookies

These soft, old-fashioned cookies are quite flavorful. With the goodness of wheat germ, they make a wholesome snack. —*Bertie Carter, Tahlequah, Oklahoma*

1/2 cup butter *or* margarine, softened
1/2 cup peanut butter
1/2 cup honey
1 egg
1 teaspoon vanilla extract
1 cup whole wheat flour
1/2 cup nonfat dry milk powder
1/2 cup wheat germ
1 teaspoon baking soda

In a mixing bowl, cream the butter, peanut butter and honey. Beat in egg and vanilla. In another bowl, combine the remaining ingredients; add to the creamed mixture. Cover and refrigerate for 30 minutes. Drop by teaspoonfuls 2 in. apart onto ungreased baking sheets. Flatten with a fork dipped in sugar. Bake at 350° for 8-10 minutes or until golden brown. Let cool on pans for 1 minute before removing to wire racks to cool completely. **Yield:** about 4 dozen.

Christmas Sugar Cookies

Sour cream keeps my favorite sugar cookies extra moist. Dress them up with a drizzle of tinted white chocolate or dip them in white chocolate, then sprinkle with crushed candy canes. —*Lisa MacLean Winslow, Arizona*

1 cup butter (no substitutes), softened
2 cups confectioners' sugar
1 egg
1/4 cup sour cream
1/4 cup honey
2 teaspoons vanilla extract
3-1/2 cups all-purpose flour
1 teaspoon baking soda
1 teaspoon cream of tartar
1/2 teaspoon ground mace
1/8 teaspoon salt
White candy coating
Green paste food coloring *or* color of your choice

In a mixing bowl, cream butter and sugar. Beat in the egg, sour cream, honey and vanilla. Combine the dry ingredients; gradually add to creamed mixture. Cover and chill for 2 hours or until easy to handle. On a lightly floured surface, roll out dough to 1/8-in. thickness. Cut with 3-in. cookie cutters dipped in flour. Place 1 in. apart on ungreased baking sheets. Bake at 325° for 8-10 minutes or until lightly browned. Remove to wire racks to cool. Melt candy coating; stir in food coloring. Drizzle over cookies. **Yield:** about 8 dozen.

Pfeffernuesse

These mild spice cookies, perfect for dunking, come from an old family recipe. —*Betty Hawkshaw Alexandria, Virginia*

1 cup butter (no substitutes), softened
1 cup sugar
2 eggs
1/2 cup light corn syrup
1/2 cup molasses
1/3 cup water
6-2/3 cups all-purpose flour
1/4 cup crushed aniseed
1 teaspoon baking soda
1 teaspoon ground cinnamon
1/2 teaspoon ground nutmeg
1/4 teaspoon ground cloves
1/4 teaspoon ground allspice
Confectioners' sugar

In a mixing bowl, cream butter and sugar. Add eggs, one at a time, beating well after each. In a bowl, combine corn syrup, molasses and water; set aside. Combine flour, aniseed, baking soda and spices; add to creamed mixture alternately with molasses mixture. Cover; refrigerate overnight. Roll into 1-in. balls. Place 2 in. apart on greased baking sheets. Bake at 400° for 11 minutes or until golden brown. Roll warm cookies in confectioners' sugar. Cool on wire racks. **Yield:** 8 dozen.

Windmill Cookie Bars

When I went to my grandma's house as a child, she was often baking Dutch windmill cookies. Like her cookies, my bars feature crisp slivered almonds. —*Edna Hoffman, Hebron, Indiana*

1 cup butter (no substitutes), softened
1 cup sugar
1 egg, *separated*
2 cups all-purpose flour
1 teaspoon ground cinnamon
1/4 teaspoon baking soda
1 cup slivered almonds

In a bowl, cream butter and sugar. Add egg yolk; mix well. Combine the flour, cinnamon and baking soda; gradually add to creamed mixture. Press into a greased 15-in. x 10-in. x 1-in. baking pan. Beat the egg white; brush over dough. Sprinkle with almonds. Bake at 350° for 20-25 minutes or until a toothpick inserted near the center comes out clean. Cool for 5 minutes and cut into bars; cool completely. **Yield:** 2-1/2 dozen.

Mocha Crackle Cookies

These cake-like cookies are better than brownies. They have crackly tops and subtle coffee flavor.
—Louise Beatty, Amherst, New York

1/2 cup butter (no substitutes)
5 squares (1 ounce *each*) unsweetened chocolate
1 tablespoon instant coffee granules
4 eggs
1/8 teaspoon salt
1 cup sugar
1 cup packed brown sugar
2 cups plus 3 tablespoons all-purpose flour
2 teaspoons baking powder
1/3 cup confectioners' sugar

In a microwave or saucepan, heat butter, chocolate and coffee until chocolate is melted; cool slightly. In a mixing bowl, combine eggs and salt. Add sugar and brown sugar. Stir in chocolate mixture; mix well. Combine flour and baking powder; gradually add to egg mixture to form a soft dough. Cover and refrigerate for 2 hours or until easy to handle. Roll dough into 3/4-in. balls. Roll in confectioners' sugar; place 2 in. apart on greased baking sheets. Bake at 350° for 12 minutes or until set. Remove to wire racks to cool. **Yield:** about 5 dozen.

Banana Crunch Bars

The distinctive taste of banana stars in these easy no-bake cereal bars. *—Ruth Anderson, Clarion, Iowa*

1 cup sugar
1 cup corn syrup
1-1/2 cups crunchy peanut butter
5 cups Banana Nut Crunch cereal
1 package (11-1/2 ounces) milk chocolate chips

In a microwave-safe bowl, combine the sugar and corn syrup. Microwave, uncovered, on high for 3-4 minutes or until sugar is dissolved. Stir in peanut butter; mix well. Add cereal; stir to coat. Press into a greased 13-in. x 9-in. x 2-in. pan. In a microwave-safe bowl, melt chocolate chips. Spread over bars. Cool before cutting. **Yield:** about 4-1/2 dozen.

Editor's Note: This recipe was tested in an 850-watt microwave.

Oatmeal Sandwich Cookies

(Pictured below)

These fun treats put a sweet fluffy filling between two chewy oatmeal cookies. They're perfect for snacking and to carry in lunch boxes. At bake sales, they always go right away. *—Jan Woodall, Cadiz, Kentucky*

1-1/2 cups shortening
2-2/3 cups packed brown sugar
4 eggs
2 teaspoons vanilla extract
2-1/4 cups all-purpose flour
2 teaspoons ground cinnamon
1-1/2 teaspoons baking soda
1 teaspoon salt
1/2 teaspoon ground nutmeg
4 cups old-fashioned oats
FILLING:
3/4 cup shortening
3 cups confectioners' sugar
1 jar (7 ounces) marshmallow creme
1 to 3 tablespoons milk

In a mixing bowl, cream shortening and brown sugar. Add eggs, one at a time, beating well after each. Beat in vanilla. Combine flour, cinnamon, baking soda, salt and nutmeg; add to creamed mixture. Stir in oats. Drop by rounded teaspoonfuls 2 in. apart onto lightly greased baking sheets. Bake at 350° for 10-12 minutes or until golden brown. Remove to wire racks to cool.

For filling, in a mixing bowl, cream shortening, sugar and marshmallow creme. Add enough milk to achieve spreading consistency. Spread filling on the bottom of half of the cookies; top with remaining cookies. **Yield:** about 4-1/2 dozen.

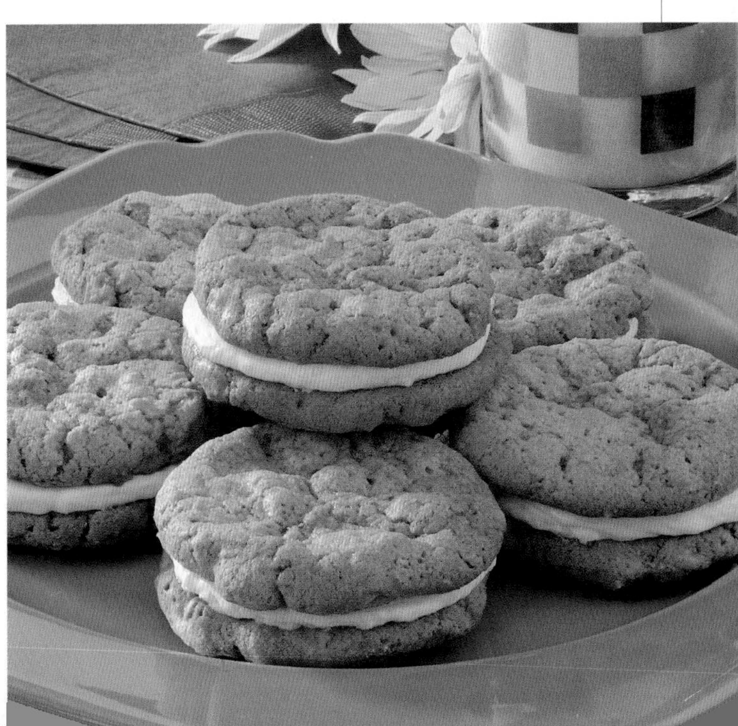

Black 'n' White Brownies

One bite of these delectable layered brownies and you'll agree the extra effort it takes to make them is well worth it. My mother won a prize with the recipe a few years ago. —Laurie Knoke, DeKalb, Illinois

3/4 cup all-purpose flour
1/2 cup sugar
1/4 teaspoon baking powder
1/4 teaspoon salt
1 cup quick-cooking oats
1 cup flaked coconut
2/3 cup butter (no substitutes), melted
2 tablespoons milk

CHOCOLATE LAYER:
1/3 cup butter
1 square (1 ounce) unsweetened chocolate
2 eggs
1 cup packed brown sugar
2 tablespoons milk
1 teaspoon vanilla extract
3/4 cup all-purpose flour
1/2 teaspoon baking powder
1/4 teaspoon salt
1/2 cup chopped walnuts

FROSTING:
4 ounces cream cheese, softened
1/4 cup butter, softened
1-1/2 teaspoons vanilla extract
2-1/4 cups confectioners' sugar
1/4 cup chopped walnuts

In a bowl, combine the first four ingredients. Stir in oats and coconut. Add butter and milk; mix well. Press into a greased 13-in. x 9-in. x 2-in. baking pan. Bake at 350° for 10-12 minutes. Remove from the oven. Reduce heat to 325°. In a saucepan, melt the butter and chocolate; cool slightly. In a mixing bowl, combine the eggs, brown sugar, milk and vanilla; mix well. Add chocolate mixture; mix well.

Combine the flour, baking powder and salt; add to chocolate mixture and mix well. Stir in walnuts. Spread evenly over crust. Bake at 325° for 25-30 minutes or until a toothpick comes out with moist crumbs (do not overbake). Cool on a wire rack. In a mixing bowl, combine the first four frosting ingredients until smooth and creamy. Spread over bars. Sprinkle with walnuts. Store in the refrigerator. **Yield:** 4 dozen.

Zucchini Granola Cookies

To use up an abundance of garden zucchini, try these wholesome, soft-textured cookies. Chocolate chips and orange peel add the right amount of sweetness. —Janice Brady, Des Moines, Washington

3/4 cup butter *or* margarine, softened
1-1/2 cups packed brown sugar
1 egg
1 tablespoon grated orange peel
1 teaspoon vanilla extract
3-1/2 cups all-purpose flour
3 cups granola cereal
1 teaspoon baking soda
1 teaspoon salt
3 cups shredded zucchini
1 package (10 to 12 ounces) semisweet chocolate *or* butterscotch chips

In a mixing bowl, cream butter and brown sugar. Beat in the egg, orange peel and vanilla. Combine flour, granola, baking soda and salt; add to creamed mixture alternately with zucchini. Stir in chips. Drop by tablespoonfuls 2 in. apart onto greased baking sheets. Bake at 350° for 8-10 minutes or until lightly browned. Remove to wire racks to cool. **Yield:** 6-1/2 dozen.

Crisp Sugar Cookies

My son Josiah enjoys making treats. This recipe is great for kids because it has two manageable time blocks—mixing and chilling the dough, then cutting out and baking the cookies. —Sharon Hildenbrand San Leandro, California

3/4 cup shortening
1 cup sugar
2 eggs
1/2 teaspoon lemon extract
2-1/2 cups all-purpose flour
1 teaspoon baking powder
1 teaspoon salt
Colored sugar

In a mixing bowl, cream shortening and sugar. Add eggs and lemon extract; mix well. Combine the flour, baking powder and salt; gradually add to creamed mixture and mix well. Cover and refrigerate for at least 2 hours or until easy to handle. On a floured surface, roll dough to 1/8-in. thickness. Cut with 2-1/2-in. cookie cutters. Place on greased baking sheets. Sprinkle with colored sugar. Bake at 400° for 7-9 minutes or until lightly browned. Cool on wire racks. **Yield:** about 4 dozen.

Almond Citrus Biscotti

Often, I'll package some of my home-baked biscotti with a mug and a special blend of coffee to give as a gift. —Claire Brogren, Winside, New York

1/2 cup butter (no substitutes), softened
1-1/2 cups sugar
4 eggs
1 tablespoon grated lemon peel
2 teaspoons grated orange peel
1 teaspoon vanilla extract
3-3/4 cups all-purpose flour
2 teaspoons baking powder
Dash salt
2 tablespoons coarsely ground almonds

In a mixing bowl, cream butter and sugar. Add 3 eggs, one at a time, beating well after each. Beat in lemon peel, orange peel and vanilla.

Combine the flour, baking powder and salt; gradually add to creamed mixture. Divide dough into four portions; shape each into an 8-in. x 2-in. rectangle on ungreased baking sheets. In a small bowl, lightly beat remaining egg; brush evenly over dough. Sprinkle with almonds.

Bake at 350° for 25-30 minutes or until lightly browned. Cool for 5 minutes. Transfer to a cutting board; cut diagonally with a serrated knife into 3/4-in. slices. Place cut side down on ungreased baking sheets. Bake for 12-14 minutes or until golden brown, turning once. Cool on wire racks. Store in an airtight container. **Yield:** about 4 dozen.

Cinnamon Anise Cookies

These Southwestern cookies have a hint of anise and cinnamon-sugar. We think they make perfect snacks.
—Viola Ward, Fruita, Colorado

2 cups shortening
1 cup plus 3 tablespoons sugar, *divided*
2 eggs
1/2 cup orange juice
2 teaspoons aniseed
6 cups all-purpose flour
1 tablespoon baking powder
3/4 teaspoon salt
1/2 teaspoon ground cinnamon

In a mixing bowl, cream shortening and 1 cup sugar. Beat in the eggs, orange juice and aniseed. Combine the flour, baking powder and salt; gradually add to creamed mixture. Cover and refrigerate for 2 hours or until easy to handle. Combine cinnamon and remaining sugar; set aside.

On a lightly floured surface, roll the dough to 1/8-in. thickness. Cut with 2-1/2-in. cookie cutters dipped in flour. Place 1 in. apart on ungreased baking sheets. Sprinkle with cinnamon-sugar. Bake at 375° for 8-10 minutes or until lightly browned. Remove to wire racks to cool. **Yield:** about 7 dozen.

Vanilla Chip Maple Cookies

(Pictured above and on page 104)

These cookies have a distinct maple flavor and stay moist and soft, although they're never in my cookie jar for long! —Debra Hogenson, Brewster, Minnesota

1 cup shortening
1/2 cup butter *or* margarine, softened
2 cups packed brown sugar
2 eggs
1 teaspoon vanilla extract
1 teaspoon maple flavoring
3 cups all-purpose flour
2 teaspoons baking soda
2 cups vanilla *or* white chips
1/2 cup chopped pecans
FROSTING:
1/4 cup butter *or* margarine, softened
4 cups confectioners' sugar
1 teaspoon maple flavoring
4 to 6 tablespoons milk
3-1/2 cups pecan halves

In a mixing bowl, cream shortening, butter and brown sugar. Add eggs, one at a time, beating well after each. Beat in vanilla and maple flavoring. Combine the flour and baking soda; gradually add to creamed mixture. Stir in vanilla chips and pecans.

Drop by rounded tablespoonfuls 2 in. apart onto ungreased baking sheets. Bake at 350° for 8-10 minutes or until golden brown. Cool for 2 minutes before removing to wire racks. In a mixing bowl, cream butter and confectioners' sugar. Beat in maple flavoring and enough milk to achieve spreading consistency. Frost cooled cookies. Top each with a pecan half. **Yield:** about 7 dozen.

Cardamom Swedish Rusks

Cardamom, which has a lemony ginger flavor, is a popular spice in Scandinavian foods. It gives a pleasantly pungent flavor to these crisp cookies. Similar to biscotti, they're great "dunkers" for a cup of steaming coffee. —Julianne Johnson, Grove City, Minnesota

1 cup butter (no substitutes), softened
1 cup sugar
2 eggs
1 tablespoon whipping cream
3/4 teaspoon almond extract
3 cups all-purpose flour
1 teaspoon baking powder
1/2 to 3/4 teaspoon ground cardamom
1/2 teaspoon salt
1/8 teaspoon baking soda

In a mixing bowl, cream butter and sugar. Add eggs, cream and extract. Combine the remaining ingredients; gradually add to creamed mixture (batter will be thick). Spoon into three greased 5-3/4-in. x 3-in. x 2-in. loaf pans. Bake at 350° for 35-40 minutes or until a toothpick inserted near the center comes out clean. Cool in pans for 10 minutes.

Remove to a cutting board; cut each loaf into nine slices with a serrated knife. Place cut side down on an ungreased baking sheet. Bake for 10 minutes. Turn slices; bake 10 minutes longer or until crisp and golden. Remove to wire racks to cool. Store in an airtight container. **Yield:** 27 cookies.

Berry Shortbread Dreams

(Pictured at far right)

Raspberry jam adds fruity sweetness to these rich-tasting cookies. They will absolutely melt in your mouth! —Mildred Sherrer, Bay City, Texas

1 cup butter (no substitutes), softened
2/3 cup sugar
1/2 teaspoon almond extract
2 cups all-purpose flour
1/3 to 1/2 cup seedless raspberry jam
GLAZE:
1 cup confectioners' sugar
2 to 3 teaspoons water
1/2 teaspoon almond extract

In a mixing bowl, cream butter and sugar. Beat in extract; gradually add flour until dough forms a ball. Cover and refrigerate for 1 hour or until easy to handle. Roll into 1-in. balls. Place 1 in. apart on ungreased baking sheets. Using the end of a wooden spoon handle, make an indentation in the center. Fill with jam. Bake at 350° for 14-18 minutes or until edges are lightly browned. Remove to wire racks to cool. Spoon additional jam into cookies if desired. Combine glaze ingredients; drizzle over cookies. **Yield:** about 3-1/2 dozen.

Coffee Shortbread

(Pictured below right)

You'll be remembered for these cookies when you serve them for a morning coffee or at a gathering. Melted chips drizzled on top make them look fancy, but they're so easy to make. —Dixie Terry, Marion, Illinois

1 cup butter (no substitutes), softened
1/2 cup packed brown sugar
1/4 cup sugar
2 tablespoons instant coffee granules
2 cups all-purpose flour
1/4 teaspoon salt
1/2 cup semisweet chocolate chips, melted
1/2 cup vanilla *or* white chips, melted

In a mixing bowl, cream butter, sugars and coffee granules. Gradually beat in flour and salt. On a lightly floured surface, roll out to 1/4-in. thickness. Cut with floured 2-in. to 3-in. cookie cutters. Place 2 in. apart on ungreased baking sheets. Bake at 300° for 20-22 minutes or until set. Remove to wire racks to cool. Drizzle with melted chips. **Yield:** about 5 dozen.

Almond Toffee Shortbread

The topping for these shortbread squares tastes like a chewy toffee bar. —Darlene Markel, Mt. Hood, Oregon

1 cup whole blanched almonds, toasted
3/4 cup confectioners' sugar, *divided*
1 cup butter (no substitutes), softened
1/4 teaspoon almond extract
1-3/4 cups all-purpose flour
1/4 teaspoon salt
1 package English toffee bits (10 ounces) *or* almond brickle chips (7-1/2 ounces)
3/4 cup light corn syrup
3/4 cup sliced almonds, *divided*
3/4 cup flaked coconut, *divided*

In a food processor or blender, place almonds and 1/4 cup sugar. Cover; process until nuts are finely ground. Set aside. In a mixing bowl, cream butter and remaining sugar until light and fluffy. Beat in extract. Combine flour, salt and ground almonds; slowly add to creamed mixture. Press into a greased 15-in. x 10-in. x 1-in. baking pan.

Bake at 350° for 20 minutes. Meanwhile, combine toffee bits and corn syrup in heavy saucepan. Cook and stir over medium heat until toffee melts. Remove from heat; stir in 1/2 cup sliced almonds and 1/2 cup coconut. Spread over hot crust. Sprinkle with remaining almonds and coconut. Bake 15 minutes or until golden and bubbly. Cool on a wire rack. Cut into squares. **Yield:** 8 dozen.

Lemon Poppy Seed Shortbread

(Pictured below)

A sprinkling of sugar adds a sparkling sweetness to tender buttery shortbread. —*Grace Yaskovic*
Branchville, New Jersey

3/4 cup butter (no substitutes), softened
1/2 cup confectioners' sugar
1 tablespoon poppy seeds
1 tablespoon lemon juice
1-1/2 cups all-purpose flour
2 teaspoons sugar

In a mixing bowl, cream butter and confectioners' sugar. Stir in poppy seeds and lemon juice. Gradually add flour; mix well. Divide dough into four portions. On a lightly floured surface, roll out each portion into a 4-in. circle. Transfer to ungreased baking sheets. Cut each circle into six wedges. Prick dough with a fork. Sprinkle with sugar. Bake at 325° for 20-25 minutes or until golden. Cool for 4 minutes before removing to wire racks. Break into wedges when cool. **Yield:** 2 dozen.

LONG ON FLAVOR. Lemon Poppy Seed Shortbread, Berry Shortbread Dreams and Coffee Shortbread (shown above, clockwise from upper right) are variations of a timeless classic that goes great with tea or coffee.

Two-Tone Fudge Brownies

(Pictured on page 105)

These moist, fudgy brownies have a scrumptious topping that tastes just like chocolate chip cookie dough! Everyone loves these brownies, and they make enough to feed a crowd. —*Rebecca Kays*
Klamath Falls, Oregon

1 cup (6 ounces) semisweet chocolate chips
1/2 cup butter *or* margarine, softened
1 cup sugar
3 eggs
1 teaspoon vanilla extract
1-1/4 cups all-purpose flour
1/4 teaspoon baking soda
3/4 cup chopped walnuts
COOKIE DOUGH LAYER:
1/2 cup butter *or* margarine, softened
1/2 cup packed brown sugar
1/4 cup sugar
3 tablespoons milk
1 teaspoon vanilla extract
1 cup all-purpose flour
1 cup (6 ounces) semisweet chocolate chips

In a microwave-safe bowl, melt chocolate chips. Cool slightly. In a mixing bowl, cream butter and sugar. Add eggs and vanilla; mix well. Stir in melted chocolate. Combine flour and baking soda; add to batter. Stir in walnuts. Spread into a greased 13-in. x 9-in. x 2-in. baking pan. Bake at 350° for 16-22 minutes or until a toothpick inserted near the center comes out clean. Cool on a wire rack.

In a mixing bowl, cream butter and sugars. Beat in milk and vanilla. Gradually add flour. Stir in chocolate chips. Drop by tablespoonfuls over cooled brownies; carefully spread over top. Cut into squares. Store in the refrigerator. **Yield:** 4 dozen.

Editor's Note: Cookie dough layer is not baked and does not contain eggs.

Almond Kiss Cookies

(Pictured on page 104)

These pretty cookies are unbelievable! They're easy to make, look elegant and are absolutely delicious. Almond, raspberry and chocolate flavors make a super combination. —*Kathy Aldrich, Webster, New York*

1/2 cup butter (no substitutes), softened
1/2 cup sugar
1/2 cup packed brown sugar
1 egg
1 teaspoon almond extract
2 cups all-purpose flour
1 teaspoon baking soda
1/4 teaspoon salt
Additional sugar
40 milk chocolate kisses with almonds
GLAZE:
1 cup confectioners' sugar
1 tablespoon milk
4 teaspoons raspberry jam
1/4 teaspoon almond extract

In a mixing bowl, cream butter and sugars. Beat in egg and extract. Combine the flour, baking soda and salt; gradually add to creamed mixture. Cover and chill for 1 hour or until easy to handle. Roll dough into 1-in. balls, then roll in additional sugar. Place 2 in. apart on ungreased baking sheets. Bake at 325° for 10-12 minutes or until golden brown. Immediately press a chocolate kiss into the center of each cookie. Cool on wire racks. Combine glaze ingredients; drizzle over cookies. **Yield:** 40 cookies.

Caramel Popcorn Bars

Need a fun last-minute school snack or bake sale item? These popular bars are sweet and chewy and can be ready in minutes. —*Ruth Burrus, Zionsville, Indiana*

8 cups popped popcorn
2 cups honey graham cereal
1 cup milk chocolate M&M's
1 cup pretzel sticks, broken
1 cup packed brown sugar
1/2 cup butter (no substitutes), cubed
1/2 cup corn syrup
2 tablespoons all-purpose flour

In a large bowl, combine popcorn, cereal, M&M's and pretzels; set aside. In a large microwave-safe bowl, combine the brown sugar, butter, corn syrup and flour. Microwave, uncovered, on high for 6 minutes or until a candy thermometer reads 244°-248° (firm-ball stage), stirring after each minute. Immediately pour over popcorn mixture and toss to coat. Press into a buttered 15-in. x 10-in. x 1-in. baking pan. Cool completely. Cut into bars. **Yield:** 2 dozen.

Chocolate Coconut Bars

It's impossible to resist these scrumptious bars. With nuts, chocolate and a creamy cheesecake-like layer, these treats taste just like homemade candy bars.
—*Carolyn Kyzer, Alexander, Arkansas*

1 tube (8 ounces) refrigerated crescent rolls
1 package (8 ounces) cream cheese, softened

1/3 cup confectioners' sugar
1 egg
3/4 cup flaked coconut
1 cup (6 ounces) semisweet chocolate chips
1/4 cup chopped nuts

Unroll crescent roll dough into one long rectangle on an ungreased baking sheet; seal seams and perforations. Roll out into a 13-in. x 9-in. rectangle, building up dough around edges. In a small mixing bowl, beat the cream cheese, sugar and egg until smooth; stir in coconut. Spread over crust.

Bake at 375° for 10-15 minutes or until cream cheese mixture is set. Immediately sprinkle with chocolate chips. Let stand for 5 minutes; spread melted chips over the top. Sprinkle with nuts. Cool completely before cutting. **Yield:** 2-1/2 dozen.

Cappuccino Cake Brownies

(Pictured on page 104)

If you like your sweets with a cup of coffee, this recipe is for you! These no-nut brownies combine a mild coffee flavor with the richness of semisweet chocolate. They're quick and easy. —*Mary Houchin Swansea, Illinois*

1 tablespoon instant coffee granules
2 teaspoons boiling water
1 cup (6 ounces) semisweet chocolate chips
1/4 cup butter *or* margarine, softened
1/2 cup sugar
2 eggs
1/2 cup all-purpose flour
1/4 teaspoon ground cinnamon

In a small bowl, dissolve coffee in water; set aside. In a microwave-safe bowl or saucepan over low heat, melt chocolate chips. In a small mixing bowl, cream butter and sugar. Beat in eggs, melted chocolate and coffee mixture. Combine flour and cinnamon; add to the creamed mixture and mix well. Pour into a greased 8-in. square baking pan. Bake at 350° for 25-30 minutes or until a toothpick inserted near the center comes out clean. Cool on a wire rack. Cut into squares. **Yield:** 16 bars.

Pear Dessert Squares

(Pictured at right)

Pears are so luscious sparked with spices and topped with graham cracker crumbs in this yummy dessert. I try to have low-sugar desserts available at family gatherings because three of my relatives are diabetic.
—*Jacquie Guarriello, Chambersburg, Pennsylvania*

✓ Uses less fat, sugar or salt. Includes Nutritional Analysis and Diabetic Exchanges.

1-1/2 pounds pears, sliced
3 tablespoons all-purpose flour, *divided*
1/4 cup unsweetened apple juice concentrate
3/4 cup reduced-fat graham cracker crumbs (about 10 squares)
1/2 teaspoon ground cinnamon
Dash ground nutmeg
3 tablespoons cold stick margarine
1/2 cup reduced-fat whipped topping
Additional ground cinnamon

In a bowl, toss pears, 1 tablespoon flour and apple juice concentrate. Spoon into an 8-in. square baking dish coated with nonstick cooking spray. In a bowl, combine crumbs, cinnamon, nutmeg and remaining flour. Cut in margarine until mixture resembles coarse crumbs. Sprinkle over pears. Bake at 375° for 30 minutes or until pears are tender and topping is light brown. Serve warm or chilled. Cut into squares; top with whipped topping and additional cinnamon. **Yield:** 9 servings.

Nutritional Analysis: One serving equals 127 calories, 5 g fat (1 g saturated fat), 0 cholesterol, 74 mg sodium, 21 g carbohydrate, 2 g fiber, 1 g protein. **Diabetic Exchanges:** 1 starch, 1/2 fruit, 1/2 fat.

Double Chocolate Cookies

When I make these yummy treats with my young grandson, Ben, I use an extra-big mixing bowl to prevent the flour and other ingredients from flying all over. He seems to enjoy making the cookies almost as much as eating them! —*Chantal Cornwall, Prince Rupert, British Columbia*

1-1/4 cups butter *or* margarine, softened
2 cups sugar
2 eggs
2 teaspoons vanilla extract
2 cups all-purpose flour
3/4 cup baking cocoa
1 teaspoon baking soda
1/2 teaspoon salt
2 cups (12 ounces) semisweet chocolate chips

In a mixing bowl, cream the butter and sugar until smooth. Beat in eggs and vanilla. Combine the flour, cocoa, baking soda and salt; gradually add to creamed mixture and mix well. Stir in chocolate chips. Drop by rounded teaspoonfuls 2 in. apart onto greased baking sheets. Bake at 350° for 8-10 minutes or until set. Cool for 2 minutes; remove from pans to wire racks. **Yield:** about 9 dozen.

Pear Crescent Cookies

(Pictured on page 104)

I first made these crescent-shaped cream cheese cookies—traditionally called "rugalach"—for my Jewish son-in-law. We all loved their wonderful texture. —*Carolyn Hayes, Marion, Illinois*

1 cup butter (no substitutes), softened
1 package (8 ounces) cream cheese, softened
2 cups all-purpose flour
1/8 teaspoon salt
1/4 cup packed brown sugar
2 teaspoons ground cinnamon
1/2 cup diced peeled pears
1/2 cup finely chopped walnuts
3/4 cup confectioners' sugar
2 tablespoons milk

In a mixing bowl, cream the butter and cream cheese. Gradually add flour and salt. Cover and refrigerate for 2 hours or until easy to handle. Combine brown sugar and cinnamon; set aside.

Divide the dough into fourths. On a floured surface, roll out each portion into a 12-in. circle. Cut into 12 wedges. Place about 1/4 teaspoon cinnamon-sugar at the wide end of each wedge. Top with about 1/2 teaspoon each pears and walnuts. Roll up, beginning at wide end. Place pointed side down 2 in. apart on ungreased baking sheets; curve ends to form a crescent.

Bake at 375° for 16-19 minutes or until lightly browned. Immediately remove to wire racks. Combine confectioners' sugar and milk; drizzle over cooled cookies. **Yield:** 4 dozen.

Pudding Sugar Cookies

This recipe, which was passed on by a friend, has become a year-round favorite at our house. For fun, substitute other flavors of pudding. —*Sharon Reed, Catlin, Illinois*

1 cup butter *or* margarine, softened
1 cup vegetable oil
1 cup sugar
1 cup confectioners' sugar
2 eggs
1 teaspoon vanilla extract
1 package (3.4 ounces) instant lemon pudding mix *or* instant pudding mix of your choice
4 cups all-purpose flour
1 teaspoon cream of tartar
1 teaspoon baking soda

In a large mixing bowl, cream the butter, oil and sugars. Beat in the eggs, vanilla and dry pudding mix. Combine the flour, cream of tartar and baking soda; gradually add to creamed mixture. Drop by tablespoonfuls 2 in. apart onto ungreased baking sheets. Flatten with a glass dipped in sugar. Bake at 350° for 12-15 minutes or until lightly browned. Remove to wire racks. **Yield:** 7 dozen.

Butterscotch Cashew Bars

(Pictured on page 104)

I knew these nutty bars were a success when I took them on our annual family vacation. My husband couldn't stop eating them...and my sister-in-law, who is a great cook, asked for the recipe. It makes a big batch, which is good, because they go quickly! —*Lori Berg, Wentzville, Missouri*

1 cup plus 2 tablespoons butter *or* margarine, softened
3/4 cup plus 2 tablespoons packed brown sugar
2-1/2 cups all-purpose flour
1-3/4 teaspoons salt

TOPPING:

- **1 package (10 to 11 ounces) butterscotch chips**
- **1/2 cup plus 2 tablespoons light corn syrup**
- **3 tablespoons butter *or* margarine**
- **2 teaspoons water**
- **2-1/2 cups salted cashew halves**

In a mixing bowl, cream the butter and brown sugar. Combine flour and salt; add to creamed mixture just until combined. Press into a greased 15-in. x 10-in. x 1-in. baking pan. Bake at 350° for 10-12 minutes or until lightly browned.

Meanwhile, combine butterscotch chips, corn syrup, butter and water in a saucepan. Cook and stir over medium heat until chips and butter are melted. Spread over crust. Sprinkle with cashews; press down lightly. Bake for 11-13 minutes or until topping is bubbly and lightly browned. Cool on a wire rack. Cut into bars. **Yield:** 3-1/2 dozen.

Raspberry Almond Bars

A co-worker's mother gave me this gem of a recipe a few years back. I can never decide what's more appealing—the attractive look of the bars or their incredible aroma while they're baking! Everyone who tries these asks for the recipe. —*Mimi Priesman, Pace, Florida*

- **1/2 cup butter *or* margarine**
- **1 package (10 to 12 ounces) vanilla *or* white chips, *divided***
- **2 eggs**
- **1/2 cup sugar**
- **1 teaspoon almond extract**
- **1 cup all-purpose flour**
- **1/2 teaspoon salt**
- **1/2 cup seedless raspberry jam**
- **1/4 cup sliced almonds**

In a saucepan, melt butter. Remove from the heat; add 1 cup chips (do not stir). In a small mixing bowl, beat eggs until foamy; gradually add sugar. Stir in chip mixture and almond extract. Combine flour and salt; add to egg mixture just until combined. Spread half of the batter into a greased 9-in. square baking pan. Bake at 325° for 15-20 minutes or until golden brown.

In a small saucepan over low heat, melt jam; spread over warm crust. Stir remaining chips into the remaining batter; drop by teaspoonfuls over the jam layer. Sprinkle with almonds. Bake 30-35 minutes longer or until a toothpick inserted near the center comes out clean. Cool on a wire rack. Cut into bars. **Yield:** 2 dozen.

Monster Chip Cookies

(Pictured above)

Welcoming "little monsters" who ring the doorbell on Halloween is one way I've shared these big treats. I've also given them as gifts from our business at Christmastime. No matter the occasion, everyone loves them! —*Judy Mabrey, Myrtle Beach, South Carolina*

- **1 cup shortening**
- **1/2 cup butter *or* margarine, softened**
- **1-1/3 cups sugar**
- **1 cup packed brown sugar**
- **4 eggs**
- **3 teaspoons vanilla extract**
- **1 teaspoon lemon juice**
- **3 cups all-purpose flour**
- **1/2 cup quick-cooking oats**
- **2 teaspoons baking soda**
- **1-1/2 teaspoons salt**
- **1 teaspoon ground cinnamon**
- **4 cups (24 ounces) semisweet chocolate chips**
- **2 cups chopped pecans *or* walnuts**

In a mixing bowl, cream shortening, butter and sugars until light and fluffy, about 5 minutes. Add eggs, one at a time, beating well after each. Add vanilla and lemon juice. Combine flour, oats, baking soda, salt and cinnamon. Add to creamed mixture; mix well. Stir in chips and nuts. Drop by 1/4 cupfuls 3 in. apart onto lightly greased baking sheets. Bake at 350° for 14-16 minutes or until lightly browned and center is set. Cool for 2 minutes before removing to wire racks. **Yield:** about 3 dozen.

Cakes & Pies

You'll fill your home with smiles as well as heavenly aromas when you make one of the 36 special selections in this chapter.

HEAVEN ON EARTH. Clockwise from upper left: Poppy Seed Strawberry Pie (p. 124), Raspberry Walnut Torte (p. 129), Texas Lime Pie (p. 118), Sour Cream Chocolate Cake (p. 119), Apricot Hazelnut Torte (p. 124) and Lemon Meringue Cake (p. 128).

Mississippi Mud Cake

(Pictured above)

Make this tempting cake, and you'll satisfy kids of all ages! A fudgy brownie-like base is topped with marshmallow creme and a nutty frosting.
—Tammi Simpson, Greensburg, Kentucky

1 cup butter *or* margarine, softened
2 cups sugar
4 eggs
1-1/2 cups self-rising flour*
1/2 cup baking cocoa
1 cup chopped pecans
1 jar (7 ounces) marshmallow creme
FROSTING:
1/2 cup butter *or* margarine, softened
3-3/4 cups confectioners' sugar
3 tablespoons baking cocoa
1 tablespoon vanilla extract
4 to 5 tablespoons milk
1 cup chopped pecans

In a mixing bowl, cream butter and sugar. Add eggs, one at a time, beating well after each addition. Combine flour and cocoa; gradually add to creamed mixture. Fold in the pecans. Transfer to a greased 13-in. x 9-in. x 2-in. baking pan. Bake at 350° for 35-40 minutes or until a toothpick inserted near the center comes out clean. Cool for 3 minutes (cake will fall in the center). Spoon the marshmallow creme over cake; carefully spread to cover top. Cool completely.

For frosting, in a mixing bowl, cream butter. Beat in confectioners' sugar, cocoa, vanilla and enough milk to achieve frosting consistency. Fold in pecans. Spread over marshmallow creme layer. Store in the refrigerator. **Yield:** 16-20 servings.

***Editor's Note:** As a substitute for *each* 1/2 cup of self-rising flour, place 3/4 teaspoon baking powder and 1/4 teaspoon salt in a 1/2-cup measuring cup. Add all-purpose flour to measure 1/2 cup.

Texas Lime Pie

(Pictured on page 116)

With the perfect balance of sweet and tart, this velvety pie is a great way to beat the Texas heat and Gulf Coast humidity. *—Diane Bell, Manvel, Texas*

3 cups graham cracker crumbs
1/2 cup packed brown sugar
2/3 cup butter *or* margarine, melted
3 cans (14 ounces *each*) sweetened condensed milk
5 egg yolks
2 cups lime juice
Whipped topping, lime slices and fresh mint, optional

In a bowl, combine cracker crumbs, brown sugar and butter. Press onto bottom and up sides of two greased 9-in. pie plates. In a mixing bowl, beat milk, egg yolks and lime juice on low for 2 minutes or until smooth and slightly thickened. Pour into prepared crusts. Bake at 350° for 18-22 minutes or until a knife inserted near center comes out clean. Cool on wire racks for 1 hour. Chill for 6 hours. Garnish with whipped topping, lime and mint if desired. **Yield:** 2 pies (6-8 servings each).

Low-Fat Chocolate Cake

This yummy cake is so chocolaty and satisfying, I sometimes enjoy it with a scoop of fat-free ice cream.
—Diana Scofield, Niceville, Florida

✓ Uses less fat, sugar or salt. Includes Nutritional Analysis and Diabetic Exchanges.

1-1/4 cups all-purpose flour
1 cup sugar
1/2 cup baking cocoa
1/4 cup cornstarch
1/2 teaspoon baking soda
1/2 teaspoon salt
4 egg whites
1 cup water
1/2 cup corn syrup
2 teaspoons confectioners' sugar

In a bowl, combine the first six ingredients. In another bowl, whisk egg whites, water and corn syrup. Stir into dry ingredients. Pour into a 9-in. square baking pan coated with nonstick cooking spray. Bake at 350° for 30-35 minutes or until a toothpick inserted near the center comes out clean. Cool on a wire rack. Dust with confectioners' sugar. **Yield:** 12 servings.

Nutritional Analysis: One serving equals 176 calories, 1 g fat (trace saturated fat), 0 cholesterol, 186 mg sodium, 42 g carbohydrate, 1 g fiber, 3 g protein. **Diabetic Exchange:** 2-1/2 starch.

Sour Cream Chocolate Cake

(Pictured on page 116)

This luscious layer cake gets wonderful moistness from sour cream. —Patsy Foster, Marion, Arkansas

4 squares (1 ounce *each*) unsweetened chocolate, melted and cooled
1 cup water
3/4 cup sour cream
1/4 cup shortening
1 teaspoon vanilla extract
2 eggs, beaten
2 cups all-purpose flour
2 cups sugar
1-1/4 teaspoons baking soda
1 teaspoon salt
1/2 teaspoon baking powder
FROSTING:
1/2 cup butter (no substitutes), softened
6 squares (1 ounce *each*) unsweetened chocolate, melted and cooled
6 cups confectioners' sugar
1/2 cup sour cream
6 tablespoons milk
2 teaspoons vanilla extract
1/8 teaspoon salt

In a mixing bowl, combine the first six ingredients; mix well. Combine the dry ingredients; gradually add to chocolate mixture. Beat on low speed just until moistened. Beat on high for 3 minutes. Pour into two greased and floured 9-in. round baking pans. Bake at 350° for 30 minutes or until a toothpick inserted near the center comes out clean. Cool for 10 minutes before removing from pans to wire racks to cool completely.

In a mixing bowl, combine frosting ingredients. Beat until smooth and creamy. Spread over cake. Store in the refrigerator. **Yield:** 12-16 servings.

Chocolate Chiffon Valentine Cake

(Pictured at right)

I first made this lovely, lightly textured cake for my husband for Valentine's Day more than 25 years ago. It's super. —Pat Eastman, Provo, Utah

1/2 cup baking cocoa
1/2 cup hot water
1-1/4 cups sugar, *divided*
3/4 cup all-purpose flour
3/4 teaspoon baking soda
1/2 teaspoon salt
4 eggs, *separated*
1/4 cup vegetable oil
1 teaspoon vanilla extract
1/4 teaspoon cream of tartar
FROSTING:
1-1/2 cups whipping cream
1/4 cup confectioners' sugar
15 small fresh strawberries, halved
Fresh mint, optional

Line two greased 9-in. heart-shaped pans with waxed paper and grease the paper; set aside. In a small bowl, combine the cocoa and water until smooth; cool. In a large bowl, combine 1 cup sugar, flour, baking soda and salt. Add egg yolks, oil, vanilla and cocoa mixture; stir until smooth.

In a small mixing bowl, beat egg whites until foamy. Add cream of tartar; beat for 1 minute. Gradually add the remaining sugar, beating until soft peaks form. Gradually fold into chocolate mixture. Pour into prepared pans. Bake at 350° for 18-20 minutes or until top springs back when lightly touched. Cool for 10 minutes before removing from pans to wire racks to cool completely; carefully remove waxed paper.

In a mixing bowl, beat cream and confectioners' sugar. Spread frosting between layers and over top and sides of cake. Spoon 1-1/2 cups of frosting into a pastry bag with a star tip. Pipe a decorative lattice design on cake top and sides. Garnish with strawberries and mint if desired. Refrigerate until serving. **Yield:** 12 servings.

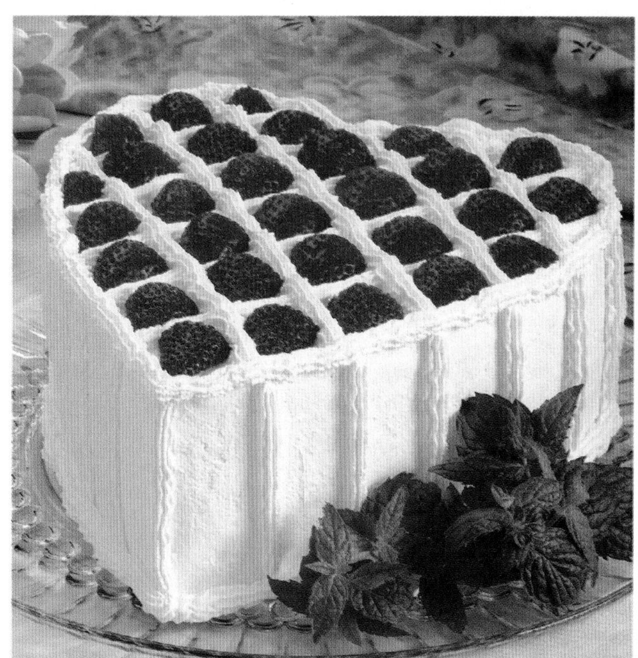

'I Wish I Had That Recipe...'

"WHILE visiting my son in California, I had dinner at the Cafe for All Seasons in San Francisco and absolutely loved their Pecan Pumpkin Pie," says Nila Towler of Baird, Texas. "It's a delicious alternative to traditional pumpkin pie! Could *Taste of Home* get the recipe?"

Chef Donna Katzl, who owns Cafe for All Seasons with husband Frank, recalls, "About 10 years ago, a gal gave me a bar cookie recipe and told me not to be put off by the cake mix in the ingredients. "I tried it and liked the taste. The next time, I made it into a pie gussied up with a caramel sauce and whipped cream.

"Our Pecan Pumpkin Pie really took off. Every year we bring it back as a dessert special in October and November. Customers can hardly wait!"

Donna—who studied with renowned chef James Beard—and Frank opened their bistro-style neighborhood cafe in 1983 "focusing on fresh, high-quality food that's simply prepared."

Located at 150 West Portal Ave., Cafe for All Seasons serves dinner 5:30 p.m. to 9:30 p.m. Monday-Saturday, 5 p.m. to 8:30 p.m. Sunday; lunch 11:30 a.m. to 2:30 p.m. Monday-Friday; breakfast/brunch 10 a.m. to 2:30 p.m. Saturday, 9 a.m. to 2:30 p.m. Sunday. Call 1-415/665-0900 for reservations.

Cafe's Pecan Pumpkin Pie

1 can (30 ounces) pumpkin pie mix
1 cup sugar
1 can (5 ounces) evaporated milk
3 eggs
2 teaspoons ground cinnamon
1/2 teaspoon salt
1 package (18-1/4 ounces) yellow cake mix
1 cup butter *or* margarine, melted
1-1/2 cups chopped pecans

CARAMEL SAUCE:

1 cup butter *or* margarine
2 cups packed brown sugar
1 cup whipping cream

TOPPING:

2 cups whipping cream
3 tablespoons confectioners' sugar
1-1/2 teaspoons vanilla extract

Line two 9-in. pie plates with waxed paper or parchment paper; coat the paper with nonstick cooking spray. Set aside.

In a mixing bowl, combine the pumpkin, sugar and milk. Beat in eggs, cinnamon and salt. Pour into prepared pans. Sprinkle with dry cake mix. Drizzle with butter. Sprinkle with pecans and press down lightly. Bake at 350° for 50-60 minutes or until golden brown. Cool for 2 hours on wire racks.

Carefully run a knife around edge of pan to loosen. Invert pies onto serving plates; remove waxed paper. Refrigerate until completely cool. In a heavy saucepan over low heat, melt butter. Add brown sugar and cream; cook and stir until sugar is dissolved. In a mixing bowl, beat cream until foamy. Beat in confectioners' sugar and vanilla until soft peaks form.

Cut pie into slices; drizzle with caramel sauce and dollop with topping. **Yield:** 2 pies (10 servings each).

Lincoln Log Cake

(Pictured above right)

My mother always made this irresistible cake roll in February to celebrate Presidents' Day.
—Mary Thomas, Hartford, Wisconsin

4 eggs, *separated*
3/4 cup sugar, *divided*
1/2 teaspoon vanilla extract
3/4 cup all-purpose flour
1 teaspoon baking powder
1/4 teaspoon salt

FROSTING:

1 cup sugar
3 tablespoons cornstarch
1/8 teaspoon salt
1 cup water
2 squares (1 ounce *each*) unsweetened chocolate, grated
2 tablespoons plus 2 teaspoons butter (no substitutes)
1 teaspoon vanilla extract

In a large mixing bowl, beat egg yolks until thick and lemon-colored. Gradually beat in 1/4 cup sugar and vanilla. In a small mixing bowl, beat egg whites until soft peaks form. Gradually add remaining sugar, beating until stiff peaks form. Fold into egg yolk mixture. Combine the flour, baking powder and salt; fold into egg mixture.

Line a greased 15-in. x 10-in. x 1-in. baking pan with waxed paper; grease the paper. Spread batter evenly into pan. Bake at 375° for 12-15 minutes or until top springs back when lightly touched. Cool 5 minutes. Turn cake onto a kitchen towel dusted with confectioners' sugar. Gently peel off waxed paper. Roll up cake in towel jelly-roll style, starting with a short side. Cool completely on a wire rack.

For frosting, combine sugar, cornstarch, salt and water in a saucepan until smooth. Bring to a boil; cook and stir for 2 minutes or until thickened. Remove from heat. Add chocolate, butter and vanilla; stir until melted.

While frosting is warm, unroll cake and spread half of frosting over cake to within 1/2 in. of edges. Roll up. Spread remaining frosting over outside of roll. Using tines of a fork, drag along sides of cake to resemble tree bark. Refrigerate for at least 1 hour before slicing. **Yield:** 12 servings.

Hot Fudge Sundae Cake

(Pictured at right)

My husband is a real chocolate lover, so I'm always on the lookout for great dessert recipes like this one, which I found years ago. Who can resist the combination of chocolate cake, ice cream and hot fudge sauce?
—Hildy Adams, Alma, Michigan

1 package (11-1/2 ounces) milk chocolate chips
1/3 cup butter *or* margarine
4 eggs, *separated*
1/3 cup all-purpose flour
1/3 cup sugar
1/2 cup slivered almonds, toasted
HOT FUDGE SAUCE:
1/2 cup sugar
1/2 cup baking cocoa
1/2 cup whipping cream
1/2 cup semisweet chocolate chips
1/4 cup butter *or* margarine
1 teaspoon vanilla extract
Vanilla ice cream

In a heavy saucepan, melt the milk chocolate chips and butter over low heat. Cool slightly. Whisk in egg yolks. Add the flour just until combined. In a small mixing bowl, beat egg whites until foamy. Gradually add sugar, beating until stiff peaks form. Fold into chocolate mixture until blended. Fold in almonds. Pour into a greased 10-in. pie plate or quiche dish. Bake at 350° for 25-30 minutes or until a toothpick comes out clean. Cool on a wire rack.

For sauce, combine sugar, cocoa and cream in a saucepan until smooth. Add semisweet chips and butter. Cook and stir over low heat until chips and butter are melted and mixture is smooth. Remove from the heat; stir in vanilla. Cut cake into wedges; top with ice cream. Drizzle cake with warm sauce. **Yield:** 12 servings.

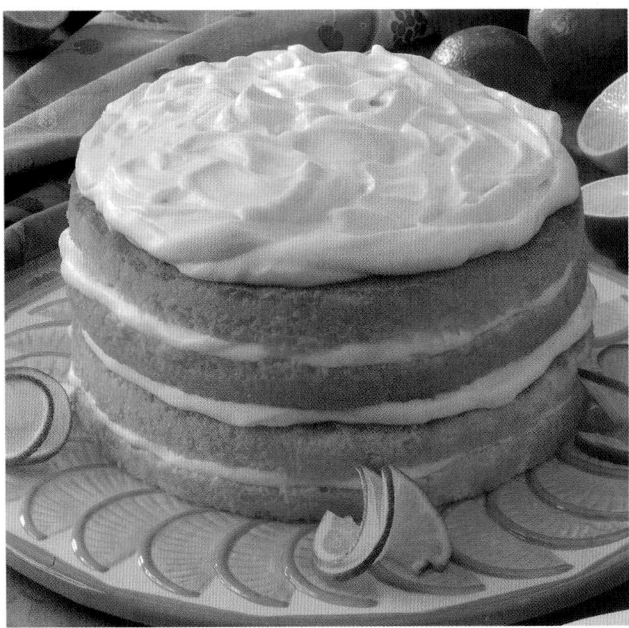

Lime Cream Torte

(Pictured above)

This impressive-looking dessert is surprisingly simple to prepare. Light and refreshing, it's a super make-ahead treat—the flavor gets better as it sits in the refrigerator. I've had many requests for the recipe.
—Theresa Tometich, Coralville, Iowa

1 package (18-1/4 ounces) butter recipe golden cake mix*
3 eggs
1/2 cup butter *or* margarine, softened
7 tablespoons water
3 tablespoons lime juice
FILLING:
1 can (14 ounces) sweetened condensed milk
1/2 cup lime juice
2 cups whipping cream, whipped
Lime slices, optional

In a mixing bowl, combine dry cake mix, eggs, butter, water and lime juice. Beat on medium speed for 4 minutes. Pour into two greased and floured 9-in. round baking pans. Bake at 375° for 20-25 minutes or until a toothpick inserted near the center comes out clean. Cool for 10 minutes before removing from pans to wire racks.

When cool, split each cake into two horizontal layers. In a bowl, combine milk and lime juice. Fold in the whipped cream. Spread about 1-1/4 cups between each layer and over top of cake. Refrigerate for at least 1 hour. Garnish with lime slices if desired. **Yield:** 10-14 servings.

***Editor's Note:** This recipe was tested with Duncan Hines Butter Recipe Golden Cake mix.

Carrot Cupcakes

To try to get my family to eat more vegetables, I often "hide" nutritional foods inside sweet treats, like these cupcakes. —Doreen Kelly, Roslyn, Pennsylvania

4 eggs
2 cups sugar
1 cup vegetable oil
2 cups all-purpose flour
2 teaspoons ground cinnamon
1 teaspoon baking soda
1 teaspoon baking powder
1 teaspoon ground allspice
1/2 teaspoon salt
3 cups grated carrots
CHUNKY FROSTING:
1 package (8 ounces) cream cheese, softened
1/4 cup butter *or* margarine, softened
2 cups confectioners' sugar
1/2 cup flaked coconut
1/2 cup chopped pecans
1/2 cup chopped raisins

In a mixing bowl, beat eggs, sugar and oil. Combine the flour, cinnamon, baking soda, baking powder, allspice and salt; gradually add to egg mixture. Stir in carrots. Fill greased or paper-lined muffin cups two-thirds full. Bake at 325° for 20-25 minutes or until a toothpick comes out clean. Cool for 5 minutes before removing from pans to wire racks.

For frosting, in a mixing bowl, beat cream cheese and butter until combined. Gradually beat in confectioners' sugar. Stir in coconut, pecans and raisins. Frost the cupcakes. Store in the refrigerator. **Yield:** 2 dozen.

Golden Lemon Pound Cake

Years ago, while pastoring a church in New Mexico, I worked in a nursing home. For a Christmas party, I baked this pound cake. Everyone raved over the treats "my wife" made. When I told them I'd made them myself, they were astonished. —Douglas Jenkins Ottawa, Kansas

2/3 cup butter-flavored shortening
1-1/4 cups sugar
2 tablespoons lemon juice
1 teaspoon lemon extract
2/3 cup milk
2-1/4 cups cake flour
1-1/4 teaspoons salt
1 teaspoon baking powder
3 eggs
Confectioners' sugar

In a mixing bowl, cream shortening and sugar. Beat in lemon juice and extract. Add milk; beat for 30 seconds. Sift cake flour, salt and baking powder; gradually add to creamed mixture. Beat on low speed for 2 minutes. Add eggs, one at a time, beating for 1 minute after each.

Pour into a greased waxed paper-lined 9-in. x 5-in. x 3-in. loaf pan. Bake at 300° for 1 hour and 30 minutes or until a toothpick comes out clean. Cool for 10 minutes before removing from pan to a wire rack to cool completely. Remove waxed paper. Dust with confectioners' sugar. **Yield:** 1 loaf.

Eggnog Pie

A holiday favorite, this creamy pie delivers wonderful eggnog flavor. It's pretty, too, with nutmeg sprinkled on top. —Florence Shaw, East Wenatchee, Washington

1 tablespoon unflavored gelatin
1/4 cup cold water
1/3 cup sugar
2 tablespoons cornstarch
1/4 teaspoon salt
2 cups eggnog*
1 teaspoon vanilla extract
1 teaspoon rum extract
1 cup whipping cream, whipped
1 pastry shell (9 inches), baked

In a small bowl, sprinkle gelatin over water; let stand 1 minute. In a saucepan, combine sugar, cornstarch and salt. Stir in eggnog until smooth. Bring to a boil; cook and stir for 2 minutes or until thickened. Stir in gelatin until dissolved. Remove from the heat; cool to room temperature. Stir in extracts; fold in whipped cream. Pour into pastry shell. Refrigerate until firm. **Yield:** 6-8 servings.

***Editor's Note:** This recipe was tested with commercially prepared eggnog.

Coconut Cream Pie

(Pictured at right)

The easy pat-in crust has a rich grain flour and is topped with old-fashioned coconut cream and a fluffy meringue. It's irresistible! —Roberta Foster Kingfisher, Oklahoma

WHOLE WHEAT CRUST:
1-1/2 cups whole wheat flour
2 teaspoons sugar
1/2 teaspoon salt
1/2 cup vegetable oil
2 tablespoons cold milk

FILLING:
2/3 cup sugar
3 tablespoons cornstarch
1 tablespoon all-purpose flour
1/2 teaspoon salt
3 cups milk
3 egg yolks, lightly beaten
3/4 cup flaked coconut
1 tablespoon butter *or* margarine
1-1/2 teaspoons vanilla extract

MERINGUE:
3 egg whites
1 cup marshmallow creme
1/4 cup flaked coconut

In a bowl, combine whole wheat flour, sugar and salt. Combine oil and milk; stir into flour mixture just until moistened (mixture will be crumbly). Press onto the bottom and up the sides of an ungreased 9-in. pie plate. Bake at 350° for 20 minutes. Cool on a wire rack.

For filling, combine sugar, cornstarch, flour and salt in a saucepan. Gradually stir in milk until smooth. Bring to a boil; cook and stir for 2 minutes or until thickened. Remove from the heat. Gradually stir 1 cup hot filling into egg yolks; return all to pan, stirring constantly. Bring to a gentle boil; cook and stir for 2 minutes. Remove from the heat; stir in coconut, butter and vanilla until butter is melted. Pour hot filling into crust.

In a mixing bowl, beat egg whites until soft peaks form. Gradually beat in marshmallow creme on high speed until stiff glossy peaks form. Spread evenly over hot filling, sealing edges to crust. Sprinkle with coconut. Bake at 350° for 12-15 minutes or until meringue is golden. Cool on a wire rack for 1 hour; refrigerate at least 3 hours before serving. Refrigerate leftovers. **Yield:** 6-8 servings.

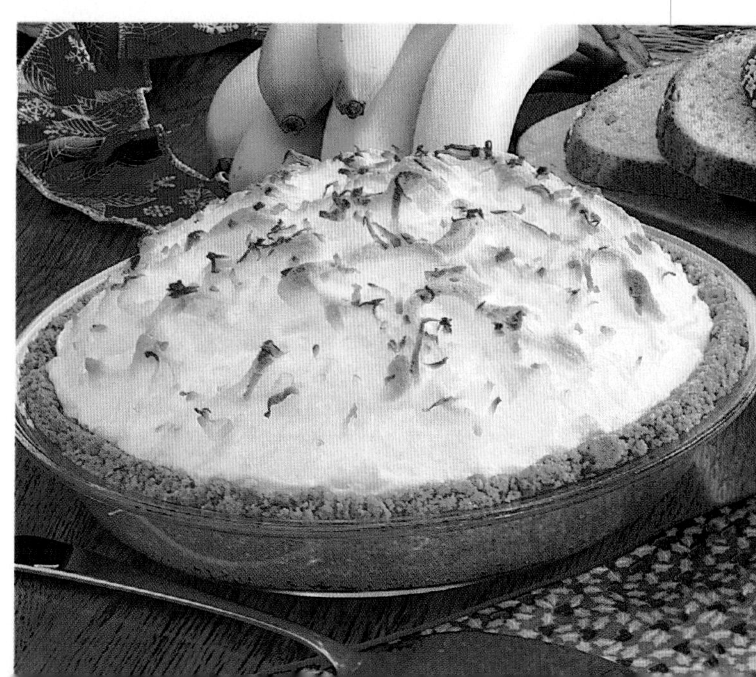

Strawberry Nut Roll

(Pictured below)

The oldest of seven children, I did a lot of cooking and baking while I was growing up. Desserts like this refreshing rolled shortcake are my favorite. The nutty cake, creamy filling and fresh strawberries make pretty swirled slices. —Judy Hayes, Peosta, Iowa

- **6 eggs, *separated***
- **3/4 cup sugar, *divided***
- **1 cup ground walnuts, toasted**
- **1/4 cup dry bread crumbs**
- **1/4 cup all-purpose flour**
- **1/8 teaspoon salt**
- **Confectioners' sugar**

FILLING:

- **1 pint fresh strawberries**
- **1 cup whipping cream**
- **2 tablespoons sugar**
- **1 teaspoon vanilla extract**
- **Confectioners' sugar**

In a mixing bowl, beat egg whites until soft peaks form. Gradually add 1/4 cup sugar, beating until stiff peaks form. Set aside. In another mixing bowl, beat egg yolks and remaining sugar until thick and lemon-colored. Combine walnuts, bread crumbs, flour and salt; add to yolk mixture. Mix well. Fold in egg white mixture.

Line a greased 15-in. x 10-in. x 1-in. baking pan with waxed paper; grease the paper. Spread batter evenly into pan. Bake at 375° for 15 minutes or until cake springs back when lightly touched. Cool for 5 minutes. Invert cake onto a kitchen towel dusted with confectioners' sugar. Gently peel off waxed paper. Roll up cake in the towel jelly-roll style, starting with a short side. Cool on a wire rack. Slice six large strawberries in half; set aside for garnish. Thinly slice remaining berries; set aside. In a mixing bowl, beat cream until soft peaks form. Gradually add sugar and vanilla, beating until stiff peaks form.

Unroll cake; spread with filling to within 1/2 in. of edges. Top with sliced berries. Roll up again. Place seam side down on serving platter. Chill until serving. Dust with confectioners' sugar. Garnish with reserved strawberries. Refrigerate leftovers. **Yield:** 12 servings.

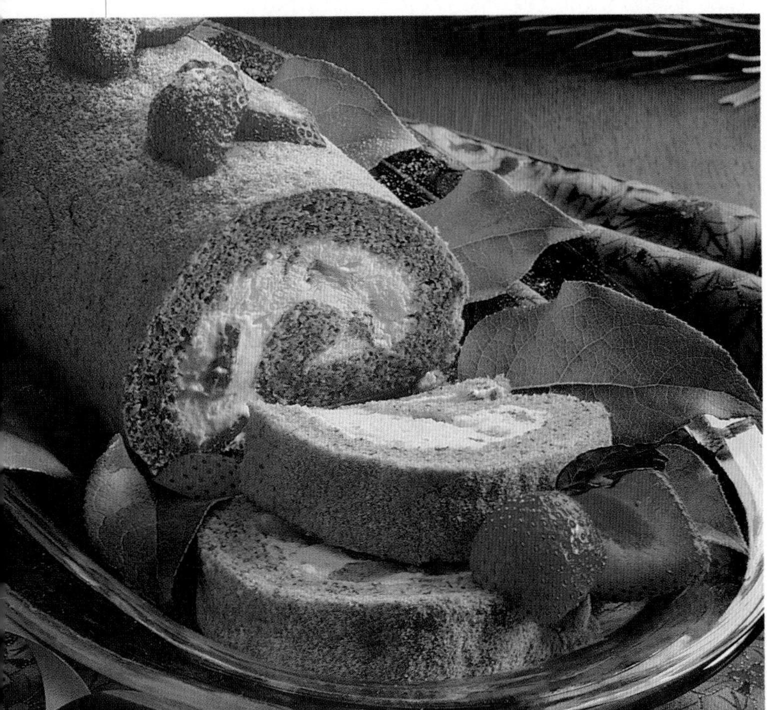

Poppy Seed Strawberry Pie

(Pictured on page 116)

The combination of flavors in this pretty dessert won me over the first time I tasted it. —Kris Sackett, Eau Claire, Wisconsin

- **1-1/3 cups all-purpose flour**
- **1 tablespoon poppy seeds**
- **1/4 teaspoon salt**
- **1/2 cup shortening**
- **3 tablespoons cold water**

FILLING:

- **2 pints strawberries, *divided***
- **2 cups whipped topping**
- **2 tablespoons honey**
- **1/4 cup slivered almonds, toasted, optional**

In a bowl, combine flour, poppy seeds and salt; cut in shortening until crumbly. Gradually add water, tossing with a fork until dough forms a ball. Roll out pastry to fit a 9-in. pie plate. Transfer pastry to plate; flute edges. Line unpricked pastry with a double thickness of heavy-duty foil. Bake at 450° for 8 minutes. Remove foil; bake 5 minutes longer. Cool on a wire rack.

Slice 1 pint of strawberries; fold into whipped topping. Spoon into pie shell. Cut remaining berries in half; arrange over top. Drizzle with honey. Sprinkle with almonds if desired. Refrigerate for at least 1 hour. **Yield:** 6-8 servings.

Apricot Hazelnut Torte

(Pictured on page 116)

Husband Gerry and I, married 36 years, love it when our children and grandchildren visit. One cake that gets "oohs" and "aahs" from the family every time is this luscious torte. It's as light as a feather and tastes heavenly. —Enid Stoehr, Emsdale, Ontario

1 cup ground hazelnuts
3/4 cup all-purpose flour
2 teaspoons baking powder
1/2 teaspoon salt
4 eggs, *separated*
2 tablespoons water
1 teaspoon vanilla extract
1 cup sugar, *divided*
2 cups whipping cream
1/4 cup confectioners' sugar
2/3 cup pureed canned apricots
1/2 cup apricot jam, warmed
Whipped cream, sliced apricots and whole *or* chopped hazelnuts, optional

In a bowl, combine hazelnuts, flour, baking powder and salt; set aside. In a mixing bowl, beat the egg yolks, water and vanilla until lemon-colored. Gradually add 3/4 cup sugar; set aside. In another mixing bowl, beat egg whites until soft peaks form. Add remaining sugar, 1 tablespoon at a time, beating until stiff peaks form. Fold a fourth of the dry ingredients into egg yolk mixture. Repeat three times. Fold in egg white mixture.

Line two greased 9-in. round baking pans with waxed paper; grease the paper. Spread batter evenly into pans. Bake at 350° for 20-25 minutes or until cake springs back when lightly touched. Cool for 10 minutes before removing from pans to wire racks to cool completely.

In a mixing bowl, beat cream and confectioners' sugar until stiff peaks form. Fold in apricots. Split each cake into two layers. Spread filling between layers and over sides of torte. Spread jam over top. Garnish with whipped cream, apricots and hazelnuts if desired. Store in the refrigerator. **Yield:** 12-14 servings.

Toffee-Mocha Cream Torte

(Pictured above right)

When you really want to impress someone, this scrumptious torte is just the thing to make! Instant coffee granules give the moist chocolate cake a mild mocha flavor...while the fluffy whipped cream layers, blended with brown sugar and crunchy toffee bits, are deliciously rich. —*Lynn Rogers*
Richfield, North Carolina

1 cup butter *or* margarine, softened
2 cups sugar
2 eggs
1-1/2 teaspoons vanilla extract
2-2/3 cups all-purpose flour
3/4 cup baking cocoa
2 teaspoons baking soda
1/4 teaspoon salt
1 cup buttermilk
2 teaspoons instant coffee granules
1 cup boiling water

TOPPING:
1/2 teaspoon instant coffee granules
1 teaspoon hot water
2 cups whipping cream
3 tablespoons light brown sugar
6 Heath candy bars (1.4 ounces *each*), crushed, *divided*

In a mixing bowl, cream butter and sugar. Beat in eggs and vanilla. Combine flour, cocoa, baking soda and salt; add to creamed mixture alternately with buttermilk. Dissolve coffee in water; add to batter. Beat for 2 minutes. Pour into three greased and floured 9-in. round baking pans. Bake at 350° for 16-20 minutes or until a toothpick inserted near center comes out clean. Cool 10 minutes before removing from pans to wire racks to cool completely.

For topping, dissolve coffee in water in a mixing bowl; cool. Add cream and brown sugar. Beat until stiff peaks form. Place bottom cake layer on a serving plate; top with 1-1/3 cups of topping. Sprinkle with 1/2 cup of crushed candy bars. Repeat layers twice. Store in the refrigerator. **Yield:** 12-14 servings.

Special Rhubarb Cake

(Pictured above)

The women at church made this for my 84th birthday. A rich vanilla sauce is served over the cake.
—Biena Schlabach, Millersburg, Ohio

2 tablespoons butter (no substitutes), softened
1 cup sugar
1 egg
2 cups all-purpose flour
1 teaspoon baking powder
1/2 teaspoon baking soda
1/2 teaspoon salt
1 cup buttermilk
2 cups chopped fresh *or* frozen rhubarb, thawed

STREUSEL TOPPING:
1/4 cup all-purpose flour
1/4 cup sugar
2 tablespoons butter, melted

VANILLA SAUCE:
1/2 cup butter
3/4 cup sugar
1/2 cup evaporated milk
1 teaspoon vanilla extract

In a mixing bowl, cream butter and sugar. Beat in egg. Combine flour, baking powder, baking soda and salt; add to creamed mixture alternately with buttermilk, beating just until moistened. Fold in the rhubarb. Pour into greased 9-in. square baking dish. Combine topping ingredients; sprinkle over batter. Bake at 350° for 40-45 minutes or until a toothpick comes out clean. Cool on a wire rack.

For sauce, melt butter in a saucepan. Add sugar and milk. Bring to a boil; cook and stir for 2-3 minutes or until thickened. Remove from the heat; stir in vanilla. Serve with cake. **Yield:** 9 servings (1-1/4 cups sauce).

Chocolate Chip Pound Cake

(Pictured on front cover)

My mom has been making this cake for years. Dotted with chips and topped with a chocolate glaze, it is absolutely divine. —Michele Strunks, Brookville, Ohio

1 cup butter (no substitutes), softened
2 cups sugar
4 eggs
1 teaspoon vanilla extract
4 cups all-purpose flour
4 teaspoons baking powder
1 teaspoon baking soda
2 cups (16 ounces) sour cream
2 cups (12 ounces) semisweet chocolate chips

GLAZE:
1/4 cup semisweet chocolate chips
2 tablespoons butter
1-1/4 cups confectioners' sugar
3 tablespoons milk
1/2 teaspoon vanilla extract

In a mixing bowl, cream butter and sugar. Add the eggs, one at a time, beating well after each addition. Beat in vanilla. Combine the flour, baking powder and baking soda; add to creamed mixture alternately with sour cream. Fold in chocolate chips. Pour into a greased and floured 10-in. fluted tube pan. Bake at 350° for 60-65 minutes or until a toothpick inserted near the center comes out clean. Cool for 10 minutes before removing from pan to a wire rack to cool completely.

For glaze, in a saucepan over low heat, melt chocolate chips and butter. Remove from the heat; whisk in confectioners' sugar, milk and vanilla until smooth. Working quickly, drizzle over cooled cake. **Yield:** 12-14 servings.

Coconut Pecan Cake

This deliciously different bundt cake won "Best of Show" when I entered it in the Laramie County Fair.
—Virginia Price, Cheyenne, Wyoming

4 eggs
3 cups sugar, *divided*
1 cup vegetable oil

3 teaspoons coconut extract, *divided*
3 cups all-purpose flour
1/2 teaspoon baking powder
1/2 teaspoon salt
1 cup buttermilk
1 cup flaked coconut
1 cup chopped pecans
1/2 cup water
2 tablespoons butter *or* margarine
Confectioners' sugar, optional

In a mixing bowl, combine eggs, 2 cups sugar, oil and 2 teaspoons extract; mix well. Combine flour, baking powder and salt; add to egg mixture alternately with buttermilk just until moistened. Stir in coconut and pecans. Spoon into a greased 10-in. fluted tube pan.

Bake at 350° for 60-70 minutes or until a toothpick inserted near the center comes out clean. Meanwhile, in a saucepan, combine the water, butter and remaining sugar. Bring to a boil; cook for 5 minutes. Remove from the heat; add remaining extract. Slowly pour hot syrup over hot cake. Cool in pan for 4 hours before removing to a serving plate. Dust with confectioners' sugar if desired. **Yield:** 10-12 servings.

Apple Cake

My husband and I are retired, so we no longer have an orchard, but we still love apples. This cake recipe is a keeper! —Leona Luecking, West Burlington, Iowa

1/4 cup butter (no substitutes), softened
1 cup sugar
1 egg
1 teaspoon vanilla extract
1 cup all-purpose flour
1 teaspoon baking soda
1/2 teaspoon ground cinnamon
1/4 teaspoon salt
1/4 teaspoon ground nutmeg
2 medium tart apples, peeled and grated
1/2 cup chopped walnuts

BUTTER SAUCE:
1/2 cup butter
1/2 cup sugar
1/2 packed brown sugar
1/2 cup half-and-half cream

In a mixing bowl, cream butter and sugar. Beat in egg and vanilla. Combine the flour, baking soda, cinnamon, salt and nutmeg; gradually add to the creamed mixture. Stir in apples and walnuts. Pour into a greased 8-in. square baking dish. Bake at 350° for 40-45 minutes or until a toothpick inserted near the center comes out clean.

Meanwhile, in a saucepan, melt butter. Stir in sugars and cream. Bring to a boil over medium heat, stirring constantly. Reduce heat. Simmer, uncovered, for 15 minutes, stirring occasionally. Serve over warm cake. **Yield:** 9 servings.

Cream Cheese Sheet Cake

(Pictured below)

This tender sheet cake with its fudgy chocolate glaze is a real crowd-pleaser. It's popular at potlucks and parties. —Gaye Mann, Washington, North Carolina

1 cup plus 2 tablespoons butter *or* margarine, softened
2 packages (3 ounces *each*) cream cheese, softened
2-1/4 cups sugar
6 eggs
3/4 teaspoon vanilla extract
2-1/4 cups cake flour

FROSTING:
1 cup sugar
1/3 cup evaporated milk
1/2 cup butter *or* margarine
1/2 cup semisweet chocolate chips

In a mixing bowl, cream butter, cheese and sugar. Add eggs, one at a time, beating well after each. Beat in vanilla. Add flour; mix well. Pour into a greased 15-in. x 10-in. x 1-in. baking pan. Bake at 325° for 30-35 minutes or until a toothpick inserted near the center comes out clean. Cool completely.

For frosting, combine sugar and milk in a saucepan; bring to a boil over medium heat. Cover and cook for 3 minutes (do not stir). Stir in butter and chocolate chips until melted. Cool slightly. Stir; spread over cake. **Yield:** 24-30 servings.

Praline Ice Cream Cake

(Pictured above)

Melted ice cream is a key ingredient in this delectable golden cake. It's been a family favorite for years—we love the pecan praline flavor. It's also a joy to serve to company, since it's not tricky to fix but always wins raves! —Joan Hallford, North Richland Hills, Texas

1 cup packed brown sugar
1/2 cup sour cream
2 tablespoons plus 1/2 cup butter *or* margarine, *divided*
2 teaspoons cornstarch
1 teaspoon vanilla extract, *divided*
2 cups vanilla ice cream, softened
2 eggs
1-1/2 cups all-purpose flour
1 cup graham cracker crumbs (about 16 squares)
2/3 cup sugar
2-1/2 teaspoons baking powder
1/2 teaspoon salt
1/2 cup chopped pecans, toasted
Whipped cream, optional

In a heavy saucepan, combine the brown sugar, sour cream, 2 tablespoons butter and cornstarch. Cook and stir over medium heat until mixture comes to a boil. Remove from the heat. Stir in 1/2 teaspoon of vanilla; set aside. Melt the remaining butter; place in a mixing bowl. Add ice cream; stir to blend. Add eggs, one at a time, beating well after each; stir in remaining vanilla.

Combine the flour, cracker crumbs, sugar, baking powder and salt; gradually add to ice cream mixture until combined. Pour into a greased 13-in. x 9-in. x 2-in. baking pan. Drizzle with half of the praline sauce. Bake at 350° for 25-30 minutes or until a toothpick inserted near the center comes out clean. Cool on a wire rack. Add pecans to remaining sauce; spoon over warm cake (sauce will not cover entire cake top). Cool in pan. Serve with whipped cream if desired. **Yield:** 15 servings.

Lemon Meringue Cake

(Pictured on page 116)

This cake tastes just like lemon meringue pie! Fresh lemon flavor shines through in the custard filling between the layers, and the light meringue frosting adds a fancy finish. It's not only a deliciously different dessert, but it's also a conversation piece! —Julie Courie, Macomb, Michigan

1 package (18-1/4 ounces) lemon *or* yellow cake mix
3 eggs
1 cup water
1/3 cup vegetable oil

FILLING:

1 cup sugar
3 tablespoons cornstarch
1/4 teaspoon salt
1/2 cup water
1/4 cup lemon juice
4 egg yolks, beaten
4 teaspoons butter *or* margarine
1 teaspoon grated lemon peel

MERINGUE:

4 egg whites
1/4 teaspoon cream of tartar
3/4 cup sugar

In a mixing bowl, combine cake mix, eggs, water and oil. Beat on low until moistened. Beat on high for 2 minutes or until blended. Pour into two greased and floured 9-in. round baking pans. Bake at 350° for 25-30 minutes or until a toothpick comes out clean. Cool for 10 minutes; remove from pans to wire racks.

For filling, combine sugar, cornstarch and salt in a saucepan. Stir in water and juice until smooth. Bring to a boil over medium heat; cook and stir 1-2 minutes or until thickened. Remove from heat. Stir a small amount of hot filling into egg yolks; return all to pan, stirring constantly. Bring to a gentle boil; cook and stir for 2 minutes. Remove from heat; stir in butter and lemon peel. Cool completely.

For meringue, in a mixing bowl, beat egg whites and cream of tartar until foamy. Gradually beat in sugar on high until stiff peaks form. To assemble, split each cake into two layers. Place bottom layer on an ovenproof serving plate; spread with a third of the filling. Repeat layers twice. Top with fourth cake layer. Spread meringue over top and sides. Bake at 350° for 10-15 minutes or until meringue is lightly browned. Serve or refrigerate. **Yield:** 12-14 servings.

Raspberry Walnut Torte

(Pictured on page 116)

I often serve this impressive cake for dinner parties or whenever a special dessert is called for. It's delicious and so pretty. —*Bonnie Malloy, Norwood, Pennsylvania*

1-1/2 cups whipping cream
3 eggs
1-1/2 cups sugar
3 teaspoons vanilla extract
1-3/4 cups all-purpose flour
1 cup ground walnuts, toasted
2 teaspoons baking powder
1/2 teaspoon salt
FROSTING:
1-1/2 cups whipping cream
1 package (8 ounces) cream cheese, softened
1 cup sugar
1/8 teaspoon salt
1 teaspoon vanilla extract
1 jar (12 ounces) raspberry preserves

In a small mixing bowl, beat cream until stiff peaks form; set aside. In a large mixing bowl, beat eggs, sugar and vanilla until thick and lemon-colored. Combine flour, walnuts, baking powder and salt; fold into egg mixture alternately with whipped cream. Pour into two greased and floured 9-in. round baking pans. Bake at 350° for 25-30 minutes or until a toothpick comes out clean. Cool for 10 minutes before removing from pans to wire racks to cool completely.

In a small mixing bowl, beat cream until stiff peaks form; set aside. In a large mixing bowl, beat cream cheese, sugar and salt until fluffy. Add vanilla; mix well. Fold in whipped cream. Split each cake into two layers. Place bottom layer on serving plate; spread with about 1/2 cup frosting. Top with second cake layer; spread with half of the raspberry preserves. Repeat layers. Frost sides of cake with frosting.

Cut a small hole in the corner of a pastry or plastic bag; insert ribbon tip No. 47. Fill bag with remaining frosting; pipe a lattice design on top of cake. Using star tip No. 32, pipe stars around top and bottom edges of cake. Store in the refrigerator. **Yield:** 16 servings.

Editor's Note: A coupler ring will allow you to easily change tips for different designs.

'I Wish I Had That Recipe...'

"THE lemon pie served at the Country Table Restaurant in Mt. Joy, Pennsylvania makes my taste buds tingle!" says Barbara Hoffner of New Holland. "I'd be so grateful if *Taste of Home* could get the recipe for this creamy dessert."

Roe and Tom Daly, owners of the popular Lancaster County dining spot, were flattered at the request. "We recently bought the restaurant from Reba and John Buckwalter—I was the bookkeeper," said Roe. "They told us this rich-tasting pie has been served at the Country Table for nearly 20 years. We sell out every time it's on the menu. Customers comment that it's not too tart and not too sweet—just perfect!"

Located at 740 East Main St., the Country Table Restaurant serves buffet, platter and family-style meals from 6 a.m. to 8 p.m. Monday through Thursday, until 9 p.m. Friday and Saturday, and is closed Sunday. There's also a bakery, deli and gift shop. For reservations, call 1-717/653-4745.

Luscious Lemon Pie

1 cup sugar
6 tablespoons cornstarch
1 cup milk
6 egg yolks, lightly beaten
1/4 cup butter *or* margarine
2 tablespoons grated lemon peel
1/2 cup lemon juice
1/2 cup sour cream
1 cup whipping cream, whipped
1 pastry shell (9 inches), baked

In a saucepan, combine the sugar and cornstarch. Stir in milk until smooth. Cook and stir over medium heat until thickened and bubbly. Reduce heat; cook and stir 2 minutes more.

Remove from the heat. Stir a small amount of hot filling into egg yolks; return all to the pan. Bring to a gentle boil; cook and stir for 2 minutes. Remove from heat; stir in butter and lemon peel. Gently stir in juice. Cool to room temperature. Fold in sour cream and whipped cream. Pour into pastry shell. Chill at least 1 hour before cutting. **Yield:** 6-8 servings.

Upside-Down German Chocolate Cake

(Pictured below)

This simple recipe yields a delectable German chocolate cake that folks will "flip over"! The tempting coconut and pecan frosting bakes under the batter and ends up on top when you turn the cake out of the pan.
—Mrs. Harold Sanders, Glouster, Ohio

1/2 cup packed brown sugar
1/4 cup butter *or* margarine
2/3 cup pecan halves
2/3 cup flaked coconut
1/4 cup evaporated milk
CAKE:
1/3 cup butter *or* margarine, softened
1 cup sugar
1 package (4 ounces) German sweet chocolate, melted
2 eggs
1 teaspoon vanilla extract
1-1/2 cups all-purpose flour
1/2 teaspoon baking soda
1/2 teaspoon baking powder
1/2 teaspoon salt
3/4 cup buttermilk
Whipped topping, optional

In a saucepan over low heat, cook and stir brown sugar and butter until sugar is dissolved and butter is melted. Spread into a greased 9-in. square baking pan. Sprinkle with pecans and coconut. Drizzle with evaporated milk; set aside.

In a mixing bowl, cream butter and sugar. Beat in chocolate, eggs and vanilla. Combine dry ingredients; add to creamed mixture alternately with buttermilk. Pour over topping in pan. Bake at 350° for 40-45 minutes or until a toothpick inserted near center comes out clean. Cool 5 minutes before inverting onto a serving plate. Serve with whipped topping if desired. **Yield:** 9 servings.

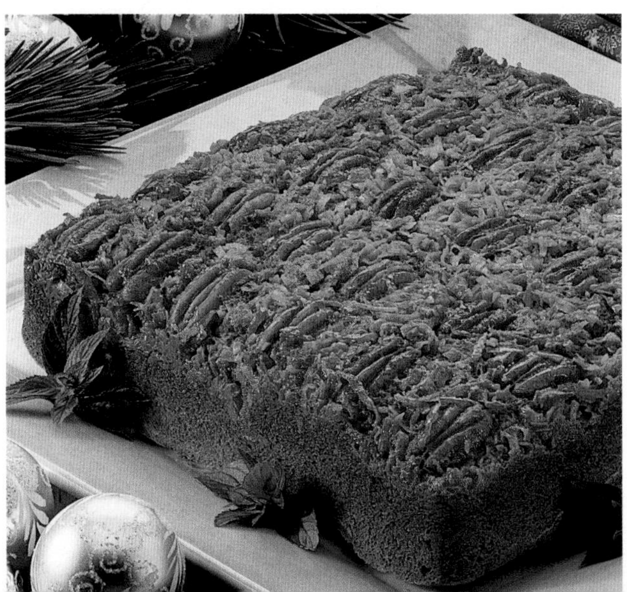

Cranberry Cake

This traditional pudding-like dessert is my mother's recipe. It's always welcomed on holidays. The moist, colorful cake is served with a rich, buttery sauce.
—Marion Lowery, Medford, Oregon

3 tablespoons butter (no substitutes), softened
1 cup sugar
1 egg
2 cups all-purpose flour
2 teaspoons baking powder
1 teaspoon ground nutmeg
1 cup milk
2 cups fresh *or* frozen cranberries, thawed
2 tablespoons grated orange *or* lemon peel
CREAM SAUCE:
1-1/3 cups sugar
1 cup whipping cream
2/3 cup butter

In a mixing bowl, cream butter and sugar. Beat in egg. Combine the flour, baking powder and nutmeg; add to the creamed mixture alternately with milk. Stir in cranberries and orange peel. Pour into a greased 11-in. x 7-in. x 2-in. baking dish. Bake at 350° for 35-40 minutes or until a toothpick inserted near the center comes out clean. Meanwhile, in a saucepan, combine sauce ingredients. Cook and stir over medium heat until heated through. Cut warm cake into squares; serve with cream sauce. **Yield:** 8-10 servings.

Chocolate Cherry Cake

This made-from-a-mix dessert tastes like you started from scratch. Cherry and almond flavors blend beautifully with the chocolate in this moist, tender cake.
—Charlene Griffin, Minocqua, Wisconsin

1 package (18-1/4 ounces) chocolate fudge cake mix
2 eggs
1 teaspoon almond extract
1 can (21 ounces) cherry pie filling
1 cup sugar
1/3 cup milk
1/3 cup butter *or* margarine
1 cup (6 ounces) semisweet chocolate chips

In a bowl, combine the cake mix, eggs and extract. Add pie filling; mix well. Spread into a greased 15-in. x 10-in. x 1-in. baking pan. Bake at 350° for 18-22 minutes or until a toothpick inserted near the center comes out clean.

Meanwhile, in a saucepan, combine sugar, milk and butter. Cook and stir until sugar is dissolved and butter is melted. Remove from the heat; stir in chocolate chips until melted. Pour over warm cake; spread evenly. Cool completely before cutting. Store in the refrigerator. **Yield:** 32 servings.

Buttermilk Chocolate Cake

My 12 children, 26 grandchildren and five great-grandchildren always request this cake for their birthdays. People call it "Imogene's Cake"!
—Imogene Koepnick, Delavan, Wisconsin

1 cup butter *or* margarine
1 cup water
2 tablespoons baking cocoa
2 cups all-purpose flour
2 cups sugar
1 teaspoon baking powder
1 teaspoon baking soda
1/2 teaspoon salt
1/2 cup buttermilk
1 teaspoon vanilla extract
2 eggs

FROSTING:

3 tablespoons butter *or* margarine
2 tablespoons baking cocoa
3 cups confectioners' sugar
1 teaspoon vanilla extract
1/8 teaspoon salt
3 to 4 tablespoons milk *or* whipping cream

In a saucepan, bring butter, water and cocoa to a boil. In a mixing bowl, combine the flour, sugar, baking powder, baking soda and salt. Add cocoa mixture; mix well. Combine buttermilk and vanilla; add to batter and mix well. Beat in eggs. Pour into a greased 13-in. x 9-in. x 2-in. baking pan. Bake at 350° for 23-27 minutes or until a toothpick comes out clean. Cool on a wire rack.

In a saucepan over medium heat, cook and stir butter and cocoa until smooth. Remove from the heat. In a small mixing bowl, combine confectioners' sugar, vanilla and salt. Add cocoa mixture and enough milk until frosting reaches desired consistency. Frost cake. **Yield:** 12-16 servings.

Pumpkin Pound Cake

(Pictured above right)

I enjoy baking from scratch and sharing my treats with others. This recipe for nicely spiced pumpkin pound cake is one I've come to rely on. It's impossible to resist a slice topped with the sweet walnut sauce.
—Jean Volk, Jacksonville, Florida

1-1/2 cups butter *or* margarine, softened
2-3/4 cups sugar
6 eggs
1 teaspoon vanilla extract
3 cups all-purpose flour
3/4 teaspoon ground cinnamon
1/2 teaspoon baking powder
1/2 teaspoon salt
1/2 teaspoon ground ginger
1/4 teaspoon ground cloves
1 cup cooked *or* canned pumpkin

WALNUT SAUCE:

1 cup packed brown sugar
1/2 cup whipping cream
1/4 cup corn syrup
2 tablespoons butter *or* margarine
1/2 cup chopped walnuts
1/2 teaspoon vanilla extract

In a mixing bowl, cream butter and sugar. Add eggs, one at a time, beating well after each addition. Stir in vanilla. Combine the dry ingredients; add to creamed mixture alternately with pumpkin, beating just until combined. Pour into two greased and floured 9-in. x 5-in. x 3-in. loaf pans.

Bake at 350° for 65-70 minutes or until a toothpick inserted near the center comes out clean. Cool for 10 minutes before removing from pans to wire racks to cool completely. For sauce, combine brown sugar, cream, corn syrup and butter in a saucepan. Bring to a boil over medium heat, stirring constantly. Reduce heat; cook and stir 5 minutes longer. Remove from the heat; stir in walnuts and vanilla. Serve warm over the cake. **Yield:** 16 servings (1-2/3 cups sauce).

Gingerbread with Lemon Sauce

(Pictured above)

I asked my mother-in-law for this recipe once I learned that this fluffy spice cake topped with tangy lemon sauce is my husband's favorite. It never fails to make us both smile. —Kristen Oak, Pocatello, Idaho

1 cup shortening
1 cup sugar
1 cup light molasses
2 eggs
3 cups all-purpose flour
1-1/2 teaspoons salt
1-1/2 teaspoons baking soda
1 teaspoon ground ginger
1 teaspoon ground cinnamon
1 cup hot water

LEMON SAUCE:

1/2 cup sugar
2 teaspoons cornstarch
Dash salt
Dash nutmeg
1 cup water
2 egg yolks, beaten
2 tablespoons butter *or* margarine
2 tablespoons lemon juice
1/2 teaspoon grated lemon peel

In a mixing bowl, combine the first four ingredients; mix well. Combine the dry ingredients; add to molasses mixture alternately with hot water. Pour into a greased 13-in. x 9-in. x 2-in. baking pan. Bake at 350° for 35-40 minutes or until a toothpick inserted near the center comes out clean. Cool on a wire rack.

Meanwhile, in a saucepan, combine the first five sauce ingredients until smooth. Bring to a boil; cook and stir for 1-2 minutes or until thickened. Remove from the heat. Stir a small amount of hot mixture into egg yolks. Return all to pan, stirring constantly. Cook and stir for 2 minutes or until a thermometer reads 160°. Remove from the heat; stir in butter, lemon juice and peel. Serve with warm cake. Refrigerate leftover sauce. **Yield:** 16-20 servings.

Daisy's Fruitcake

To an apple cake recipe, I added pecans and candied fruits. —Daisy Corene McHorse, San Saba, Texas

3 cups chopped peeled tart apples (about 2 large)
2 cups sugar
1/2 cup apple juice
3 eggs
3/4 cup vegetable oil
1 teaspoon vanilla extract
3 cups all-purpose flour
2 teaspoons apple pie spice
1 teaspoon baking soda
1 teaspoon salt
2 cups coarsely chopped pecans
1/2 pound candied red cherries, halved
1/2 pound candied green cherries, halved
1/2 pound diced candied pineapple

Line three 8-in. x 4-in. x 2-in. loaf pans with waxed paper; grease the paper and set aside. In a large mixing bowl, combine apples, sugar and apple juice; let stand for 15 minutes. In a bowl, combine the eggs, oil and vanilla. Add to apple mixture; mix well. Combine the flour, apple pie spice, baking soda and salt; add to apple mixture and mix well. Fold in pecans, cherries and pineapple. Pour into prepared pans.

Bake at 350° for 55-65 minutes or until a toothpick inserted near center comes out clean. Cool for 10 minutes before removing from pans to wire racks. Remove waxed paper. Cool completely. **Yield:** 3 loaves.

Editor's Note: Fruitcakes may be baked in eight 5-3/4-in. x 3-in. x 2-in. loaf pans for 40-45 minutes.

Cranberry Torte

Besides being eye-catching and delicious, this pretty pink treat is conveniently made ahead and frozen. —Pat Waymire, Yellow Springs, Ohio

1-1/4 cups graham cracker crumbs (about 20 squares)
1/4 cup finely chopped pecans
1-1/4 cups sugar, *divided*

6 tablespoons butter *or* margarine, melted
1-1/2 cups ground fresh *or* frozen cranberries
1 tablespoon orange juice concentrate
1 teaspoon vanilla extract
1/8 teaspoon salt
1 cup whipping cream

TOPPING:

1/2 cup sugar
1 tablespoon cornstarch
3/4 cup fresh *or* frozen cranberries
2/3 cup water

In a bowl, combine cracker crumbs, pecans, 1/4 cup sugar and butter. Press onto bottom and 1 in. up sides of a 9-in. springform pan. Bake at 375° for 8-10 minutes or until lightly browned. In a bowl, combine cranberries, orange juice concentrate, vanilla, salt and remaining sugar. In a mixing bowl, beat cream until soft peaks form. Fold into cranberry mixture. Pour into crust. Freeze until firm.

For topping, combine sugar and cornstarch in a saucepan. Stir in cranberries and water until blended. Bring to a boil. Reduce heat; cook and stir until berries pop and mixture is thickened, about 5 minutes; cool. Let torte stand at room temperature for 10 minutes before slicing. Serve with topping. **Yield:** 12-14 servings.

Butterscotch Apple Cake

My family often requests this old-fashioned cake when we get together. It's easy to make and yet tastes so incredibly good. —*Beth Struble, Bryan, Ohio*

3 eggs
1-1/4 cups vegetable oil
1 teaspoon vanilla extract
2-1/2 cups all-purpose flour
2 cups sugar
2 teaspoons baking powder
1 teaspoon salt
1 teaspoon baking soda
1 teaspoon ground cinnamon
4 medium tart apples, peeled and chopped (4 cups)
1 cup chopped pecans
1 package (11 ounces) butterscotch chips

In a mixing bowl, beat the eggs, oil and vanilla. Combine the flour, sugar, baking powder, salt, baking soda and cinnamon; add to egg mixture and mix well. Stir in the apples and pecans. Pour into an ungreased 13-in. x 9-in. x 2-in. baking dish. Sprinkle with butterscotch chips. Bake at 325° for 40-45 minutes or until a toothpick inserted near the center comes out clean. Cool on a wire rack. **Yield:** 12-15 servings.

Nutty Fudge Torte

(Pictured below)

This dessert is so yummy and beautiful, you'd never guess it's easy to make. It never fails to draw compliments. —*Kay Berg, Lopez Island, Washington*

1/2 cup semisweet chocolate chips
1/3 cup sweetened condensed milk
1 package (18-1/4 ounces) devil's food cake mix
1/3 cup vegetable oil
1 teaspoon ground cinnamon
1 can (15 ounces) sliced pears, drained
2 eggs
1/3 cup chopped pecans, toasted
2 teaspoons water
1/4 cup hot caramel ice cream topping, warmed
1/2 teaspoon milk
Whipped cream *or* vanilla ice cream and additional toasted pecans, optional

In a microwave, melt chocolate chips with condensed milk; stir until smooth. Set aside. In a mixing bowl, combine cake mix, oil and cinnamon until crumbly. Set aside 1/2 cup for topping. In a blender or food processor, process pears until smooth; add to remaining cake mixture with eggs. Beat on medium speed for 2 minutes. Pour into a greased 9-in. springform pan. Drop melted chocolate by tablespoonfuls over batter.

Combine pecans, water and reserved cake mixture; crumble over chocolate. Bake at 350° for 45-50 minutes or until a toothpick comes out clean. Cool for 10 minutes. Carefully run a knife around sides of pan to loosen. Cool completely on a wire rack. Remove sides of pan. Combine caramel topping and milk until smooth; drizzle on serving plates. Top with a slice of torte. If desired, serve with whipped cream or ice cream and sprinkle with pecans. **Yield:** 12-14 servings.

Just Desserts

Turn here for a great selection of desserts—from crisps to cheesecakes.

CAPTIVATING CONFECTIONS. Clockwise from upper left: Lemon Ice Cream (p. 142), Coconut Peach Dessert (p. 143), Butterscotch Delight (p. 145), Mint Chip Ice Cream (p. 142), Rich Chocolate Pudding (p. 141) and Pumpkin Cheesecake with Sour Cream Topping (p. 146).

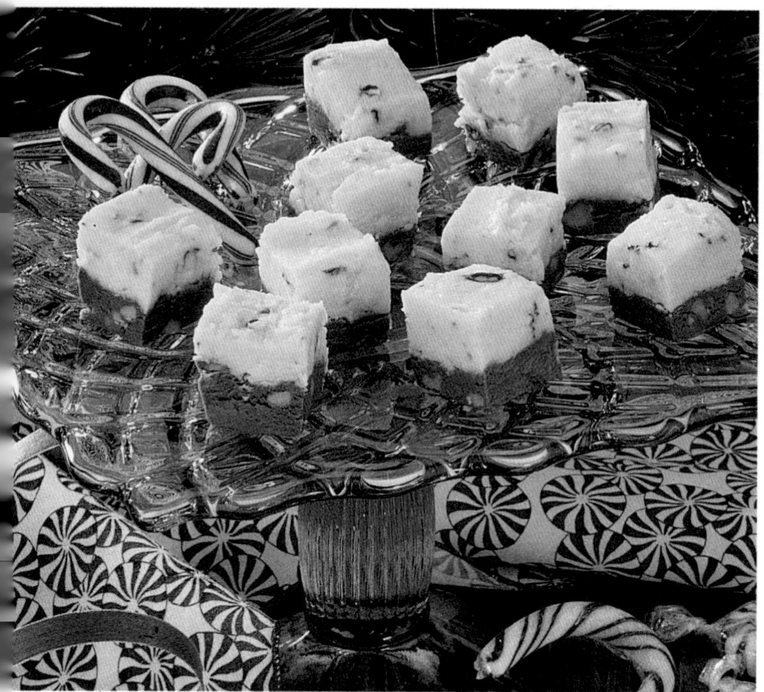

Peppermint Fudge

(Pictured above)

Three great flavors—nuts, chocolate and peppermint—combine in a delightful manner in this scrumptious fudge. The two distinct layers are eye-catching.
—Connie Denmark, Macon, Illinois

1-1/2 teaspoons butter (no substitutes), softened
2 ounces cream cheese, softened
2 cups confectioners' sugar
3 tablespoons baking cocoa
1/2 teaspoon milk
1/2 teaspoon vanilla extract
1/4 cup chopped nuts
PEPPERMINT LAYER:
2 ounces cream cheese, softened
2 cups confectioners' sugar
1/2 teaspoon milk
1/2 teaspoon peppermint extract
1/4 cup crushed peppermint candy

Line the bottom and sides of an 8-in. x 4-in. x 2-in. loaf pan with foil. Grease foil with 1-1/2 teaspoons butter; set aside. In a small mixing bowl, beat cream cheese. Gradually beat in confectioners' sugar, cocoa, milk and vanilla. Stir in the nuts. Spread into prepared pan. Chill for 1 hour or until firm.

For peppermint layer, beat cream cheese in a small mixing bowl. Gradually beat in confectioners' sugar, milk and extract. Stir in peppermint candy. Spread evenly over chocolate layer. Chill for 1 hour or until firm. Using foil, lift fudge from pan. Gently peel off foil. Cut into squares. **Yield:** 1-1/4 pounds.

Banana Split Ice Cream

This tasty lightened-up ice cream dessert has all the flavors of a banana split. It's a real treat.
—Carol Dale, Greenville, Texas

✓ Uses less fat, sugar or salt. Includes Nutritional Analysis and Diabetic Exchanges.

5 cups fat-free milk, *divided*
1 cup egg substitute
2 cans (14 ounces *each*) fat-free sweetened condensed milk
2 medium ripe bananas, mashed
2 tablespoons lime juice
1 tablespoon vanilla extract
3/4 cup fat-free chocolate ice cream topping
1/2 cup chopped pecans
1/4 cup chopped maraschino cherries

In a heavy saucepan, combine 2-1/2 cups fat-free milk and egg substitute. Cook and stir over low heat until mixture is thick enough to coat a metal spoon and reaches at least 160°, about 10 minutes. Remove from the heat; set pan in ice and stir to cool quickly. Pour into a large bowl; stir in condensed milk and remaining fat-free milk. Cover and refrigerate overnight. Combine bananas, lime juice and vanilla; stir into milk mixture.

Fill ice cream freezer two-thirds full; freeze according to manufacturer's directions. Refrigerate remaining mixture until ready to freeze. Spoon each batch into a large freezer-safe container; gently fold in chocolate topping, pecans and cherries. Store in refrigerator freezer. **Yield:** about 2-1/2 quarts.

Nutritional Analysis: One serving (1/2 cup) equals 193 calories, 3 g fat (0 saturated fat), 4 mg cholesterol, 111 mg sodium, 35 g carbohydrate, 1 g fiber, 8 g protein. **Diabetic Exchanges:** 1-1/2 fruit, 1 milk, 1 fat.

Danish Apple Pizza

Here in Oregon, we are blessed with beautiful tasty apples. This pizza-style dessert is fun and fills the kitchen with a wonderful aroma while it's in the oven.
—Helen White, Eugene, Oregon

2-1/2 cups all-purpose flour
1 teaspoon salt
1 cup shortening
1/2 cup milk
1 egg, *separated*
1 cup crushed cornflakes
6 medium tart apples, peeled and thinly sliced
1 cup sugar
1-1/2 to 2 teaspoons ground cinnamon

Additional sugar, optional
GLAZE:
1/2 cup confectioners' sugar
1/4 teaspoon vanilla extract
2 to 3 teaspoons hot water

In a bowl, combine flour and salt. Cut in shortening until crumbly. Combine milk and egg yolk; mix well. Gradually add to dry ingredients until dough forms a ball. Cover and refrigerate for at least 1 hour. On a lightly floured surface, roll out half of pastry to fit an ungreased 13-in. pizza pan. Sprinkle with cornflakes. Top with apples. Combine sugar and cinnamon; sprinkle over apples. Roll out remaining pastry to fit top of pie. Place over apples; cut slits in top. Seal pastry and flute edges if desired. Brush with beaten egg white. Sprinkle with additional sugar if desired.

Bake at 350° for 40-45 minutes or until golden. For glaze, combine confectioners' sugar, vanilla and enough water to achieve desired consistency. Drizzle over pizza. **Yield:** 12-16 servings.

Strawberry Rhubarb Crunch

There's no tastier way to get all the good nutrition of oats—including B vitamins and iron—than a serving of this sweet, tasty crunch. It doesn't get soggy like some crunches do. —*Frances Poste*
Wall, South Dakota

2 cups all-purpose flour
2 cups packed brown sugar
1 cup cold butter *or* margarine
2 cups quick-cooking oats
6 cups sliced fresh *or* frozen rhubarb, thawed
1 cup sugar
2 tablespoons cornstarch
1 cup water
1 teaspoon vanilla extract
1 package (3 ounces) strawberry gelatin
Vanilla ice cream, optional

In a bowl, combine flour and brown sugar. Cut in butter until crumbly. Stir in the oats. Press half into a greased 13-in. x 9-in. x 2-in. baking dish; top with rhubarb. In a saucepan, combine sugar and cornstarch; stir in water until smooth. Bring to a boil; cook and stir for 2 minutes or until thickened. Remove from the heat; stir in vanilla. Pour over rhubarb. Sprinkle with gelatin powder. Top with remaining crumb mixture.

Bake at 350° for 40-45 minutes or until rhubarb is tender and topping is golden brown. Serve with ice cream if desired. **Yield:** 12-15 servings.

'I Wish I Had That Recipe...'

"EVERY TIME I dine at the Blue Coat Inn in Dover, Delaware, I think about the peach crisp dessert even before I order my meal," says Marie Nemphos from King of Prussia, Delaware.

Marlene Koutoufaris, co-owner of the inn with husband John, gladly shares the recipe.

"Delaware Peach Crisp is one of our most popular desserts. It was created by John, who is a chef, and a friend when we opened the inn in 1967. The inn was named for the uniforms worn by Colonel John Haslet and his troops. They marched from Dover's Green to join General George Washington in the War for Independence in 1776."

At 800 N. State St. in Dover, the Blue Coat Inn serves lunch from 11:30 a.m. and dinner from 4:30 p.m. Tuesday through Saturday. On Sundays, brunch is served from noon to 2 p.m. and dinner from noon to 9 p.m. It's closed Mondays. Phone 1-302/674-1776.

Delaware Peach Crisp

1 can (29 ounces) sliced peaches
1 cup packed brown sugar
2 tablespoons cornstarch
2 tablespoons honey
1/2 teaspoon ground cinnamon
1/4 teaspoon ground nutmeg
1/2 cup lemon juice
1/2 cup raisins
1/2 cup chopped pecans
TOPPING:
1 cup all-purpose flour
1/2 cup sugar
1/2 cup butter *or* margarine, melted
Vanilla ice cream, optional

Drain peaches, reserving the syrup in a saucepan; set peaches aside. Stir brown sugar, cornstarch, honey, cinnamon and nutmeg into the peach syrup until smooth. Bring to a boil; cook and stir for 2 minutes or until thickened. Add lemon juice, raisins, pecans and reserved peaches. Pour into a greased 2-qt. baking dish. For topping, combine flour, sugar and butter. Sprinkle over peach mixture. Bake at 350° for 35 minutes. Serve with ice cream if desired. **Yield:** 6 servings.

Strawberry Banana Dessert

(Pictured below)

Like springtime on a plate, this eye-catching dessert has a bright cheery color and plenty of fruity flavor.
—Margaret Kuntz, Bismarck, North Dakota

✓ Uses less fat, sugar or salt. Includes Nutritional Analysis and Diabetic Exchanges.

3 medium firm bananas, sliced
1 prepared angel food cake (16 ounces), cut into 1-inch cubes
1 pint fresh strawberries, halved
1 package (.6 ounce) sugar-free strawberry gelatin
2 cups boiling water
1-1/2 cups cold water
1 carton (8 ounces) reduced-fat whipped topping, thawed

Layer banana slices and cake cubes in a 13-in. x 9-in. x 2-in. dish coated with nonstick cooking spray. Place strawberries over cake and press down gently. In a bowl, dissolve gelatin in boiling water; stir in cold water. Pour over strawberries. Refrigerate for 3 hours or until set. Frost with whipped topping. **Yield:** 16 servings.

Nutritional Analysis: One serving equals 138 calories, 2 g fat (2 g saturated fat), 0 cholesterol, 168 mg sodium, 27 g carbohydrate, 1 g fiber, 3 g protein. **Diabetic Exchanges:** 1 starch, 1 fruit.

Baklava

The recipe for this traditional Greek strudel uses phyllo dough, which is not difficult to work with. Just have your ingredients ready to go and follow the directions on the package. The results are scrumptious and well worth the effort. *—Judy Losecco*
Buffalo, New York

1-1/2 pounds finely chopped walnuts
1/2 cup sugar
1/2 teaspoon ground cinnamon
1/8 teaspoon ground cloves
2 packages (16 ounces *each*) phyllo dough
1 pound butter (no substitutes), melted, *divided*

SYRUP:
2 cups sugar
2 cups water
1 cup honey
1 tablespoon grated lemon *or* orange peel

In a bowl, combine walnuts, sugar, cinnamon and cloves; set aside. Brush a 15-in. x 10-in. x 1-in. baking pan with some of the butter. Unroll each package of phyllo sheets; trim each stack to fit into pan. Cover dough with plastic wrap and a damp cloth while assembling. Place one sheet of phyllo into pan; brush with butter. Repeat 14 times. Spread with 2 cups walnut mixture. Layer with five sheets of phyllo, brushing with butter between each. Spread with remaining walnut mixture. Top with one sheet of phyllo; brush with butter. Repeat 14 times. Cut into 2-1/2-in. squares; cut each square in half diagonally. Brush remaining butter over top.

Bake at 350° for 40-45 minutes or until golden brown. Meanwhile, in a saucepan, bring the syrup ingredients to a boil. Reduce heat; simmer for 10 minutes. Strain and discard peel; cool to lukewarm. Pour syrup over warm baklava. **Yield:** 4 dozen.

Banana Pudding Crunch

I give a twist to a traditional comfort food by adding a crunchy meringue-nut topping. It's a dressed-up dessert that's so easy to prepare. *—Joanie Ward*
Brownsburg, Indiana

2 cups cold milk
2 packages (3.4 ounces *each*) instant vanilla pudding mix
1/2 cup sour cream
2 medium firm bananas, sliced
1 cup sugar
1 cup chopped pecans

1 egg, beaten

In a bowl, combine milk, pudding mix and sour cream; whisk until mixture begins to thicken, about 1 minute. Fold in bananas. Pour into a 1-1/2-qt. serving bowl. Cover and refrigerate. For topping, combine sugar, pecans and egg; spoon onto a greased 15-in. x 10-in. x 1-in. baking pan. Bake at 350° for 20 minutes or until browned and crunchy. Cool. Using a spatula, loosen pecan mixture from pan and break into small pieces. Sprinkle over pudding just before serving. **Yield:** 6-8 servings.

Tart Lemon Sorbet

On hot summer days, nothing seems to satisfy like the tartness of lemons. This light, refreshing sorbet is one of my favorite ways to use that puckery fruit.
—Susan Garoutte, Georgetown, Texas

3 cups water
1-1/2 cups sugar
1-1/2 cups lemon juice
1 tablespoon grated lemon peel

In a saucepan, bring water and sugar to a boil. Cook and stir until the sugar is dissolved, about 5 minutes. Cool. Add the lemon juice and peel; mix well. Pour into the cylinder of an ice cream freezer; freeze according to manufacturer's directions. Remove from the freezer 10 minutes before serving. **Yield:** about 1 quart.

Caramel Praline Cheesecake

(Pictured above right)

I wowed my wife, Carla, and a group of her friends with this luscious dessert, the finale to a fabulous meal I fixed for the 12 women. I often cater dinners and luncheons at church. *—Mark Jones, Clovis, California*

14 graham cracker squares
1/2 cup chopped pecans, toasted
6 tablespoons butter (no substitutes), melted

FILLING:

4 packages (8 ounces *each*) cream cheese, softened
1-1/2 cups sugar
1/4 cup all-purpose flour
5 eggs
2 cups (16 ounces) sour cream
1/4 cup milk

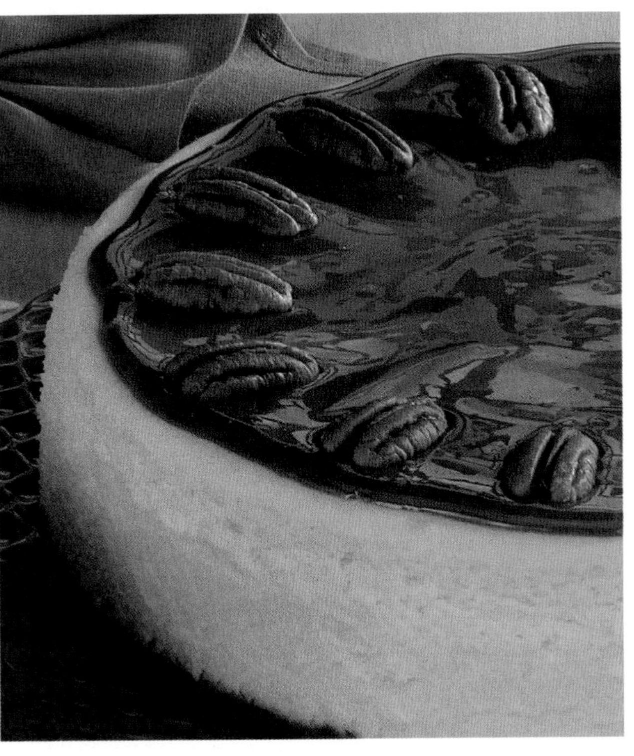

1 tablespoon vanilla extract

TOPPING:

1 cup sugar, *divided*
1 cup whipping cream
1 tablespoon butter (no substitutes)
1 teaspoon vanilla extract
1/2 cup pecan halves, toasted

In a food processor or blender, combine graham crackers and pecans; cover and process until fine and crumbly. Stir in butter. Press onto the bottom of an ungreased 10-in. springform pan. Chill for 30 minutes. In a mixing bowl, beat cream cheese and sugar until smooth. Beat in flour. Add eggs, beating on low speed just until combined. Stir in sour cream, milk and vanilla. Pour into crust. Bake at 325° for 75-80 minutes or until center is almost set. Cool on a wire rack for 10 minutes. Carefully run a knife around edge of pan to loosen; cool for 1-1/2 hours. Chill.

For topping, heat 1/2 cup sugar in a heavy saucepan over medium-low heat, without stirring, until melted and golden brown, about 15 minutes. Reduce heat to low; gradually add cream and remaining sugar (melted sugar will harden). Cook and stir until sugar is completely melted. Continue cooking, without stirring, over medium heat until a candy thermometer reaches 225°. Remove from the heat; stir in butter and vanilla. Cool to room temperature. Spread topping evenly over cheesecake (do not scrape sides of pan). Garnish with pecan halves. Chill overnight. Remove sides of pan. Refrigerate leftovers. **Yield:** 12-14 servings.

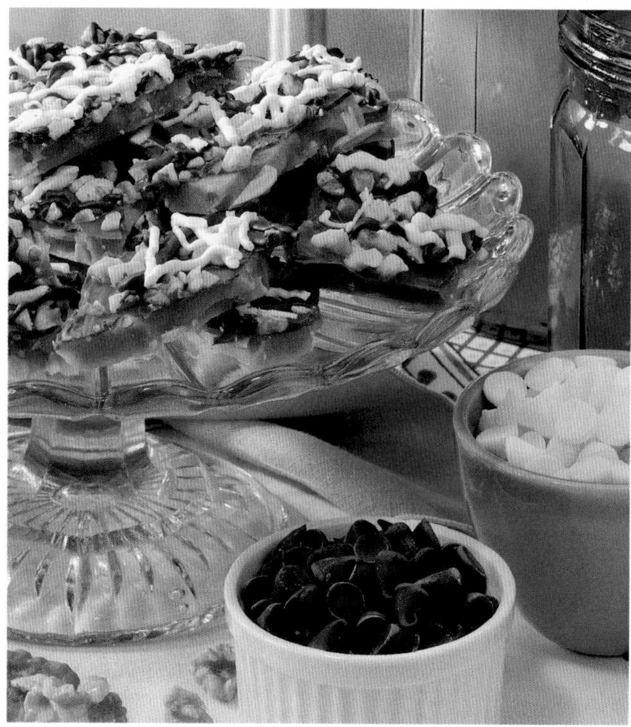

Three-Chip English Toffee

(Pictured above)

With its melt-in-your-mouth texture and scrumptiously rich flavor, this is the ultimate toffee! Drizzled on top are three kinds of melted chips, plus a sprinkling of walnuts. Packaged in colorful tins, these pretty pieces make great gifts. —Lana Petfield, Richmond, Virginia

1/2 teaspoon plus 2 cups butter (no substitutes), *divided*
2 cups sugar
1 cup slivered almonds
1 cup milk chocolate chips
1 cup chopped walnuts
1/2 cup semisweet chocolate chips
1/2 cup vanilla *or* white chips
1-1/2 teaspoons shortening

Butter a 15-in. x 10-in. x 1-in. baking pan with 1/2 teaspoon butter. In a heavy saucepan over medium-low heat, bring sugar and remaining butter to a boil, stirring constantly. Cover and cook for 2-3 minutes.

Uncover; add almonds. Cook and stir with a clean spoon until a candy thermometer reads 300° (hard-crack stage) and mixture is golden brown. Pour into prepared pan (do not scrape sides of saucepan). Surface will be buttery. Cool for 1-2 minutes. Sprinkle with milk chocolate chips. Let stand for 1-2 minutes; spread chocolate over the top. Sprinkle with walnuts; press down gently with the back of a spoon. Chill for 10 minutes.

In a microwave or heavy saucepan, melt semisweet chips; stir until smooth. Drizzle over walnuts. Refrigerate for 10 minutes. Melt vanilla chips and shortening; stir until smooth. Drizzle over walnuts. Cover and refrigerate for 1-2 hours. Break into pieces. **Yield:** about 2-1/2 pounds.

Editor's Note: We recommend that you test your candy thermometer before each use by bringing water to a boil; the thermometer should read 212°. Adjust your recipe temperature up or down based on your test. If toffee separates during cooking, add 1/2 cup hot water and stir vigorously. Bring back up to 300° and proceed as recipe directs.

Pineapple Crisp

This recipe's combination of coconut and pineapple is delightful! —Karen Bourne, Magrath, Alberta

1-1/2 cups flaked coconut
1 cup all-purpose flour
1 cup packed brown sugar
1/2 cup butter *or* margarine, melted
1/8 teaspoon salt

FILLING:

3/4 cup sugar
3 tablespoons cornstarch
1 can (8 ounces) crushed pineapple, undrained
1 tablespoon lemon juice
1 tablespoon butter *or* margarine

In a bowl, combine the coconut, flour, brown sugar, butter and salt. Press 1-1/2 cups into a greased 9-in. square baking pan; set remaining mixture aside. In a saucepan, combine the filling ingredients. Bring to a boil; cook and stir for 2 minutes or until thickened and bubbly. Cool; spread over crust. Sprinkle with reserved coconut mixture. Bake at 350° for 25-30 minutes or until golden brown. Cool on a wire rack. **Yield:** 9 servings.

Strawberry Gelatin Dessert

I love desserts and strawberries, so I try to combine the two whenever possible. This light, fluffy gelatin treat goes over well. —Virginia Myers, Altamont, Illinois

✓ Uses less fat, sugar or salt. Includes Nutritional Analysis and Diabetic Exchanges.

1 cup graham cracker crumbs (about 16 squares)
1 tablespoon sugar
2 tablespoons butter *or* stick margarine, melted
2 cups sliced fresh strawberries

2 tablespoons sugar
1 package (.3 ounce) sugar-free strawberry gelatin
1 cup boiling water
4 cups miniature marshmallows
1/2 cup fat-free milk
1 carton (8 ounces) reduced-fat whipped topping

In a bowl, combine cracker crumbs, sugar and butter. Press into a greased 9-in. square baking dish. Bake at 350° for 10 minutes or until golden brown. Cool on a wire rack. Combine strawberries and sugar in a small bowl; let stand for 20 minutes. In another bowl, dissolve gelatin in water. Drain berries, reserving the juice; add enough water to juice to measure 1 cup. Stir berries and juice mixture into gelatin. Refrigerate until partially set.

Meanwhile, combine marshmallows and milk in a saucepan. Cook and stir over low heat until blended and smooth. Cool to room temperature, about 15 minutes. Fold in whipped topping, then gelatin mixture. Pour into prepared crust. Refrigerate for 4 hours or until firm. **Yield:** 9 servings.

Nutritional Analysis: One serving equals 243 calories, 7 g fat (5 g saturated fat), 7 mg cholesterol, 150 mg sodium, 41 g carbohydrate, 1 g fiber, 2 g protein. **Diabetic Exchanges:** 2 starch, 1 fruit, 1/2 fat.

Pumpkin Cheesecake

My wife and I think this is a perfect ending to a good meal. The cheesecake is smooth and creamy.
—DeWhitt Sizemore, Woodlawn, Virginia

1-1/2 cups graham cracker crumbs (about 24 squares)
1 tablespoon sugar
5 tablespoons butter *or* margarine, melted

FILLING:
3 packages (8 ounces *each*) cream cheese, softened
1 cup sugar
1 teaspoon vanilla extract
3 eggs
1 cup cooked *or* canned pumpkin
1/2 teaspoon ground cinnamon
1/4 teaspoon ground nutmeg
1/4 teaspoon ground allspice
Whipped cream

In a small bowl, combine cracker crumbs and sugar; stir in the butter. Press onto the bottom and 2 in. up the sides of a greased 9-in. springform pan. Bake at 350° for 5 minutes. Cool on a wire rack. In a mixing bowl, beat cream cheese, sugar and vanilla until smooth. Add eggs, pumpkin and spices; beat just until combined. Pour into crust.

Bake at 350° for 1 hour or until center is almost set. Cool on a wire rack for 10 minutes. Carefully run a knife around edge of pan to loosen; cool 1 hour longer. Refrigerate until completely cooled (center will fall). Remove sides of pan just before serving. Garnish with whipped cream. **Yield:** 12 servings.

Rich Chocolate Pudding

(Pictured below and on page 134)

Creamy, smooth and fudgy, this dessert is a true chocolate indulgence. With just four ingredients, it might be the easiest from-scratch pudding you'll ever make.
—Verna Hainer, Aurora, Colorado

2 cups (12 ounces) semisweet chocolate chips
1/3 cup confectioners' sugar
1 cup milk
1/4 cup butter *or* margarine
Whipped topping and miniature semisweet chocolate chips, optional

Place chocolate chips and confectioners' sugar in a blender; cover and process until chips are coarsely chopped. In a saucepan over medium heat, bring milk and butter to a boil. Add to blender; cover and process until chips are melted and mixture is smooth. Pour into six individual serving dishes. Refrigerate. Garnish with whipped topping and miniature chips if desired. **Yield:** 6 servings.

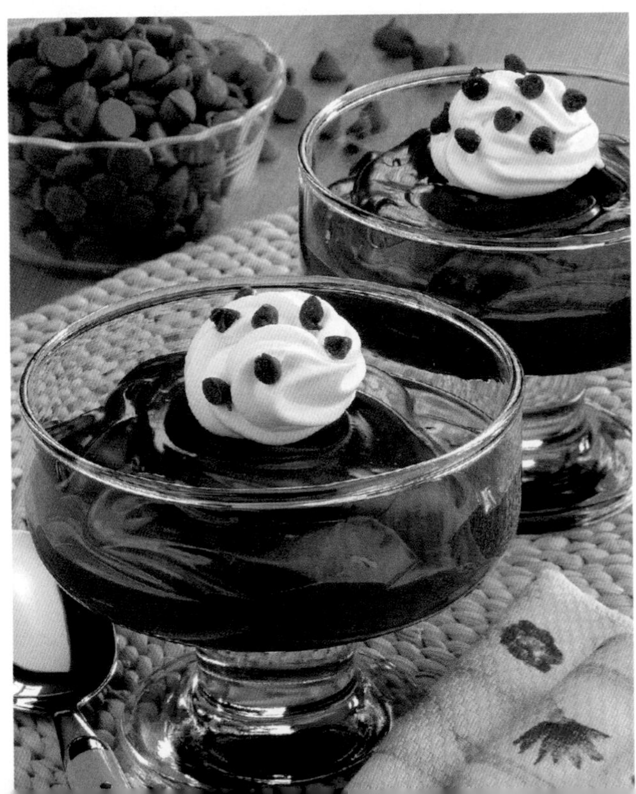

Mint Chip Ice Cream

(Pictured below and on page 135)

We have a milk cow, so homemade ice cream has become a regular treat for our family. This version is very creamy with a mild mint flavor that goes well with the mini chocolate chips. It was an instant hit with my husband and our two little girls. —Farrah McGuire Springdale, Washington

3 eggs, lightly beaten
1-3/4 cups milk
3/4 cup sugar
Pinch salt
1-3/4 cups whipping cream
1 teaspoon vanilla extract
1/4 teaspoon peppermint extract
4 drops green food coloring, optional
1/2 cup miniature semisweet chocolate chips

In a saucepan, combine eggs, milk, sugar and salt. Cook and stir over medium heat until mixture reaches 160° and coats a metal spoon. Cool to room temperature. Stir in cream, vanilla, peppermint extract and food coloring if desired. Refrigerate for 2 hours. Stir in chocolate chips. Fill ice cream freezer cylinder two-thirds full; freeze according to the manufacturer's directions. Refrigerate remaining mixture until ready to freeze. **Yield:** 1-1/2 quarts.

Lemon Ice Cream

(Pictured on page 134)

What better use could there be for fresh lemon juice than to make refreshing ice cream? I love this recipe because it's delicious and not at all tricky to make. —Nancy Schantz, San Angelo, Texas

1 package (3 ounces) cream cheese, softened
3 cups sugar
1 package (3 ounces) lemon gelatin
2 cups half-and-half cream
2/3 cup lemon juice
1 teaspoon vanilla extract
1/2 teaspoon lemon extract
1 cup whipping cream, whipped
8 to 10 cups milk
Yellow food coloring, optional

In a mixing bowl, combine the cream cheese, sugar and gelatin; mix well. Add half-and-half, lemon juice and extracts; beat until smooth. Fold in the whipped cream. Stir in enough milk to measure 1 gallon. Add food coloring if desired. Freeze in batches according to manufacturer's directions. Refrigerate extra mixture until it can be frozen. Allow to ripen in ice cream freezer or firm up in refrigerator freezer for 2-4 hours before serving. Remove from freezer 10 minutes before serving. **Yield:** 1 gallon.

Almond Custard

I like to fix this rich custard on Saturday to serve with Sunday dinner. It always gets rave reviews! —Suzanne McKinley, Lyons, Georgia

3-1/3 cups milk, *divided*
1-1/2 cups sugar
6 egg yolks, beaten
1-1/2 teaspoons unflavored gelatin
1 teaspoon almond extract
1 teaspoon vanilla extract
2 cups whipping cream, whipped
1/2 cup sliced almonds, toasted

In a double boiler, combine 3 cups milk and sugar; add egg yolks. Cook and stir over medium heat for 10 minutes or until mixture coats the back of a metal spoon and a thermometer reads 160°. In a saucepan, combine gelatin and remaining milk; let stand for 1 minute. Heat on low until gelatin is dissolved. Stir into custard. Chill until partially set.

Stir in the extracts. Fold in whipped cream. Pour into a shallow serving dish. Refrigerate until set, about 45 minutes. Sprinkle with almonds before serving. **Yield:** 8-10 servings.

Coconut Peach Dessert

(Pictured on page 134 and on back cover)

If you enjoy peaches and coconut, you're sure to like this sweet, fruity pizza-style treat. —*Inez Orsburn Demotte, Indiana*

1-1/3 cups flaked coconut
1/2 cup chopped almonds
1/3 cup sugar
2 tablespoons all-purpose flour
1/8 teaspoon salt
2 egg whites, lightly beaten
1/2 teaspoon almond extract

TOPPING:

2 cups whipped cream
4 cups sliced fresh *or* frozen peaches, thawed
1/2 cup sugar *or* honey

In a bowl, combine the first five ingredients. Stir in egg whites and extract. Line a baking sheet with foil; grease foil well. Spread coconut mixture into a 9-in. circle on foil. Bake at 325° for 20-25 minutes or until lightly browned. Cool on a wire rack. Refrigerate overnight. Place the crust on a serving plate; spread with whipped cream. Combine peaches and sugar; spoon over cream. Cut into wedges. Serve immediately. **Yield:** 6-8 servings.

Deluxe Chip Cheesecake

(Pictured above right)

Once, when my husband and I were asked to make a dessert for a "traveling basket" for our church, we prepared this luscious layered treat. We ended up keeping it and contributing another sweet treat instead! —*Kari Gollup, Madison, Wisconsin*

1-1/2 cups vanilla wafer crumbs
1/2 cup confectioners' sugar
1/4 cup baking cocoa
1/3 cup butter *or* margarine, melted

FILLING:

3 packages (8 ounces *each*) cream cheese, softened
3/4 cup sugar
1/3 cup sour cream
3 tablespoons all-purpose flour
1 teaspoon vanilla extract

1/4 teaspoon salt
3 eggs
1 cup butterscotch chips, melted
1 cup semisweet chocolate chips, melted
1 cup vanilla *or* white chips, melted

TOPPING:

1 tablespoon *each* butterscotch, semisweet and vanilla chips
1-1/2 teaspoons shortening

In a bowl, combine wafer crumbs, confectioners' sugar, cocoa and butter. Press onto the bottom and 1-1/2 in. up the sides of a greased 9-in. springform pan. Bake at 350° for 7-9 minutes or until set. Cool on a wire rack.

In a mixing bowl, beat cream cheese and sugar until smooth. Add sour cream, flour, vanilla and salt; mix well. Add eggs; beat on low speed just until combined. Remove 1-1/2 cups batter to a bowl; stir in butterscotch chips. Pour over crust. Add chocolate chips to another 1-1/2 cups batter; carefully spoon over butterscotch layer. Stir vanilla chips into remaining batter; spoon over chocolate layer.

Bake at 350° for 55-60 minutes or until center is almost set. Cool on a wire rack for 10 minutes. Carefully run a knife around edge of pan to loosen. Cool for 1 hour. For topping, place each flavor of chips and 1/2 teaspoon shortening in three small microwave-safe bowls. Microwave on high for 25 seconds; stir. Heat in 10- to 20-second intervals, stirring until smooth. Drizzle over cheesecake. Chill for at least 3 hours. Remove sides of pan. Refrigerate leftovers. **Yield:** 12-14 servings.

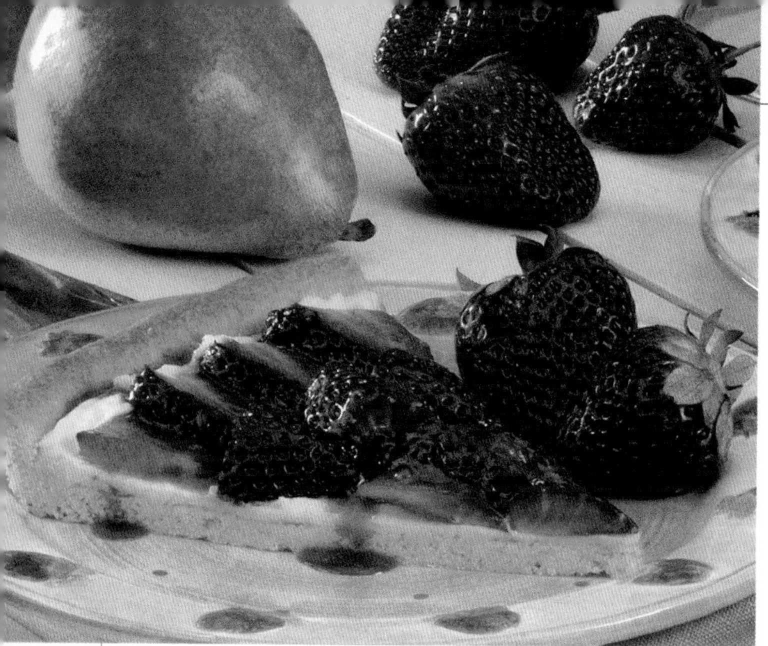

Strawberry Pizza

(Pictured above)

Both strawberry and cheesecake lovers will delight in this dreamy treat. My family requests this sweet fruit pizza every strawberry season. —*Kara Cook Elk Ridge, Utah*

6 tablespoons butter *or* margarine, softened
1/2 cup sugar
1 egg
1/2 teaspoon vanilla extract
1/4 teaspoon almond extract
1-1/4 cups all-purpose flour
1/2 teaspoon baking powder
1/2 teaspoon salt

FILLING:

1 package (8 ounces) cream cheese, softened
1/2 cup confectioners' sugar
2 cups sliced fresh strawberries
1 cup sugar
1/4 cup cornstarch
2 cups crushed strawberries

In a mixing bowl, cream butter and sugar for 2 minutes. Beat in egg and extracts. Combine flour, baking powder and salt; gradually add to creamed mixture and mix well. Cover and refrigerate for 1 hour. On a floured surface, roll dough into a 13-in. circle. Transfer to an ungreased 12-in. pizza pan. Build up edges slightly. Bake at 350° for 18-22 minutes or until lightly browned. Cool completely.

In a mixing bowl, beat the cream cheese and confectioners' sugar until smooth. Spread over crust. Arrange sliced strawberries on top. In a saucepan, combine the sugar, cornstarch and crushed berries until blended. Bring to a boil; cook and stir for 2 minutes or until thickened. Cool slightly. Spoon over strawberries. Refrigerate until serving. **Yield:** 12-16 servings.

Brownie Toffee Trifle

I'm hoping to write my own cookbook soon, and this favorite confection will surely be included. —*Barb Stewart, McDonalds Corners, Ontario*

1 package fudge brownie mix (13-inch x 9-inch pan size)
4 teaspoons instant coffee granules
1/4 cup warm water
1-3/4 cups cold milk
1 package (3.4 ounces) instant vanilla pudding mix
2 cups whipped topping
1 package (11 ounces) vanilla *or* white baking chips
3 Heath candy bars (1.55 ounces *each*), chopped

Prepare and bake brownies according to package directions, using a 13-in. x 9-in. x 2-in. baking pan. Cool; cut into 3/4-in. cubes. Dissolve coffee granules in warm water. In a mixing bowl, beat milk and pudding mix on low speed for 2 minutes. Beat in coffee mixture. Fold in whipped topping.

In a 3-qt. trifle glass or bowl, layer half of the brownie cubes, pudding, vanilla chips and candy bars. Repeat layers. Cover and refrigerate for at least 1 hour before serving. **Yield:** 10-12 servings.

Poached Pears with Vanilla Sauce

This dessert is a great ending to a special-occasion meal. Whole pears are lightly spiced and chilled, then served with a heavenly custard sauce. —*Al Latimer Bentonville, Arkansas*

2-1/3 cups sugar, *divided*
2 teaspoons cornstarch
1 cup milk
1/2 cup whipping cream
4 egg yolks, lightly beaten
1 teaspoon vanilla extract
10 cups water, *divided*
2 tablespoons lemon juice, *divided*
6 medium firm pears, stems attached
1 teaspoon grated lemon peel
1 cinnamon stick (3 inches)
3 whole cloves

In a heavy 2-qt. saucepan, combine 1/3 cup sugar and cornstarch; gradually stir in milk and cream until smooth. Bring to a boil over medium heat; cook and stir for 2 minutes. Remove from the heat. Gradually add a small amount of hot mixture to egg yolks; return all to the pan, stirring constantly. Cook and stir over medium-low heat for

15 minutes or until mixture thickens slightly (do not boil). Stir in vanilla. Pour into a bowl; place a piece of waxed paper or plastic wrap on top of sauce. Cover and refrigerate.

In a large bowl, combine 6 cups water and 1 tablespoon lemon juice. Carefully peel pears, leaving stems attached. Immediately plunge pears into lemon water. In a large saucepan, combine lemon peel, and the remaining sugar, water and lemon juice. Bring to a boil. Add cinnamon stick, cloves and pears. Reduce heat; cover and simmer for 20-25 minutes or until pears are tender.

Carefully remove pears to a plate. Discard cinnamon stick and cloves. Drizzle syrup over pears. Loosely cover and refrigerate for 2-3 hours. To serve, place pears on dessert plates; drizzle with chilled vanilla sauce. **Yield:** 6 servings.

Butterscotch Delight

(Pictured on page 135 and on back cover)

This creamy layered dessert is popular whenever I serve it. —Barbara Edgemon, Belleview, Florida

- **1/2 cup cold butter *or* margarine**
- **1 cup all-purpose flour**
- **1 cup finely chopped walnuts**
- **1 package (8 ounces) cream cheese, softened**
- **1 cup confectioners' sugar**
- **1 carton (8 ounces) frozen whipped topping, thawed, *divided***
- **3-1/2 cups cold milk**
- **2 packages (3.5 ounces *each*) instant butterscotch pudding mix**
- **1/2 cup coarsely chopped walnuts**

In a bowl, cut butter into flour; stir in the finely chopped walnuts. Press into a greased 13-in. x 9-in. x 2-in. baking pan. Bake at 350° for 20 minutes or until golden brown. Cool on a wire rack. In a mixing bowl, beat the cream cheese and sugar. Fold in 1 cup whipped topping. Spread over crust. In another bowl, beat milk and pudding mix for 2 minutes or until thickened. Spread over cream cheese layer. Spread with the remaining whipped topping; sprinkle with coarsely chopped walnuts. Chill until set. **Yield:** 12-15 servings.

Pear Melba Dumplings

(Pictured at right and on back cover)

I substituted pears in a favorite apple dumpling recipe, then added a raspberry sauce. Yum! —Doreen Kelly Roslyn, Pennsylvania

- **2 cups all-purpose flour**
- **1-1/4 teaspoons salt**
- **1/2 teaspoon cornstarch**
- **2/3 cup butter-flavored shortening**
- **4 to 5 tablespoons cold water**
- **6 small ripe pears, peeled and cored**
- **6 tablespoons brown sugar**
- **1/4 teaspoon ground cinnamon**
- **2 tablespoons milk**
- **1 tablespoon sugar**

RASPBERRY SAUCE:

- **1 tablespoon sugar**
- **1 tablespoon cornstarch**
- **2 tablespoons water**
- **1 package (10 ounces) frozen raspberries, thawed**
- **1/4 teaspoon almond extract**

Ice cream, optional

In a bowl, combine flour, salt and cornstarch. Cut in shortening until mixture resembles coarse crumbs. Stir in water until pastry forms a ball. On a floured surface, roll into a 21-in. x 14-in. rectangle. Cut into six squares. Place one pear in center of each square. Pack pear centers with brown sugar; sprinkle with cinnamon. Brush edges of squares with milk; fold up corners to center and pinch to seal. Place in a greased 15-in. x 10-in. x 1-in. baking pan. Brush with milk; sprinkle with sugar.

Bake at 375° for 35-40 minutes or until golden brown. Meanwhile, in a saucepan, combine sugar, cornstarch and water until smooth. Add raspberries. Bring to a boil; cook and stir for 2 minutes or until thickened. Remove from the heat; stir in extract. Serve warm over warm dumplings with ice cream if desired. **Yield:** 6 servings.

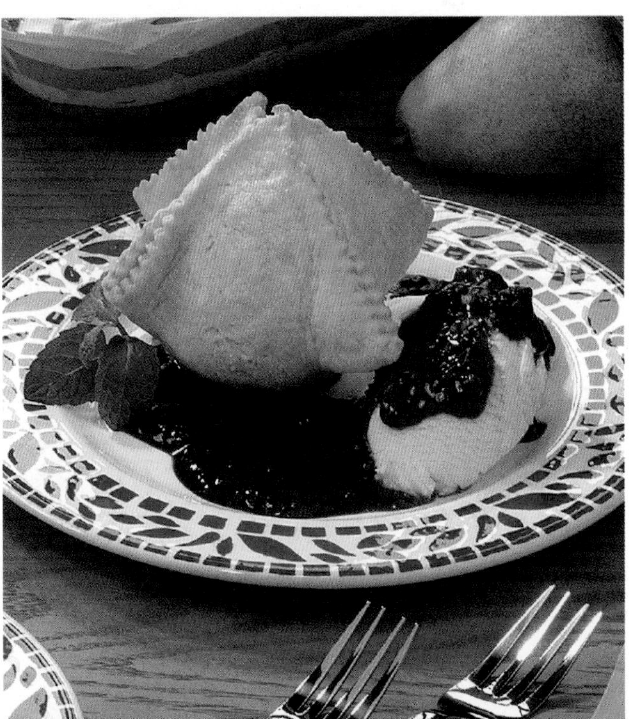

Peanut Butter Puddingwiches

(Pictured below)

If you like frozen ice cream sandwiches, you'll love the homemade goodness of these peanut buttery pudding treats. The filling is smooth and scrumptious, and the graham crackers stay crisp. They're handy to have in the freezer. —*Darlene Markel, Salem, Oregon*

✓ Uses less fat, sugar or salt. Includes Nutritional Analysis and Diabetic Exchanges.

1-1/2 cups peanut butter, *divided*
3 cups cold milk, *divided*
1 package (3.9 ounces) instant chocolate pudding mix
2 cups whipped topping, *divided*
1 package (3.4 ounces) instant vanilla pudding mix
32 whole graham crackers

Line two 13-in. x 9-in. x 2-in. pans with foil; set aside. In a mixing bowl, combine 3/4 cup peanut butter and 1-1/2 cups milk until smooth. Slowly beat in chocolate pudding mix until blended; fold in 1 cup whipped topping. Pour into one prepared pan; freeze until firm. Repeat with vanilla pudding and remaining peanut butter, milk and whipped topping. Pour into second pan; freeze until firm.

Break or cut graham crackers into squares. Cut frozen pudding mixture into 32 squares, about 2-1/2 in. x 2-1/4 in.; place each square between two crackers. Wrap in plastic wrap. Freeze overnight. **Yield:** 32 sandwiches.

Nutritional Analysis: One sandwich (prepared with fat-free milk, sugar-free chocolate pudding and reduced-fat whipped topping) equals 216 calories, 9 g fat (2 g saturated fat), 0 cholesterol, 324 mg sodium, 28 g carbohydrate, 2 g fiber, 6 g protein. **Diabetic Exchanges:** 2 starch, 1 fat.

Pumpkin Cheesecake with Sour Cream Topping

(Pictured on page 134)

Why not surprise Thanksgiving guests with this luscious creamy cheesecake instead of the traditional pie? —*Dorothy Smith, El Dorado, Arkansas*

1-1/2 cups graham cracker crumbs (about 24 squares)
1/4 cup sugar
1/3 cup butter *or* margarine, melted

FILLING:

3 packages (8 ounces *each*) cream cheese, softened
1 cup packed brown sugar
1 can (15 ounces) solid-pack pumpkin
2 tablespoons cornstarch
1-1/4 teaspoons ground cinnamon
1/2 teaspoon ground nutmeg
1 can (5 ounces) evaporated milk
2 eggs

TOPPING:

2 cups (16 ounces) sour cream
1/3 cup sugar
1 teaspoon vanilla extract
Additional ground cinnamon, optional

In a bowl, combine crumbs and sugar; stir in butter. Press onto the bottom and 1-1/2 in. up the sides of a greased 9-in. springform pan. Bake at 350° for 5-7 minutes or until set. Cool for 10 minutes. In a mixing bowl, beat cream cheese and brown sugar until smooth. Add the pumpkin, cornstarch, cinnamon and nutmeg; mix well. Gradually beat in milk and eggs just until blended. Pour into crust.

Bake at 350° for 55-60 minutes or until center is almost set. Combine the sour cream, sugar and vanilla; spread over filling. Bake 5 minutes longer. Cool on a wire rack for 10 minutes. Carefully run a knife around edge of pan to loosen; cool 1 hour longer. Chill overnight. Remove sides of pan; let stand at room temperature for 30 minutes before slicing. Sprinkle with cinnamon if desired. Refrigerate leftovers. **Yield:** 12-14 servings.

Editor's Note: Even a tight-fitting springform pan may leak. To prevent drips, place the filled springform on a baking sheet in the oven.

Flaky Apricot Pastries

This tender fruit-filled pastry melts in your mouth. The logs can be made ahead of time and frozen. Then just thaw at room temperature before warming them.
—Ed Patterson, Greenville, Texas

3 packages (3 ounces *each*) cream cheese, softened
1 cup butter (no substitutes), softened
2 cups all-purpose flour
1/4 cup sugar
1 teaspoon ground cinnamon
1/2 cup apricot preserves
4 teaspoons ground pecans
GLAZE:
1 cup confectioners' sugar
2 tablespoons butter *or* margarine, softened
1 to 2 tablespoons milk

In a mixing bowl, beat cream cheese and butter. Add flour; mix well. Divide dough into four pieces. Cover and refrigerate for 2 hours. On a floured surface, roll each portion of dough into a 12-in. x 8-in. rectangle. Combine sugar and cinnamon; sprinkle over dough. Spread with preserves; sprinkle with pecans. Roll up tightly, starting with a short side; pinch ends. Place seam side down on a greased baking sheet. Using a sharp knife, make three slashes across the top of each roll.

Bake at 350° for 28-32 minutes or until golden brown. Remove to wire racks to cool. Combine glaze ingredients; drizzle over pastries. **Yield:** 4 pastries.

Chocolate Hazelnut Truffles

I've given these delectable candies with a nutty surprise inside to teachers and friends.
—Debra Pedrazzi, Ayer, Massachusetts

3/4 cup confectioners' sugar
2 tablespoons baking cocoa
4 milk chocolate candy bars (1.55 ounces *each*)
6 tablespoons butter (no substitutes)
1/4 cup whipping cream
24 whole hazelnuts
1 cup ground hazelnuts, toasted

In a bowl, sift together confectioners' sugar and cocoa; set aside. In a saucepan, melt candy bars and butter. Add the cream and reserved cocoa mixture. Cook and stir over medium-low heat until mixture is thickened and smooth. Pour into an 8-in. square dish. Cover and refrigerate overnight. Using a melon baller or spoon, shape candy into 1-in. balls; press a hazelnut into each. Reshape balls and roll in ground hazelnuts. Store in an airtight container in the refrigerator. **Yield:** 2 dozen.

Melon Ambrosia

(Pictured above)

Each time I serve this light and refreshing dessert, it gets wonderful reviews. With three kinds of melon, it's lovely and colorful but so simple to prepare.
—Edie DeSpain, Logan, Utah

✓ Uses less fat, sugar or salt. Includes Nutritional Analysis and Diabetic Exchanges.

1 cup watermelon balls *or* cubes
1 cup cantaloupe balls *or* cubes
1 cup honeydew balls *or* cubes
1/3 cup lime juice
2 tablespoons sugar
2 tablespoons honey
1/4 cup flaked coconut, toasted
Fresh mint, optional

In a bowl, combine melon balls. In another bowl, combine the lime juice, sugar and honey; pour over melon and toss to coat. Cover and refrigerate for at least 1 hour. Sprinkle with coconut. Garnish with mint if desired. **Yield:** 4 servings.

Nutritional Analysis: One serving (3/4 cup) equals 137 calories, 4 g fat (3 g saturated fat), 0 cholesterol, 12 mg sodium, 29 g carbohydrate, 2 g fiber, 1 g protein. **Diabetic Exchange:** 2 fruit.

Potluck Pleasers

Whether you're headed to a family reunion or a church supper, turn here for large-quantity favorites that will spark smiles and appetites.

PLENTY TO PASS. Clockwise from upper left: No-Knead Knot Rolls (p. 162), Oven-Barbecued Spareribs (p. 162), Pistachio Orange Asparagus (p. 159) and Rhubarb Meringue Dessert (p. 163).

Mocha Walnut Brownies

(Pictured above)

These rich cake-like brownies are generously topped with a scrumptious mocha frosting. They're an excellent dessert to serve to company or to share when you need a dish to pass. Be sure to hold back a few if you want leftovers! —Jill Bonanno, Prineville, Oregon

4 squares (1 ounce *each*) unsweetened chocolate
1 cup butter (no substitutes)
2 cups sugar
4 eggs
1 teaspoon vanilla extract
1-1/4 cups all-purpose flour
1/2 teaspoon baking powder
1/2 teaspoon salt
1 cup chopped walnuts

MOCHA FROSTING:

4 cups confectioners' sugar
1/2 cup butter (no substitutes), melted
1/3 cup baking cocoa
1/4 cup strong brewed coffee
2 teaspoons vanilla extract

In a saucepan over low heat, melt chocolate and butter; stir until smooth. Remove from heat. Add sugar and mix well. Add eggs, one at a time, beating well after each. Stir in vanilla. Combine flour, baking powder and salt; add to chocolate mixture just until combined. Stir in walnuts. Pour into a greased 13-in. x 9-in. x 2-in. baking pan. Bake at 375° for 30 minutes or until a toothpick inserted near the center comes out clean. Cool on a wire rack. Combine frosting ingredients in a bowl; mix well. Spread over brownies. **Yield:** about 2 dozen.

Crowd-Size Spaghetti Sauce

This is the best sauce I've ever made. The flavors blend so well. It's especially handy for a large group. —Donna Bennett, Bramalea, Ontario

4 pounds ground beef
4 large onions, chopped
4 garlic cloves, minced
4 cans (28 ounces *each*) diced tomatoes, undrained
2 cans (15 ounces *each*) tomato paste
1 can (29 ounces) tomato sauce
2 cups water
2 cans (4-1/4 ounces *each*) chopped ripe olives, drained
2 cans (4 ounces *each*) mushroom stems and pieces, drained
1/2 cup minced fresh parsley
1/4 cup packed brown sugar
2 tablespoons dried basil
2 tablespoons salt
4 teaspoons dried oregano
2 teaspoons pepper

In several large kettles, cook the beef, onions and garlic over medium heat until meat is no longer pink; drain. Add the remaining ingredients; cover and simmer for 4 hours, stirring occasionally. **Yield:** 65-70 servings (8 quarts).

Yeast Dinner Rolls

Ever since I was a child, fresh-from-the-oven yeast breads and rolls have been my absolute favorite. These melt in your mouth. —Earlene McEvers, Herrin, Illinois

✓ Uses less fat, sugar or salt. Includes Nutritional Analysis and Diabetic Exchanges.

1 package (1/4 ounce) active dry yeast
1-1/2 cups warm water (110° to 115°)
1 can (12 ounces) evaporated milk
2 eggs
1/3 cup sugar
1/4 cup butter *or* stick margarine, melted
2 teaspoons salt
8 to 8-1/2 cups all-purpose flour
Additional melted butter *or* margarine, optional

In a large mixing bowl, dissolve yeast in warm water. Add milk, eggs, sugar, butter, salt and 4 cups flour until smooth. Add enough remaining flour to form a soft dough. Turn onto a floured surface; knead until smooth and elastic, about 6-8 minutes. Place in a greased bowl, turning once to grease top.

Cover and let rise in a warm place until doubled, about 1-1/2 hours. Punch dough down; divide into four portions. Shape each into eight rolls; place

20 rolls in a greased 13-in. x 9-in. x 2-in. baking pan. Place 12 rolls in a greased 8-in. square baking pan. Cover and let rise in a warm place until doubled, about 20-30 minutes. Bake at 375° for 15-20 minutes or until golden brown. Brush with butter if desired. Serve warm. **Yield:** 32 rolls.

Nutritional Analysis: One roll (prepared with margarine and fat-free evaporated milk) equals 148 calories, 2 g fat (trace saturated fat), 15 mg cholesterol, 179 mg sodium, 27 g carbohydrate, 1 g fiber, 5 g protein. **Diabetic Exchange:** 2 starch.

Coconut Cherry Snack Cake

This cake will satisfy any sweet tooth. It's packed with goodies. —Barbara Birk, St. George, Utah

1-1/2 cups butter *or* margarine, softened
3 cups sugar
6 eggs
2 teaspoons vanilla extract
1 teaspoon almond extract
2-3/4 cups all-purpose flour
1 cup flaked coconut
1 cup walnuts *or* pecans, chopped
1 jar (10 ounces) maraschino cherries, chopped and well drained

In a mixing bowl, cream the butter and sugar. Add eggs, one at a time, beating well after each addition. Beat in extracts. Add flour; beat until blended. Fold in coconut, nuts and cherries. Spread into two greased 13-in. x 9-in. x 2-in. baking pans. Bake at 350° for 30-35 minutes or until a toothpick inserted near the center comes out clean. Cool on wire racks. **Yield:** 2 cakes (16-20 servings each).

Barbecue Sauce for Pork

We raise hogs and cattle, so we've tried plenty of barbecue recipes. Smothered in sauce, this pork gets rave reviews from everyone who tastes it.
—Debbie Kokes, Tabor, South Dakota

1 gallon ketchup
4 cups sugar
2-2/3 cups white vinegar
1/2 cup dried minced onion
2 tablespoons pepper
4-1/2 teaspoons garlic powder
1 to 3 teaspoons hot pepper sauce, optional

In a large kettle or Dutch oven, combine all ingredients. Cook over medium-high heat until heated through. Serve over pork. **Yield:** 4-1/2 quarts.

Broccoli Ham Roll-Ups

(Pictured below)

My mother made these flavorful rolls for me when I came home from the hospital with each of my two children. They can be frozen before baking and pulled out of the freezer for a quick meal or a handy potluck dish.
—Susan Simmons, Norwalk, Iowa

1 package (10 ounces) frozen chopped broccoli
1 can (10-3/4 ounces) condensed cream of mushroom soup, undiluted
1 cup dry bread crumbs
1/4 cup shredded cheddar cheese
1 tablespoon chopped onion
1-1/2 teaspoons diced pimientos
1/8 teaspoon rubbed sage
1/8 teaspoon dried rosemary, crushed
1/8 teaspoon dried thyme
Dash pepper
12 slices fully cooked ham (1/8 inch thick)

Cook broccoli according to package directions; drain. In a bowl, combine soup, bread crumbs, cheese, onion, pimientos and seasonings. Add broccoli; mix well. Spoon 1/4 cup mixture onto each ham slice. Roll up and place in an ungreased 13-in. x 9-in. x 2-in. baking dish. Cover and bake at 350° for 40 minutes or until heated through. **Yield:** 12 servings.

Lemon Cheesecake Squares

(Pictured below)

Whether I'm hosting friends or sending a plate to work with my husband, these creamy elegant cheesecake squares are always a hit. It's a wonderful make-ahead dessert that easily serves a large group.
—Peggy Reddick, Cumming, Georgia

3/4 cup shortening
1/3 cup packed brown sugar
1-1/4 cups all-purpose flour
1 cup rolled oats
1/4 teaspoon salt
1/2 cup seedless raspberry jam
FILLING:
4 packages (8 ounces *each*) cream cheese, softened
1-1/2 cups sugar
1/4 cup all-purpose flour
4 eggs
1/3 cup lemon juice
4 teaspoons grated lemon peel

In a mixing bowl, cream shortening and brown sugar. Combine the flour, oats and salt; gradually add to creamed mixture. Press dough into a greased 13-in. x 9-in. x 2-in. baking dish. Bake at 350° for 15-18 minutes or until golden brown. Spread with jam.

For filling, beat the cream cheese, sugar and flour until fluffy. Add the eggs, lemon juice and peel just until blended. Carefully spoon over jam. Bake at 350° for 30-35 minutes or until center is almost set. Cool on a wire rack. Cover and store in the refrigerator. **Yield:** 20 servings.

Peanut Butter Sheet Cake

A minister's wife gave me this recipe, which my family just loves. —Brenda Jackson, Garden City, Kansas

2 cups all-purpose flour
2 cups sugar
1 teaspoon baking soda
1/2 teaspoon salt
1 cup water
3/4 cup butter *or* margarine
1/2 cup chunky peanut butter*
1/4 cup vegetable oil
2 eggs
1/2 cup buttermilk
1 teaspoon vanilla extract
GLAZE:
2/3 cup sugar
1/3 cup evaporated milk
1 tablespoon butter *or* margarine
1/3 cup chunky peanut butter*
1/3 cup miniature marshmallows
1/2 teaspoon vanilla extract

In a large mixing bowl, combine the flour, sugar, baking soda and salt; set aside. In a saucepan, bring water and butter to a boil; stir in peanut butter and oil until blended. Add to dry ingredients; mix well. Combine eggs, buttermilk and vanilla; add to peanut butter mixture and mix well. Pour into a greased 15-in. x 10-in. x 1-in. baking pan. Bake at 350° for 16-20 minutes or until a toothpick inserted near the center comes out clean.

Meanwhile, combine sugar, milk and butter in a saucepan. Bring to a boil, stirring constantly; cook and stir for 2 minutes. Remove from the heat; stir in peanut butter, marshmallows and vanilla until marshmallows are melted. Spoon over warm cake and carefully spread over the top. Cool completely. **Yield:** 20-24 servings.

***Editor's Note:** Reduced-fat or generic brands of peanut butter are not recommended for this recipe.

Roasted Vegetables

With a little up-front preparation, you can include this delicious, colorful side dish on a holiday buffet without any last-minute fuss. *—Cathryn White Newark, Delaware*

✓ Uses less fat, sugar or salt. Includes Nutritional Analysis and Diabetic Exchanges.

5 cups cubed unpeeled red potatoes (about 1-1/2 pounds)
7 medium carrots, cut into 1/2-inch slices
4 medium parsnips, peeled and cut into 1/2-inch slices

- **2 medium turnips, peeled and cut into 1/2-inch cubes**
- **1 cup fresh *or* frozen pearl onions**
- **1 medium red onion, cut into 1/2-inch wedges and halved**
- **3 tablespoons butter *or* margarine, melted**
- **3 tablespoons olive *or* vegetable oil**
- **1 tablespoon dried thyme**
- **2 teaspoons salt**
- **1/2 teaspoon pepper**
- **2-1/2 cups brussels sprouts, halved**
- **3 to 4 garlic cloves, quartered**

In a roasting pan, combine the first six ingredients. In a small bowl, combine the butter, oil, thyme, salt and pepper. Drizzle over vegetables; toss to coat. Cover and bake at 425° for 30 minutes. Add brussels sprouts and garlic. Bake, uncovered, for 30-45 minutes or until vegetables are tender, stirring frequently. **Yield:** 20 servings.

Nutritional Analysis: One 3/4-cup serving (prepared with stick margarine) equals 107 calories, 4 g fat (trace saturated fat), 0 cholesterol, 281 mg sodium, 17 g carbohydrate, 3 g fiber, 2 g protein. **Diabetic Exchanges:** 1 starch, 1/2 fat.

Creamy Floret Bake

A college professor gave me the recipe for this special side dish years ago. My family always requests it for Thanksgiving.—Patricia Potter, Manassas, Virginia

- **1 large head cauliflower, broken into florets (4 cups)**
- **1 medium bunch broccoli, cut into florets (4 cups)**
- **1/4 cup butter *or* stick margarine**
- **1/4 cup all-purpose flour**
- **2 cups half-and-half cream**
- **2 tablespoons grated orange peel**
- **1/2 teaspoon salt**
- **1/4 teaspoon ground nutmeg**
- **1/4 teaspoon white pepper**
- **1/4 cup shredded cheddar cheese**

In a saucepan, bring 1 in. of water to a boil; add cauliflower. Reduce heat; cover and simmer for 10-12 minutes or until crisp-tender. In another saucepan, bring 1 in. of water to a boil; add broccoli. Reduce heat; cover and simmer for 8-10 minutes or until crisp-tender. Drain vegetables and rinse with cold water.

Melt butter in a saucepan. Stir in flour until smooth. Gradually add cream. Bring to a boil; cook and stir for 2 minutes or until thickened. Stir in orange peel, salt, nutmeg and pepper. Arrange cauliflower and broccoli in alternate rows in a 13-in. x 9-in. x 2-in. baking dish. Top with cream sauce and cheese. Bake, uncovered, at 325° for 20-25 minutes or until heated through. **Yield:** 12 servings.

Onion Cheese Bread

Biscuit mix is the handy base for this tender, pretty quick bread that never fails to disappear in a snap!
—Betty Lee, Ocala, Florida

- **1 cup chopped onion**
- **4 teaspoons vegetable oil**
- **3 cups biscuit/baking mix**
- **2 eggs**
- **1 cup milk**
- **1-1/2 cups (6 ounces) shredded cheddar cheese, *divided***
- **6 teaspoons dried parsley flakes, *divided***
- **2 tablespoons butter *or* margarine, melted**

In a skillet, saute onion in oil until tender. Place biscuit mix in a bowl. Combine eggs and milk; stir into biscuit mix just until combined. Stir in the onion, 1 cup of cheese and 4 teaspoons of parsley. Spread the batter into two greased 8-in. round baking pans. Sprinkle with remaining cheese and parsley. Drizzle with butter. Bake at 400° for 15-20 minutes or until cheese is melted and top of bread is lightly browned. **Yield:** 12-16 servings.

Clam Chowder for a Crowd

This flavorful soup is popular at church camp and our family reunions. It has a thinner broth than most chowders.—Mrs. Lynn Richardson, Bauxite, Arkansas

- **10 quarts water**
- **3 tablespoons salt**
- **8 pounds red potatoes, peeled and cubed**
- **6 large onions, chopped**
- **1 cup butter *or* margarine**
- **4 large carrots, grated**
- **16 cans (6-1/2 ounces *each*) minced clams**
- **3 cans (12 ounces *each*) evaporated milk**
- **1/2 cup minced fresh parsley**
- **1 to 2 tablespoons pepper**
- **2 pounds bacon, cooked and crumbled**

In several large kettles, bring water and salt to a boil. Add potatoes; cook until tender (do not drain). In another large pan, saute onions in butter until tender. Add onions and carrots to potato mixture; heat through. Drain clams if desired. Stir clams, milk, parsley and pepper into vegetable mixture; heat through. Just before serving, stir in bacon. **Yield:** 60-65 servings (about 15 quarts).

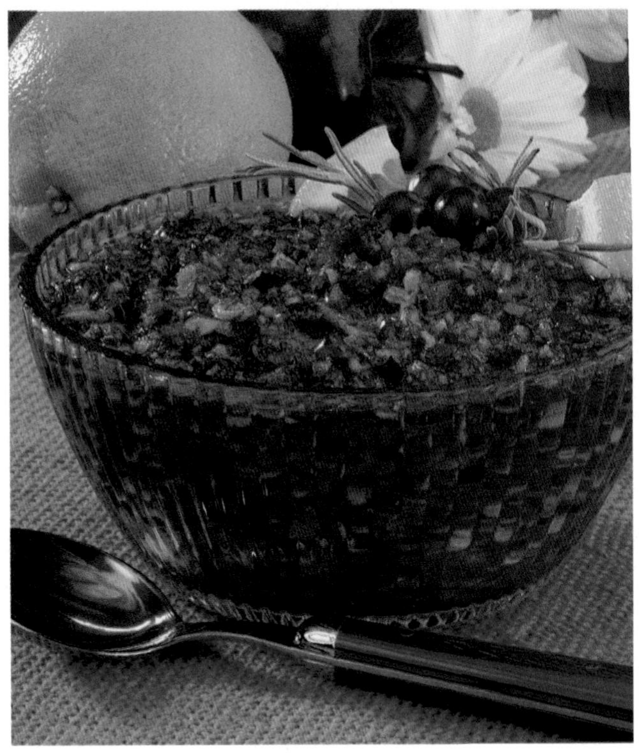

Cranberry Fruit Relish

(Pictured above)

Rich color, a perky texture and tongue-tingling flavor make this relish a feast for the eyes and the taste buds. It's lovely for a special dinner, a ladies luncheon or as a stand-alone salad topped with cottage cheese. It's also a great way to use up holiday cranberries.
—Henryetta Lewis, Santa Fe, New Mexico

3-1/2 cups fresh *or* frozen cranberries
1 medium naval orange, peeled and sectioned
1 medium apple, cut into wedges
1-1/2 cups sugar
1 can (8 ounces) crushed pineapple, drained
3/4 teaspoon ground ginger
1/2 teaspoon ground nutmeg

Place the cranberries, orange and apple in a blender or food processor; cover and process until chunky. Transfer to a bowl; stir in sugar, pineapple, ginger and nutmeg. Cover and refrigerate for at least 2 hours. **Yield:** about 4 cups.

Frozen Strawberry Pie

This sweet-tart treat is well received at church picnics and family get-togethers. Cream cheese makes it melt-in-your-mouth good.
—Gary Kleisley
Royal Palm Beach, Florida

2 packages (8 ounces *each*) cream cheese, softened
1 can (12 ounces) frozen pink lemonade concentrate, thawed
2 packages (20 ounces *each*) frozen unsweetened strawberries, thawed
2 cartons (12 ounces *each*) frozen whipped topping, thawed
3 graham cracker crusts (10 inches *each*)
Fresh strawberries and additional whipped topping, optional

In a large mixing bowl, beat the cream cheese until smooth. Gradually beat in the pink lemonade concentrate. Mash the strawberries; add to the cream cheese mixture and mix well. Fold in the whipped topping. Spoon into graham cracker crusts. Freeze until firm. Remove from the freezer 10-15 minutes before serving. Garnish with strawberries and whipped topping if desired. **Yield:** 3 pies (8 servings each).

Sausage Mushroom Dressing

When a crowd's coming over and I'm serving turkey, I always make this dressing. My children and guests almost pass over the bird in favor of this savory stuffing each holiday.
—Mary Coleman
Norwood, Massachusetts

6 bacon strips, diced
1 pound fresh mushrooms, sliced
1 large onion, chopped
2 celery ribs, chopped
2 to 3 garlic cloves, minced
1/2 cup butter *or* margarine
1 teaspoon rubbed sage
1/2 teaspoon salt
1/4 teaspoon pepper
28 cups cubed day-old bread (about 3 pounds sliced bread)
1 pound bulk pork sausage, cooked and drained
2-1/4 to 2-1/2 cups chicken broth

In a large skillet, cook bacon until crisp. Remove to paper towels to drain. Reserve 2 tablespoons drippings. Saute the mushrooms, onion, celery and garlic in the reserved drippings and butter until tender. Stir in the sage, salt and pepper. In large bowls, combine the mushroom mixture, bread cubes, sausage, broth and bacon; toss to coat. Transfer to two greased 13-in. x 9-in. x 2-in. baking dishes. Cover and bake at 350° for 45 minutes. Uncover; bake 10-15 minutes longer or until lightly browned. **Yield:** 2 casseroles (12-16 servings each).

Cheesy Carrot Casserole

Carrots become everyone's favorite vegetable when they're prepared this way. Crisp golden bread cubes and a cheesy sauce ensure this dish is a hit every time I serve it. —*Carol Wilson, Dixon, Illinois*

4 pounds carrots, cut into 1/2-inch slices
1-1/4 cups chopped onions
11 tablespoons butter *or* margarine, *divided*
5 tablespoons all-purpose flour
1/2 teaspoon salt
1/2 teaspoon celery salt
1/2 teaspoon ground mustard
1/8 teaspoon pepper
2-1/2 cups milk
10 ounces process American cheese, cubed
5-1/2 cups cubed day-old bread

Place carrots in a Dutch oven or large kettle and cover with water; bring to a boil. Reduce heat; cover and simmer until tender, about 10 minutes. Drain and set aside. In a large saucepan, saute onions in 4 tablespoons butter until tender. Stir in the flour, salt, celery salt, mustard and pepper until smooth. Gradually add milk. Bring to a boil; cook and stir for 2 minutes. Stir in cheese until melted. Add carrots and stir to coat.

Transfer to a greased 13-in. x 9-in. x 2-in. baking dish. Melt remaining butter; toss with bread cubes. Sprinkle over carrots. Bake, uncovered, at 350° for 40-50 minutes or until heated through. **Yield:** 18 servings.

Peanutty Caramel Bars

These quick-to-fix bars are sure to satisfy any sweet tooth. You'll be pleasantly surprised by the number of people who ask for "just one more". —*Charlene Bennett, Clearville, Pennsylvania*

1 package (14 ounces) caramels
1/4 cup water
3/4 cup peanut butter, *divided*
4 cups Cheerios
1 cup salted peanuts
1 cup semisweet *or* milk chocolate chips
1/2 cup butter *or* margarine, softened

In a large microwave-safe bowl, heat caramels, water and 1/2 cup peanut butter on high for 1 minute; stir. Microwave 1-2 minutes longer or until melted. Add cereal and peanuts; stir until coated. Spread into a greased 13-in. x 9-in. x 2-in. pan; set aside. In another microwave-safe bowl, heat chips, butter and remaining peanut butter on high for 30-60 seconds or until melted. Spread over cereal mixture. Refrigerate before cutting. **Yield:** about 3 dozen.

Editor's Note: This recipe was tested in an 850-watt microwave with Hershey caramels. Reduced-fat or generic brands of peanut butter are not recommended for this recipe.

Slow-Cooked Beans

(Pictured below)

This flavorful bean dish adds nice variety to any buffet because it's a bit different than traditional baked beans. It's a snap to prepare, since it uses convenient canned beans and prepared barbecue sauce and salsa. —*Joy Beck, Cincinnati, Ohio*

4 cans (15-1/2 ounces *each*) great northern beans, rinsed and drained
4 cans (15 ounces *each*) black beans, rinsed and drained
2 cans (15 ounces *each*) butter beans, rinsed and drained
2-1/4 cups barbecue sauce
2-1/4 cups salsa
3/4 cup packed brown sugar
1/2 to 1 teaspoon hot pepper sauce

In a 5-qt. slow cooker, gently combine all ingredients. Cover and cook on low for 2 hours or until heated through. **Yield:** 16 servings.

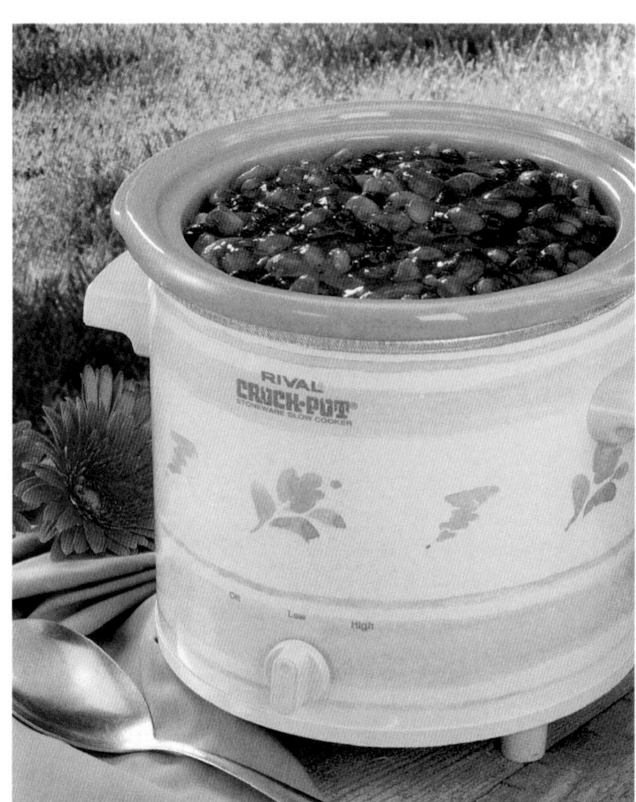

Pumpkin Knot Rolls

(Pictured below)

These light and tender rolls always disappear fast at the big holiday dinners I host. Pumpkin gives them an unexpected flavor that fits right in with Thanksgiving or Christmas. —*Dianna Shimizu Issaquah, Washington*

2 packages (1/4 ounce *each*) active dry yeast
1 cup warm milk (110° to 115°)
1/3 cup butter *or* margarine, softened
1/2 cup sugar
1 cup cooked *or* canned pumpkin
3 eggs
1-1/2 teaspoons salt
5-1/2 to 6 cups all-purpose flour
1 tablespoon cold water
Sesame *or* poppy seeds, optional

In a mixing bowl, dissolve yeast in warm milk. Add the butter, sugar, pumpkin, 2 eggs, salt and 3 cups flour. Beat until smooth. Stir in enough remaining flour to form a soft dough. Turn onto a lightly floured surface; knead until smooth and elastic, about 6-8 minutes. Place in a greased bowl, turning once to grease top. Cover and let rise in a warm place until doubled, about 1 hour.

Punch dough down. Turn onto a lightly floured surface; divide in half. Shape each portion into 12 balls. Roll each ball into a 10-in. rope; tie into a knot and tuck ends under. Place 2 in. apart on greased baking sheets. Cover and let rise until doubled, about 30 minutes.

In a small bowl, beat water and remaining egg. Brush over rolls. Sprinkle with sesame or poppy seeds if desired. Bake at 350° for 15-17 minutes or until golden brown. Remove from pans to wire racks. **Yield:** 2 dozen.

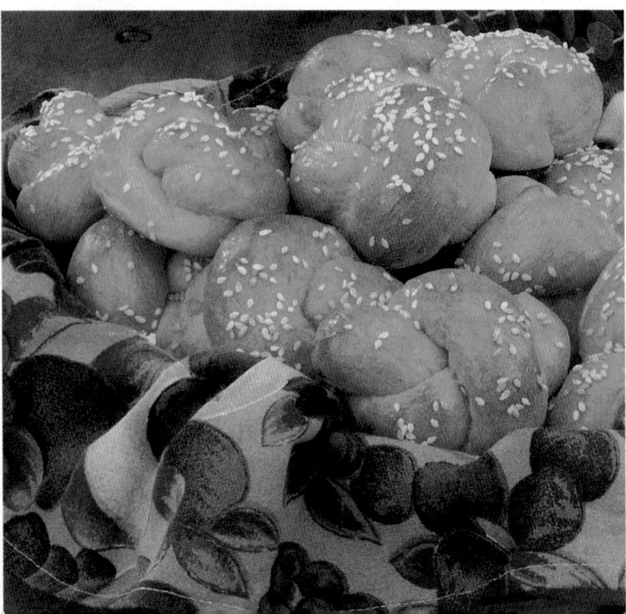

Picnic Macaroni Salad

This is the best-tasting macaroni salad ever! When I fix a batch, I serve myself a portion right away because if I wait until I get to the table, I know it will be all gone. —*Judith Hunt, Goldsboro, North Carolina*

2 packages (16 ounces *each*) elbow macaroni, cooked and drained
8 medium carrots, chopped
2 medium tart green apples, chopped
2 medium green peppers, chopped
2 small onions, chopped
3 cups mayonnaise *or* salad dressing
1/3 cup prepared mustard
1/4 cup cider vinegar
1/4 cup sugar
2 teaspoons garlic salt
2 teaspoons salt
1 teaspoon pepper
12 hard-cooked eggs, sliced
1 teaspoon seafood seasoning

In a large bowl, combine the first five ingredients. In a small bowl, combine the mayonnaise, mustard, vinegar, sugar, garlic salt, salt and pepper. Pour over macaroni mixture; toss to coat. Top with egg slices; sprinkle with seafood seasoning. Cover and refrigerate for at least 3 hours. **Yield:** 30-32 servings.

Coconut Ice Cream

This refreshing ice cream is a special treat on a warm summer day. —*Sandi Pichon, Slidell, Louisiana*

6 cups half-and-half cream
2 cups milk
1-1/2 cups sugar
1/8 teaspoon salt
5 eggs
5 egg yolks
2 cups whipping cream
2 teaspoons coconut extract
1-1/2 teaspoons vanilla extract
3 cups flaked coconut

In a large saucepan, combine the first four ingredients. Cook over medium heat for 10 minutes or until sugar is dissolved. Remove from the heat. In a bowl, beat the eggs and yolks. Stir 1 cup hot cream mixture into eggs; return all to the pan, stirring constantly. Cook and stir until slightly thickened and a thermometer reads 160°. Cool. Refrigerate overnight.

In a bowl, beat whipping cream and extracts until stiff peaks form. Fold into egg mixture with coconut. Fill cylinder of ice cream freezer two-thirds full; freeze according to manufacturer's directions.

Refrigerate remaining mixture until ready to freeze. Transfer to a 4-qt. freezer container; freeze for at least 4 hours before serving. **Yield:** about 3 quarts.

Frosted Peanut Butter Bars

These bars go a long way at big gatherings, plus they taste great. —Sharon Smith, Muskegon, Michigan

1/2 cup peanut butter
1/3 cup shortening
1-1/2 cups packed brown sugar
2 eggs
1 teaspoon vanilla extract
1-1/2 cups all-purpose flour
1-1/2 teaspoons baking powder
1/2 teaspoon salt
1/4 cup milk
FROSTING:
2/3 cup creamy peanut butter
1/2 cup shortening
4 cups confectioners' sugar
1/3 to 1/2 cup milk
TOPPING:
1/4 cup semisweet chocolate chips
1 teaspoon shortening

In a mixing bowl, cream first three ingredients. Beat in eggs and vanilla. Combine the flour, baking powder and salt; gradually add to creamed mixture. Add milk; mix well. Transfer to a greased 15-in. x 10-in. x 1-in. baking pan. Bake at 350° for 16-20 minutes or until a toothpick inserted near the center comes out clean. Cool. For frosting, in a mixing bowl, cream first three ingredients. Gradually beat in enough milk to achieve spreading consistency. Frost bars. Melt chocolate chips and shortening; stir until smooth. Drizzle over frosting. Refrigerate. **Yield:** 5 dozen.

Classic Creamy Coleslaw

After eating this coleslaw with a chicken dinner at an auction, I convinced the lady who made it to share the recipe. —Martha Artyomenko, Beaver Bay, Minnesota

3 large heads cabbage, shredded (about 48 cups)
3 large carrots, shredded (about 2-1/2 cups)
2 cups mayonnaise *or* salad dressing
1 cup sugar
1/4 cup white vinegar
2 tablespoons celery seed
1 tablespoon salt
2 teaspoons garlic powder

In several large bowls, combine the cabbage and carrots. In another bowl, combine the remaining ingredients. Stir into the cabbage mixture. Cover and refrigerate for at least 1 hour. Toss before serving. **Yield:** 30-35 servings (about 3/4 cup each).

Peachy Tossed Salad

(Pictured above)

I serve this great salad when the lettuce in my garden is fresh. —April Neis, Lone Butte, British Columbia

✓ Uses less fat, sugar or salt. Includes Nutritional Analysis and Diabetic Exchanges.

1/4 cup orange juice
2 tablespoons cider vinegar
2 tablespoons plain yogurt
1 tablespoon grated orange peel
2 teaspoons sugar
1/2 teaspoon garlic powder
1/2 teaspoon salt
1/4 teaspoon pepper
1/2 to 3/4 cup olive *or* canola oil
8 cups torn fresh spinach
8 cups torn Bibb *or* Boston lettuce
4 medium fresh peaches, peeled and sliced
4 bacon strips, cooked and crumbled

In a blender or food processor, combine first eight ingredients. While processing, gradually add oil in a steady stream. Process until sugar is dissolved. In a salad bowl, combine spinach, lettuce, peaches and bacon. Drizzle with dressing; toss to coat. Serve immediately. **Yield:** 16 servings.

Nutritional Analysis: One 1-cup serving (prepared with 1/2 cup oil) equals 92 calories, 8 g fat (1 g saturated fat), 1 mg cholesterol, 113 mg sodium, 5 g carbohydrate, 1 g fiber, 2 g protein. **Diabetic Exchanges:** 1 vegetable, 1 fat.

Pinwheel Pizza Loaf

(Pictured above)

This simple rolled meat loaf has the scrumptious flavor of pizza. It's especially popular with my kids and their friends. —Rhonda Touchet, Jennings, Louisiana

2 eggs
Salt and pepper to taste
3 pounds lean ground beef
6 thin slices deli ham
2 cups (8 ounces) shredded mozzarella cheese
1 jar (14 ounces) pizza sauce

In a large bowl, beat eggs, salt and pepper. Crumble beef over eggs and mix well. On a piece of heavy-duty foil, pat beef mixture into a 12-in. x 10-in. rectangle. Cover with ham and cheese to within 1/2 in. of edges. Roll up jelly-roll style, starting with a short side and peeling away foil while rolling. Seal seam and ends.

Place loaf seam side down in a greased 13-in. x 9-in. x 2-in. baking dish. Top with pizza sauce. Bake, uncovered, at 350° for 1-1/4 hours or until meat is no longer pink and a meat thermometer reads 160°. Let stand for 10 minutes before slicing. **Yield:** 12 servings.

Holiday Baked Ham

I've made this ham many times over the years for my children and grandchildren. They're all very fond of it. Honey, brown sugar and pan juices create a succulent glaze. —Mary Padgett, Savannah, Georgia

1 fully cooked bone-in ham (10 to 12 pounds)
2 teaspoons whole cloves, *divided*
1 large onion, chopped
2 garlic cloves, minced
1 teaspoon dried oregano
1 teaspoon dried basil
1/2 teaspoon pepper
1 cup packed brown sugar, *divided*
1/2 cup minced fresh parsley
3 cups ginger ale
1 cup honey
1 can (16 ounces) pineapple slices, drained

Remove skin from ham; score the surface, making diamond shapes 1/2 in. deep. Insert a clove in every other diamond; set remaining cloves aside. Place ham on a rack in a shallow roasting pan. Combine onion, garlic, oregano, basil and pepper; pat onto ham. Combine 1/2 cup brown sugar and parsley; sprinkle over top of ham. Pour ginger ale around ham. Bake, uncovered, at 350° for 2 hours, basting often. Remove ham from pan; set aside. Drain pan juices, reserving 3 tablespoons.

For glaze, combine honey, remaining brown sugar and reserved pan juices in a bowl. Increase oven temperature to 400°. Return ham to pan. Insert remaining cloves into ham. Spoon half of the glaze over ham. Bake for 20 minutes. Place pineapple on ham; drizzle with remaining glaze. Bake 30 minutes longer or until a meat thermometer reads 140°. Let stand for 15 minutes before carving. **Yield:** 30 servings.

Baked Potato Casserole

I wanted a great all-around side dish for special meals. When I made this one, friends and neighbors told me it's the one. —Karen Berlekamp, Maineville, Ohio

5 pounds red potatoes, cooked and cubed
1 pound sliced bacon, cooked and crumbled
4 cups (1 pound) cubed cheddar cheese
4 cups (1 pound) shredded sharp cheddar cheese
1 large onion, finely chopped
1 cup mayonnaise*
1 cup (8 ounces) sour cream
1 tablespoon minced chives
1 teaspoon salt
1/2 teaspoon pepper

In a large bowl, combine potatoes and bacon. In another bowl, combine the remaining ingredients; add to potato mixture and toss gently to coat. Transfer to a greased 4-1/2-qt. baking dish. Bake, uncovered, at 325° for 50-60 minutes or until bubbly and lightly browned. **Yield:** 20-24 servings.

***Editor's Note:** Light or fat-free mayonnaise may not be substituted for regular mayonnaise.

Potluck Fruit Salad

Light and creamy, this tasty fruit salad gets gobbled up with gusto at every gathering. I can count on taking home an empty bowl. —Fran Du Bay, Corrales, New Mexico

✓ Uses less fat, sugar or salt. Includes Nutritional Analysis and Diabetic Exchanges.

1 can (20 ounces) pineapple chunks
2/3 cup sugar
2 tablespoons all-purpose flour
1/4 cup orange juice
2 tablespoons lemon juice
2 eggs, lightly beaten
2 cups whipped topping
3 pints fresh strawberries, sliced
6 cups green grapes
6 medium firm bananas, cut into 1/2-inch slices
6 kiwifruit, peeled, halved and sliced

Drain pineapple, reserving juice; set pineapple aside. In a saucepan, combine sugar and flour. Stir in the orange juice, lemon juice and reserved pineapple juice. Bring to a boil. Remove from the heat. Stir a small amount of hot mixture into eggs; return all to the pan, stirring constantly. Bring to a boil; cook and stir for 2 minutes or until thickened.

Cool to room temperature, stirring several times, about 20 minutes. Fold in whipped topping. In a large bowl, combine strawberries, grapes, bananas, kiwi and pineapple. Add dressing; toss. Serve immediately. **Yield:** 30 servings.

Nutritional Analysis: One 3/4-cup serving (prepared with reduced-fat whipped topping) equals 99 calories, 1 g fat (1 g saturated fat), 14 mg cholesterol, 5 mg sodium, 22 g carbohydrate, 2 g fiber, 1 g protein. **Diabetic Exchange:** 1-1/2 fruit.

Sweet Pepper French Dressing

Back when I prepared meals for 100 senior citizens at a time, they liked the way this tangy dressing perked up a salad. —Elsie McHenry, Gridley, California

2 cups sugar
2-1/2 teaspoons salt
2-1/2 teaspoons ground mustard
2-2/3 cups vegetable oil
2-2/3 cups cider vinegar
2 medium green peppers, finely chopped
2 jars (4 ounces *each*) sliced pimientos, drained and finely chopped
2-1/2 teaspoons grated onion

In a large bowl, combine the first five ingredients. Stir in green peppers, pimientos and onion. Stir frequently while serving. **Yield:** about 2 quarts.

Pistachio Orange Asparagus

(Pictured below and on page 148)

We're so pleased to have finally gotten an asparagus bed established! Now when I have a bounty of those tender spears, I pull out this recipe. Orange and pistachios complement the asparagus beautifully. —Janice Mitchell, Aurora, Colorado

2 pounds fresh asparagus, trimmed
6 tablespoons coarsely chopped pistachios
3/4 cup butter *or* margarine
1/4 cup orange juice
2 teaspoons grated orange peel
Dash pepper

In a saucepan, bring 1 in. of water to a boil; place asparagus in a steamer basket over water. Cover and steam for 5 minutes or until crisp-tender; drain. Place asparagus on a serving platter and keep warm. In a skillet over medium heat, cook pistachios in butter for 3-4 minutes or until lightly browned. Add orange juice and peel; heat through. Pour over asparagus. Sprinkle with pepper. **Yield:** 12 servings.

Summer Veggie Salad

(Pictured above)

For a deliciously different salad, I suggest this lightly dressed version without lettuce. It's especially good when I use fresh bounty from our garden.
—Kimberly Walsh, Fishers, Indiana

1 cup thinly sliced carrots
1 cup fresh green beans, cut into 2-inch pieces
1 cup fresh sugar snap peas
1 cup thinly sliced zucchini
1 cup thinly sliced yellow summer squash
1/2 cup thinly sliced green onions
1/2 cup chopped sweet red pepper
1 can (2-1/4 ounces) sliced ripe olives, drained

DRESSING:
6 tablespoons olive *or* vegetable oil
4-1/2 teaspoons lemon juice
1 tablespoon red wine vinegar *or* cider vinegar
1 tablespoon minced fresh parsley
1-1/2 teaspoons sugar
1 garlic clove, minced
1/8 teaspoon salt
Dash pepper
1/4 cup shredded Parmesan cheese, optional

In a large saucepan, bring 4 in. of water to a boil. Add carrots, beans and peas; cook for 4 minutes. Drain and rinse in cold water. Place in a bowl; add zucchini, summer squash, onions, red pepper and olives. In a jar with a tight-fitting lid, combine oil, lemon juice, vinegar, parsley, sugar, garlic, salt and pepper; shake well. Pour over vegetable mixture and toss to coat. Refrigerate for up to 1 hour. Just before serving, sprinkle with Parmesan cheese if desired. **Yield:** 12 servings.

Chocolate Peanut Butter Cookies

Sandwich cookies are always a hit, and homemade ones like these that feature peanut butter and chocolate are guaranteed to please! Whenever we visit out-of-town friends, they ask if we'll bring a batch of these cookies. *—Vickie Rhoads, Eugene, Oregon*

2 cups butter *or* margarine
1/4 cup shortening
2 cups baking cocoa
1 cup chocolate syrup
1/2 cup peanut butter
6 eggs
5 cups sugar
5 teaspoons vanilla extract
5 cups all-purpose flour
3 teaspoons baking soda
1 teaspoon salt

FILLING:
1/2 cup butter *or* margarine, softened
1 cup chunky peanut butter
1 cup milk
2 teaspoons vanilla extract
11 cups confectioners' sugar

In a saucepan over low heat, melt butter and shortening. Remove from the heat; stir in cocoa, chocolate syrup and peanut butter until smooth. Cool.

In a large mixing bowl, beat eggs and sugar until lemon-colored. Beat in the chocolate mixture and vanilla. Combine the flour, baking soda and salt; gradually add to creamed mixture. Drop by teaspoonfuls 2 in. apart onto ungreased baking sheets. Flatten with a glass dipped in sugar. Bake at 350° for 10-12 minutes or until surface cracks. Cool for 2 minutes before removing to wire racks.

In a mixing bowl, beat butter and peanut butter. Beat in milk and vanilla. Gradually add confectioners' sugar, beating until blended. Spread on the bottom of half of the cookies; top with remaining cookies. **Yield:** 11 dozen.

Lemon Avocado Salad Dressing

This creamy dressing, with its bold lemon flavor, is a refreshing change of pace—it's not one you'll see on

grocery store shelves. My uncle in California shared the recipe with me. It's also a good dip.
—Bernice Morris, Marshfield, Missouri

1 medium ripe avocado, peeled and mashed
1/4 cup water
2 tablespoons sour cream
2 tablespoons lemon juice
1 tablespoon minced fresh dill *or* 1 teaspoon dill weed
2 teaspoons olive *or* vegetable oil
1 garlic clove, minced
1/2 teaspoon seasoned salt
1/2 teaspoon honey
Salad greens, cherry tomatoes, sliced cucumbers and sweet red and yellow pepper strips

In a blender, combine the first nine ingredients; cover and process until smooth. Serve with salad greens, tomatoes, cucumbers and peppers. Store in the refrigerator. **Yield:** 1 cup.

Editor's Note: For a thinner consistency, stir in additional water.

Parmesan Herb Chicken

With a golden Parmesan cheese and herb coating, these tender chicken breasts make a tempting and hearty main dish. They're really very little fuss. Just coat them and bake. *—Phyllis Joann Schmalz Kansas City, Kansas*

2 cups grated Parmesan cheese
1/4 cup minced fresh parsley
2 tablespoons dried oregano
2 teaspoons paprika
1 teaspoon salt
1 teaspoon pepper
12 bone-in chicken breast halves
1 cup butter *or* margarine, melted

In a shallow dish, combine the first six ingredients. Dip chicken in butter, then coat with Parmesan mixture. Place in two greased 15-in. x 10-in. x 1-in. baking pans. Bake, uncovered, at 350° for 40-45 minutes or until the juices run clear. **Yield:** 12 servings.

Roasted Fan-Shaped Potatoes

These wonderful oven-roasted potatoes are very pretty to serve—the partially cut slices spread out in the shape of a fan. Folks at a potluck can easily take as many slices as they want. *—Eunice, Stoen Decorah, Iowa*

12 large baking potatoes
1/2 teaspoon salt
1/2 cup butter *or* margarine, melted, *divided*
6 tablespoons dry bread crumbs
6 tablespoons shredded Parmesan cheese

With a sharp knife, slice potatoes thinly but not all the way through, leaving slices attached at the bottom. Place potatoes in a greased shallow baking dish. Sprinkle with salt; brush with 1/4 cup butter. Bake, uncovered, at 425° for 30 minutes. Brush potatoes with remaining butter and sprinkle with bread crumbs. Bake 20 minutes longer. Sprinkle with Parmesan cheese. Bake 5-10 minutes more or until potatoes are tender and golden brown. **Yield:** 12 servings.

Peanut Butter Oat Bars

With their yummy chocolate and butterscotch topping, these chewy bars are sure to satisfy any sweet tooth! Since the recipe makes a big batch, the treats are perfect for potlucks and bake sales. *—Dawn Eggers Hollister, California*

2/3 cup butter *or* margarine, melted
1/4 cup peanut butter
1 cup packed brown sugar
1/4 cup light corn syrup
1/4 teaspoon vanilla extract
4 cups quick-cooking oats
TOPPING:
1 cup milk chocolate chips
1/2 cup butterscotch chips
1/3 cup peanut butter

In a mixing bowl, combine the butter, peanut butter, brown sugar, corn syrup and vanilla; gradually add the oats. Press into a greased 13-in. x 9-in. x 2-in. baking pan. Bake at 400° for 12-14 minutes or until edges are golden brown. Cool on a wire rack for 5 minutes. Meanwhile, for topping, melt chips and peanut butter in a microwave or saucepan. Stir until blended; spread over warm bars. Cool completely; refrigerate for 2-3 hours before cutting. **Yield:** 4 dozen.

Editor's Note: This recipe does not contain flour.

Homemade Peanut Butter

To make your own peanut butter, chop plain or dry roasted peanuts in a blender. When nuts are very finely ground, add a bit of vegetable oil, processing until mixture reaches spreading consistency.

Meaty Spinach Manicotti

(Pictured above)

Be prepared to share this recipe! Everyone who tries it asks for it. —*Pat Schroeder, Elkhorn, Wisconsin*

2 packages (8 ounces *each*) manicotti shells
1/4 cup butter *or* margarine
1/4 cup all-purpose flour
2-1/2 cups milk
3/4 cup grated Parmesan cheese
1 pound bulk Italian sausage
4 cups diced cooked chicken *or* turkey
2 packages (10 ounces *each*) frozen chopped spinach, thawed and squeezed dry
2 eggs, beaten
1 cup (4 ounces) shredded mozzarella cheese
2 cans (26-1/2 ounces *each*) spaghetti sauce
1/4 cup minced fresh parsley

Cook manicotti according to package directions. Meanwhile, melt butter in a saucepan. Stir in the flour until smooth. Gradually add milk. Bring to a boil; cook and stir for 2 minutes or until thickened. Stir in Parmesan cheese until melted; set aside. Drain manicotti; set aside. In a skillet, cook the sausage over medium heat until no longer pink; drain. Add the chicken, spinach, eggs, mozzarella cheese and 3/4 cup white sauce. Stuff into manicotti shells.

Spread 1/2 cup spaghetti sauce in each of two ungreased 13-in. x 9-in. x 2-in. baking dishes. Top with manicotti. Pour remaining spaghetti sauce over the top. Reheat the remaining white sauce, stirring constantly. Pour over spaghetti sauce. Bake, uncovered, at 350° for 45-50 minutes. Sprinkle with parsley. **Yield:** 14-16 servings.

Oven-Barbecued Spareribs

(Pictured on page 148)

Folks will go back for seconds once they get a bite of these tender, mildly tangy ribs. Expect compliments, not leftovers! —*Lynn Gaston, Selma, Alabama*

10 pounds pork spareribs, cut into serving-size pieces
2 large onions, chopped
1 cup finely chopped celery
2 cups ketchup
1 cup apple juice
1 cup water
1/2 cup lemon juice
1/4 cup packed brown sugar
1/4 cup ground mustard
1/4 cup cider vinegar
1/4 cup Worcestershire sauce
2 tablespoons paprika
2 tablespoon prepared horseradish
1/4 to 1/2 teaspoon cayenne pepper

Place ribs in a single layer in large baking pans. Bake, uncovered, at 350° for 30 minutes. Drain, reserving 1/4 cup drippings. Turn ribs. Bake 30 minutes longer. Meanwhile, in a saucepan, saute onions and celery in reserved drippings until tender. Stir in the remaining ingredients; bring to a boil. Drain ribs; pour sauce over ribs. Cover and bake for 15 minutes; turn ribs and baste. Bake 15 minutes longer or until tender. **Yield:** 12 servings.

No-Knead Knot Rolls

(Pictured on page 148)

My mom, Velma Perkins, loved to serve these light, golden rolls when I was growing up on our Iowa farm. The dough rises in the refrigerator overnight. —*Toni Hilscher, Omaha, Nebraska*

2 packages (1/4 ounce *each*) active dry yeast
2 cups warm water (110° to 115°)
1/2 cup sugar
2 teaspoons salt
6 to 6-1/2 cups all-purpose flour
1 egg
1/2 cup shortening
1/2 cup butter *or* margarine, softened

In a mixing bowl, dissolve yeast in warm water. Add the sugar, salt and 2 cups flour. Beat on medium speed for 2 minutes. Add egg and shortening; mix well. Stir in enough remaining flour to form a soft dough (do not knead). Cover and refrigerate overnight.

Punch dough down and divide into four portions. Cover three pieces with plastic wrap. Roll remaining portion into a 14-in. x 12-in. rectangle. Spread 2 tablespoons butter over dough. Fold in half lengthwise; cut into 12 strips. Tie each strip into a knot; tuck and pinch ends under. Place 2 in. apart on greased baking sheets. Repeat with remaining dough. Cover and let rise until doubled, about 1 hour. Bake at 400° for 10-12 minutes or until golden brown. **Yield:** 4 dozen.

Coconut Sweet Potato Bake

Yummy ingredients give sweet potatoes a special holiday appeal. —Jan Pavkov, Doylestown, Ohio

8 cans (2 pounds 8 ounces *each*) cut sweet potatoes, drained
1 pound butter *or* margarine
1 cup sugar
1 cup milk
4 teaspoons ground cinnamon
1 teaspoon ground nutmeg
1 package (14 ounces) flaked coconut
2 teaspoons vanilla extract
6 cups miniature marshmallows

Divide sweet potatoes among four greased 13-in. x 9-in. x 2-in. baking dishes. In a large saucepan over medium heat, combine butter, sugar, milk, cinnamon and nutmeg; cook and stir until butter is melted and mixture is smooth. Remove from the heat; stir in coconut and vanilla. Pour over sweet potatoes. Cover and bake at 350° for 45 minutes. Uncover; sprinkle each with 1-1/2 cups marshmallows. Bake 5-10 minutes longer or until marshmallows just begin to puff and melt. **Yield:** about 50 servings (about 1/2 cup each).

Rhubarb Meringue Dessert

(Pictured on page 148)

I hear so many nice comments when I serve this springtime dessert. —Jessica Moch, Bismarck, North Dakota

2 cups all-purpose flour
2 tablespoons sugar
1 cup cold butter *or* margarine

FILLING:

2 cups sugar
1/3 cup all-purpose flour
1 teaspoon salt
6 egg yolks, beaten
1 cup whipping cream
5 cups sliced fresh *or* frozen rhubarb, thawed

MERINGUE:

6 egg whites
1/2 teaspoon cream of tartar
3/4 cup sugar
1 teaspoon vanilla extract

In a bowl, combine flour and sugar; cut in butter until crumbly. Press into a greased 13-in. x 9-in. x 2-in. baking dish. Bake at 350° for 20 minutes. Cool on a wire rack while preparing filling. In a bowl, combine sugar, flour and salt. Stir in egg yolks and cream. Add rhubarb. Pour over crust. Bake at 350° for 50-60 minutes or until set. In a mixing bowl, beat egg whites and cream of tartar on medium speed until soft peaks form. Gradually beat in sugar, a tablespoon at a time, until stiff peaks form. Beat in vanilla. Spread over hot filling. Bake for 12-15 minutes or until golden. Cool on a wire rack. Refrigerate for 1-2 hours before serving. Refrigerate leftovers. **Yield:** 12-15 servings.

Marinated Vegetable Salad

When my family went to visit my grandmother in Nebraska, she made this easy-to-prepare dish for us. We loved it! —Rachael Montague, Sebastopol, California

✓ Uses less fat, sugar or salt. Includes Nutritional Analysis and Diabetic Exchanges.

2 cups sugar
1-3/4 cups cider vinegar
1/4 cup vegetable oil
1 tablespoon salt
1 small head cauliflower, broken into florets
3 medium carrots, grated
2 celery ribs, thinly sliced
1 green pepper, chopped
1 medium onion, chopped
1 can (15-1/4 ounces) white *or* shoepeg corn, drained
1 can (14-1/2 ounces) French-style green beans, drained
1 can (14 ounces) bean sprouts, drained
1 can (8 ounces) sliced water chestnuts, drained and halved
1 jar (4-1/2 ounces) sliced mushrooms, drained

In a saucepan, combine the sugar, vinegar, oil and salt. Bring to boil. Remove from the heat; cool to room temperature. In a large bowl, combine the remaining ingredients. Add dressing; toss to coat. Cover and chill for at least 2 hours. Serve with a slotted spoon. **Yield:** 25 servings.

Nutritional Analysis: One serving (2/3 cup) equals 89 calories, 2 g fat (trace saturated fat), 0 cholesterol, 405 mg sodium, 17 g carbohydrate, 2 g fiber, 2 g protein. **Diabetic Exchanges:** 1 starch, 1/2 fat.

Taco Braid

(Pictured below)

This pretty braided sandwich loaf is a winner! My daughter entered the recipe in a state 4-H beef cooking contest and won a trip to the national competition. It seems to rate tops with most folks who taste it.
—Lucile Proctor, Panguitch, Utah

1 teaspoon active dry yeast
2 tablespoons sugar, *divided*
3/4 cup warm water (110° to 115°), *divided*
2 tablespoons butter *or* margarine, softened
2 tablespoons nonfat dry milk powder
1 egg, beaten
1/2 teaspoon salt
2 cups all-purpose flour

FILLING:
1 pound lean ground beef
1/4 cup sliced fresh mushrooms
1 can (8 ounces) tomato sauce
2 tablespoons taco seasoning
1 egg, beaten
1/2 cup shredded cheddar cheese
1/4 cup sliced ripe olives

In a mixing bowl, dissolve yeast and 1 teaspoon sugar in 1/2 cup water; let stand for 5 minutes. Add butter, milk powder, egg, salt and remaining sugar and water. Stir in enough flour to form a soft dough. Turn onto a floured surface; knead until smooth and elastic, about 6-8 minutes. Place in a greased bowl, turning once to grease top. Cover and let rise in a warm place until doubled, about 1 hour.

In a skillet, cook beef and mushrooms over medium heat until meat is no longer pink; drain. Stir in tomato sauce and taco seasoning. Set aside 1 tablespoon beaten egg. Stir remaining egg into beef mixture. Cool completely. Punch dough down. Turn onto a lightly floured surface; roll into a 15-in. x 12-in. rectangle. Place on a greased baking sheet. Spread filling lengthwise down center third of rectangle. Sprinkle with cheese and olives.

On each long side, cut 1-in.-wide strips about 2-1/2 in. into center. Starting at one end, fold alternating strips at an angle across filling. Pinch ends to seal and tuck under. Cover and let rise for 30 minutes. Brush with reserved egg. Bake at 350° for 20-25 minutes or until golden brown. Remove from pan to a wire rack. **Yield:** 12-16 servings.

Pickle Pea Salad

Pickle relish adds unique flavor to this perky salad. Cubes of cheddar cheese and sliced hard-cooked eggs dress it up.—Kathryn Fleener, Louisville, Illinois

7 cans (15-1/4 ounces *each*) peas, drained
6 hard-cooked eggs, chopped
1 jar (16 ounces) dill pickle relish
1 pound cheddar cheese, cubed
1 medium onion, chopped
1 jar (32 ounces) mayonnaise
1/4 cup sugar
1/4 cup cider vinegar
2 teaspoons salt
1 can (12 ounces) salted peanuts, coarsely chopped
Sliced hard-cooked eggs, optional

In a large bowl, combine the first five ingredients. Combine the mayonnaise, sugar, vinegar and salt; mix well. Pour over pea mixture; toss to coat. Cover and refrigerate for at least 2 hours. Just before serving, stir in the chopped peanuts. Garnish with egg slices if desired. **Yield:** 50-55 servings (about 1/2 cup each).

Hearty Ham Loaf

I volunteered to cook for a regular group meeting of senior citizens. Attendance increased from 35 to more than 100, thanks in part to tasty dishes like this one. Ham, pork and beef combine to form tender, meaty slices in this loaf. *—Luella Feck, Bexley, Ohio*

3 eggs
2 cups milk

1-1/2 cups crushed saltines (about 35 crackers)
1-1/2 cups graham cracker crumbs (about 24 squares)
1 teaspoon onion salt
1 teaspoon salt
1/4 teaspoon pepper
3 pounds ground fully cooked ham
1 pound ground beef
1 pound ground pork
SWEET TANGY SAUCE:
2 cans (10-3/4 ounces *each*) condensed tomato soup, undiluted
2-1/2 cups packed brown sugar
1/2 cup cider vinegar
2 tablespoons ground mustard

In a large bowl, combine eggs, milk, cracker crumbs, onion salt, salt and pepper. Add meat; mix well. Shape into three loaves, about 9 in. x 3-1/2 in. x 1-3/4 in. each. Transfer to greased 9-in. x 5-in. x 3-in. loaf pans. Bake at 350° for 1 to 1-1/4 hours or until a meat thermometer reads 160°. In a saucepan, combine sauce ingredients. Cook and stir until sugar is dissolved. Serve with ham loaves. **Yield:** 3 loaves and 4 cups sauce (8 servings each).

Hot Turkey Sandwiches

This is a deliciously different entree when you're cooking for a crowd. Tender, shredded turkey is smothered in a basil cream sauce. Folks appreciate the change of pace from traditional turkey and gravy.
—Janice Bilek, Holland, Michigan

3 bone-in turkey breasts (6 to 7 pounds *each*)
3 cups sliced fresh mushrooms
3 cups thinly sliced green onions
1-1/2 cups butter *or* margarine
3/4 cup all-purpose flour
3 to 4 tablespoons dried basil
1 tablespoon salt
1 teaspoon pepper
6 cups chicken broth
3 cups whipping cream
50 sandwich rolls, split

Place turkey on racks in roasting pans. Bake, uncovered, at 325° for 2 hours or until a meat thermometer reads 170°, basting several times with pan drippings. Cover and let stand for 10 minutes. Shred turkey.

In several Dutch ovens or large pans, saute mushrooms and onions in butter until tender. Stir in flour, basil, salt and pepper until blended. Gradually stir in broth. Bring to a boil; cook and stir for 2 minutes or until thickened and bubbly. Add the turkey and heat through. Stir in cream; heat through. Spoon 1/2 cup onto each roll. **Yield:** 50 servings.

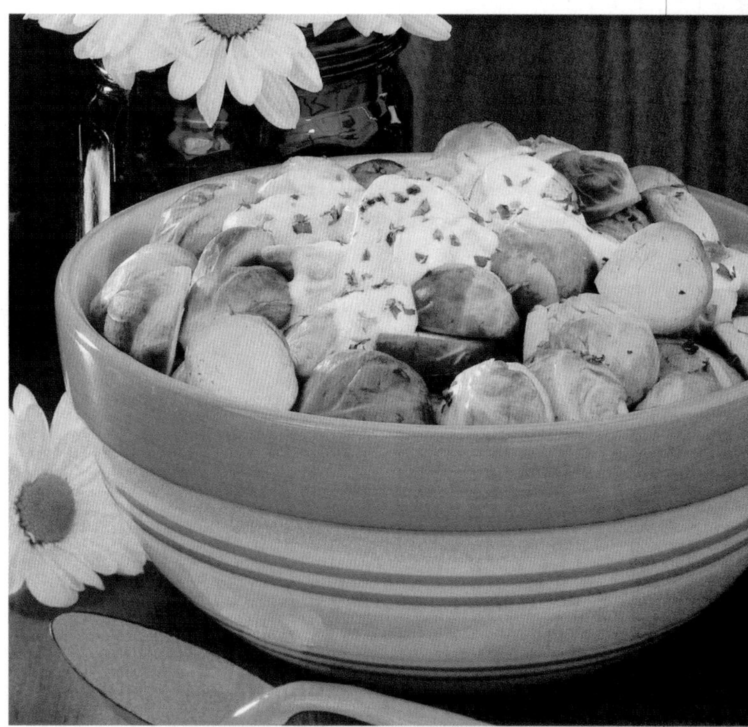

Sprouts with Sour Cream

(Pictured above)

I never really cared for brussels sprouts, but this wonderful recipe I received from a friend changed my mind. The slightly sweet sauce turns the tender veggies into a special change-of-pace side dish.
—Mary Devlin, Etobicoke, Ontario

2 pounds fresh brussels sprouts, halved
1/2 cup chopped onion
2 tablespoons butter *or* margarine
1 tablespoon all-purpose flour
1 tablespoon brown sugar
1/2 teaspoon salt
1/2 teaspoon ground mustard
1/2 cup milk
1 cup (8 ounces) sour cream
Minced fresh parsley

Add 1 in. of water and brussels sprouts to a saucepan; bring to a boil. Reduce heat; cover and simmer for 8-10 minutes or until tender. Meanwhile, in another saucepan, saute onion in butter until tender. Stir in flour, brown sugar, salt and mustard until blended. Gradually stir in milk. Bring to a boil; boil for 1 minute. Reduce heat. Stir in sour cream; heat through. Drain the sprouts; place in a serving bowl. Top with sauce. Sprinkle with parsley. **Yield:** 12 servings.

Cooking for One or Two

These perfectly portioned recipes will satisfy hearty appetites but won't leave you with a week's worth of leftovers.

JUST THE RIGHT SIZE. Clockwise from upper left: Tuna Salad Pockets (p. 181); Cherry Cream Cheese Tarts, Basil Vinaigrette and Salisbury Steak for Two (pp. 182 and 183); Toasted Angel Food Cake, Saucy Brussels Sprouts and Crispy Dijon Chicken (pp. 168 and 169); Hearty Stuffed Potatoes (p. 172); Spiced Ham Steak and Potato Vegetable Medley (p. 174).

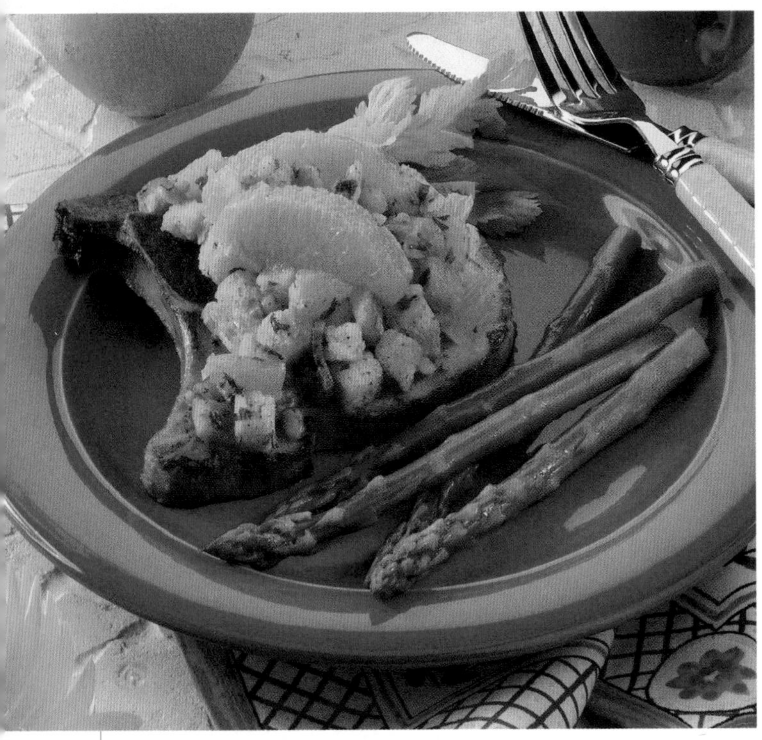

Smoked Pork Chops with Dressing

(Pictured above)

Tender smoked pork chops are a nice change of pace topped with a delicious, moist dressing. A hint of orange flavor adds interest. —*Rebecca Baird*
Salt Lake City, Utah

- **1 large navel orange**
- **2 smoked bone-in pork rib chops (3/4 inch thick and about 1 pound)**
- **1-1/2 teaspoons vegetable oil**
- **1/4 cup thinly sliced celery**
- **2 tablespoons finely chopped onion**
- **2 tablespoons minced fresh parsley**
- **3 tablespoons butter *or* margarine**
- **1 cup seasoned croutons**
- **1/4 cup coarsely chopped walnuts**
- **1/4 teaspoon pepper**
- **2 tablespoons chicken broth**

Grate 1 teaspoon orange peel; set aside. Peel and section the orange. Set four segments aside; coarsely chop remaining segments and set aside. In a skillet, brown pork chops on both sides in oil. Place chops in an ungreased 9-in. square baking dish; set aside. In the same skillet, saute the celery, onion and parsley in butter until tender. Add the croutons, walnuts and pepper; cook for 1-2 minutes. Stir in broth and reserved chopped orange and peel. Cook 1 minute longer.

Spoon dressing over chops; top with reserved oranges. Cover; bake at 350° for 30-35 minutes or until a meat thermometer reads 160°. **Yield:** 2 servings.

Crispy Dijon Chicken

(Pictured below right and on page 166)

I know you'll relish this doubly delicious dish as much as I do. Yogurt and mustard give golden oven-baked chicken a tangy taste, while cornflake crumbs provide plenty of crunch. I love the convenience of this baked chicken entree. —*Ella West*
Lake Charles, Louisiana

- **1/4 cup plain yogurt**
- **1/2 teaspoon salt-free herb seasoning blend**
- **1/2 teaspoon lemon juice**
- **1/2 teaspoon Dijon mustard**
- **1/2 cup cornflake crumbs**
- **1/4 cup grated Parmesan cheese**
- **2 bone-in chicken breast halves**

In a shallow bowl, combine the yogurt, seasoning blend, lemon juice and Dijon mustard. In another bowl, combine the cornflake crumbs and Parmesan cheese. Roll the chicken in yogurt mixture, then in crumb mixture. Place in a greased 8-in. square baking pan. Bake, uncovered, at 350° for 35-45 minutes or until chicken juices run clear. **Yield:** 2 servings.

Saucy Brussels Sprouts

(Pictured at right and on page 166)

Brussels sprouts are extra special dressed up for the holidays in a mild white sauce dotted with bright-red pimientos. —*Margery Bryan, Royal City, Washington*

- **1 package (10 ounces) frozen brussels sprouts**
- **1 tablespoon finely chopped onion**
- **1 tablespoon butter *or* margarine**
- **2 teaspoons brown sugar**
- **1 teaspoon all-purpose flour**
- **1/4 teaspoon salt**
- **1/4 teaspoon ground mustard**
- **Dash pepper**
- **1/4 cup milk**
- **1/4 cup sour cream**
- **1 jar (2 ounces) diced pimientos, drained**

Cook the brussels sprouts according to package directions. Meanwhile, in a saucepan, saute onion in butter until tender. Stir in brown sugar, flour, salt, mustard and pepper until blended. Gradually add milk. Bring to a boil; cook and stir for 1 minute. Reduce heat to low. Drain sprouts; cut in half. Add to sauce and heat through. Stir in sour cream and pimientos. **Yield:** 2 servings.

Toasted Angel Food Cake

(Pictured below and on page 166)

A scrumptious dessert just for one is even more satisfying if it's quick and easy like this fun treat.
—Tammy Clark, Duvall, Washington

1 tablespoon cream cheese, softened
2 slices angel food cake (3/4 inch thick)
1 to 2 teaspoons raspberry preserves
2 teaspoons butter *or* margarine, softened
Confectioners' sugar

Spread cream cheese on one slice of cake; spread preserves on second slice. Place slices together, sandwich-style. Spread butter on outsides of cake. In a skillet over medium heat, toast cake on both sides until lightly browned and cream cheese is melted. Dust with confectioners' sugar. Serve immediately. **Yield:** 1 serving.

SMALL YIELD, BIG IMPRESSION. You'll have no leftovers but lots of compliments with a meal of Crispy Dijon Chicken, Saucy Brussels Sprouts and Toasted Angel Food Cake (shown above).

Mini Sweet Potato Casserole

Orange peel, cinnamon and coconut season this delightfully different sweet potato dish. Since it's tasty and nutritious, it's one of my favorite holiday recipes. This perfectly portioned casserole pairs well with many entrees. —Bob Breno, Strongsville, Ohio

1 medium sweet potato
2 tablespoons butter *or* margarine, melted, *divided*
1 tablespoon raisins
1/2 teaspoon grated orange peel
1/8 teaspoon salt
1/8 teaspoon ground cinnamon
Dash ground nutmeg
2 tablespoons flaked coconut

Place the sweet potato in a saucepan; cover with water. Bring to a boil; reduce heat. Cover and simmer for 30-40 minutes or just until tender; drain. When cool enough to handle, peel the sweet potato and place it in a bowl; mash. Stir in 1 tablespoon butter, raisins, orange peel, salt, cinnamon and nutmeg. Transfer to a greased 1-1/2-cup baking dish. Toss the coconut with remaining butter; sprinkle over the top. Bake, uncovered, at 350° for 25-30 minutes or until golden brown. **Yield:** 2 servings.

Quick Baked Apple

Baked apples are so simple to make...and this version has a yummy filling of chopped nuts, raisins and coconut. I enjoy this fruity dessert served warm with a scoop of vanilla ice cream. But I know you'll agree it's just as delicious served by itself. —Judi Klee Nebraska City, Nebraska

1 teaspoon finely chopped nuts
1 teaspoon raisins
1 teaspoon flaked coconut
1 medium tart apple
Dash ground cinnamon
2 tablespoons apple juice
1-1/2 teaspoons maple syrup

In a small bowl, combine nuts, raisins and coconut; set aside. Core apple and peel the top third; place in a microwave-safe dish. Fill center with nut mixture. Sprinkle with cinnamon. Pour apple juice into dish and syrup over apple. Cover and microwave on high for 2-3 minutes or until apple is tender, basting and rotating every minute. Serve warm. **Yield:** 1 serving.

Editor's Note: This recipe was tested in an 850-watt microwave.

Stuffed Pork Chops

(Pictured at right)

A savory stuffing and gravy make these chops nice enough for a birthday dinner or other special occasion. It's usually just my husband and I who enjoy these moist tender chops, but I've been known to triple the recipe for our grown children and their families. —Shirley Itz, Fredericksburg, Texas

2 tablespoons chopped celery
2 tablespoons chopped onion
2 tablespoons butter *or* margarine, *divided*
1/2 cup seasoned stuffing croutons
3 tablespoons milk
1 teaspoon minced fresh parsley
1/4 teaspoon paprika
1/8 teaspoon salt
1/8 teaspoon pepper
2 boneless pork loin chops (1 inch thick)
3/4 cup beef broth
1 to 2 tablespoons cornstarch
2 tablespoons cold water

In a skillet, saute celery and onion in 1 tablespoon butter until tender. Transfer to a bowl. Add croutons, milk, parsley, paprika, salt and pepper. Cut a pocket in each pork chop; fill with stuffing. In a skillet, brown chops in remaining butter. Transfer to a greased 9-in. square baking dish. Pour broth into dish. Cover and bake at 350° for 30-35 minutes or until a meat thermometer reads 160°. Remove chops and keep warm.

Pour the pan drippings into a saucepan; bring to a boil. Combine cornstarch and water until smooth; gradually stir into drippings. Cook and stir for 2 minutes or until thickened. Serve with the pork chops. **Yield:** 2 servings.

Maple Carrots

(Pictured above right)

Nutritious carrots are extra sweet and appealing in this simple-to-fix recipe. Tarragon and maple syrup might seem like an odd combination, but those flavors combine well in this side dish. —Beatrice Fulton Bellevue, Washington

1-1/2 cups sliced carrots
1 tablespoon maple syrup
1/8 to 1/4 teaspoon dried tarragon

Place 1 in. of water in a saucepan; add the carrots. Bring to a boil. Reduce heat; cover and simmer for 3-4 minutes or until tender. Drain. Stir in syrup and tarragon. **Yield:** 2 servings.

TABLE FOR TWO. Treat yourself and someone special to a super meal of Stuffed Pork Chops, Maple Carrots and Li'l Pecan Pies (shown above).

Li'l Pecan Pies

(Pictured above)

These tempting little tarts have all the rich traditional taste of a full-size pecan pie in a much smaller package. The tarts are perfect for two. —Christine Boitos Livonia, Michigan

1/2 cup all-purpose flour
1/8 teaspoon salt
3 tablespoons shortening
4 teaspoons cold water
FILLING:
1/3 cup pecan halves
1 egg
1/3 cup corn syrup
1/3 cup packed brown sugar
1/2 teaspoon vanilla extract
Whipped cream, optional

In a bowl, combine flour and salt; cut in shortening until crumbly. Gradually add water, tossing with a fork until dough forms a ball. Cover and refrigerate for at least 30 minutes. Divide dough in half. Roll each half into a 6-in. circle. Transfer to two 4-1/2-in. tart pans; fit pastry into pans, trimming if necessary.

Arrange pecans in shells. In a bowl, combine egg, corn syrup, brown sugar and vanilla; mix well. Pour over pecans. Place shells on a baking sheet. Bake at 375° for 35-40 minutes or until a knife inserted near the center comes out clean. Cool on a wire rack. Top with whipped cream if desired. **Yield:** 2 servings.

Hearty Stuffed Potatoes

(Pictured above and on page 166)

Packed with cheddar and cottage cheeses and hard-cooked egg, these potatoes make a terrific light lunch all by themselves. You can also offer them as a side dish with roast beef. —*Lorraine Danz*
New Holland, Pennsylvania

- **2 medium baking potatoes**
- **1/2 cup cottage cheese**
- **3 tablespoons mayonnaise**
- **2 teaspoons prepared mustard**
- **1/2 teaspoon dill weed**
- **1/4 to 1/2 teaspoon salt**
- **1/8 teaspoon pepper**
- **1/2 cup plus 1 tablespoon shredded cheddar cheese, *divided***
- **1 hard-cooked egg, chopped**
- **1 plum tomato, thinly sliced**

Bake the potatoes at 375° for 1 hour or until tender. Cool. Cut a thin slice off the top of each potato. Scoop out the pulp, leaving a thin shell. In a bowl, mash the pulp with cottage cheese, mayonnaise, mustard, dill, salt and pepper. Stir in 1/2 cup of the cheddar cheese and egg. Spoon into potato shells. Top with the remaining cheese. Place on a baking sheet. Bake at 375° for 25-30 minutes or until heated through. Garnish with the tomato slices. **Yield:** 2 servings.

Denver Omelet Scramble

For breakfast, lunch or dinner, this savory scramble loaded with potatoes, ham, vegetables and cheese is a satisfying entree any time of day. —*Ron Gardner*
Grand Haven, Michigan

- **1 cup sliced peeled uncooked potato**
- **1/2 cup diced fully cooked ham**
- **1/2 cup *each* chopped onion, green pepper and sweet red pepper**
- **1 can (4 ounces) mushroom stems and pieces, drained**
- **1 tablespoon butter *or* margarine**
- **1 teaspoon salt**
- **4 eggs, lightly beaten**
- **1/2 cup shredded cheddar cheese**

Place potato slices in a saucepan; cover with water. Bring to a boil. Cook until tender; drain. In a skillet, saute the potato, ham, onion, peppers and mushrooms in butter for 6-8 minutes or until vegetables are tender. Sprinkle with salt. Pour eggs over top. Cook and stir until the eggs are completely set. Sprinkle with cheese. **Yield:** 2 servings.

Apricot Pork Chops

The pork and fruit flavors blend wonderfully in this entree, which is great for family or special occasions. It has such a terrific flavor that folks will think you fussed. —*Mrs. Thomas Allison*
Redmond, Washington

- **2 bone-in pork loin chops (1-1/4 inches thick)**
- **2 tablespoons chopped onion**
- **2 tablespoons butter *or* margarine**
- **1-1/2 cups soft bread crumbs**
- **1/2 cup chopped dried apricots**
- **1/2 teaspoon salt**
- **1/8 teaspoon pepper**
- **2 tablespoons plus 1/2 cup water, *divided***
- **1 tablespoon vegetable oil**
- **2 tablespoons white wine vinegar *or* cider vinegar**

Cut a pocket in each chop by slicing from the fat side almost to the bone; set aside. In a skillet, saute onion in butter until tender. Stir in the bread crumbs, apricots, salt and pepper. Add 2 tablespoons water; toss to coat. Stuff chops. In a skillet, brown chops in oil. Combine vinegar and remaining water; pour over chops. Bring to a boil. Reduce heat; cover and simmer for 20-25 minutes or until a meat thermometer reads 160°. **Yield:** 2 servings.

Macaroni Egg Salad

This tasty dish proves you don't have to feed a crowd to enjoy that delicious picnic salad flavor.
—Ruth Wimmer, Bland, Virginia

1 cup uncooked elbow macaroni
1/4 cup mayonnaise
1 teaspoon sugar
1 teaspoon cider vinegar
1/2 teaspoon salt
1/2 teaspoon prepared mustard
Dash pepper
1 celery rib, chopped
2 tablespoons chopped onion
1 hard-cooked egg, chopped

Cook macaroni according to package directions. Drain and rinse in cold water. In a bowl, combine the mayonnaise, sugar, vinegar, salt, mustard and pepper. Stir in celery and onion. Fold in macaroni and egg. Refrigerate until serving. **Yield:** 2 servings.

Salsa Squash

You can't beat this combination of sweet squash, zippy salsa and eye-catching orange color for a fun side dish.
—Marilyn Young, Riverside, Ohio

1 pound butternut squash, peeled, seeded and cubed
1/4 cup finely chopped onion
1 garlic clove, minced
1 tablespoon butter *or* margarine
2/3 cup salsa
1/2 teaspoon salt
1/2 cup shredded cheddar cheese, *divided*

In a saucepan, bring 1 in. of water to a boil; place squash in a steamer basket over water. Reduce heat; cover and steam for 10-15 minutes or until tender. Meanwhile, in a large saucepan, saute onion and garlic in butter until tender. Stir in salsa, salt and squash cubes.

Spoon half of the mixture into a greased 1-qt. baking dish. Sprinkle with 1/4 cup cheese. Top with remaining squash mixture. Cover and bake at 400° for 15 minutes. Uncover; top with remaining cheese. Bake 5 minutes longer or until cheese is melted. **Yield:** 2 servings.

Butternut Squash Basics

Buy butternut squash that have coarse, hard rinds and that feel heavy for their size.

Pork Tenderloin Stir-Fry

(Pictured below)

This flavorful stir-fry is ideal for serving two. The combination of tender meat and crunchy vegetables is so satisfying.
—Shelly McCallum, Aylmer, Ontario

✓ Uses less fat, sugar or salt. Includes Nutritional Analysis and Diabetic Exchanges.

1/2 pound pork tenderloin, thinly sliced
2 teaspoons canola oil
4 fresh mushrooms, sliced
3 green onions, sliced
1/4 cup frozen peas
3/4 cup thinly sliced cabbage
4 ounces canned bean sprouts
2 garlic cloves, minced
1 teaspoon ground ginger
1/2 teaspoon sugar
1 tablespoon soy sauce
Hot cooked rice

In a skillet, stir-fry pork in oil until no longer pink. Add mushrooms, onions and peas; stir-fry for 1 minute. Add cabbage, bean sprouts, garlic, ginger and sugar; stir-fry for 2 minutes. Stir in soy sauce. Serve over rice. **Yield:** 2 servings.

Nutritional Analysis: One serving (prepared with reduced-sodium soy sauce; calculated without rice) equals 254 calories, 9 g fat (2 g saturated fat), 67 mg cholesterol, 334 mg sodium, 14 g carbohydrate, 4 g fiber, 29 g protein. **Diabetic Exchanges:** 3 lean meat, 1 starch.

Pot Roast for Two

(Pictured above)

A satisfying pot roast dinner doesn't have to feed an army, as this recipe proves. I love the bold combination of spices in this moist, flavorful meal-in-one dish. —*Judy Armstrong, Norwell, Massachusetts*

2 beef eye of round steaks
2 small carrots, cut into 3/4-inch chunks
2 small potatoes, peeled and cut into 1/2-inch slices
1 celery rib, coarsely chopped
1 small onion, sliced
1 can (14-1/2 ounces) diced tomatoes, undrained
1/4 cup beef broth
2 garlic cloves, thinly sliced
2 teaspoons onion soup mix
1 teaspoon salt
1/2 teaspoon Italian seasoning
1/4 teaspoon pepper
1/8 teaspoon aniseed
1/8 teaspoon *each* ground cinnamon, ginger and nutmeg
Dash ground cloves

Place steaks in an ungreased 2-1/2-qt. baking dish. Top with carrots, potatoes, celery and onion. Combine the tomatoes, broth, garlic, soup mix and seasonings; pour over vegetables. Cover and bake at 350° for 1-1/2 to 1-3/4 hours or until meat and vegetables are tender. **Yield:** 2 servings.

Spiced Ham Steak

(Pictured below right and on page 166)

My husband loves ham, but I get bored cooking it the same old way. I wanted something easy and tasty, so I came up with this zippy sauce that really perks up a plain ham steak. —*Karla Foisy*
Minneapolis, Minnesota

1 fully cooked ham steak (about 8 ounces and 1/2 inch thick)
4-1/2 teaspoons lime juice
1 tablespoon grated Parmesan cheese
1 tablespoon sour cream
1-1/2 teaspoons all-purpose flour
1 teaspoon vegetable oil
1/4 teaspoon garlic salt
1/4 teaspoon Cajun seasoning
1/4 teaspoon curry powder
1/4 teaspoon dried savory

Place ham steak on a lightly greased broiler pan; broil 4 in. from the heat for 5 minutes. In a small bowl, combine the lime juice, Parmesan cheese, sour cream, oil, garlic salt, Cajun seasoning, curry powder and savory; mix well. Turn ham steak; spread with sauce. Broil 5 minutes longer or until lightly browned and bubbly. Cut in half to serve. **Yield:** 2 servings.

Potato Vegetable Medley

(Pictured at right and on page 166)

Vegetables star in this fresh-tasting and colorful side dish. The mild seasoning lets their natural goodness come through. Just because you're cooking a small portion doesn't mean you can't use a variety of produce. —*Edna Hoffman, Hebron, Indiana*

2 medium red potatoes, quartered
2 medium carrots, halved lengthwise and quartered
1 small onion, cut into 8 wedges
1/4 cup chicken broth
1 teaspoon seasoned salt, *divided*
1 medium zucchini, quartered and cut into 1-inch slices
1 tablespoon minced fresh parsley

In a greased 1-qt. baking dish, combine the potatoes, carrots, onion, broth and 1/2 teaspoon seasoned salt. Cover and bake at 400° for 30 minutes. Stir in zucchini and remaining seasoned salt. Bake 5-10 minutes longer or until vegetables are tender. Sprinkle with parsley. **Yield:** 2 servings.

Apricot Berry Shortcake

(Pictured below)

This fun and convenient alternative to traditional strawberry shortcake features some of summer's finest fruits. It's a delightful dessert that's easy to assemble using purchased sponge cakes. —*Marion Lowery Medford, Oregon*

1 cup fresh raspberries *and/or* blackberries
1 tablespoon sugar
Dash ground nutmeg
1/4 cup apricot jam
1 teaspoon butter *or* margarine
Dash salt
2 individual round sponge cakes
Whipped cream

In a small bowl, combine the berries, sugar and nutmeg. Cover and refrigerate for 1 hour. In a saucepan, heat jam, butter and salt on low until butter is melted. In a microwave, warm the sponge cakes on high for 20 seconds; place on serving plates. Top with berry mixture; drizzle with apricot sauce. Top with a dollop of whipped cream. **Yield:** 2 servings.

PERFECT PAIRING of flavor and freshness is this meal for two: Spiced Ham Steak, Potato Vegetable Medley and Apricot Berry Shortcake (shown above).

Tuna Patty Sandwiches

Here's a tasty way to dress up canned tuna in a hot sandwich. The patties are simple to assemble.
—Ruth Wimmer, Bland, Virginia

1 egg
1/2 teaspoon prepared mustard
1/4 cup dry bread crumbs
1 can (6 ounces) tuna, drained and flaked
1 tablespoon vegetable oil
2 sandwich rolls, split

In a bowl, combine the egg, mustard, bread crumbs and tuna; mix well. Shape into four patties (mixture will be soft). In a skillet over medium heat, fry patties in oil on both sides until lightly browned. Place two patties on each roll. **Yield:** 2 servings.

Green Chili Grilled Cheese

I make grilled cheese often when it's too hot to use the oven. Here an old standby gets a Southwestern twist. *—Emily Hockett, Federal Way, Washington*

4 slices bread
4 slices cheddar cheese
1 can (4 ounces) chopped green chilies, drained
2 tablespoons butter *or* margarine, softened

Top two slices of bread with two slices of cheese; sprinkle with chilies. Top with remaining bread. Butter the outsides of sandwiches. In a large skillet over medium heat, cook sandwiches on both sides until golden brown and cheese is melted. **Yield:** 2 servings.

Lemon Sponge Pudding

You'll want to pucker up and kiss the cook once you try this comforting pudding bursting with lemon flavor.
—Evelyn Kating, Pryor, Oklahoma

1/3 cup sugar
2 teaspoons all-purpose flour
1/3 cup milk
2 tablespoons lemon juice
1 teaspoon lemon peel
1 egg, *separated*
Confectioners' sugar

In a bowl, combine sugar and flour. Stir in milk, lemon juice and peel. Beat egg yolk; add to lemon mixture. In a mixing bowl, beat egg white until stiff peaks form; fold into lemon mixture. Place two ungreased 6-oz. custard cups in an 8-in. square baking pan. Divide lemon mixture between the cups. Pour hot water into pan to a depth of 1 in. Bake, uncovered, at 325° for 35-40 minutes or until a knife inserted near the center comes out clean. Dust with confectioners' sugar. Serve immediately. **Yield:** 2 servings.

Tater Tot Taco Salad

(Pictured at right)

Since I love potatoes and my husband and I both enjoy the flavor of tacos, this fun dish is a tasty meal-in-one for the two of us. *—Eleanor Mielke*
Mitchell, South Dakota

2 cups frozen miniature Tater Tots
1/2 pound ground beef
2 tablespoons taco seasoning
1/2 cup shredded cheddar cheese
1/4 cup sliced ripe *or* stuffed olives
1 cup shredded lettuce
2 tablespoons taco sauce
1/4 cup sour cream

Bake Tater Tots according to package directions. Meanwhile, in a large skillet, cook beef over medium heat until no longer pink; drain. Stir in taco seasoning. Divide Tater Tots between two serving plates or bowls. Top with taco mixture, cheese, olives, lettuce, taco sauce and sour cream. **Yield:** 2 servings.

Rye Drop Biscuits

(Pictured at right)

My husband, Ken, and I like these rich, rugged, melt-in-your-mouth biscuits with any meal. They're so easy to make. *—Nancy Zimmerman*
Cape May Court House, New Jersey

1/3 cup all-purpose flour
1/4 cup rye flour
1 tablespoon brown sugar
1 teaspoon baking powder
1/4 teaspoon dried parsley flakes
1/8 teaspoon salt
1/4 cup cold butter *or* margarine
1 egg
1 tablespoon milk

In a bowl, combine the first six ingredients. Cut in butter until mixture resembles coarse crumbs. Stir

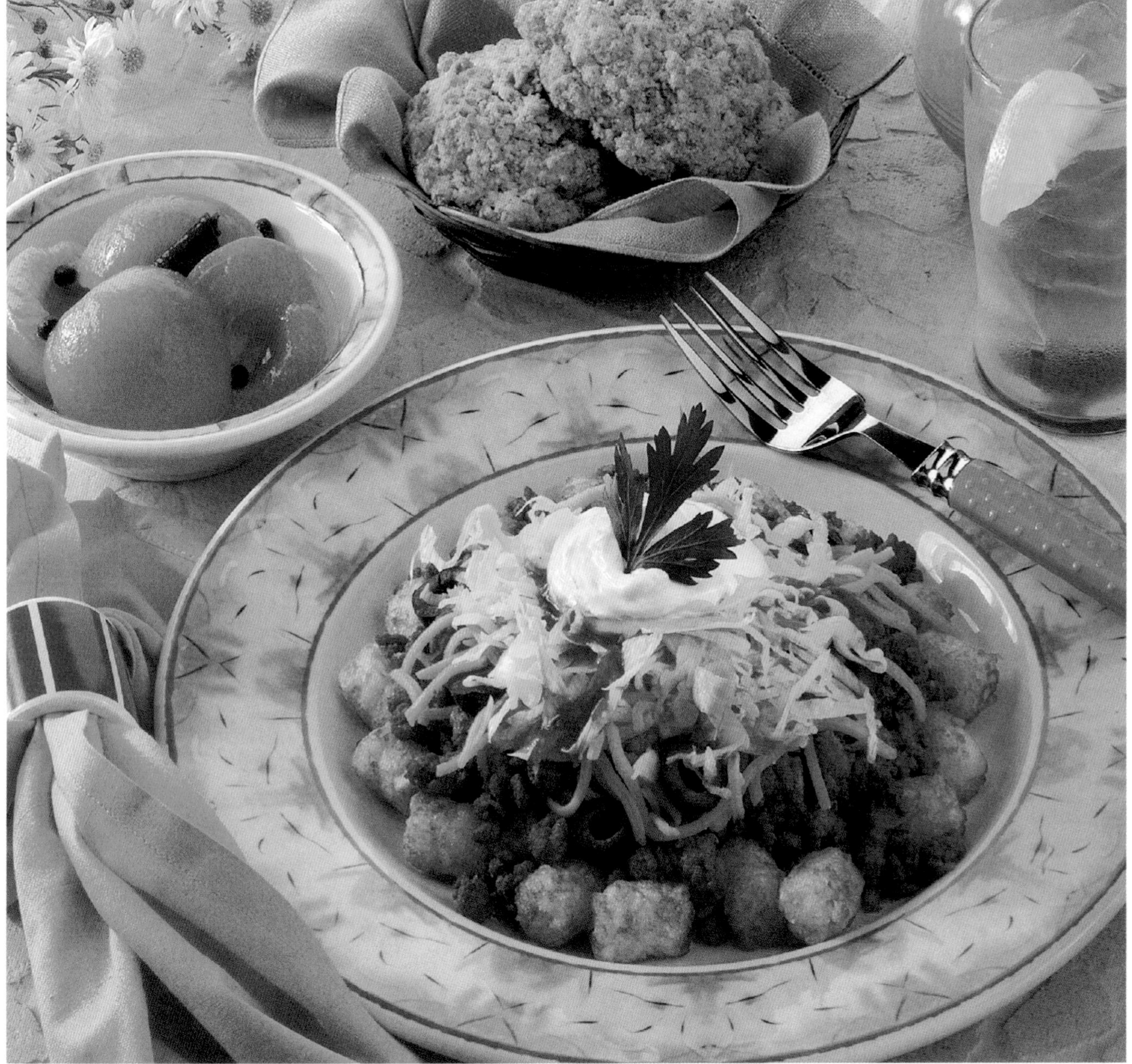

A TASTY TRIO of Tater Tot Taco Salad, Rye Drop Biscuits and Spiced Apricots (shown above) makes one marvelous meal just perfect for two.

in the egg and milk just until combined. Drop by 1/4 cupfuls 2 in. apart onto a greased baking sheet. Bake at 400° for 7-10 minutes or until golden brown. Remove to a wire rack. **Yield:** 4 biscuits.

Spiced Apricots

(Pictured above)

I've been cooking for big gatherings for years...and now that I'm widowed, it's hard to cook for just one or two. That's why I appreciate simple recipes like this one, which turns canned apricots into a special side dish. —*Trudy Barth, Niceville, Florida*

1 can (15 ounces) apricot halves
2 tablespoons cider vinegar
6 whole allspice
1 cinnamon stick (3 inches)

Drain apricots, reserving syrup. Set apricots aside. In a saucepan, combine the syrup, vinegar, allspice and cinnamon. Bring to a boil. Reduce heat; cover and simmer for 15 minutes. Remove from the heat; stir in apricots. Cover and let stand for 30 minutes, stirring occasionally. Drain if desired. Serve warm or cold. **Yield:** 2 servings.

Stuffed Chicken Breasts

(Pictured below)

This moist chicken with its savory filling makes a special entree for two, yet it's not tricky to prepare. The recipe can easily be doubled. —*Katherine Suter Prescott, Arizona*

3/4 cup chopped tart apple
1/2 cup finely chopped fully cooked ham
1/4 cup chopped fresh mushrooms
1/4 cup chopped red onion
2 tablespoons vegetable oil, *divided*
2 tablespoons Dijon mustard
1/3 cup dry bread crumbs
1/4 teaspoon lemon-pepper seasoning
2 large boneless skinless chicken breast halves
2 tablespoons all-purpose flour

HARVEST A BUSHEL of compliments with such fall favorites as Stuffed Chicken Breasts, Scalloped Potatoes and Date-Filled Baked Apple (shown above).

In a small saucepan, saute the apple, ham, mushrooms and onion in 1 tablespoon oil until onion and apple are tender. Stir in mustard, bread crumbs and lemon-pepper. Flatten chicken breasts to 1/4-in. thickness; top each with the apple mixture. Roll up and secure with toothpicks. Coat with flour. In a skillet, brown chicken in remaining oil. Place in an 8-in. square baking dish. Bake, uncovered, at 350° for 20-30 minutes or until juices run clear. **Yield:** 2 servings.

Scalloped Potatoes

(Pictured at left)

These potatoes are mildly cheesy, creamy and comforting—just like Mom used to make, only less of them!
—Edith Jennings, Prairie City, Iowa

2 tablespoons butter *or* margarine
2 tablespoons all-purpose flour
1 cup milk
1/4 cup shredded cheddar cheese
1/2 teaspoon salt
1/4 teaspoon Worcestershire sauce
1/8 teaspoon pepper
2 medium potatoes, peeled and thinly sliced
Paprika, optional

In a small saucepan, melt butter over medium heat. Stir in flour until smooth. Gradually add milk. Bring to a boil; cook and stir for 2 minutes or until thickened. Reduce heat; add the cheese, salt, Worcestershire sauce and pepper. Cook and stir until cheese is melted. Place potatoes in a greased 1-qt. baking dish. Top with sauce. Cover and bake at 350° for 25 minutes. Uncover; bake 20 minutes longer or until potatoes are tender. Sprinkle with paprika if desired. **Yield:** 2 servings.

Date-Filled Baked Apple

(Pictured at left)

It's hard to say what's more appealing—the homey aroma of this treat baking in the oven or the mouth-watering flavor of the warm apple, sweet dates and crunchy walnuts.
—Dorothy Pritchett
Wills Point, Texas

4-1/2 teaspoons brown sugar, *divided*
1 tablespoon chopped dates
1-1/2 teaspoons chopped walnuts
1/8 teaspoon ground cinnamon
1 large tart apple
1/4 cup water
Whipped cream

In a small bowl, combine 1-1/2 teaspoons brown sugar, dates, walnuts and cinnamon. Peel top half of apple and remove core; place in a small baking dish. Fill with date mixture. Combine water and remaining brown sugar; pour over apple. Cover and bake at 400° for 35-40 minutes or until the apple is tender, basting occasionally. Serve warm with whipped cream. **Yield:** 1 serving.

Coconut Carrot Salad

Why eat a plain carrot when this super salad is such a snap to make? The coconut makes this salad taste like a tropical treat. It keeps meals interesting to fix something special for yourself once in a while.
—Evelyn Schwartz, Quincy, Illinois

1 medium carrot, shredded
1/4 cup finely chopped apple
1/4 cup flaked coconut
2 tablespoons sour cream
1-1/2 teaspoons honey
1 teaspoon lemon juice

In a bowl, combine all ingredients; mix well. Cover and refrigerate until serving. **Yield:** 1 serving.

Italian Potato Pancake

Seasoned with basil and oregano and sprinkled with mozzarella cheese, this potato pancake variation is almost like an Italian potato patty. —Celeste Rossmiller
Denver, Colorado

1 medium potato, peeled and grated
2 tablespoons chopped onion
2 tablespoons whole wheat flour
1 egg
1/4 teaspoon dried basil
1/4 teaspoon dried oregano
Salt and pepper to taste
1 tablespoon olive *or* vegetable oil
Shredded mozzarella cheese

Rinse grated potato in cold water; drain thoroughly. In a bowl, combine potato, onion, flour, egg, basil, oregano, salt and pepper. In a skillet, heat oil; add potato mixture. Cover and cook over medium-low heat for 5-7 minutes or until golden brown. Turn; sprinkle with cheese. Cover and cook over low heat 5 minutes longer. **Yield:** 1 serving.

Chicken Vegetable Soup

(Pictured above)

I love eating a big bowl of this colorful, fresh-tasting soup on a winter's day. What a great way to warm up!
—Ruth Wimmer, Bland, Virginia

2 cups chicken broth
1 cup fresh *or* frozen corn
1 small celery rib, chopped
1 small carrot, chopped
1 small onion, chopped
1 cup cubed cooked chicken
1/2 cup canned diced tomatoes
Salt and pepper to taste

In a saucepan, combine the first five ingredients. Bring to a boil. Reduce heat; cover and simmer for 25-30 minutes or until vegetables are tender. Stir in the chicken, tomatoes, salt and pepper; heat through. **Yield:** 2 servings.

Hamburger Stroganoff

This classic stick-to-your-ribs mainstay is really very little fuss. To add color, I sprinkle a bit of parsley on top when serving it.
—Elie Wren
Farmington Hills, Michigan

1/2 pound ground beef
1/4 cup chopped onion
1 tablespoon all-purpose flour
1/2 teaspoon salt
1/8 teaspoon pepper
1 can (4-1/2 ounces) mushroom stems and pieces, undrained
1/2 cup condensed cream of chicken soup, undiluted
1/2 cup sour cream
Hot cooked noodles

In a skillet, cook beef and onion over medium heat until meat is no longer pink; drain. Stir in flour, salt and pepper until blended. Add mushrooms; cook and stir over low heat for 5 minutes. Stir in the soup; simmer, uncovered, for 10 minutes. Stir in sour cream; heat through. Serve over noodles. **Yield:** 2 servings.

Creamy Tomato Soup

A few handy pantry items inspired me to create this fresh-tasting tomato soup. It's super easy...and oh-so-good!
—Gail Westing, Landfall, Minnesota

1 can (8 ounces) tomato sauce
1 tablespoon butter *or* margarine
1/8 to 1/4 teaspoon onion powder
Dash pepper
2 cups milk

In a saucepan, combine the first four ingredients. Bring to a simmer over medium heat. Gradually stir in milk; cook and stir until heated through (do not boil). **Yield:** 2 servings.

Apple Puff Pancake

For a light breakfast, lunch or brunch entree, this fluffy baked pancake is very little fuss. It's economical, too.
—Sharon Emery, New Burnside, Illinois

1/2 cup all-purpose flour
1/8 teaspoon salt
2 eggs
1/2 cup milk
1 tablespoon butter *or* margarine, melted
1 medium tart apple, peeled and chopped
1/2 cup apple jelly
1/8 teaspoon ground cinnamon

In a mixing bowl, combine flour and salt. Add eggs, milk and butter. Pour into a greased 8-in. square baking pan. Bake at 400° for 20-25 minutes or until lightly browned. Meanwhile, combine the chopped apple, jelly and cinnamon in a saucepan. Cook and stir until jelly is melted. Cut pancake into fourths; place two pieces on each plate. Top with apple mixture. **Yield:** 2 servings.

Pork Broccoli Stir-Fry

This dish has lots of eye-catching color, a nice combination of tender meat and crisp vegetables, and wonderful garlic flavor. —*Nadia Boutin Sylvester, Cookshire, Quebec*

1/2 pound pork tenderloin, thinly sliced
1 tablespoon vegetable oil
1-1/2 cups sliced broccoli florets
1/2 cup julienned green pepper
1/2 cup julienned sweet red pepper
3 garlic cloves, minced
1 cup sliced fresh mushrooms
2 tablespoons cornstarch
1 cup chicken broth
4 teaspoons soy sauce
Hot cooked rice

In a skillet, stir-fry pork in oil for 3 minutes or until no longer pink. Remove and keep warm. In the same skillet, stir-fry broccoli for 2-3 minutes. Add peppers and garlic; cook for 2 minutes. Stir in the mushrooms; cook 1-2 minutes longer. Combine the cornstarch, broth and soy sauce until smooth; stir into skillet. Bring to a boil; cook and stir for 2 minutes or until thickened. Return pork to the pan; heat through. Serve over rice. **Yield:** 2 servings.

Pepperoni Pizza Pita

With its no-fuss pita crust, this pizza makes a quick meal for one. And if you're serving a family, individual pizzas are perfect—everyone can choose their own toppings! —*Jeannette Derner, Newport News, Virginia*

✓ Uses less fat, sugar or salt. Includes Nutritional Analysis and Diabetic Exchanges.

2 tablespoons pizza sauce
1 whole pita bread (6 inches)
6 pepperoni slices
2 fresh mushrooms, sliced
1/4 cup shredded mozzarella cheese

Spread pizza sauce over pita bread. Top with pepperoni, mushrooms and cheese. Place on an ungreased baking sheet. Bake at 400° for 4-6 minutes or until cheese is melted. **Yield:** 1 serving.

Nutritional Analysis: One serving (prepared with turkey pepperoni and part-skim mozzarella cheese) equals 275 calories, 6 g fat (3 g saturated fat), 25 mg cholesterol, 756 mg sodium, 38 g carbohydrate, 2 g fiber, 16 g protein. **Diabetic Exchanges:** 2 starch, 2 lean meat.

Tuna Salad Pockets

(Pictured below and on page 166)

Yogurt in place of mayonnaise gives these easy-to-assemble sandwiches a lighter, refreshing touch. Celery and walnuts add crunch. I keep this salad on hand for a fast, satisfying lunch. —*Ethel Bazoian, Los Angeles, California*

1 can (6 ounces) tuna, drained and flaked
1/4 cup thinly sliced celery
1/4 cup chopped walnuts
1/4 cup plain yogurt
3 tablespoons sweet pickle relish
1 green onion, sliced
2 pita breads (6 inches), halved

In a small bowl, combine the first six ingredients. Spoon into pitas. **Yield:** 2 servings.

Salisbury Steak for Two

(Pictured below and on page 166)

These tender beef patties with golden gravy are quick to prepare, but they taste like old-fashioned comfort food. I make this meaty entree often.
—Sharon Manus, Smyrna, Tennessee

✓ Uses less fat, sugar or salt. Includes Nutritional Analysis and Diabetic Exchanges.

1 egg
1 slice bread, torn into small pieces
1 tablespoon finely chopped onion
1/2 pound ground beef
2 teaspoons vegetable oil, optional
1 can (10-3/4 ounces) condensed golden mushroom *or* cream of mushroom soup, undiluted
1/2 cup water
1 jar (4-1/2 ounces) whole mushrooms, drained *or* 3/4 cup sliced fresh mushrooms
Dash pepper

In a bowl, combine egg, bread and onion. Add beef; mix well. Shape into two patties. In a nonstick skillet over medium heat, brown patties on both sides in oil if desired; drain. Combine the soup, water, mushrooms and pepper; pour over patties. Bring to a boil. Reduce heat; cover and simmer until meat is no longer pink. **Yield:** 2 servings.

Nutritional Analysis: One serving (prepared with egg substitute, lean ground beef, reduced-fat cream of mushroom soup and fresh mushrooms and without oil) equals 342 calories, 13 g fat (4 g saturated fat), 42 mg cholesterol, 814 mg sodium, 25 g carbohydrate, 4 g fiber, 30 g protein. **Diabetic Exchanges:** 3 lean meat, 1-1/2 starch, 1 fat.

IDEAL FARE FOR A PAIR. Why not prepare a delicious dinner of Salisbury Steak for Two, Basil Vinaigrette over greens and Cherry Cream Cheese Tarts (shown above)? It's certain to be a memorable meal.

Basil Vinaigarette

(Pictured below left and on page 166)

A splash of this delicate dressing lets the goodness of fresh salad greens shine through. —*Vivian Haen Menomonee Falls, Wisconsin*

1/4 cup olive *or* vegetable oil
4-1/2 teaspoons red wine vinegar *or* cider vinegar
1/4 teaspoon ground mustard
1/4 teaspoon dried basil
1/8 teaspoon garlic powder
Salt and pepper to taste

In a jar with a tight-fitting lid, combine all ingredients; shake well. Serve over salad greens. **Yield:** 1/4 cup.

Cherry Cream Cheese Tarts

(Pictured at left and on page 166)

You can make these tasty tarts with just five ingredients. —*Cindi Lynn Mitchell, Waring, Texas*

✓ Uses less fat, sugar or salt. Includes Nutritional Analysis and Diabetic Exchanges.

1 package (3 ounces) cream cheese, softened
1/4 cup confectioners' sugar
1/8 to 1/4 teaspoon almond *or* vanilla extract
2 individual graham cracker shells
1/4 cup cherry pie filling

In a small mixing bowl, beat the cream cheese, sugar and extract until smooth. Spoon into shells. Top with pie filling. Refrigerate. **Yield:** 2 servings.

Nutritional Analysis: One tart (prepared with reduced-fat cream cheese and reduced-sugar cherry pie filling) equals 295 calories, 14 g fat (6 g saturated fat), 24 mg cholesterol, 279 mg sodium, 37 g carbohydrate, 1 g fiber, 6 g protein. **Diabetic Exchanges:** 2 starch, 2 fat, 1-1/2 fruit.

Cinnamon-Spice French Toast

Cinnamon and nutmeg give French toast an extra tasty twist. —*Angela Sansom, New York, New York*

1 egg
1/4 cup milk
1/2 teaspoon sugar
1/4 to 1/2 teaspoon ground cinnamon
1/8 teaspoon ground nutmeg
2 slices day-old whole wheat *or* white bread
2 teaspoons butter *or* margarine
Maple syrup

In a shallow bowl, beat egg, milk, sugar, cinnamon and nutmeg. Add bread, one slice at a time, and soak both sides. Melt butter on a griddle over medium heat; cook bread until golden brown on both sides and cooked through. Serve with syrup. **Yield:** 1 serving.

Pepper Steak for One

Have a taste for pepper steak? This small-quantity recipe yields savory and satisfying results. —*Rita Winterberger, Huson, Montana*

4 ounces beef round steak
1 tablespoon vegetable oil
1/4 cup sliced green pepper
1/4 cup thinly sliced green onions
1 small garlic clove, minced
1 tablespoon cornstarch
1/3 cup water
2 teaspoons soy sauce

Pound steak to tenderize; cut into 1/4-in. strips. In a skillet, brown steak in oil over medium-high heat. Add green pepper, onions and garlic; stir-fry for 2-3 minutes. Combine cornstarch, water and soy sauce until smooth; add to skillet. Bring to a boil; cook and stir for 1 minute or until thickened. **Yield:** 1 serving.

Spinach Catfish Skillet

Nestled in a skillet with colorful nutritious carrots and spinach, this catfish fillet comes out perfectly moist. —*Sharon McComas, Kansas City, Missouri*

10 baby carrots
2 teaspoons vegetable oil
1/4 cup thinly sliced onion
1 catfish fillet (about 6 ounces)
1 package (6 ounces) fresh baby spinach
2 tablespoons white wine vinegar *or* cider vinegar
1/4 teaspoon sugar

In a skillet, stir-fry carrots in oil for 1-2 minutes or until crisp-tender. Add onion; cook and stir for 1 minute. Add catfish; cook for 2-3 minutes on each side. Add spinach. Sprinkle with vinegar and sugar. Cover and cook for 5 minutes or until fish flakes easily with a fork. Remove to a warm serving dish; spoon pan juices over fillet. **Yield:** 1 serving.

'My Mom's Best Meal'

Six cooks share the secrets of those special dinners only Mom could make. Now, you can create memorable meals, too!

SWEET MEMORIES. Clockwise from upper left: Down-Home Dinner (p. 206), Casual Country Fare (p. 198), Old-Style German Supper (p. 190) and Italian Birthday Meal (p. 194).

Sunday dinners were special times showcasing Mom's incredible knack for fixing great, farm-fresh fare.

By Sandy Jenkins, Elkhorn, Wisconsin

EVERY SUNDAY seemed like a holiday when I was growing up because Mom always fixed a feast.

My mom (Ruth Poritz Celia, above, of Pell Lake, Wisconsin) was raised on a dairy farm and regularly helped cook for crowds, whether it was for a family gathering or a gang of threshers.

She was in her element preparing a big meal for my father, sister, three brothers, me and any of our friends who just happened to be hanging around at dinnertime. Those who stayed always walked away from the table happy and full!

Since my parents had a farm, we raised all our own meat and vegetables. Mom even made homemade bread and butter weekly. Between the fresh ingredients and the care she put into her cooking and baking, everything tasted delicious.

My favorite meal is one that Mom made frequently since it was also one my father requested often. She used recipes handed down from her mother.

Mom's Duck with Cherry Sauce is a mouth-watering main dish. The thick cherry sauce complements the tender duck so nicely.

Alongside, she served Scalloped Corn, a hearty side dish with garden-fresh flavor. There was no need to tell us to eat our vegetables—we did so gladly.

Lime Pear Gelatin added a light fruity touch to the meal. We kids, especially, considered it an ideal salad.

And for a festive finale, Mom prepared her scrumptious Cranberry Raisin Pie. Dotted with plump raisins and rosy red cranberries, this lovely pie is so good topped with a scoop of homemade ice cream.

These days, Mom enjoys cooking for her grandchildren. She continues to satisfy our appetites with wonderful food and nourish our spirits with her love.

PICTURED AT LEFT: Duck with Cherry Sauce, Scalloped Corn, Pear Lime Gelatin and Cranberry Raisin Pie (recipes are on the next page).

Keeping Corn Fresh

Fresh sweet corn is best if used the day you buy it. It can be stored for no more than 1 day in a plastic bag in the refrigerator.

Scalloped Corn

This comforting casserole features sunny corn kernels tucked into a creamy custard. My mom got this recipe, and many other excellent ones, from her mother. By the time this dish got around the table, my father, sister, brothers and I would have almost scraped it clean.

4 cups fresh *or* frozen corn
3 eggs, beaten
1 cup milk
1 cup crushed saltines (about 30 crackers), *divided*
3 tablespoons butter *or* margarine, melted
1 tablespoon sugar
1 tablespoon finely chopped onion
Salt and pepper to taste

In a large bowl, combine the corn, eggs, milk, 3/4 cup cracker crumbs, butter, sugar, onion, salt and pepper. Transfer to a greased 1-1/2-qt. baking dish. Sprinkle with remaining cracker crumbs. Bake, uncovered, at 325° for 1 hour or until a knife inserted near the center comes out clean. **Yield:** 6 servings.

Duck with Cherry Sauce

My mom prepared this golden tender roast duck often for Sunday dinner when I was growing up. It was one of my dad's favorite meals. The cherry sauce stirs up easily and makes this dish doubly delightful.

1 domestic duckling (4 to 5 pounds)
1 jar (12 ounces) cherry preserves
1 to 2 tablespoons red wine vinegar *or* cider vinegar
Bing cherries, star fruit and kale, optional

Prick skin of duckling well and place, breast side up, on a rack in a shallow roasting pan. Tie drumsticks together. Bake, uncovered, at 325° for 2 hours or until juices run clear and a meat thermometer reads 180°. (Drain fat from pan as it accumulates.)

Cover and let stand for 20 minutes before carving. Meanwhile, for sauce, combine preserves and vinegar in a small saucepan. Cook and stir over medium heat until heated through. Serve with duck. Garnish platter with fruit and kale if desired. **Yield:** 4-5 servings.

Pear Lime Gelatin

This jolly gelatin salad is a light and refreshing treat. My mom knew that fruit served in this form would get gobbled right up. The bowl looked like a sparkling jewel on our dinner table.

✓ Uses less fat, sugar or salt. Includes Nutritional Analysis and Diabetic Exchanges.

1 can (29 ounces) pear halves in juice
1 package (3 ounces) lime gelatin
1 package (3 ounces) cream cheese, cubed
1 cup whipped topping

Drain pears, reserving juice; set pears aside. Measure the juice; add water if needed to equal 1-1/2 cups. Pour into a saucepan; bring to a boil. Add gelatin; stir until dissolved. Gradually add cream cheese, whisking until smooth. Cover and refrigerate until cool. Mash reserved pears; fold into gelatin mixture. Fold in whipped topping. Pour into a 6-cup serving bowl. Refrigerate until set. **Yield:** 6 servings.

Nutritional Analysis: One serving (prepared with sugar-free gelatin and reduced-fat cream cheese and whipped topping) equals 172 calories, 3 g fat (2 g saturated fat), 5 mg cholesterol, 398 mg sodium, 21 g carbohydrate, 2 g fiber, 8 g protein. **Diabetic Exchanges:** 2 fruit, 1 fat.

Cranberry Raisin Pie

Even though it was difficult, we saved room for dessert when my mom made this festive holiday pie.

2 cups all-purpose flour
1 teaspoon salt
1/2 cup vegetable oil
5 tablespoons cold water
FILLING:
1-1/2 cups sugar
1/4 cup all-purpose flour
1/2 teaspoon ground cinnamon
1/4 teaspoon salt
1/4 teaspoon ground nutmeg
1 cup orange juice
2-2/3 cups fresh *or* frozen cranberries
1 cup raisins
Milk, optional

In a bowl, combine flour and salt. In another bowl, combine oil and water. Gradually add to flour mixture, stirring with a fork until blended. Shape into a ball; divide dough in half so one ball is slightly larger than the other. Roll out larger ball between two sheets of waxed paper to fit a 9-in. pie plate. Transfer pastry to pie plate; trim pastry even with edge. Set aside.

For filling, combine sugar, flour, cinnamon, salt and nutmeg in a saucepan; gradually stir in orange juice until smooth. Stir in cranberries and raisins; bring to a boil. Reduce heat; cook and stir over medium heat until thickened, about 5 minutes. Pour into crust. Roll out remaining dough between two sheets of waxed paper. Cut slits in pastry or use a 1-1/2-in. holly leaf cutter to make a design. Place over filling. Trim, seal and flute edges. Brush pastry with milk if desired.

Bake at 400° for 35-40 minutes or until golden brown and filling is bubbly. Cool on a wire rack. Refrigerate leftovers. **Yield:** 6-8 servings.

With traditional German Sauerbraten as the main dish, Mom serves up a dinner that's truly wunderbar!

By Cathy Eland, Hightstown, New Jersey

MY MOTHER is known throughout our family as an excellent cook, and with good reason.

When I was growing up, Mom (Norma Wyckoff from Brick, New Jersey, above) worked for a deli preparing all sorts of salads and sandwiches. But she still loved to make special dinners for my father, brother, sister and me.

Her family was German, and Mom learned a lot by working in the kitchen with *her* mom, who also loved to cook. Oma (that's German for grandmother) was a good teacher, and the two created many happy memories as well as delicious meals.

Now whenever we all get together, we unanimously request that Mom fix our favorite old-world meal.

German Sauerbraten is a traditional main dish that is tender and flavorful when it's cooked to perfection. The tempting aroma of the spiced beef roast always draws us into the kitchen.

Ginger, vinegar, onions, cloves and pickling spices create a marinade that turns into a rich, tasty gravy. Dad especially enjoys pouring the gravy over Mom's Potato Dumplings. These mild little dumplings are hearty and delightful with just a hint of nutmeg.

Sweet-Sour Red Cabbage is a colorful and crunchy side dish that really tingles your taste buds. We always go back for seconds.

It's not easy, but we try to save room for dessert when Mom makes her wonderful Sour Cream Peach Kuchen. The crust is tender, and the filling is fresh-tasting and lightly sweet. It can even be made with canned peaches when fresh ones are not in season.

This meal takes a bit of effort to prepare, but Mom doesn't mind since she knows we savor every bite. Mom and I are thrilled to share these recipes so your family can enjoy what is, for us, a true taste of home.

PICTURED AT LEFT: German Sauerbraten, Sweet-Sour Red Cabbage, Potato Dumplings and Sour Cream Peach Kuchen (recipes are on the next page).

German Sauerbraten

Our family loves it when Mom prepares this wonderful old-world dish. The tender beef has a bold blend of mouth-watering seasonings. It smells so good in the oven and tastes even better!

2 teaspoons salt
1 teaspoon ground ginger
1 beef top round roast (about 4 pounds)
2-1/2 cups water
2 cups cider vinegar
2 medium onions, sliced
1/3 cup sugar
2 tablespoons mixed pickling spices
1 teaspoon whole peppercorns
8 whole cloves
2 bay leaves
2 tablespoons vegetable oil
14 to 16 gingersnaps, crushed

Combine salt and ginger; rub over roast. Place in a deep glass bowl. In a saucepan, combine water, vinegar, onions, sugar, pickling spices, peppercorns, cloves and bay leaves; bring to a boil. Pour over roast; turn to coat. Cover and refrigerate for 2 days, turning twice a day.

Remove roast, reserving marinade; pat roast dry. In a large kettle or Dutch oven, brown roast on all sides in oil. Strain marinade, reserving half of the onions and seasonings. Pour 1 cup of marinade and reserved onions and seasonings over roast (cover and refrigerate remaining marinade). Bring to a boil. Reduce heat; cover and simmer for 3 hours or until meat is tender.

Strain cooking liquid, discarding the onions and seasonings. Measure liquid; if necessary, add enough reserved marinade to equal 3 cups. Pour into a saucepan; bring to a rolling boil. Add gingersnaps; simmer until gravy is thickened. Slice roast and serve with gravy. **Yield:** 12-14 servings.

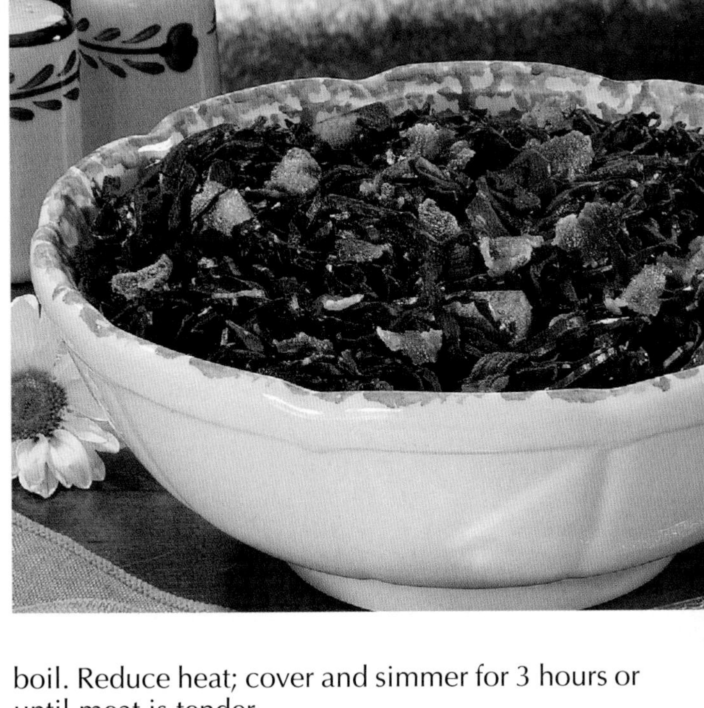

Sweet-Sour Red Cabbage

This crunchy eye-catching cooked cabbage is seasoned with a flavorful blend of vinegar, spices and bacon.

1/2 cup cider vinegar
1/4 cup sugar
1/4 cup packed brown sugar
1 medium head red cabbage, shredded (10 cups)
2 bacon strips, diced
1 medium tart apple, peeled and chopped
1/2 cup chopped onion
1/4 cup water
2 tablespoons white wine vinegar *or* additional cider vinegar
1/2 teaspoon salt
1/4 teaspoon pepper
1/8 teaspoon ground cloves

In a large bowl, stir the cider vinegar and sugars until sugars are dissolved. Add cabbage; toss to coat. Let stand for 5-10 minutes. Meanwhile, in a large skillet over medium heat, cook bacon until crisp. Remove with a slotted spoon, reserving drippings.

In the drippings, saute the apple and onion until tender. Add the water and cabbage mixture. Bring to a boil. Reduce the heat; cover and simmer for 30-35 minutes. Stir in the remaining ingredients. Simmer, uncovered, for 5 minutes or until tender. Sprinkle with the reserved bacon just before serving. **Yield:** 8-10 servings.

Potato Dumplings

With a few additional basic ingredients, my mom transforms potatoes into these delightful dumplings. This authentic German side dish is so hearty and comforting. We love the dumplings in sauerbraten gravy.

3 pounds russet potatoes
2 eggs
1 cup all-purpose flour, *divided*
1/2 cup dry bread crumbs
1 teaspoon salt
1/4 teaspoon ground nutmeg
Dash pepper
Minced fresh parsley, optional

Place potatoes in a saucepan and cover with water; bring to a boil. Reduce heat; cover and simmer for 30-35 minutes or until tender. Drain well. Refrigerate for 2 hours or overnight. Peel and grate potatoes. In a bowl, combine the eggs, 3/4 cup flour, bread crumbs, salt, nutmeg and pepper. Add potatoes; mix with hands until well blended. Shape into 1-1/2-in. balls; roll in remaining flour.

In a large kettle, bring salted water to a boil. Add the dumplings, a few at a time, to boiling water. Simmer, uncovered, until the dumplings rise to the top; cook 2 minutes longer. Remove dumplings with a slotted spoon to a serving bowl. Sprinkle with parsley if desired. **Yield:** 10 servings.

Sour Cream Peach Kuchen

For an old-fashioned treat, there's nothing that beats my mom's peach kuchen. With a melt-in-your-mouth crust and a lightly sweet filling, this dessert is perfect after a big meal. Sweetened sour cream tops it off.

3 cups all-purpose flour
1-1/4 cups sugar, *divided*
1/2 teaspoon baking powder
1/4 teaspoon salt
1 cup cold butter *or* margarine
2 cans (29 ounces *each*) sliced peaches, drained *or* 13 small fresh peaches, peeled and sliced
1 teaspoon ground cinnamon

TOPPING:
4 egg yolks
2 cups (16 ounces) sour cream
2 to 3 tablespoons sugar
1/4 teaspoon ground cinnamon

In a bowl, combine the flour, 1/4 cup sugar, baking powder and salt; cut in butter until mixture resembles coarse crumbs. Press onto the bottom and 1 in. up the sides of a greased 13-in. x 9-in. x 2-in. baking dish. Arrange peaches over crust. Combine cinnamon and remaining sugar; sprinkle over peaches. Bake at 400° for 15 minutes.

Meanwhile, in a bowl, combine egg yolks and sour cream. Spread over peaches. Combine sugar and cinnamon; sprinkle over top. Bake 30-35 minutes longer or until golden. Serve warm or cold. Store leftovers in the refrigerator. **Yield:** 12 servings.

Birthday girl chooses Mom's luscious beef lasagna with frosted carrot cake for her special family supper.

By Kim Orr, Louisville, Kentucky

I REMEMBER my mom (Cindy Robbins, above, of Waynesville, Ohio) always making sure we had a home-cooked meal when we were growing up, no matter how busy the day.

Mom is a self-taught cook who enjoys preparing foods for family, friends and church dinners. Everyone loves to gather at my parents' home, since she fixes delicious meals and always makes them extra-special with a festively set table.

When my sister and I were younger, Mom would make us our favorite dinner on our birthdays. I always chose lasagna. I loved to watch her assemble this dish layer by layer. The aroma while it was baking in the oven was mouth-watering! Her recipe card is yellow and worn now, but it doesn't matter. Mom can practically make this lasagna in her sleep!

To go with this hearty main course, she would fix a crusty loaf of Chive Garlic Bread. Those savory slices were ideal with an Italian meal.

We all looked forward to a crispy lettuce salad draped with her chunky and flavorful Thousand Island Salad Dressing.

Each year, I requested Old-Fashioned Carrot Cake for my birthday dessert. Since it was *my* special day, I always asked for seconds of this yummy layer cake. Lucky for me, Mom never said "no" to the birthday girl. The moist cake was chock-full of sweet carrots and topped with a rich cream cheese frosting.

I could not have been blessed with a more wonderful role model both in and out of the kitchen. Mom has taught me that bringing a family together for a meal is one of the most wonderful opportunities we have for sharing. Both of us are pleased to share this meal with you. Don't wait for a birthday to try it!

PICTURED AT LEFT: Mom's Lasagna, Chive Garlic Bread, Thousand Island Salad Dressing and Old-Fashioned Carrot Cake (recipes are on the next page).

Mom's Lasagna

This recipe is one of my mom's specialties. It's a hearty main dish that gets requested time and time again. The from-scratch sauce makes it more flavorful and softer-textured than other versions.

1 pound ground beef
2 garlic cloves, minced
1-1/2 cups water
1 can (15 ounces) tomato sauce
1 can (6 ounces) tomato paste
1/2 to 1 envelope onion soup mix
1 teaspoon dried oregano
1/2 teaspoon sugar
1/4 teaspoon pepper
9 lasagna noodles, cooked and drained
2 cups (16 ounces) small-curd cottage cheese
4 cups (16 ounces) shredded mozzarella cheese
2 cups grated Parmesan cheese

In a large saucepan, cook beef and garlic over medium heat until meat is no longer pink; drain. Stir in the water, tomato sauce and paste, soup mix, oregano, sugar and pepper. Bring to a boil. Reduce heat; cover and simmer for 30 minutes.

Spoon 1/2 cup meat sauce into a greased 13-in. x 9-in. x 2-in. baking dish. Layer with three noodles and a third of the cottage cheese, mozzarella, meat sauce and Parmesan cheese. Repeat layers twice.

Cover and bake at 350° for 40 minutes or until bubbly and heated through. Uncover; bake 5-10 minutes longer. Let stand for 10 minutes before cutting. **Yield:** 12 servings.

Chive Garlic Bread

A purchased loaf of French bread gets a real boost with a few simple ingredients. Garlic and chives make the savory slices irresistible. Along with lasagna or another Italian meal, we munch them until the last crumbs have vanished!

1/4 cup butter *or* margarine, softened
1/4 cup grated Parmesan cheese
2 tablespoons snipped chives
1 garlic clove, minced
1 loaf (1 pound) French bread, cut into 1-inch slices

In a bowl, combine the butter, Parmesan cheese, chives and garlic. Spread on one side of each slice of bread; wrap in a large piece of heavy-duty foil. Seal the edges. Place on a baking sheet. Bake at 350° for 25-30 minutes or until heated through. **Yield:** 12 servings.

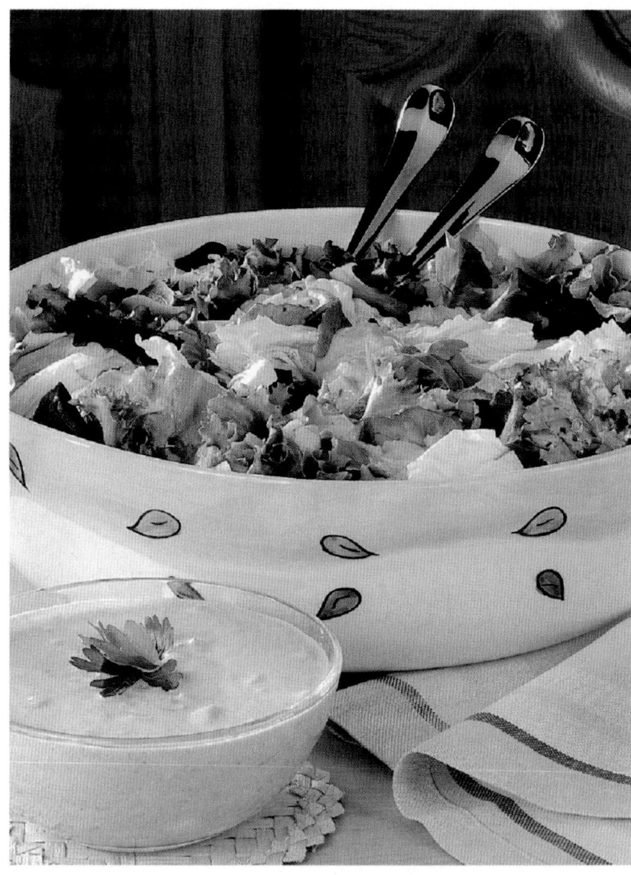

Thousand Island Salad Dressing

This comforting homemade dressing is chock-full of tasty ingredients, including chopped onion, celery and hard-cooked eggs. It's a delightful topping for any crisp green salad.

1 cup mayonnaise *or* salad dressing
1/4 cup chili sauce
2 hard-cooked eggs, chopped
2 tablespoons chopped green onion
2 tablespoons chopped celery
4-1/2 teaspoons finely chopped onion
1 teaspoon paprika
1/2 teaspoon salt

In a bowl, combine all ingredients; mix well. Cover and refrigerate until serving. Serve over salad greens. **Yield:** 1-1/2 cups.

Old-Fashioned Carrot Cake

A pleasingly moist cake, this treat is the one I requested that my mom make each year for my birthday. It's dotted with sweet carrots and a hint of cinnamon. The fluffy, buttery cream cheese frosting is scrumptious with chopped walnuts stirred in. One piece of this cake is never enough!

4 eggs
2 cups sugar
1-1/2 cups vegetable oil
2 cups all-purpose flour
2 to 3 teaspoons ground cinnamon
1 teaspoon baking powder
1 teaspoon baking soda
1/4 teaspoon salt
1/4 teaspoon ground nutmeg
2 cups grated carrots
FROSTING:
1/2 cup butter *or* margarine, softened
1 package (3 ounces) cream cheese, softened
3-3/4 cups confectioners' sugar
1 teaspoon vanilla extract
2 to 3 tablespoons milk
1 cup chopped walnuts
Carrot curls and additional walnuts, optional

In a mixing bowl, combine eggs, sugar and oil; mix well. Combine flour, cinnamon, baking powder, baking soda, salt and nutmeg; beat into egg mixture. Stir in carrots.

Pour into two greased and floured 9-in. round baking pans. Bake at 350° for 35-40 minutes or until a toothpick inserted near the center comes out clean. Cool for 10 minutes before removing from pans to wire racks.

For frosting, in a mixing bowl, cream butter and cream cheese. Gradually beat in confectioners' sugar and vanilla. Add enough milk to achieve desired consistency. Stir in walnuts. Spread frosting between layers and over top and sides of cake. Garnish with carrot curls and walnuts if desired. Refrigerate leftovers. **Yield:** 12 servings.

Mom's barbecued beef and pork sandwiches are so good and so well-known, they're named after her!

By Pat Cole, Polebridge, Montana

MY MOTHER is a person who loves to feed people. She is known for setting out trays of food as soon as someone enters her home.

When my older brothers, sister and I were growing up, Mom (Betty Dillon, above, from Park Ridge, Illinois) worked full-time in a factory, so she had to be creative with meal preparation. She set it up so that dinner could easily be completed by us kids.

On weekends, she fixed a big meal with lots of ethnic variety. Her mother was Polish and her mother-in-law was Irish, so she had plenty of influence.

Mom's also a great baker. Our friends loved to come to our house because there were always fresh, homemade cookies.

To commemorate Mom's 90th birthday, I put together a cookbook with her best recipes to share with family members and friends.

My favorite meal is one that is well-known throughout our extended family. Her beef and pork barbecue (fondly known as Betty's Barbecue) makes savory sandwiches that can't be beat.

Creamy Potato Salad and Tangy Coleslaw are two classic accompaniments to those sandwiches. She made big batches because we all went back for seconds—plus we'd gladly accept any leftovers she wanted to send home with us.

Mom's Frosted Shortbread, topped with a layer of chocolate and a sprinkling of walnuts, is a scrumptious, fitting finale for any meal.

Before my husband and I moved to a remote cabin in the woods, I was sure to get those recipes in writing from Mom (who usually cooks from memory).

Now a widow, grandma and great-grandma, Mom is still busy cooking and baking for those she loves. She and I are pleased to share these recipes with you and your family.

PICTURED AT LEFT: Betty's Barbecue, Tangy Coleslaw, Creamy Potato Salad and Frosted Shortbread (recipes are on the next page).

Creamy Potato Salad

Mildly seasoned with onion and dill, Mom's delightfully different potato salad is pretty, too, with the red potatoes left unpeeled. Of course, that also means it's quicker to make than traditional potato salad!

✓ Uses less fat, sugar or salt. Includes Nutritional Analysis and Diabetic Exchanges.

7-1/2 cups cubed red potatoes (about 2-1/2 pounds)
1 hard-cooked egg, chopped
3 celery ribs, chopped
3/4 cup chopped onion
2 tablespoons finely chopped green pepper
3/4 cup mayonnaise
1/4 cup sour cream
1 to 1-1/2 teaspoons salt
1/4 teaspoon pepper
1/8 to 1/4 teaspoon dill weed
Sliced hard-cooked egg, paprika and fresh dill sprigs, optional

Place potatoes in a large saucepan or Dutch oven; cover with water. Cover and bring to a boil. Reduce heat; cook for 20-30 minutes or until tender. Drain and cool.

Place potatoes in a large bowl. Add chopped egg, celery, onion and green pepper. In a small bowl, combine mayonnaise, sour cream, salt, pepper and dill. Pour over potato mixture and toss gently to coat. Cover and refrigerate until serving. Garnish with egg, paprika and dill if desired. **Yield:** 12 servings.

Nutritional Analysis: One 1-cup serving (prepared with fat-free mayonnaise, reduced-fat sour cream and 1 teaspoon salt) equals 114 calories, 1 g fat (1 g saturated fat), 19 mg cholesterol, 320 mg sodium, 24 g carbohydrate, 2 g fiber, 3 g protein. **Diabetic Exchanges:** 1 starch, 1 vegetable.

Betty's Barbecue

For a fun sandwich filling that's perfect for a picnic or potluck, try these sweetly spicy barbecue sandwiches. My 90-year-old mother came up with this outdoor specialty, which combines chunks of tender pork and beef. It's one of my family's favorites.

1 boneless beef rump roast (3 to 4 pounds)
1 pork tenderloin (1 pound)
2 cups water
1 envelope onion soup mix
1 garlic clove, minced
1/4 cup chopped celery with leaves
1/2 cup barbecue sauce
1/2 cup ketchup
1 tablespoon brown sugar
10 to 14 sandwich buns, split

Place beef and pork in a Dutch oven. Combine the water, soup mix and garlic; pour over meat. Cover and bake at 325° for 2-1/2 to 3 hours or until meat is very tender. Remove meat; cool. Cut into small cubes. Skim fat from drippings. Saute celery in the drippings until tender. Add the barbecue sauce, ketchup and brown sugar; bring to a boil. Stir in cubed meat; heat through. Serve on buns. **Yield:** 10-14 servings.

Frosted Shortbread

My mom has always known that homemade cookies have a special appeal that can't be duplicated by the store-bought variety. Even today, she keeps us grown-up kids well stocked with fresh-from-the-oven treats such as this tender shortbread.

1 cup butter (no substitutes), softened
1 cup packed brown sugar
1 egg yolk
1 teaspoon vanilla extract
2 cups all-purpose flour
1/4 teaspoon salt
4 milk chocolate candy bars (1.55 ounces *each*), broken into rectangles
1/2 cup chopped walnuts

In a mixing bowl, cream butter and brown sugar. Add egg yolk and vanilla; mix well. Combine flour and salt; add to creamed mixture. Press into a greased 15-in. x 10-in. x 1-in. baking pan. Bake at 350° for 15-18 minutes or until golden brown. Immediately place candy bar pieces over crust. Let stand for 1 minute or until softened; spread chocolate evenly. Sprinkle with walnuts. Cool. Cut into squares. **Yield:** 3 dozen.

Tangy Coleslaw

The fresh flavor and crunchy texture of garden vegetables star in this tart, colorful coleslaw. Lightly dressed with vinegar and oil, it's a refreshing salad. My mom fixed it often when I was growing up.

6 cups shredded cabbage
4 medium carrots, shredded
4 celery ribs, chopped
1/2 cup finely chopped green pepper
1/2 cup finely chopped onion
1/2 cup cider vinegar
1/4 cup vegetable oil
1/4 cup sugar
1-1/2 teaspoons salt
1/4 teaspoon pepper
1/4 teaspoon paprika

In a large bowl, combine the cabbage, carrots, celery, green pepper and onion. In a small bowl, combine vinegar, oil, sugar, salt, pepper and paprika. Pour over cabbage mixture and toss to coat. Cover and refrigerate until serving. **Yield:** 10 servings.

Customized Coleslaw

To make store-bought coleslaw taste homemade, add shredded cheese, apple, carrots or bell pepper.

Mom's tender chicken dinner filled the house with a wonderful aroma that was topped only by the meal's taste.

By Barbara Wheeler, Sparks Glencoe, Maryland

WHEN WE were growing up, my sister, Sandy, my brother, Ed, and I were lucky enough to have a mom who was a full-time homemaker. Mom (Barbara "Be Be" Mead, above, of Avalon, New Jersey) has always been devoted to her family.

My mother delights in creating flavorful meals... and even leftovers become a fun smorgasbord when she assembles them. The kitchen is still her favorite room of the house, and the tempting aromas of dishes she's cooking or baking from scratch tend to draw in friends and family. You can tell she enjoys what she's doing and takes pride in serving a tasty supper.

Trying to identify just one meal as Mom's best is really hard, but we all especially enjoy her Baked Chicken. It's so tender and flavorful. A sauce made of ketchup, lemon juice, brown sugar and spices coats every piece with wonderful flavor.

Scored Potatoes make an excellent side dish. They're simple to prepare yet look like extra care went into them. In Mom's case that's true, of course.

Mom's Caesar Salad is a real classic. The homemade dressing makes it extra fresh-tasting.

We all try to save room for dessert, especially when Mom makes her famous Picnic Chocolate Cake. It's moist and chocolaty, and tastes great alone or with a big scoop of vanilla ice cream plopped on top.

Mom learned most of her kitchen skills from her aunt and grandmother, and I'm happy to say she passed along many of her secrets to us kids. She and Dad have been married more than 50 years.

My husband, our son and I love to be invited to share a meal at my parents' house. We always feel welcome. The only trouble is it's hard to decide what's better—the food or the company!

PICTURED AT LEFT: Baked Chicken, Scored Potatoes, Caesar Salad and Chocolate Picnic Cake (recipes are on the next page).

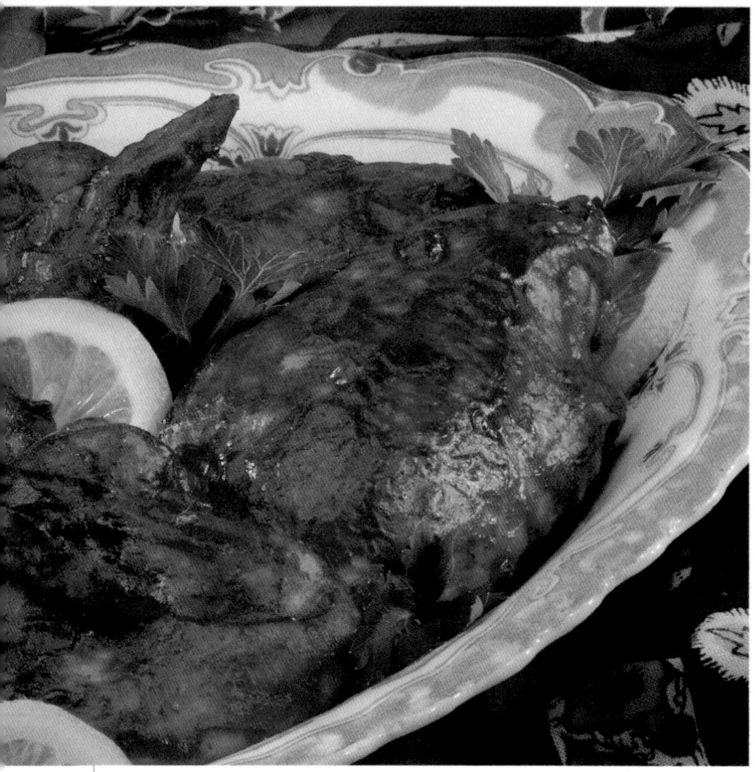

Scored Potatoes

These well-seasoned baked potatoes are a fun alternative to plain baked potatoes. It's easy to help yourself to just the amount you want, too, since the potato halves are scored into sections. My mom serves them alongside many different kinds of meat.

4 large baking potatoes
2 tablespoons butter *or* margarine, melted, *divided*
1/8 teaspoon paprika
1 tablespoon minced fresh parsley
Salt and pepper to taste

With a sharp knife, cut the potatoes in half lengthwise. Slice each half widthwise six times, but not all the way through; fan potatoes slightly. Place in a shallow baking dish. Brush the potatoes with 1 tablespoon melted butter. Sprinkle with paprika, parsley, salt and pepper. Bake, uncovered, at 350° for 50 minutes or until the potatoes are tender. Drizzle with the remaining butter. **Yield:** 4 servings.

Baked Chicken

A tangy from-scratch sauce makes this tender chicken extra flavorful. My mom is an excellent cook who has fixed delicious dishes like this one for years. If you're in a hurry, just prepare it ahead and pop it in the oven when you get home.

1 broiler/fryer chicken (3 pounds), cut up
1 tablespoon all-purpose flour
1/4 cup water
1/4 cup packed brown sugar
1/4 cup ketchup
2 tablespoons white vinegar
2 tablespoons lemon juice
2 tablespoons Worcestershire sauce
1 small onion, chopped
1 teaspoon ground mustard
1 teaspoon paprika
1 teaspoon chili powder
1/2 teaspoon salt
1/8 teaspoon pepper

Place chicken in a greased 13-in. x 9-in. x 2-in. baking dish. In a saucepan, whisk flour and water until smooth. Stir in brown sugar, ketchup, vinegar, lemon juice and Worcestershire sauce. Bring to a boil; cook and stir for 2 minutes or until thickened. Stir in the remaining ingredients. Pour over chicken. Cover and refrigerate for 2-4 hours. Remove from the refrigerator 30 minutes before baking. Bake, uncovered, at 350° for 35-45 minutes or until chicken juices run clear. **Yield:** 4 servings.

Caesar Salad

This classic recipe can't be beat! When Mom's cooking, our whole family looks forward to this refreshing salad that's tossed with a tangy homemade dressing.

3 tablespoons olive *or* vegetable oil
4-1/2 teaspoons lemon juice
1 teaspoon prepared mustard
1 garlic clove, minced
6 cups torn romaine

2/3 cup Caesar salad croutons
1/2 cup shredded Parmesan cheese
Coarsely ground pepper to taste

In a jar with a tight-fitting lid, combine the oil, lemon juice, mustard and garlic; shake well. In a salad bowl, combine the romaine, croutons, Parmesan cheese and pepper. Drizzle with dressing and toss to coat. **Yield:** 4 servings.

Salad Solutions

- When buying lettuce or other salad greens, look for those that are crisp and blemish-free.
- Greens will last longer if you wash them as soon as you get them home.
- An easy way to clean most greens is to cut off the bottom to separate the leaves, then put them in a large container of water. Swish the greens around with your hands, then let them sit for a few minutes so any dirt can sink to the bottom.
- To clean iceberg lettuce, first remove the core. To do so, hit the core against the countertop, then twist and remove the core. Pour cold water into the hole and swish around. Turn the head of lettuce over to drain the water.
- Thoroughly dry greens before eating or storing. If you don't have a salad spinner, shake off excess water and blot greens dry with paper towel.
- Store clean greens wrapped loosely in dry paper towels and sealed tightly in a plastic bag. Remove excess air. Greens will keep 1 week.

Chocolate Picnic Cake

Rich, moist and chocolaty, this scrumptious cake is very versatile. It freezes well...and the chocolate chip topping makes it easy to pack in lunches and carry along to picnics. At home, we like it topped with vanilla ice cream.

2 squares (1 ounce *each*) unsweetened chocolate
1-1/4 cups all-purpose flour
1/2 teaspoon baking soda
1/2 teaspoon salt
1 egg
1 cup sugar
3/4 cup cold water
1/3 cup vegetable oil
1 cup (6 ounces) semisweet chocolate chips

In a microwave, melt chocolate; cool for 10 minutes. Combine the flour, baking soda and salt; set aside. In a mixing bowl, beat the egg and sugar. Beat in the water and oil. Stir in melted chocolate and dry ingredients; mix until blended. Pour batter into a greased 8-in. square baking pan. Sprinkle with chocolate chips. Bake at 350° for 32-38 minutes or until a toothpick inserted near the center comes out clean. Cool on a wire rack. **Yield:** 9 servings.

For this longtime Italian cook, making great family suppers is a labor of love that earns praise and appreciation.

By Jeanne Voss, Anaheim Hills, California

MY MOM (Pat Voss, above) has been a proud homemaker since the day she and my dad got married 45 years ago.

Of Italian descent, Mom can make a day of meal planning, grocery shopping and cooking. She thinks nothing of working hours in the kitchen preparing a meal for her family in La Mirada, California.

When my two brothers and I were growing up, we'd walk in the door after school and always be greeted by wonderful aromas wafting from the kitchen.

She taught us kids to cook at an early age. When most of my friends were earning their Girl Scout cooking badges by making something simple like hamburgers, Mom insisted I prepare chicken tetrazzini, antipasto salad and cream puffs!

Mom has many specialties, but my absolute favorite meal starts with her flavorful Tangy Country-Style Ribs. Smothered in a sweet and zesty sauce, those tender ribs are irresistible.

In Bacon-Tomato Spinach Salad, oregano perks up the creamy homemade dressing. It's served with a pretty mixture of spinach, red onion, tomatoes and bacon.

Her golden Sally Lunn Batter Bread bakes up high and as light as a feather. It tastes as good as it smells.

Cream Cheese Finger Cookies are sure to melt in your mouth. They're a nutty old-fashioned treat.

The love of cooking is one of the best gifts Mom could have given me. I enjoy fixing meals for my husband, Robert, and our son, Andrew. We're fortunate to live close to my parents so we can still enjoy dinner at their house regularly.

Mom and I enjoyed sharing our favorite recipes with you, and we hope they will become part of your treasured collection, too.

PICTURED AT LEFT: Tangy Country-Style Ribs, Bacon-Tomato Spinach Salad, Sally Lunn Batter Bread and Cream Cheese Finger Cookies (recipes are on the next page).

Tangy Country-Style Ribs

There are never any leftovers when my mom fixes these tender sweet-and-sour ribs. She doubles the batch when our family gets together so there'll be enough for each of us to take some home for our freezers.

4 pounds boneless country-style pork ribs
1 medium onion, chopped
2 tablespoons vegetable oil
1 cup chili sauce
1/2 cup water
1/4 cup lemon juice
2 tablespoons brown sugar
2 tablespoons white vinegar
2 tablespoons ketchup
1 tablespoon Worcestershire sauce
Dash salt and pepper
Hot cooked rice

Place ribs on a rack in a shallow roasting pan. Cover and bake at 325° for 30 minutes. Meanwhile, in a skillet, saute onion in oil until tender. Add the chili sauce, water, lemon juice, brown sugar, vinegar, ketchup, Worcestershire sauce, salt and pepper. Reduce heat; simmer, uncovered, for 5 minutes or until slightly thickened.

Drain ribs; brush with some of the sauce. Bake, uncovered, for 1 to 1-1/2 hours, brushing occasionally with sauce. Serve with hot cooked rice. **Yield:** 8 servings.

Bacon-Tomato Spinach Salad

Mom always knew how to get us kids to eat our vegetables! This lovely salad combines spinach, tomatoes, red onions and bacon, served with a creamy homemade dressing. It's a classic side dish we've enjoyed for years and never tire of.

16 cups torn fresh spinach (about 12 ounces)
12 cherry tomatoes, halved
6 bacon strips, cooked and crumbled
1/4 cup julienned red onion
CREAMY OREGANO DRESSING:
1 cup mayonnaise
1 to 2 tablespoons white vinegar
2 teaspoons dried oregano
Salt and pepper to taste

In a large bowl, combine the spinach, tomatoes, bacon and onion. In a small bowl, whisk the dressing ingredients until smooth. Serve with salad. **Yield:** 8 servings.

Sally Lunn Batter Bread

The tantalizing aroma of this golden loaf baking always draws people into my mother's kitchen. With its circular shape, it's a pretty bread, too. I've never seen it last more than 2 hours out of the oven!

1 package (1/4 ounce) active dry yeast
1/2 cup warm water (110° to 115°)
1 cup warm milk (110° to 115°)
1/2 cup butter *or* margarine, softened
1/4 cup sugar
2 teaspoons salt
3 eggs
5-1/2 to 6 cups all-purpose flour
HONEY BUTTER:
1/2 cup butter (no substitutes), softened
1/2 cup honey

In a mixing bowl, dissolve yeast in warm water. Add the milk, butter, sugar, salt, eggs and 3 cups flour. Beat until smooth. Stir in enough remaining flour to form a soft dough (do not knead). Place in a greased bowl, turning once to grease top. Cover and let rise in a warm place until doubled, about 1 hour.

Stir dough down. Spoon into a greased and floured 10-in. tube pan. Cover and let rise until doubled, about 1 hour. Bake at 400° for 25-30 minutes or until golden brown. Remove from pan to a wire rack.

Combine the honey butter ingredients until smooth. Serve with bread. **Yield:** 12-16 servings.

Cream Cheese Finger Cookies

These melt-in-your-mouth cookies are one of my mom's specialties. Made with cream cheese and butter, they're very rich...and the pecans add wonderful flavor. They're great with a hot cup of coffee or a tall glass of cold milk.

1/2 cup butter (no substitutes), softened
4 ounces cream cheese, softened
1 teaspoon vanilla extract
1-3/4 cups all-purpose flour
1 tablespoon sugar
Dash salt
1 cup finely chopped pecans
Confectioners' sugar

In a mixing bowl, cream butter and cream cheese. Beat in vanilla. Combine the flour, sugar and salt; gradually add to creamed mixture. Stir in pecans (dough will be crumbly). Shape tablespoonfuls into 2-in. logs. Place 2 in. apart on ungreased baking sheets. Bake at 375° for 12-14 minutes or until lightly browned. Roll warm cookies in confectioners' sugar; cool on wire racks. **Yield:** 2 dozen.

Perfect Cookies

For accurate temperatures, always use a good oven thermometer. A mercury thermometer will outlast metal spring-style thermometers, which are less expensive but can become unreliable after a jolt. Mercury thermometers can be found in kitchen-supply stores. If you're baking more than one sheet at a time, ensure even browning by switching the sheets from top to bottom and front to back halfway through the baking time.

Editors' Meals

Taste of Home magazine is edited by 1,000 cooks across North America. On the following pages, you'll "meet" six of those cooks who share a family-pleasing meal.

FAMILY FARE. Clockwise from upper left: A Savory Salmon Menu (p. 216), Holiday Ham Dinner (p. 220), Perfect Patio Party (p. 224) and A Feast for Thanksgiving (p. 232).

Christmas in the Country

Impressive yet simple to prepare, this holiday dinner is a great-tasting family tradition. Don't count on a lot of leftovers!

By Lise Thomson, Magrath, Alberta

OUR CHRISTMAS celebration is flavored with family fun, holiday traditions from my native Denmark and a festive menu made up of favorite recipes.

We live on the farm where my husband, Merrill, was raised and have four children and four grandchildren. I came to Canada from Denmark in 1970 and still decorate our Christmas tree like we did when I was a girl, with dozens of small Danish flags and *real* candles!

Serving a special holiday meal is another tradition I happily carry on. French Onion Soup, No-Fuss Beef Roast, Creamy Mashed Potatoes, Carrots Supreme and Cherry Almond Cheesecake are festive foods that leave family and guests full and happy when they get up from the table. This meal is so good and easy that I also used it for my son's wedding dinner.

We begin our festive feast with French Onion Soup. This version has a slightly sweet flavor that makes it unique.

I've tried many ways to prepare rib roast, but No-Fuss Beef Roast is the most foolproof way I've found. It turns out so well, there's no need to worry it will fail when you have company.

Party-Perfect Potatoes

A big fan of mashed potatoes, I dress them up as Creamy Mashed Potatoes for special occasions. I mix in cream cheese and garlic, then top the mixture with green onions and paprika.

I often serve them when we have company, and they win raves! For the past 15 years, Merrill and I have held dinner parties with two other couples every 6 to 8 weeks. We try new recipes on each other, including many from both *Taste of Home* and *Quick Cooking*.

There are seldom any leftovers when Carrots Supreme is on the table. My motto is: If it's all gone, then we had a good time! The crumb topping on this saucy casserole has a hint of cheese. It goes so well with the roast beef.

Dessert is a delectable "crown" to a nice dinner. Marbled slices of Cherry Almond Cheesecake are so pretty topped with cherry filling. Since this dessert needs to chill overnight, I make it a day ahead.

Prize-Winning Pudding

Speaking of sweets, on Christmas Eve our family participates in another holiday tradition from Denmark. We put one almond in a big bowl of rice pudding and everyone gets a spoonful. The person who comes up with the almond gets a prize.

I can remember playing this game as a child, and now our grandchildren look forward to it! They are such fun. We can "wind them up" and then later turn them over to their parents to deal with!

I learned basic cooking skills from my mother. We did not have much money when I was growing up, but Mom always made sure the food tasted good. When I came to Canada, I really paid attention to how food was cooked and served here, and there have been many people who helped me along the way.

I love cookbooks and will take one to bed to read like most people would a novel. My other interests include working with dried flowers, sewing, gardening and traveling. The problem is there is never much time for travel when you live on a farm!

My biggest hobby is my family. We have great times together. Our oldest son, Craig, his wife and three children live here on the farm and work with us. Chad and his wife live in Coaldale, 35 minutes north. Clark is in Oakland, California.

Daughter La Dean, her husband and their child live on another farm we own. She comes to help out during harvest and when we need her to help move our cattle out on grass. It takes 10 to 15 horseback riders to trail the herd.

I can hardly wait to prepare my favorite meal when my family gathers at our house each Christmas. I'll be delighted if you try my holiday recipes and they please your family, too.

PICTURED AT LEFT: Creamy Mashed Potatoes, French Onion Soup, Carrots Supreme, Cherry Almond Cheesecake and No-Fuss Beef Roast (recipes are on the next page).

No-Fuss Beef Roast

I just coat the beef roast with a dry rub to spark the flavor, then stick it in the oven.

1-1/2 teaspoons seasoned salt
1 teaspoon garlic powder
1/2 teaspoon onion powder
1/4 teaspoon cayenne pepper
1 beef rib roast (4 to 6 pounds)
1/2 cup butter *or* margarine, cubed

Combine the first four ingredients; rub over roast. Place roast, fat side up, in a roasting pan. Dot with butter. Bake, uncovered, at 350° for 1-3/4 to 3 hours or until meat reaches desired doneness (for medium-rare, a meat thermometer should read 145°; medium, 160°; well-done, 170°). Let stand for 10-15 minutes before carving. Thicken pan drippings for gravy if desired. **Yield:** 6-8 servings.

Editor's Note: One envelope of meat marinade seasoning mix may be substituted for the seasoned salt, garlic powder, onion powder and cayenne.

French Onion Soup

(Pictured on page 212)

When my husband asked me to make this soup for a dinner at church, I prepared a huge pot and counted on having some left for us. But he came home with an empty pan and many requests for the recipe!

6 cups thinly sliced onions
1 tablespoon sugar
1/2 teaspoon pepper
1/3 cup vegetable oil
6 cups beef broth
8 slices French bread (3/4 inch thick), toasted
1/2 cup shredded Parmesan *or* Swiss cheese

In a Dutch oven or soup kettle over medium-low heat, cook onions, sugar and pepper in oil for 20 minutes or until onions are caramelized, stirring frequently. Add the broth; bring to a boil. Reduce heat; cover and simmer for 30 minutes. Ladle soup into ovenproof bowls. Top each with a slice of French bread; sprinkle with cheese. Broil until cheese is melted and serve. **Yield:** 8 servings.

Carrots Supreme

This creamy carrot casserole is always a hit. An easy-to-fix but very special side dish, it goes well with almost any meat or poultry.

✓ Uses less fat, sugar or salt. Includes Nutritional Analysis and Diabetic Exchanges.

8 cups sliced carrots
1 small onion, chopped
1 tablespoon butter *or* margarine
1 can (10-3/4 ounces) condensed cream of mushroom soup, undiluted
1 can (4 ounces) mushroom stems and pieces, drained
1/2 cup grated Parmesan cheese
1 cup soft bread crumbs

Place carrots in a saucepan and cover with water. Bring to a boil. Reduce heat; cover and cook until tender. Meanwhile, in a small skillet, saute onion in butter until tender. Drain carrots; add onion, soup, mushrooms and Parmesan cheese. Transfer to a greased 2-1/2-qt. baking dish. Sprinkle with bread crumbs. Bake, uncovered, at 350° for 30-35 minutes or until heated through. **Yield:** 8 servings.

Nutritional Analysis: One 1-cup serving (prepared with stick margarine and reduced-fat soup) equals 142 calories, 4 g fat (2 g saturated fat), 7 mg cholesterol, 420 mg sodium, 22 g carbohydrate, 5 g fiber, 5 g protein. **Diabetic Exchanges:** 2 vegetable, 1-1/2 starch, 1 fat.

Creamy Mashed Potatoes

I love potatoes—mashed ones especially. This company-worthy version is great with roast beef.

5 pounds potatoes, peeled and cubed
3 garlic cloves, peeled
1 package (3 ounces) cream cheese, softened
1/2 cup milk
2 tablespoons butter *or* margarine
1 to 1-1/2 teaspoons salt
1/4 teaspoon pepper
1/4 cup chopped green onions, optional
1/8 teaspoon paprika, optional

Place potatoes and garlic in a saucepan; cover with water. Bring to a boil. Reduce heat; cover and cook for 20-25 minutes or until potatoes are very tender. Drain well. Place potatoes and garlic in a mixing bowl. Add cream cheese, milk, butter, salt and pepper; beat until smooth. Transfer to a serving bowl; sprinkle with onions and paprika if desired. **Yield:** 6-8 servings.

Cherry Almond Cheesecake

Cherry marbling and topping bring a holiday look to this lovely dessert.

1 cup ground almonds
1/3 cup graham cracker crumbs (about 6 squares)
1/4 cup butter *or* margarine, melted
3 packages (8 ounces *each*) cream cheese, softened
1 can (14 ounces) sweetened condensed milk
3 eggs
1 can (21 ounces) cherry pie filling, *divided*

In a small bowl, combine almonds and cracker crumbs; stir in butter. Press onto the bottom of a greased 9-in. springform pan; set aside. In a mixing bowl, beat the cream cheese and milk until smooth. Add eggs; beat on low just until combined. Pour into prepared crust. Refrigerate 1/2 cup pie filling for garnish. Drop remaining pie filling by teaspoonfuls onto cream cheese mixture; cut through batter with a knife to swirl the filling.

Bake at 325° for 50-55 minutes or until center is almost set. Cool on wire rack for 10 minutes. Carefully run a knife around edge of pan to loosen; cool 1 hour longer. Chill overnight. Remove sides of pan. Cut cheesecake into slices; garnish with reserved pie filling. Refrigerate leftovers. **Yield:** 12 servings.

Camélier panaché
Jacinthe d'Orient

A Savory Salmon Menu

Mixing and matching favorite recipes, this avid cook has come up with a "can't miss" menu that's perfect for a special-occasion family meal or for company.

By Kathy Schrecengost, Oswego, New York

I'VE ALWAYS liked to try new foods. But it wasn't until I was 20 and began working as a waitress in a local restaurant that I discovered a passion for cooking.

Since then, I've been cooking up a storm. Besides making meals for my husband, Steve, and our sons, Zac and Drazen, I've operated a small catering business and now am food editor for our city's newspaper.

My favorite menu is one I often serve when company's coming. Serving a first course of soup gives the feeling of "we're out to dinner" and takes the edge off guests' appetites. My creamy Garlic Soup is a great meal-starter.

Salmon is readily available and makes an attractive entree for guests. Even people who aren't crazy about other types of fish comment on how much they enjoy the subtle flavor of my Maple Teriyaki Salmon Fillets. New York maple syrup is showcased in this dish, blending beautifully with soy sauce to produce a teriyaki flavor.

Browning the thin egg noodles in Noodle Rice Pilaf adds color and interest. Plus, you can throw in slivered almonds, diced apricots or other ingredients.

Spinach tops my list of greens since it's so tasty and good for you. At its best in Spinach Salad with Oranges, the leaves are tossed with pretty mandarin oranges, sliced mushrooms, crisp bacon and a tangy homemade dressing. At Thanksgiving and Christmastime, I'll frequently throw in some dried cranberries for a festive touch.

Our family fondly refers to the Poppy Seed Bundt Cake as "Matthew's Grandma's Poppy Seed Cake". We first tasted it at son Zac's preschool introduction dinner. The recipe came from the grandmother of one of his classmates. She was delighted to share it.

While I try to use as few convenience foods as I can in my cooking, I'm not adverse to starting with a mix when the end result has such wonderful "from scratch" taste.

Like most of my menus, this one came together as I mixed and matched recipes I'm constantly trying. I make it a point to prepare a couple of new things every week. It keeps mealtime interesting and gives the kids variety.

To get them to try something they've never tasted, I sometimes put a small dish on the table, saying it's "just for Mom and Dad". Usually they get curious and want to taste it, too!

Came to Cooking Late

Since I didn't start cooking as a child, I suppose you could call me a "late bloomer" in the kitchen. But after I started working in that restaurant years ago, I realized I wanted to spend as much time as I could with foods. So after returning from my honeymoon, I started a catering business with my best friend.

We had such fun with the business, doing everything from birthday parties to weddings. I remember one particularly crazy day when, with the help of my husband, we did *three* parties.

It was the hottest day of the summer and halfway through the second party, one of our electric woks went on the fritz. Somehow we managed to pull it off, only to promise ourselves that we would never commit to more than one party per day again!

Family obligations have since prompted us to put the catering business on the back burner. I now serve as food editor at our local newspaper. My job includes a weekly column with recipes, restaurant interviews and reporting on food-related events in town.

I've been fortunate enough to have recipes published in other well-known food-related magazines. But when people ask me which publication I use most, I always say *Taste of Home.*

It is so "user friendly" and consistently great. I often take the whole magazine along when I go to get groceries!

You could do the same when you try this easy, pleasing salmon meal. It's been a winner for me, and I hope you'll enjoy it, too.

PICTURED AT LEFT: Maple Teriyaki Salmon Fillets, Noodle Rice Pilaf, Spinach Salad with Oranges and Poppy Seed Bundt Cake (recipes are on the next page).

Maple Teriyaki Salmon Fillets

A marinade made with maple syrup and apple juice is used to baste these salmon fillets while they're broiled or grilled. It glazes the fish nicely and adds a mild sweetness.

1/3 cup apple juice
1/3 cup maple syrup
3 tablespoons soy sauce
2 tablespoons finely chopped onion
2 garlic cloves, minced
4 salmon fillets (about 2 pounds)

In a bowl, combine the first five ingredients. Remove 1/2 cup for basting; cover and refrigerate. Pour remaining marinade into a large resealable plastic bag. Add salmon; seal bag and turn to coat. Refrigerate for 1-3 hours. Drain and discard marinade. Broil salmon 4 in. from the heat for 5 minutes. Baste with reserved marinade. Broil 10 minutes longer or until fish flakes easily with a fork, basting frequently. **Yield:** 4 servings.

Spinach Salad with Oranges

The tangy dressing for this refreshing salad has the right sweet-tart balance to suit my taste—and others who try it agree!

1 package (10 ounces) fresh spinach, torn
1 can (11 ounces) mandarin oranges, drained
1 cup sliced fresh mushrooms
3 bacon strips, cooked and crumbled

DRESSING:

3 tablespoons ketchup
2 tablespoons cider vinegar
1-1/2 teaspoons Worcestershire sauce
1/4 cup sugar
2 tablespoons chopped onion
1/8 teaspoon salt
Dash pepper
1/2 cup vegetable oil

In a large salad bowl, toss spinach, oranges, mushrooms and bacon; set aside. In a blender or food processor, combine the ketchup, vinegar, Worcestershire sauce, sugar, onion, salt and pepper; cover and process until smooth. While processing, gradually add oil in a steady stream. Serve with salad. **Yield:** 4-6 servings (about 3/4 cup dressing).

Garlic Soup

(Not pictured)

This recipe can be prepared a day ahead and can easily be doubled or tripled. I garnish each serving with a dab of sour cream. By adding chicken and rice, you can turn it into a main course.

2 small onions, chopped
3 garlic cloves, minced
1/2 cup butter *or* margarine
6 tablespoons all-purpose flour
6 cups chicken broth
1/4 to 1/2 teaspoon cayenne pepper

In a large saucepan, saute onions and garlic in butter until tender, about 2-3 minutes. Stir in flour until blended. Gradually add broth. Bring to a boil; cook and stir for 2 minutes or until thickened. Reduce heat; simmer, uncovered, for 15 minutes. Stir in cayenne. **Yield:** 4-6 servings.

Noodle Rice Pilaf

My dad was Armenian, and when I was growing up, we always had a side dish similar to this tasty noodle and rice pilaf.

1/4 cup butter *or* margarine
1 cup long grain rice
1/2 cup uncooked fine egg noodles *or* vermicelli
2-3/4 cups chicken broth
2 tablespoons minced fresh parsley

In a saucepan, melt butter. Add the rice and noodles; cook and stir until lightly browned, about 3 minutes. Stir in broth; bring to a boil. Reduce heat; cover and simmer for 20-25 minutes or until the broth is absorbed and rice is tender. Stir in the parsley. **Yield:** 4 servings.

Poppy Seed Bundt Cake

It tastes so "old-fashioned" that you might be tempted not to tell anyone this cake starts with a mix! A hint of coconut and the tender texture make it simply delicious. All you need to dress it up is a dusting of confectioners' sugar.

1 package (18-1/4 ounces) yellow cake mix
1 package (3.4 ounces) instant coconut cream pudding mix
1 cup water
1/2 cup vegetable oil
3 eggs
2 tablespoons poppy seeds
Confectioners' sugar

In a mixing bowl, combine cake and pudding mixes, water, oil and eggs. Beat on low speed until moistened. Beat on medium for 2 minutes. Stir in the poppy seeds. Pour into a greased and floured 10-in. fluted tube pan. Bake at 350° for 48-52 minutes or until a toothpick inserted near center comes out clean. Cool for 10 minutes before removing from pan to a wire rack to cool completely. Dust with confectioners' sugar. **Yield:** 12-15 servings.

Storing Poppy Seeds

To keep poppy seeds fresh, store them in an airtight container in the refrigerator or freezer.

Holiday Ham Dinner

Say "Happy Easter" with her delectable down-home dinner. It's also a mighty good menu for whenever you have a taste for ham and all the fixin's!

By Lavonne Hartel, Williston, North Dakota

IT'S A JOY for me to cook a mouth-watering holiday meal. For Easter, I like to serve Raisin Sauce for Ham, Golden Au Gratin Potatoes, Carrot Parsnip Stir-Fry, Lemon Refresher and Butterscotch Torte.

Together, these family-favorite foods fit my personal guidelines for an attractive, appetizing meal: Serve something hot and something cold, something crisp and something soft, and always make it colorful!

Ham—always a great entree for a group—is easily dressed up with tangy Raisin Sauce. Some years ago, my husband, Duane, and I were asked to prepare a banquet for parents' night at our church's youth camp. We served ham, and I mixed up this sweet-tart sauce using ingredients I found in the cupboard.

Since then, it has become a favorite of ours. The raisins cook up plump and soft in this simple sauce. It perks up the flavor of a mild-tasting ham...and complements a saltier one.

Creamy Casserole

After tasting Golden Au Gratin Potatoes at a potluck, I eagerly requested the recipe for this creamy, rich-tasting casserole with crunchy topping.

I've prepared it often, most recently for Christmas dinner at the RV resort in Apache Junction, Arizona, where we spend 4 months each winter. The park owner furnished ham for everyone and we all brought a dish to pass. What fun and fellowship! These folks have become just like family.

Cooking in our 32-foot motor home is like playing house. We use compact kettles with removable handles for storage, mini spatulas, soup ladles and stackable lightweight serving bowls.

I miss my three ovens at home, but by using the small oven, a 6-quart roaster oven and our grill, we can even entertain on the road! Our five children and eight grandchildren live in Colorado, and we visit them on the way to and from Arizona.

The kids always loved fried grated carrots. One day I remembered how good fried parsnips, fresh from the garden, were when I was a child. So I added some to the carrots and came up with Carrot Parsnip Stir-Fry.

For everyday meals, I grate the carrots and parsnips. But cutting the vegetables into thin julienne strips makes them fancier for a special occasion.

Thirst-Quenching Beverage

Lemon Refresher, the fruity beverage served with my Easter meal, was a recipe I brought to a "punch party" 30 years ago. My group of friends had decided we needed some new punch recipes and each of us found a different one to try.

Mine was popular, and still is, because it truly is refreshing and not too sweet. I served it at both our daughters' wedding receptions.

Best made the day before you serve it, Butterscotch Torte is yummy and old-fashioned. The tender graham cracker cake's taste improves with age. With its fluffy whipped cream filling and luscious butterscotch sauce drizzled over, this torte is a fine finale for a festive dinner.

I began cooking while I was growing up, one of eight children, on a North Dakota prairie farm. Attending rural country schools, I was the only one in my class for several years—with one of my sisters as my teacher! Total enrollment ranged from 3 to 12 students.

High school meant boarding in Watford City, 23 miles from home. After attending college in Kansas and finishing my degree in North Dakota, I taught school and married the local telephone man.

Through the years, I've cooked for a variety of large groups including family reunions, scores of church friends and neighbors, and the local Head Start program. I like food to taste good and be fun. I still remember the time I baked a meat loaf "cake" frosted with mashed potatoes. The Head Start kids were so surprised.

I hope you'll have fun trying my Easter menu or mixing and matching the recipes here with favorites of your own.

PICTURED AT LEFT: Raisin Sauce for Ham, Carrot Parsnip Stir-Fry, Golden Au Gratin Potatoes and Butterscotch Torte (recipes are on the next page).

Raisin Sauce for Ham

The raisins cook up plump and soft in this savory golden sauce that dresses up ham for Easter dinner or anytime. A hint of lemon balances the fruit's sweetness. You can mix up this accompaniment in minutes.

1/2 cup packed brown sugar
2 tablespoons cornstarch
1 teaspoon ground mustard
1-1/2 cups water
1/2 cup raisins
2 tablespoons white vinegar
2 tablespoons lemon juice
1/4 teaspoon grated lemon peel
2 tablespoons butter *or* margarine

In a saucepan, combine first three ingredients. Stir in water, raisins, vinegar, lemon juice and peel until blended. Bring to a boil; cook and stir for 2 minutes or until thickened. Stir in butter until melted. Serve warm over sliced ham. **Yield:** 2 cups.

Lemon Refresher

(Not pictured)

It's hard to believe I started making this tart punch 30 years ago. It's definitely a tried-and-true recipe!

1-1/2 cups sugar
1/3 cup lemon juice
2 cups milk
1 tablespoon lemon extract
1/2 teaspoon grated lemon peel, optional
2 liters lemon-lime soda, chilled

In a mixing bowl, beat sugar and lemon juice on high speed for 3 minutes or until sugar is partially dissolved. Gradually add milk, beating constantly on high. Stir in the lemon extract and peel if desired. Refrigerate until ready to serve. Stir in soda just before serving. Serve over ice. **Yield:** 3 quarts.

Golden Au Gratin Potatoes

During the many years I've made this creamy potato dish, I haven't run into anyone who didn't like it! The sauce is flavorful and just the right consistency.

1 can (10-3/4 ounces) condensed cream of chicken soup, undiluted
1 cup (8 ounces) sour cream
3/4 cup butter *or* margarine, melted, *divided*
3 tablespoons dried minced onion
1/2 teaspoon salt
1 package (32 ounces) frozen Southern-style hash brown potatoes, thawed
2-1/2 cups shredded cheddar cheese
2-1/2 cups crushed cornflakes

In a large bowl, combine the soup, sour cream, 1/2 cup butter, onion and salt. Stir in the potatoes and cheese. Transfer to a greased 13-in. x 9-in. x 2-in. baking dish. Toss the cornflakes and remaining butter; sprinkle over potatoes. Bake, uncovered, at 350° for 50-60 minutes or until heated through. **Yield:** 8-10 servings.

Carrot Parsnip Stir-Fry

Orange carrot slivers and yellow parsnips make a pretty and different side dish. If parsnips aren't available, you could substitute rutabagas or turnips. Usually, I saute the vegetables until they are crisp-tender. But they're also good quite well-cooked, almost browned.

1-1/2 pounds parsnips, peeled and julienned
1/4 cup butter *or* margarine
2 pounds carrots, julienned
2 tablespoons dried minced onion

In a large skillet, saute the parsnips in butter for 3-4 minutes. Add the carrots and onion; cook and stir until vegetables are tender, about 10-15 minutes. **Yield:** 8 servings.

Butterscotch Torte

This recipe makes plenty of yummy butterscotch sauce, so you can drizzle some over the top and have extra to serve on the side. The cake is best when served the day after it's made.

6 eggs, *separated*
1-1/2 cups sugar
2 teaspoons vanilla extract
2 cups graham cracker crumbs
1 cup finely chopped nuts
1 teaspoon baking powder
TOPPING/FILLING:
1 cup packed brown sugar
1 tablespoon all-purpose flour
Dash salt
1/4 cup orange juice
2 tablespoons water
1 egg, beaten
1/4 cup butter *or* margarine
1 teaspoon vanilla extract
2 cups whipping cream
1/4 cup confectioners' sugar

Line three greased 9-in. round baking pans with waxed paper and grease the paper; set aside. In a small mixing bowl, beat egg whites on high speed until stiff peaks form; set aside. In a large mixing bowl, beat egg yolks and sugar until thick and lemon-colored. Add vanilla; mix well. Combine cracker crumbs, nuts and baking powder; fold into egg yolk mixture. Gradually fold in egg whites. Pour into prepared pans. Bake at 325° for 20-25 minutes or until lightly browned. Cool for 10 minutes before removing from pans to wire racks.

For topping, combine brown sugar, flour and salt in a saucepan. Stir in orange juice and water until smooth; bring to a boil. Reduce heat; cook and stir for 2 minutes or until slightly thickened. Stir some of the hot mixture into beaten egg; return to pan, stirring constantly. Cook and stir until nearly boiling; reduce heat. Cook and stir 1-2 minutes longer (do not boil). Remove from the heat; stir in butter and vanilla. Cool completely.

In a mixing bowl, beat cream until soft peaks form. Beat in confectioners' sugar until stiff. Place one cake layer on a serving plate; spread with a third of whipped cream. Repeat layers twice. Drizzle some of topping over cake. Serve remaining topping with cake. Refrigerate. **Yield:** 12 servings.

Perfect Patio Party

"Dining out" is what this cook enjoys most in summer. Grilled pork roast and homegrown garden bounty star in her mouth-watering menu.

By Christine Wilson, Sellersville, Pennsylvania

OUR GRILL gets put to good use, especially during the summer months! My husband, Don, and I enjoy casual outdoor entertaining around our pool. Plus, our family prefers meat grilled.

When we've invited relatives or friends to our home for dinner, I know I can't miss with a menu of Grilled Rosemary Pork Roast, Home-Style Mashed Potatoes, Walnut-Cheese Spinach Salad, Raspberry Iced Tea and Blueberry Orange Cheesecake.

The idea for my Grilled Rosemary Pork Roast came about when I entered a local pork company's recipe contest several years ago. I decided to complement the tender pork with garlic, rosemary and apples.

I was fortunate to have everything come out well and be chosen as a finalist! To make things even better, my mom—Ann Nace from Perkasie, Pennsylvania—also placed in the contest.

Childhood Cook

I've lived in this area all my life. Coming from a family of seven, I took an interest in cooking at an early age. It was a job I could do to help out around the house.

I strive to be as good a cook as my mom. The joke in our family is that she and Dad don't go out to dinner often because my dad will pick through his meal and is never as satisfied as when Mom has cooked something. He is so spoiled!

I've also been influenced by my grandmothers. One was Pennsylvania Dutch; her specialty was apple dumplings. The other was Czechoslovakian —she made the most fantastic nut rolls!

Served with my pork roast, Home-Style Mashed Potatoes are a takeoff on a menu item from the restaurant at a golf course where Don and I play. Keeping the red skins on makes this dish eye-appealing and more nutritious, too.

After tasting a store-bought raspberry vinaigrette dressing, I thought, "I can make that." Don't we all do that sometimes? So I developed a homemade dressing for my Walnut-Cheese Spinach Salad, which we like even better than the store-bought kind.

Time for Tea

A co-worker of mine from England gave me a tip on making the best iced tea: The sugar should be added first to make a syrup before adding the tea bags. Try it and see if you taste a difference. I often serve Raspberry Iced Tea with lemon slices.

We grow raspberries, blueberries, herbs and flowers in our garden. With our abundant berry crop, I prepare jams to give throughout the year as gifts.

Backyard berries are also featured in luscious Blueberry Orange Cheesecake. It's one of the many recipes I've collected from Mom over the years. We are big cheesecake fans. This is lighter than the traditional version. I sometimes trim this dessert with nasturtiums, which are pretty and edible flowers.

Currently, I work as a teaching assistant at a middle school, helping out in a variety of classes, including Family and Consumer Science. Many students do well because they are motivated by getting to eat what they make! In the past, I've worked in a school cafeteria and have baked for caterers.

My husband is always ready with a compliment for my cooking. Don also likes to cook—Cajun meals, breads and grilling are his specialties.

An electric tower lineman for 25 years, he always came home very hungry. We have two daughters, Donna and Amber. Donna is married to Scott Fogel, a policeman. We adore their toddler, Devon.

I look forward to our frequent family mini excursions. I also like to swim, read and help with the Sellersville Fire Department Ladies Auxiliary events. Our group serves banquets and puts on bake sales and craft fairs to help raise money for the department, of which Don is chief.

For your next summer gathering, consider serving my seasonal supper featuring fresh flavors.

PICTURED AT LEFT: Raspberry Iced Tea, Grilled Rosemary Pork Roast, Home-Style Mashed Potatoes, Blueberry Orange Cheesecake and Walnut-Cheese Spinach Salad (recipes on the next page).

Grilled Rosemary Pork Roast

When the family's coming or we're expecting guests for dinner, I often serve this flavorful grilled pork roast. Apple and honey complement the rosemary and garlic.

✓ Uses less fat, sugar or salt. Includes Nutritional Analysis and Diabetic Exchanges.

3 medium tart apples, peeled and chopped
1 cup unsweetened apple cider *or* juice
3 green onions, chopped
3 tablespoons honey
1 to 2 tablespoons minced fresh rosemary *or* 1 to 2 teaspoons dried rosemary, crushed
2 garlic cloves, minced
1 boneless pork loin roast (3 pounds)

In a saucepan, combine the first six ingredients; bring to a boil. Reduce heat; simmer, uncovered, for 5 minutes. Cool slightly. Place pork roast in a large resealable plastic bag; add half of the marinade. Cover and refrigerate overnight, turning occasionally. Transfer the remaining marinade to a bowl; cover and refrigerate.

Drain and discard marinade. Grill roast, covered, over indirect medium-low heat for 1-1/2 to 2 hours or until a meat thermometer reads 160°, turning occasionally. Let stand for 10 minutes before slicing. Heat reserved marinade; serve with pork. **Yield:** 8 servings.

Nutritional Analysis: One serving equals 312 calories, 9 g fat (3 g saturated fat), 94 mg cholesterol, 79 mg sodium, 19 g carbohydrate, 2 g fiber, 37 g protein. **Diabetic Exchanges:** 3-1/2 lean meat, 1 starch, 1 fat.

Home-Style Mashed Potatoes

Leaving the tender skins on the spuds not only saves time, it sparks the taste and adds color to these hearty mashed potatoes.

3 pounds red potatoes, quartered
2 teaspoons salt, *divided*
1/4 to 1/2 cup milk
5 tablespoons butter *or* margarine
1/4 teaspoon white pepper

Place potatoes in a large saucepan or Dutch oven; cover with water. Add 1 teaspoon salt. Cover and bring to a boil. Reduce heat; cook for 20-30 minutes or until very tender. Drain potatoes well and place in a large mixing bowl. Add 1/4 cup milk, butter, pepper and remaining salt. Beat on low speed until potatoes are light and fluffy, adding remaining milk if needed. **Yield:** 8 servings.

Raspberry Iced Tea

(Pictured on page 224)

One sip and you'll likely agree this is the best flavored tea you've ever tasted.

8-1/4 cups water, *divided*
2/3 cup sugar
5 individual tea bags
3 to 4 cups unsweetened raspberries

In a large saucepan, bring 4 cups water to a boil. Stir in sugar until dissolved. Remove from the heat; add tea bags. Steep for 5-8 minutes. Discard tea bags. Add 4 cups water. In another saucepan, bring raspberries and remaining water to a boil. Reduce heat; simmer, uncovered, for 3 minutes. Strain and discard pulp. Add raspberry juice to the tea mixture. Serve over ice. **Yield:** about 2 quarts

Walnut-Cheese Spinach Salad

Tangy homemade raspberry vinaigrette dressing gives a summery flavor—and a pretty pink-red tint—to this salad that's special enough to serve to company.

2 cups unsweetened raspberries
1/3 cup sugar
1/3 cup vegetable oil
2 tablespoons white wine vinegar *or* cider vinegar
1/4 teaspoon Worcestershire sauce, optional
1 package (6 ounces) fresh baby spinach
1 small red onion, thinly sliced and separated into rings
1/2 to 1 cup crumbled feta cheese
1/2 cup chopped walnuts

In a saucepan over medium heat, bring raspberries and sugar to a boil. Cook for 1 minute. Strain and discard pulp. In a blender, combine the raspberry juice, oil, vinegar and Worcestershire sauce if desired; cover and process until smooth. In a salad bowl, combine the spinach, onion, cheese and walnuts. Drizzle with desired amount of dressing; toss to coat. Refrigerate any remaining dressing. **Yield:** 8 servings.

Blueberry Orange Cheesecake

I'm always quick to give my mom credit for this lovely dessert recipe when people compliment me on it.

1-1/2 cups graham cracker crumbs
2 tablespoons all-purpose flour
2 tablespoons brown sugar
6 tablespoons butter *or* margarine, melted

FILLING:

4 cups cream-style cottage cheese, undrained
1-1/2 cups sugar
1/2 cup all-purpose flour
3/4 cup whipping cream
3 tablespoons orange juice concentrate
1/2 teaspoon vanilla extract
1/8 teaspoon salt
5 eggs

TOPPING:

1 cup (8 ounces) sour cream
2 tablespoons confectioners' sugar
1 cup fresh blueberries
Fresh mint

In a small bowl, combine the cracker crumbs, flour and brown sugar; stir in butter. Press onto the bottom and 2-1/2 in. up the sides of a greased 9-in. springform pan; set aside. In a blender, cover and process cottage cheese until smooth. Transfer to a large mixing bowl; beat in sugar. Beat in the next five ingredients. Add eggs; beat on low speed just until combined. Pour over crust.

Bake at 350° for 70-75 minutes or until center is almost set. Cool on a wire rack for 10 minutes. Carefully run a knife around edge of pan to loosen. Cool for 1 hour. Chill overnight. Remove sides of pan. In a small bowl, combine sour cream and confectioners' sugar; spread over cake. Garnish with blueberries and mint. **Yield:** 12 servings.

Comforting Sunday Fare

Gathering family recipes into a cookbook for her newlywed daughter, this avid cook wouldn't dare omit a Sunday dinner that features "Mom's meat loaf"!

By Sue Call, Beech Grove, Indiana

I'M BUSY putting together a special collection of recipes for my newly married daughter, Lora. It inspired me to share this well-loved menu that I've served frequently as Sunday dinner.

I can always count on satisfied smiles and compliments whenever I serve Bacon-Topped Meat Loaf, Emerald Rice, Citrus Cabbage Slaw, Herbed Onion Bread and Chocolate Cheesecake. Lora, her husband, Kevin, our son, Michael, and my husband, Lee, all enjoy this delicious meal.

Since I work full-time, I like to cook a big meal on Sunday. For 20 years, I've been an administrative secretary in a hospital. Often we invite the kids, friends or relatives to come over after church.

Meat Loaf Is a Mainstay

One of our favorite foods is meat loaf. I'd tried many recipes before I found one that, with a few changes, met everyone's approval. For years, Bacon-Topped Meat Loaf has been a delicious standard at our house.

We think the seasoning is perfect and love the added flavor of cheese and bacon. If there should be any leftovers, it makes great sandwiches.

I think you'll enjoy Emerald Rice, too. This pretty side dish is dressed up with spinach and cheese. It's tasty with the meat loaf and is also a great accompaniment for other meats.

Since I don't like to plan too many last-minute dishes when guests are coming, I decided Citrus Cabbage Slaw was another classic for Lora's cookbook. You can assemble it ahead and mix it just before serving, which is a plus when entertaining.

Most people don't think of coleslaw as having fruit and cauliflower in it. So this version is different and pleasant.

PICTURED AT LEFT: Citrus Cabbage Slaw, Herbed Onion Bread, Emerald Rice, Chocolate Cheesecake and Bacon-Topped Meat Loaf (recipes are on the next page).

Warm slices of Herbed Onion Bread have a fine texture and are speckled with minced onion, dill and poppy seeds for a savory flavor. The wonderful aroma that fills the house makes guests think you've worked for hours baking for them.

Chocolate Lover's Choice

When I know a chocolate lover is coming for dinner, there's no question about dessert. It has to be Chocolate Cheesecake, which is almost like a deliciously smooth piece of fudge.

I adapted a friend's recipe, substituting chocolate cookie crumbs for the graham crackers she used in her crust. For me and my family, the more chocolate, the better!

None of the recipes in this menu are complicated, I've assured Lora. She's never taken much interest in cooking until recently. So I was pleased when she said she wants to be able to prepare meals so she and Kevin don't have to eat out all the time.

My own mother never used a recipe! Growing up on a farm and helping her make meals for our family of eight, I learned by adding a dash of this and a dab of that. It wasn't until I got married that I started reading cookbooks.

Cooking has become my favorite hobby. I enjoy trying new recipes and adapting them to my family's likes and dislikes.

Lee is my willing taste-tester. I can count on him for an honest opinion.We also have a great kitchen arrangement—I cook and he washes the dishes! That suits me just fine.

I sometimes take samples of new recipes to the hospital for my co-workers to critique. Several of my personal recipes have been used in the hospital cafeteria, which is very flattering.

Located just outside of Indianapolis, our town of Beech Grove is the home of Amtrak's Maintenance Shops, where cars are repaired. Lee has worked there for many years.

I've tried many delicious recipes from *Taste of Home*, and being a field editor has been a lot of fun. People I hardly know come up to me and ask about the magazine.

Thanks for letting me tell you about myself and my family and give you a taste of our favorite Sunday dinner at the Calls.

Bacon-Topped Meat Loaf

My family loves meat loaf—this one in particular. I created the recipe after trying and adjusting many other recipes over the years.

1/2 cup chili sauce
2 eggs, lightly beaten
1 tablespoon Worcestershire sauce
1 medium onion, chopped
1 cup (4 ounces) shredded cheddar cheese
2/3 cup dry bread crumbs
1/2 teaspoon salt
1/4 teaspoon pepper
2 pounds lean ground beef
2 bacon strips, halved

In a bowl, combine the first eight ingredients. Crumble beef over mixture; mix well. Shape into a loaf in an ungreased 13-in. x 9-in. x 2-in. baking dish. Top with bacon. Bake, uncovered, at 350° for 70-80 minutes or until meat is no longer pink and a meat thermometer reads 160°. Drain; let stand 10 minutes before cutting. **Yield:** 8 servings.

Emerald Rice

(Pictured on page 228)

Half-and-half cream and cheddar cheese give this rice dish its down-home flavor.

✓ Uses less fat, sugar or salt. Includes Nutritional Analysis and Diabetic Exchanges.

3 cups cooked rice
1 package (10 ounces) frozen chopped spinach, thawed and squeezed dry
1 cup (4 ounces) shredded cheddar cheese
1 cup half-and-half cream
1/2 cup chopped onion
1 tablespoon butter
1 teaspoon salt

In a bowl, combine all ingredients. Transfer to a greased 1-1/2-qt. baking dish. Cover and bake at 350° for 25-35 minutes or until heated through. **Yield:** 8 servings.

Nutritional Analysis: One 3/4-cup serving (prepared with reduced-fat cheese and fat-free milk instead of cream) equals 151 calories, 4 g fat (2 g saturated fat), 12 mg cholesterol, 437 mg sodium, 22 g carbohydrate, 2 g fiber, 8 g protein. **Diabetic Exchange:** 1-1/2 starch.

Citrus Cabbage Slaw

A hint of mustard in the vinaigrette-style dressing sparks the flavor in this change-of-pace coleslaw.

✓ Uses less fat, sugar or salt. Includes Nutritional Analysis and Diabetic Exchanges.

5 cups shredded cabbage
1 can (11 ounces) mandarin oranges, drained
1 cup cauliflowerets
1 can (8 ounces) unsweetened pineapple chunks, drained
1/2 cup chopped green pepper
2/3 cup sugar
1/3 cup white vinegar
1/3 cup vegetable oil
1 tablespoon water
2 teaspoons finely chopped onion
1 teaspoon salt

1 teaspoon prepared mustard
1/2 teaspoon celery seed

In a large bowl, toss the first five ingredients. In another bowl, combine remaining ingredients. Stir into cabbage mixture. Cover; refrigerate 2 hours. Toss just before serving. **Yield:** 8 servings.

Nutritional Analysis: One serving (1/2 cup) equals 195 calories, 9 g fat (1 g saturated fat), 0 cholesterol, 314 mg sodium, 28 g carbohydrate, 2 g fiber, 2 g protein. **Diabetic Exchanges:** 1 vegetable, 1 fruit, 1 fat, 1/2 starch.

Herbed Onion Bread

I really enjoy the convenience of my bread machine and use it often. This is one of my best recipes.

1 cup plus 1 tablespoon water (70° to 80°)
2 tablespoons butter *or* margarine, softened
1-1/4 teaspoons salt
3 cups bread flour
2 teaspoons dried minced onion
1-1/2 teaspoons dill weed
1 teaspoon poppy seeds
2 tablespoons nonfat dry milk powder
2 tablespoons sugar
1-1/2 teaspoons active dry yeast

In bread machine pan, place all ingredients in order suggested by manufacturer. Select basic bread setting. Choose crust color and loaf size if available. Bake according to bread machine directions (check dough after 5 minutes of mixing; add 1 to 2 tablespoons of water or flour if needed). **Yield:** 1 loaf (1-1/2 pounds).

Editor's Note: If your bread machine has a time-delay feature, we recommend you do not use it for this recipe.

Chocolate Cheesecake

Everyone's a chocolate lover when it comes to this special dessert. "It melts in your mouth!" and "Very smooth and fudgy!" are typical comments I've heard.

1 cup crushed chocolate wafer crumbs
3 tablespoons sugar
3 tablespoons butter *or* margarine, melted

FILLING:

2 cups (12 ounces) semisweet chocolate chips
2 packages (8 ounces *each*) cream cheese, softened
3/4 cup sugar
2 tablespoons all-purpose flour
2 eggs
1 teaspoon vanilla extract
Strawberries and white chocolate shavings, optional

In a small bowl, combine cookie crumbs and sugar; stir in butter. Press onto the bottom of a greased 9-in. springform pan; set aside. In a saucepan over low heat, melt the chocolate chips; stir until smooth. Set aside. In a mixing bowl, beat cream cheese and sugar until smooth. Add flour and beat well. Add eggs; beat on low just until combined. Stir in vanilla and melted chocolate just until blended. Pour over crust.

Bake at 350° for 40-45 minutes or until center is almost set. Cool on a wire rack for 10 minutes. Carefully run a knife around edge of pan to loosen; cool 1 hour longer. Chill overnight. Remove sides of pan. Garnish slices with strawberries and chocolate shavings if desired. Refrigerate leftovers. **Yield:** 12 servings.

Editor's Note: Even a tight-fitting springform pan may leak. To prevent drips, place the filled springform on a baking sheet in the oven.

A Feast for Thanksgiving

Two good friends cook up a tasty and treasured tradition that started more than 20 years ago and keeps growing! A fabulous meal is counted among the blessings.

By Ardis Rollefson, Jackson Hole, Wyoming

FOR NEARLY 25 years, my family has gotten together with friends Diane and Alan Galbraith to celebrate Thanksgiving. We alternate homes for the holiday and always have a full house—with up to 20 around the table!

Through the years, we have watched our children become adults...have seen countless girlfriends and boyfriends come and go (some stayed and became spouses!)...and have entertained guests outside our families who otherwise would have been alone on this glorious holiday.

But one thing has remained the same—the menu. Diane and I need only a quick phone call to iron out the details about who's doing what.

Family-Favorite Menu

Among the ever-popular holiday foods are Turkey with Chestnut Stuffing, Creamed Onions and Carrots, Raspberry Gelatin Ring, Molasses Yeast Rolls and Apple Crumb Pie.

We always dress up for dinner. When I'm hosting (I've been a widow for 24 years), the table is set with gorgeous Haviland china that was brought over from France in 1915. It's an inheritance from my husband Max's family.

As we gather around the pretty table, we say individual prayers before the sumptuous feast. Our showstopper is oven-roasted Turkey with Chestnut Stuffing. We always get a large one, but we learned not to get too carried away after serving a 42-pounder one year! It was almost too much to handle.

The marvelous dressing is Diane's mother's recipe. She was raised in the East, and the chestnuts are a Dutch touch from New York's Hudson River Valley. There's plenty of stuffing to stuff the bird and extra to bake separately. And, of course, we serve giblet gravy over mashed potatoes as well.

My Creamed Onions and Carrots can be made in advance, which eases pressure on the big day and helps meld the flavors. It's a pleasant dish with a mild onion taste, one of several sides we serve, including buttered green peas, scalloped baked corn and sweet potato casserole.

Homegrown Raspberries Add Zip

Since I raise and freeze my own raspberries, they star in my Raspberry Gelatin Ring, which has a luscious layer of complementary cream cheese.

Molasses Yeast Rolls—tender golden-brown buns—are made with whole wheat, taking me back to my roots. The recipe comes from my youngest brother's wife, Mrs. Melvin (Dorelee) Hodenfield, who lives on the family farm where I grew up near Ray, North Dakota.

We raised a variety of grains, though mostly spring wheat. I remember helping Dad in the field during harvest. Mom, an excellent baker and cook, was my role model in the kitchen. Since both of my parents were of Norwegian heritage, many of her dishes had a Scandinavian flair.

By the time I was 10, I could put dinner on the table for our family of six and the hired man. Accustomed to Mom's excellent meals, my brothers were always finding fault with some little thing about the dishes I prepared. When I was about to be married, my brother Curt told Max, "Well, you're getting a good cook!"

That was the closest thing to a compliment about food that I had ever gotten from any of my brothers!

We serve Thanksgiving dinner about 3 p.m. but wait until evening for dessert. My mom's Apple Crumb Pie is always among the choices. The yummy pastry crumb topping makes this special-occasion pie extra fancy.

As we gather around the table these days, great conversation and a sing-along make each Thanksgiving memorable. Although my children live in California, Wyoming and Montana, one or more of them usually visits for the holiday.

This Thanksgiving meal always reminds me that life is good—and it's time to reflect on my many blessings.

PICTURED AT LEFT: Turkey with Chestnut Stuffing, Molasses Yeast Rolls, Raspberry Gelatin Ring, Creamed Onions and Carrots and Apple Crumb Pie (recipes are on the next page).

Turkey with Chestnut Stuffing

With delicious chopped chestnuts in the savory stuffing, this golden roasted bird is a "must" on the menu.

1 pound chestnuts
2 cups chopped celery
2 cups chopped onions
1/2 cup butter *or* margarine
1 package (16 ounces) bulk pork sausage, cooked and drained
1 package (16 ounces) crushed seasoned stuffing
1 can (14-1/2 ounces) chicken broth
1 cup water
1 turkey (18 to 20 pounds)
2 tablespoons vegetable oil

In a large saucepan or Dutch oven, bring 2 qts. of water to boil. Cut an "X" in each chestnut; drop into boiling water. Return to a boil; cook for 5 minutes. Remove from the heat; peel outer shell and inner layer. Coarsely chop chestnuts; set aside. In a skillet, saute celery and onions in butter until tender. Transfer to a large bowl; add sausage, stuffing and chestnuts. Add broth and water; toss to mix.

Loosely stuff turkey just before roasting. Skewer openings; tie drumsticks together. Place breast side up on a rack in a roasting pan. Brush with oil. Bake, uncovered, at 325° for 4-1/4 to 4-3/4 hours or until a meat thermometer reads 180° for turkey and 165° for stuffing, basting occasionally with pan drippings. Cover loosely with foil if turkey browns too quickly.

Cover and let stand for 20 minutes before removing the stuffing and carving the turkey. If desired, thicken pan drippings for gravy. **Yield:** 18 servings (9-10 cups stuffing).

Editor's Note: Stuffing can be prepared as directed and baked in a greased 3-qt. baking dish. Cover; bake at 325° for 40 minutes. Uncover and bake 10 minutes longer or until lightly browned.

Raspberry Gelatin Ring

Besides being wonderfully tasty, this refreshing salad with a cream cheese layer is pretty, too.

1 package (6 ounces) raspberry gelatin
1-1/2 cups boiling water
2 packages (10 ounces *each*) frozen sweetened raspberries, thawed and drained
2 cans (8 ounces *each*) crushed pineapple, undrained
1/4 teaspoon salt
1 package (8 ounces) cream cheese, softened
1/2 cup sour cream

In a bowl, dissolve gelatin in water. Stir in the raspberries, pineapple and salt. Pour half into an 8-cup ring mold coated with nonstick cooking spray; refrigerate for 30 minutes or until firm. Let remaining gelatin mixture stand at room temperature. In a mixing bowl, beat cream cheese and sour cream until smooth. Carefully spread over gelatin in mold; top with remaining gelatin mixture. Refrigerate for 6 hours or until firm. **Yield:** 12 servings.

Creamed Onions and Carrots

(Pictured on page 232)

Preparing this side dish a day ahead of time gives the pleasant flavors time to meld, plus it makes the holiday itself easier on me!

8 cups water
2 pounds pearl onions
2 tablespoons butter *or* margarine
3 tablespoons all-purpose flour

1-1/4 cups whipping cream
1/2 teaspoon salt
1/4 teaspoon pepper
2 cups shredded carrots

In a Dutch oven or large kettle, bring water to a boil. Add onions; boil for 3 minutes. Drain and rinse in cold water; peel and set aside. In a large saucepan, melt butter. Stir in flour until smooth. Gradually add cream, salt and pepper. Bring to a boil; cook and stir for 2 minutes or until thickened. Stir in carrots and onions. Transfer to a greased 2-qt. baking dish. Bake, uncovered, at 325° for 30-40 minutes or until vegetables are tender. **Yield:** 12 servings.

Molasses Yeast Rolls

This recipe, from my youngest brother's wife, evokes memories of learning to cook and bake with my mom.

1 package (1/4 ounce) active dry yeast
3/4 cup warm water (110° to 115°)
1/2 teaspoon honey
1-1/2 cups warm milk (110° to 115°)
1/2 cup molasses
1/4 cup butter *or* margarine, softened
1 egg, beaten
1-1/2 teaspoons salt
3 cups whole wheat flour
4-1/2 cups all-purpose flour

In a large mixing bowl, dissolve yeast in water. Add honey; let stand for 5 minutes. Add the milk, molasses, butter, egg, salt and whole wheat flour. Beat until smooth. Stir in enough all-purpose flour to form a soft dough.Turn onto a floured surface; knead until smooth and elastic, about 6-8 minutes.

Place in a greased bowl, turning once to grease top. Cover and let rise in a warm place until doubled, about 1 hour.

Punch dough down. Turn onto a lightly floured surface; divide into 24 pieces. Shape each into a 10-in. rope. Shape each rope into an "S"; coil ends until they touch the center. Place 2 in. apart on greased baking sheets. Cover and let rise until doubled, about 35 minutes. Bake at 375° for 12-15 minutes or until golden brown. Remove from pans to wire racks. **Yield:** 2 dozen.

Apple Crumb Pie

I carefully brown the topping for this special-occasion pie under the broiler to give it extra eye appeal.

Pastry for single-crust pie (9 inches)
6 cups chopped peeled tart apples (about 6 medium)
2 tablespoons butter *or* margarine, melted
2 tablespoons sour cream
4 teaspoons lemon juice
1/2 cup sugar
1 tablespoon all-purpose flour
1/2 teaspoon ground cinnamon
1/2 teaspoon ground nutmeg

TOPPING:

1/2 cup all-purpose flour
1/2 cup sugar
1/4 cup cold butter *or* margarine

Line a 9-in. pie plate with pastry; flute edges. In a bowl, combine the next eight ingredients. Spoon into pastry shell. In another bowl, combine flour and sugar; cut in butter until crumbly. Sprinkle over filling. Bake at 375° for 45-50 minutes or until filling is bubbly and apples are tender. Cool on a wire rack. **Yield:** 6-8 servings.

Meals in Minutes

In a hurry? Mix and match these recipes to make countless meals that are ready to eat in 30 minutes or less.

FAST 'N' FLAVORFUL. Clockwise from upper left: Steak Fajitas Put a Sizzle in Supper (p. 242), Chicken Grills to a Summer Sensation (p. 244), Chili Puts Zip in Autumn Burgers (p. 246) and Flavors Blend to Make Chicken Special (p. 240).

Cranberries Add Festive Flair to Pork Dinner

IF HOLIDAY hustle and bustle keep your time in the kitchen to a minimum, a satisfying, quick meal may be just the gift to give yourself and your family!

The menu here is made up of favorite recipes shared by three great cooks and combined in our test kitchen. You can have the entire meal ready to serve in just 30 minutes.

Maria Brennan of Waterbury, Connecticut suggests Cranberry Pork Medallions for the entree. "This tender, juicy pork with its festive cranberry glaze is quick and easy to prepare," Maria says. "But it tastes so special and looks so good, everyone will think you went to a lot of fuss."

Honey-Mustard Salad Dressing has only four ingredients, but it's big on flavor. Says Joanne Hof of Los Alamos, New Mexico, "My family loves this thick, tangy golden topping over a mixture of fresh greens and mushrooms."

Chocolate Raisin Truffles are recommended by Diane Hixon of Niceville, Florida.

"I've always enjoyed store-bought chocolate-covered raisins, but they're costly," Diane shares. "These sweet morsels have wonderful homemade flavor, plus they're inexpensive to make. I sometimes give them to friends as holiday gifts. They're so pretty and tasty, they're a pleasant surprise that's hard to resist."

Cranberry Pork Medallions

1 pork tenderloin (about 1 pound), cut into 1/2-inch slices
3 tablespoons olive *or* vegetable oil
1 medium onion, finely chopped
1 garlic clove, minced
3 tablespoons sugar
3/4 cup apple juice
1/2 cup cranberry juice
1/2 cup fresh *or* frozen cranberries
2 teaspoons Dijon mustard
1/2 teaspoon minced fresh rosemary *or* 1/8 teaspoon dried rosemary, crushed
Additional cranberries and fresh rosemary, optional

In a nonstick skillet, cook pork in oil for 3-4 minutes on each side or until golden brown. Remove and set aside. In the same skillet, saute onion, garlic and sugar until onion is caramelized and tender. Stir in the apple juice, cranberry juice, cranberries, mustard and rosemary. Bring to a boil. Reduce heat; simmer, uncovered, for 5-6 minutes or until sauce is reduced by half. Return pork to pan; heat through. Garnish with additional cranberries and rosemary if desired. **Yield:** 3 servings.

Honey-Mustard Salad Dressing

3 tablespoons honey
2 tablespoons Dijon mustard
1/4 cup cider vinegar
1/2 cup vegetable oil
Salad greens and sliced fresh mushrooms

In a small bowl, combine honey and mustard until smooth. Add vinegar; whisk until blended. Slowly add oil while beating with whisk. Serve over salad greens and mushrooms. **Yield:** 1 cup.

Chocolate Raisin Truffles

1 cup milk chocolate chips
1/4 cup light corn syrup
2 tablespoons confectioners' sugar
1-1/2 teaspoons vanilla extract
1-1/2 cups raisins
Nonpareils, sprinkles *and/or* ground nuts

In a microwave-safe bowl, melt chocolate chips at 70% power for 1-2 minutes, stirring often. Stir in the corn syrup, sugar and vanilla until smooth. Add raisins; stir until evenly coated. Drop by teaspoonfuls onto a buttered baking sheet. Roll in nonpareils, sprinkles or nuts. **Yield:** 2-1/2 dozen.

Editor's Note: This recipe was tested in an 850-watt microwave.

Substituting Syrups

You can substitute dark corn syrup if you're out of light. Dark syrup adds color and bolder flavor.

HONEY PIE
LITTLE KISS

Flavors Blend to Make Chicken Special

SPENDING TIME preparing an elaborate meal is no problem for those who like to cook *and* have time to spend in the kitchen. But some days, speed can be the crucial ingredient in what foods you whip up for your hungry clan.

The complete-meal menu here is comprised of family favorites from three great cooks. The ingredients are readily available any time of year, plus you can have the entire meal ready to serve in just 30 minutes or less!

Baked Garlic Chicken is a quick oven entree for lovely golden breaded chicken breasts. "The coating keeps the meat moist and well-seasoned," assures Mary Lou Wayman of Salt Lake City, Utah. "It's a simple recipe that tastes like it took a lot more work than it really did."

Salad with Buttermilk Dressing is suggested by Vivian Haen of Menomonee Falls, Wisconsin. "My family has requested this creamy dressing over garden-fresh salad greens for years," she says, "and I haven't had to disappoint them yet! Peppers provide added color and crunch."

Raspberry Pear Delight is a fast-to-fix yet fancy-looking dessert that's a perfect ending to just about any type of meal—from simple to special-occasion, says Marion Tipton of Phoenix, Arizona. "This is one dessert my family just adores. Chocolate and raspberries were made for each other!"

Baked Garlic Chicken

1/3 cup mayonnaise*
1/4 cup grated Parmesan cheese
3 to 4 tablespoons savory herb with garlic soup mix
4 boneless skinless chicken breast halves
2 tablespoons dry bread crumbs

In a bowl, combine mayonnaise, Parmesan cheese and soup mix. Place the chicken in a greased 11-in. x 7-in. x 2-in. baking dish. Spread with the mayonnaise mixture. Sprinkle with bread crumbs. Bake, uncovered, at 400° for 20-25 minutes or until juices run clear and a meat thermometer reads 170°. **Yield:** 4 servings.

***Editor's Note:** Light or fat-free mayonnaise may not be substituted for regular mayonnaise.

Salad with Buttermilk Dressing

3/4 cup buttermilk
3/4 cup mayonnaise
1 tablespoon minced fresh parsley
1/2 teaspoon sugar
1/2 teaspoon ground mustard
1/4 teaspoon onion powder
1/4 teaspoon garlic powder
1/4 teaspoon pepper
Assorted salad greens, sweet yellow pepper strips and sliced cucumbers *or* vegetables of your choice

In a bowl, whisk together the buttermilk, mayonnaise, parsley, sugar, mustard, onion powder, garlic powder and pepper. Serve over salad greens and fresh vegetables. Refrigerate leftover dressing. **Yield:** 1-1/2 cups.

Raspberry Pear Delight

1 package (10 ounces) frozen sweetened raspberries, thawed
1 can (15 ounces) pear halves, drained
1 pint raspberry sorbet *or* sherbet
Hot fudge ice cream topping
Fresh raspberries and mint, optional

In a blender or food processor, puree the raspberries; strain the seeds. Pour onto four dessert plates or into shallow bowls. Top with pears and a scoop of sorbet. Drizzle with hot fudge topping. Garnish with fresh berries and mint if desired. **Yield:** 4 servings.

Cooking Chicken

• Reduce shrinkage in boneless chicken breasts by removing the clearly visible white tendon.

• Add fiber to the coating of fried or baked chicken by mixing oat bran with the seasonings.

• To spark the flavor of a mild dish, rub the whole chicken or pieces with a paste of fresh herbs (tarragon, rosemary and/or thyme are classic choices), minced garlic and olive oil.

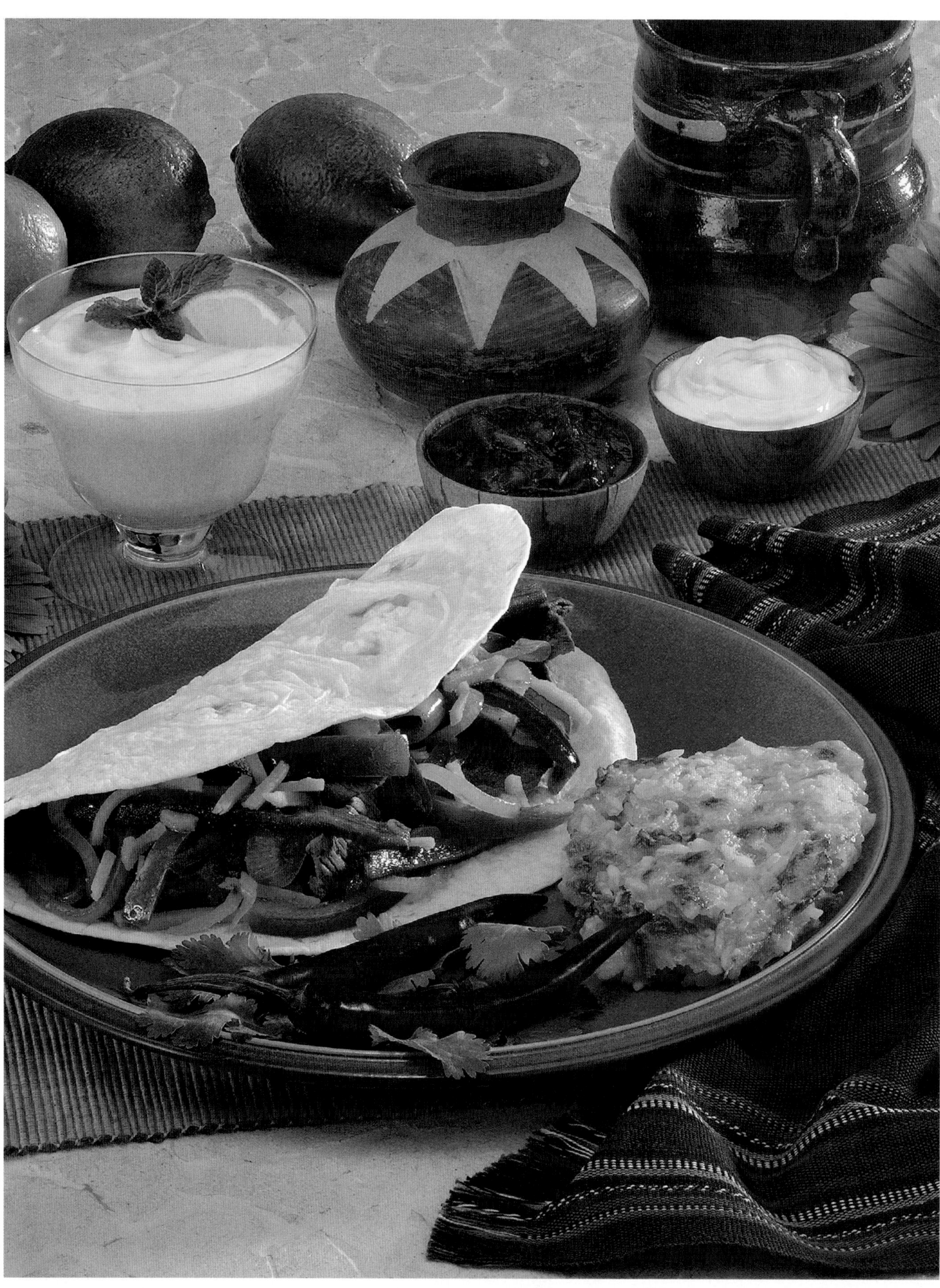

Steak Fajitas Put A Sizzle in Supper

WHEN YOU WANT lots of flavor in just a little time, reach for this zesty yet simple menu. The whole Southwestern-style meal—start to finish—takes a mere 30 minutes to make.

Tender strips of sirloin pick up plenty of spicy flavor in Steak Fajitas. The beef is marinated briefly in orange juice seasoned with cayenne pepper and cumin before being sauteed with onions and peppers and stuffed into tortillas.

"These colorful, hot sandwiches are speedy and satisfying," says Shirley Hilger of Lincoln, Nebraska.

A side dish that's sure to hit the spot is Green Chili Rice from Sandra Hanson of Emery, South Dakota. As a mother of triplets, she often relies on fast dishes.

"With only five ingredients, this rich and creamy rice casserole mixes up in a snap. I always get requests for the recipe," Sandra says.

Top off the meal with Simple Lime Mousse, featuring the perfect pairing of zesty lime and fluffy whipped cream.

"It's light and refreshing," assures Shirley Glaab of Hattiesburg, Mississippi, "especially after a meal that's left your taste buds tingling."

That's one thing *this meal* is guaranteed to do!

Steak Fajitas

1/4 cup orange juice
1/4 cup white vinegar
4 garlic cloves, minced
1 teaspoon seasoned salt
1 teaspoon dried oregano
1 teaspoon ground cumin
1/4 teaspoon cayenne pepper
1 pound boneless beef sirloin steak, cut into 1/4-inch strips
1 medium onion, thinly sliced
1 medium green pepper, thinly sliced
1 medium sweet red pepper, thinly sliced
2 tablespoons vegetable oil, *divided*
4 to 6 flour tortillas (10 inches), warmed
Shredded cheddar cheese, picante sauce and sour cream, optional

In a large resealable plastic bag, combine the first seven ingredients; add the beef. Seal bag and turn to coat; set aside. In a skillet, saute onion and peppers in 1 tablespoon oil until crisp-tender; remove and set aside.

Drain and discard marinade. In the same skillet, cook beef in remaining oil for 2-4 minutes or until it reaches desired doneness. Return vegetables to pan; heat through. Spoon mixture onto tortillas. If desired, top with cheese and serve with picante sauce and sour cream. **Yield:** 4-6 servings.

Green Chili Rice

1 can (10-3/4 ounces) condensed cream of celery soup, undiluted
1 cup (8 ounces) sour cream
1 can (4 ounces) chopped green chilies
1 cup (4 ounces) shredded cheddar cheese
1-1/2 cups uncooked instant rice

In a bowl, combine the soup, sour cream, chilies and cheese. Stir in rice. Transfer to a greased shallow 1-1/2-qt. baking dish. Bake, uncovered, at 350° for 20 minutes or until rice is tender. **Yield:** 4-6 servings.

Simple Lime Mousse

1 cup whipping cream
1/4 cup sugar
2 tablespoons lime juice
1 tablespoon grated lime peel
1 teaspoon vanilla extract
Lime slices and fresh mint, optional

In a mixing bowl, combine the cream, sugar, lime juice, peel and vanilla. Beat on high speed until soft peaks form, about 4 minutes. Spoon into dessert dishes. Garnish with lime and mint if desired. **Yield:** 4 servings.

Luscious Limes

For best flavor, pick brightly colored fruit with smooth skin. Avoid hard or shriveled skin.

Chicken Grills to a Summer Sensation

EVEN FOLKS who truly love to cook may want to spend less time in the kitchen on warm, sunny days. Since fresh air builds appetites, a fast-to-fix menu is especially appropriate.

The complete meal here is made up of favorites from three great cooks and was combined by our test kitchen staff. You can have everything ready to serve in just half an hour.

Grilled Chicken Over Spinach is suggested by Michelle Krzmarzick of Redondo Beach, California.

"With two young children to keep me busy, it's essential to have a few 'ready-in-minutes' dishes for days when I'm short on time," she says. "This is a recipe I've pieced together and added my own touches to. It really satisfies my family."

Biscuit Bites couldn't be easier. Convenient refrigerated biscuits are sprinkled with Parmesan cheese and onion powder, then baked.

"These savory bites are wonderful with soup, a main dish or even as a snack," says Joy Beck of Cincinnati, Ohio. "We like to munch on them instead of popcorn when watching television."

Peachy Fruit Dip served with fresh strawberries, grapes and pieces of melon is a refreshing summer dessert or side dish. "It's even great for breakfast or brunch," shares Barbara Nowakowski of North Tonawanda, New York, "and it's so colorful!"

Grilled Chicken Over Spinach

✓ Uses less fat, sugar or salt. Includes Nutritional Analysis and Diabetic Exchanges.

1 to 2 tablespoons olive *or* canola oil
1 tablespoon cider vinegar
1 garlic clove, minced
1 teaspoon dried thyme
1/2 teaspoon dried oregano
1/2 teaspoon cayenne pepper
1/4 teaspoon salt
Dash pepper
4 boneless skinless chicken breast halves (1 pound)

SAUTEED SPINACH:

1 green onion, finely chopped
1 to 2 garlic cloves, minced
1 to 2 tablespoons olive *or* canola oil
1/2 pound fresh mushrooms, sliced
1 package (10 ounces) fresh spinach, torn

In a bowl, combine the oil, vinegar, garlic, thyme, oregano, cayenne pepper, salt and pepper; mix well. Spoon over the chicken. Grill, uncovered, over medium heat for 7 minutes on each side or until the juices run clear. In a large skillet, saute the onion and garlic in oil for 1 minute. Stir in the mushrooms; saute for 3-4 minutes or until tender. Add the spinach and saute for 2 minutes or until wilted. Transfer to a serving platter; top with chicken. **Yield:** 4 servings.

Nutritional Analysis: One serving (prepared with a total of 2 tablespoons oil) equals 237 calories, 10 g fat (2 g saturated fat), 73 mg cholesterol, 268 mg sodium, 6 g carbohydrate, 3 g fiber, 31 g protein. **Diabetic Exchanges:** 3-1/2 lean meat, 1 vegetable.

Biscuit Bites

1 tube (12 ounces) refrigerated buttermilk biscuits
2 tablespoons grated Parmesan cheese
1 teaspoon onion powder

Cut each biscuit into thirds; place biscuit pieces on a greased baking sheet. Combine Parmesan cheese and onion powder; sprinkle over biscuits. Bake at 400° for 7-8 minutes or until golden brown. **Yield:** 5 servings.

Peachy Fruit Dip

1 can (15-1/4 ounces) sliced *or* halved peaches, drained
1/2 cup marshmallow creme
1 package (3 ounces) cream cheese, cubed
1/8 teaspoon ground nutmeg
Assorted fresh fruit

In a blender or food processor, combine the first four ingredients; cover and blend until smooth. Serve with fruit. **Yield:** 1-3/4 cups.

Chili Puts Zip In Autumn Burgers

WARM WEATHER in autumn can easily convince you to stop and enjoy the great outdoors, even if you have indoor chores on your to-do list.

This fast-to-fix menu gets you in and out of the kitchen in less than 30 minutes, so you can quickly get back to your favorite lawn or garden spot.

The meal is made up of favorites from three great cooks and then combined in our test kitchen.

Chili Burgers are hearty, easy-to-assemble sandwiches suggested by Sue Ross of Casa Grande, Arizona.

"Savory chili and french-fried onions are a fun alternative to traditional burger toppings like ketchup and mustard," she says. "Melted cheddar cheese is the creamy crowning touch."

The recipe for Rosemary Peas 'n' Squash comes from Emily Chaney of Penobscot, Maine.

"The beauty of this recipe is that I can substitute *any* vegetables and still have a terrific side dish," she notes. "I grow fresh rosemary and use it to season whatever garden bounty I harvest. Since zucchini is abundant almost every year, this recipe puts that to good use."

Sally Kendrick says she can hardly wait for fresh berries to come in season, so she can make Berries with Custard Sauce for her family.

"Although it's simple to make, this dessert is the No. 1 favorite at my house," says the Bishop, California cook. "And when I serve it to guests, I'm always asked for the recipe. You can use strawberries, raspberries, blueberries, blackberries—whatever's in season."

Chili Burgers

1 pound ground beef
1-1/2 teaspoons chili powder
1 can (15 ounces) chili with beans
4 hamburger buns, split and toasted
1/2 cup shredded cheddar cheese
1 can (2.8 ounces) french-fried onions

In a bowl, combine beef and chili powder. Shape into four patties. Pan-fry, grill or broil until meat is no longer pink. Meanwhile, in a saucepan, bring chili to a boil. Reduce heat; simmer for 5 minutes or until heated through. Place burgers on bun bottoms; top with chili, cheese and onions. Replace bun tops. **Yield:** 4 servings.

Rosemary Peas 'n' Squash

1 medium yellow summer *or* pattypan squash
1 medium zucchini
1 tablespoon butter *or* margarine
1/4 pound fresh *or* frozen sugar snap peas
1 tablespoon minced fresh rosemary *or* 1 teaspoon dried rosemary, crushed
Salt and pepper to taste

Cut squash into 1-in. chunks. In a large skillet, melt butter. Saute squash, peas and rosemary until vegetables are crisp-tender, about 5 minutes. Sprinkle with salt and pepper. **Yield:** 4 servings.

Berries with Custard Sauce

1/2 cup sugar
2 tablespoons cornstarch
1/4 teaspoon salt
1-1/2 cups milk
4 eggs, beaten
1/2 cup sour cream
1-1/2 teaspoons vanilla extract
Assorted fresh berries

In a saucepan, combine the sugar, cornstarch and salt. Gradually stir in milk until smooth. Bring to a boil over medium heat, stirring constantly. Add a small amount to eggs; return all to pan, stirring constantly. Cook and stir for 2-1/2 minutes or until the mixture reaches 160°.

Remove from the heat; stir in the sour cream and vanilla. Set the saucepan in ice and stir the mixture for 5 minutes. Cover and refrigerate until serving. Serve over berries. **Yield:** about 2 cups sauce.

Berry Good Berries

To make sure grocery store berries are fresh, check the bottom of the container. If the basket is see-through, look for unripe, bruised or moldy berries. If the container is cardboard, watch for juice stains that would indicate some berries are crushed (and possibly rotten).

Crab Adds Elegance To Fish Fillets

WHEN cooler days signal the start of the pre-holiday season, even dedicated cooks can't always spend as much time in the kitchen as they'd like. That's when hearty, fast-to-fix meals come in handy.

Ready to serve in just 30 minutes, the complete menu here combines recipes from three super cooks.

Crab-Topped Fish Fillets are elegant enough for company but truly no-fuss.

"We live in south Florida, where fish is abundant," says Mary Tuthill of Ft. Myers Beach. "We like to get together with friends in the afternoon, so I often need to whip up a quick dinner when we get home. This special fish is one of my husband's favorites."

Three-Cheese Potato Bake is a comforting dish that's ready in a snap. The recipe comes from Lois Buffalow of Grandview, Missouri.

Green Beans with Radishes is a side dish with a flavorful twist.

"The fresh green beans are so pretty mixed with crisp radish slices," says Marlene Muckenhirn, the Delano, Minnesota cook who shares the mouth-watering recipe. "The lemon-butter sauce is an unexpected but tasty touch."

Crab-Topped Fish Fillets

1 pound sole, orange roughy *or* cod fillets
1 can (6 ounces) crabmeat, drained, flaked and cartilage removed *or* 1 cup imitation crabmeat, chopped
1/2 cup grated Parmesan cheese
1/2 cup mayonnaise
1 teaspoon lemon juice
Paprika, optional
1/3 cup slivered almonds, toasted

Place fillets in a greased 8-in. square baking dish. Bake, uncovered, at 350° for 18-22 minutes or until fish flakes easily with a fork. Meanwhile, in a bowl, combine the crab, Parmesan cheese, mayonnaise and lemon juice.

Drain cooking juices from baking dish; spoon crab mixture over fillets. Broil 5 in. from the heat for 5 minutes or until topping is lightly browned. Sprinkle with paprika if desired and almonds. **Yield:** 4 servings.

Three-Cheese Potato Bake

2-2/3 cups chicken broth
2/3 cup milk
1/4 cup butter *or* margarine
1/4 teaspoon pepper
2-2/3 cups mashed potato flakes
1/3 cup shredded Monterey Jack cheese
1/3 cup shredded cheddar cheese
1/3 cup cubed process American cheese
2 tablespoons snipped chives
1/4 cup sour cream, optional

In a large saucepan, combine the broth, milk, butter and pepper; bring to a boil. Remove from the heat; stir in potato flakes. Let stand for 30 seconds; fluff with a fork.

Transfer to a greased 1-qt. baking dish. Top with the three cheeses. Bake, uncovered, at 350° for 20 minutes or until cheese is melted. Sprinkle with chives. Serve with sour cream if desired. **Yield:** 4 servings.

Green Beans with Radishes

✓ Uses less fat, sugar or salt. Includes Nutritional Analysis and Diabetic Exchanges.

1 pound fresh green beans
2 tablespoons thinly sliced green onion
2 tablespoons butter *or* stick margarine
1 teaspoon lemon juice
1 teaspoon soy sauce
1/4 cup sliced radishes

Place fresh green beans in a large saucepan and cover with water; bring to a boil. Cook, uncovered, for 8-10 minutes or until crisp-tender; drain.

In a skillet, saute onion in butter just until tender. Stir in the beans, lemon juice and soy sauce; cook and stir mixture until heated through. Just before serving, sprinkle with the sliced radishes. **Yield:** 4 servings.

Nutritional Analysis: One 1-cup serving (prepared with reduced-sodium soy sauce) equals 90 calories, 6 g fat (4 g saturated fat), 16 mg cholesterol, 118 mg sodium, 9 g carbohydrate, 4 g fiber, 2 g protein. **Diabetic Exchanges:** 2 vegetable, 1 fat.

Enjoy Seasonal Meals in Minutes... Year-Round!

The 12 time-saving menus on the following pages were created by the Taste of Home test kitchen staff with your busy schedule in mind. These meals will satisfy your family the whole year through.

DON'T YOU MISS those sincere compliments when you serve your family a frozen dinner instead of a home-cooked meal because you're short on time?

The 12 menus on the following pages (36 recipes in all) show you that complete meals can be homemade, delicious and fast any time of year.

Each and every recipe was created and kitchen-tested just for you by the staff of *Taste of Home*, so you can serve your family savory, well-rounded meals even on your busiest days. Each meal takes 30 minutes or less to prepare—and was planned with a specific season in mind.

Chase away the winter blahs with warm and wonderful Curry Crab Sandwiches, Speedy Vegetable Soup and Smooth Vanilla Shakes (recipes on pages 252 and 253).

Create heartfelt memories on Valentine's Day with a steak dinner for that special someone. Herbed Beef Tenderloin, Parmesan Bow Ties and Quick Chocolate Cream (recipes on pages 254 and 255) would tempt even Cupid.

Celebrate summer with grilled favorites such as Tangy Turkey Kabobs and Corn 'n' Pepper Packets, then cool off the clan with Peanut Butter Sundaes (recipes are on pages 266 and 267) for dessert.

With the 36 fabulous recipes on the following pages, the possibilities for fast, flavorful foods year-round are endless.

ALL 12 MONTHS are covered in this chapter with meals that include, clockwise from upper left: Springtime Favorites (p. 256), Southwest Selections (p. 264), Fabulous Fall Fare (p. 270) and Twists on the Traditional (p. 272).

Winter Warm-Up

CHASE AWAY the winter chills with this classic midday combination. Instead of offering ordinary lunchmeat and canned soup, serve the family hot Curry Crab Sandwiches and a bowl brimming with Speedy Vegetable Soup. For dessert, banana adds a tropical taste to Smooth Vanilla Shakes.

Curry Crab Sandwiches

Hearty sandwiches are always a speedy supper solution. This hot and tasty version dresses up plain crabmeat with a blend of seasonings and cheese.

1 package (8 ounces) imitation crabmeat, chopped
1/3 cup mayonnaise
1/4 cup finely chopped celery
1/4 cup finely chopped onion
1 tablespoon prepared mustard
1/4 teaspoon seasoned salt
1/4 teaspoon curry powder
1/8 teaspoon pepper
4 sandwich rolls, split
1 cup (4 ounces) shredded cheddar cheese
Butter *or* margarine, softened

In a bowl, combine the crabmeat, mayonnaise, celery, onion, mustard and seasonings. Spread 1/2 cup crab mixture on the bottom of each roll. Sprinkle with cheese. Spread butter on cut side of roll tops. Broil both halves of sandwiches 4 in. from the heat for 3-4 minutes or until cheese is melted and crab mixture is bubbly. **Yield:** 4 servings.

Speedy Vegetable Soup

Don't think you have time to make homemade soup on hurried, hectic days? You can with this simple recipe! Frozen mixed vegetables simmer in a seasoned canned broth for a mere 25 minutes, so you can ladle out hearty servings in no time.

1/4 cup chopped onion
1/4 cup chopped celery
1 tablespoon butter *or* margarine
1 can (14-1/2 ounces) vegetable broth
1 can (14-1/2 ounces) diced tomatoes, undrained
2 cups frozen mixed vegetables
1 tablespoon sugar
1/4 teaspoon ground marjoram
1/8 teaspoon pepper
Seasoned salad croutons

In a large saucepan, saute the onion and celery in butter until tender. Add the broth, tomatoes, veg-

etables and seasonings; bring to a boil. Reduce heat; simmer, uncovered, for 20-25 minutes or until vegetables are tender. Sprinkle with croutons. **Yield:** 4 servings.

Smooth Vanilla Shakes

Rich and creamy shakes are sure to round out a meal. They also make a great anytime snack. Pudding mix, yogurt and banana make this a deliciously different treat you'll enjoy around the clock.

- **2 cups cold milk**
- **1/3 cup instant vanilla pudding mix**
- **1 carton (8 ounces) vanilla yogurt**
- **1-1/2 cups vanilla ice cream**
- **1 small ripe banana**

Place all ingredients in a blender. Cover and process until smooth. Pour into chilled glasses. Serve immediately. **Yield:** 4 servings.

Special Steak Dinner

THERE'S a lot at stake when Valentine's Day rolls around! But you won't go wrong by offering loved ones savory Herbed Beef Tenderloin. Parmesan Bow Ties and your family's favorite fresh cooked vegetable are the perfect sides, while cool Quick Chocolate Cream really rounds out the rich meal.

Herbed Beef Tenderloin

When winter weather doesn't allow for grilling outdoors, simply bake your steaks instead! Bread crumbs and seasonings seal in the meat's juices with wonderful results.

2 tablespoons seasoned bread crumbs
1/2 teaspoon garlic salt
1/2 teaspoon each dried basil, oregano and thyme
1/4 teaspoon fennel seed, crushed
1/4 teaspoon pepper
4 beef tenderloin steaks (1 inch thick)

Combine bread crumbs and seasonings. Rub or sprinkle on both sides of steaks. Place steaks in an ungreased 13-in. x 9-in. x 2-in. baking pan. Bake, uncovered, at 425° for 25-28 minutes or until meat reaches desired doneness (for rare, a meat thermometer should read 140°; medium, 160°; well-done, 170°). **Yield:** 4 servings.

Parmesan Bow Ties

This fuss-free side dish calls for just four ingredients that you can easily keep in your pantry and refrigerator. Serve it on special occasions as well as for everyday dinners.

2 cups uncooked bow tie pasta
1/4 cup zesty Italian salad dressing
1/4 cup shredded Parmesan cheese
1 tablespoon minced fresh parsley

Cook noodles according to package directions; drain. Transfer to a serving bowl. Add the remaining ingredients; toss to coat. **Yield:** 4 servings.

Quick Chocolate Cream

Sometimes a creamy chocolate dessert is all you need to end a satisfying meal. This fantastic finale will surely disappear before your eyes, so you may want to double the recipe.

2/3 cup hot fudge sauce
1/2 cup sour cream
1/4 teaspoon almond extract, optional

1 cup whipping cream, whipped
Additional hot fudge sauce and sliced almonds, optional

In a bowl, combine fudge sauce, sour cream and extract if desired. Fold in the whipped cream. Spoon into dessert dishes. Drizzle with additional fudge sauce and sprinkle with almonds if desired. **Yield:** 4 servings.

Basic Green Beans

Green beans are a superb side dish for any meal. To cook green beans, place them in a saucepan; cover with water. Bring to a boil. Cook, uncovered, for 8 to 10 minutes or until crisp-tender. Drizzle with melted butter or margarine.

Springtime Favorites

WHEN SPRING arrives, the pace around your house likely picks up. So you can rely on Ranch Skillet Dinner, which cooks on the stovetop in no time. Add a simple Tossed Salad with Lime Vinaigrette and easy-to-make Cheery Cherry Pastries for a complete meal in minutes.

Ranch Skillet Dinner

With ground beef, packaged potatoes, cheese and frozen mixed vegetables, this skillet supper is a true meal in one. Just add a simple side salad for a dinner that's guaranteed to satisfy.

1 pound ground beef
1/2 cup chopped onion
2-1/3 cups hot water
2/3 cup milk
1 package (5.6 ounces) ranch potatoes*
2 cups frozen mixed vegetables, cut green beans *or* corn
1/4 cup shredded cheddar cheese

In a skillet, cook beef and onion over medium heat until meat is no longer pink; drain. Stir in water, milk and potatoes with contents of sauce mix. (Discard potato topping mix or save for another use.) Bring to a boil. Reduce heat; cover and simmer for 12 minutes, stirring occasionally. Add the vegetables; cover and cook for 4 minutes or until potatoes and vegetables are tender. Sprinkle with cheese. **Yield:** 4 servings.

***Editor's Note:** The butter listed on the potato package is not used in this recipe.

Tossed Salad with Lime Vinaigrette

A unique lime vinaigrette adds just the right amount of tang, making this tossed salad stand out from any others. Mix and match your favorite salad greens and veggies.

4 cups torn salad greens
1 small tomato, cut into wedges
1/2 cup sliced cucumber
1/4 cup vegetable oil
1/4 cup lime juice
2 teaspoons sugar
1 teaspoon grated onion
1/2 teaspoon grated lime peel
1/4 teaspoon salt

In a salad bowl, toss the greens, tomato and cucumber. In a jar with a tight-fitting lid, combine the oil, lime juice, sugar, onion, lime peel and salt; shake well. Pour over salad and toss to coat. **Yield:** 4 servings.

Cheery Cherry Pastries

Refrigerated crescent rolls are the secret to the fast success of these cherry pastries. They're perfect for breakfast, lunch, dinner and snacks.

1 tube (8 ounces) refrigerated crescent rolls
3/4 cup cherry pie filling
1/8 teaspoon almond extract
1 tablespoon milk
1 tablespoon sugar

Unroll crescent dough and separate into triangles; place on a greased baking sheet. Combine the pie filling and almond extract; place a rounded tablespoon in the center of bottom half of triangle. Fold the right point of the wide end of triangle over pie filling to left point; seal bottom seam. Bring top point over the pie filling to left point; seal left seam (filling will show). Brush with milk; sprinkle with sugar. Bake at 400° for 12-14 minutes or until golden brown. **Yield:** 8 pastries.

Tempting Trio

AS SOON AS the days start getting longer, reach for this sunny dinner! Broiling the Honey Garlic Chicken a bit lends to its light golden color. Citrus Rice Pilaf is the perfect accompaniment to any meal. And Pineapple Angel Dessert is a fresh alternative to chocolate sweets.

Honey Garlic Chicken

The mellow flavor of chicken pairs well with honey, orange juice and garlic. Broiling for a few minutes gives the chicken an attractive golden color.

4 boneless skinless chicken breast halves
2 tablespoons honey
2 tablespoons orange *or* lemon juice
1 tablespoon vegetable oil
1/2 teaspoon salt
Dash pepper
1 to 2 garlic cloves, minced

Place chicken in a greased 13-in. x 9-in. x 2-in. baking pan. Combine the remaining ingredients; pour over chicken. Bake, uncovered, at 400° for 15 minutes. Broil 4 to 6 in. from the heat for 5-7 minutes or until juices run clear, brushing occasionally with sauce. **Yield:** 4 servings.

Citrus Rice Pilaf

Food doesn't have to be made from scratch to have great homemade taste. Here, a packaged rice mix gets added flair and flavor from crunchy snow peas and water chestnuts.

1 package (6.9 ounces) chicken-flavored rice mix
2 tablespoons butter *or* margarine
2-3/4 cups water
1 package (6 ounces) frozen snow peas
1 can (8 ounces) sliced water chestnuts, drained
1 to 2 tablespoons orange marmalade
1/4 teaspoon pepper

In a large skillet, saute rice mix in butter until golden brown. Stir in water and contents of rice seasoning packet. Bring to a boil. Reduce heat; cover and simmer for 15 minutes. Stir in peas, water chestnuts, marmalade and pepper. Cover and cook for 3-4 minutes or until rice and vegetables are tender. **Yield:** 4 servings.

Pineapple Angel Dessert

Sprinkling slices of angel food cake with confectioners' sugar and broiling gives each bite a sweet and

crunchy texture. Be sure to watch closely so the sugar doesn't burn.

- **2 cans (8 ounces *each*) crushed pineapple, drained**
- **2 tablespoons sugar**
- **2 tablespoons whipping cream**
- **1/8 teaspoon ground cinnamon**
- **Dash ground ginger**
- **4 slices prepared angel food cake (1 inch thick)**
- **Confectioners' sugar**
- **Toasted coconut**

In a small saucepan, combine the pineapple, sugar, cream, cinnamon and ginger. Cook and stir over medium heat for 5 minutes. Meanwhile, place the cake on a baking sheet and sprinkle with confectioners' sugar. Broil 6 in. from the heat for 3-4 minutes or until golden brown. Serve sauce over the cake; sprinkle with coconut. **Yield:** 4 servings.

Country Breakfast

DON'T THINK you have time to prepare a hearty morning meal? Put away the cold cereal and think again! You'll soon be digging into hearty Dilly Asparagus Frittata and Sausage Potato Skillet. Honey Fruit Salad can be tossed together in mere minutes.

Dilly Asparagus Frittata

A frittata is an easy breakfast or brunch entree because there's no stirring like scrambled eggs require.

2 tablespoons butter *or* margarine
8 eggs
1 cup cooked chopped asparagus
1 cup (4 ounces) shredded cheddar cheese, *divided*
1/2 teaspoon dill weed
1/2 teaspoon salt
1/8 teaspoon pepper

In an 8-in. ovenproof skillet, melt butter. In a bowl, beat eggs. Stir in asparagus, 3/4 cup of cheese, dill, salt and pepper. Pour into skillet. Cook, without stirring, over medium-low heat for 8 minutes. Remove from the heat; sprinkle with remaining cheese. Bake at 425° for 6-8 minutes or until a knife inserted near the center comes out clean. Cut into wedges. **Yield:** 4 servings.

Sausage Potato Skillet

Sausage and potatoes are conveniently cooked in the same skillet, so you dirty only one pan.

1 package (8 ounces) brown-and-serve sausage links
2 tablespoons water
2 tablespoons vegetable oil
3 cups frozen shredded hash brown potatoes
1/2 cup chopped sweet red *or* green pepper
1/4 cup chopped onion
Salt and pepper to taste

Cut sausage links into bite-size pieces. In a covered skillet, cook sausage in water and oil over medium heat for 5 minutes. Remove sausage with a slotted spoon and keep warm. Carefully add potatoes, red pepper and onion to pan. Cover and cook for 5 minutes. Uncover; cook 5-6 minutes longer or until potatoes are tender. Return sausage to pan; heat through. **Yield:** 4 servings.

Honey Fruit Salad

A light honey and lime dressing brings out the won-

derful flavor of canned and fresh fruits. This is a colorful addition to any early-morning meal.

- **1 can (11 ounces) mandarin oranges, drained**
- **1 can (8 ounces) pineapple chunks, drained**
- **1 cup green grapes**
- **1 cup halved fresh strawberries**
- **1 medium firm banana, sliced**
- **3 tablespoons honey**
- **2 teaspoons lime juice**
- **1/4 teaspoon grated lime peel**
- **1/4 teaspoon vanilla extract**
- **1/4 teaspoon poppy seeds**

Fresh mint, optional

In a large bowl, combine fruit. In a small bowl, combine honey, lime juice, peel and vanilla. Pour over fruit; toss. Sprinkle with poppy seeds. Garnish with mint if desired. **Yield:** 4 servings.

Fun-in-the-Sun Supper

COOKING CAN really be a day at the beach, especially with these fast-to-fix recipes. With a touch of chili powder, Chili Chicken Strips and Zesty Corn and Beans spice up summer days. No-bake Butterscotch Oatmeal Bites keep your kitchen cool and are great for on-the-go snacking. A walk along the beach—or through a park—is a great after-dinner treat.

Chili Chicken Strips

Instead of ordinary bread crumbs, seasoned crushed corn chips coat these slightly crunchy chicken fingers. If your family likes food with some zip, use the full 1-1/2 teaspoons of chili powder.

3/4 cup crushed corn chips
2 tablespoons dry bread crumbs
1 tablespoon all-purpose flour
1 to 1-1/2 teaspoons chili powder
1/2 teaspoon seasoned salt
1/2 teaspoon poultry seasoning
1/4 teaspoon pepper
1/4 teaspoon paprika
1 egg
1-1/2 pounds boneless skinless chicken breasts, cut into 1/2-inch strips
4 tablespoons butter *or* margarine, *divided*

In a shallow bowl, combine the first eight ingredients. In another shallow bowl, beat egg. Dip chicken strips in egg, then coat with corn chip mixture. In a large skillet, cook half of the chicken in 2 tablespoons butter for 8-10 minutes or until the juices run clear. Repeat with remaining chicken and butter. **Yield:** 6 servings.

Zesty Corn and Beans

When you're in the mood for Mexican food, reach for this easy stovetop recipe. The tomato, corn and bean mixture can also be refrigerated and eaten as a relish without the rice.

1 can (14-1/2 ounces) Cajun *or* Mexican diced tomatoes, undrained
2 cups frozen corn
1 cup canned black beans, rinsed and drained
1/4 teaspoon dried oregano
1/4 teaspoon chili powder
Hot cooked rice

In a saucepan, combine the tomatoes, corn, beans, oregano and chili powder. Cook over medium heat for 6-8 minutes or until the corn is tender, stirring occasionally. Serve over hot cooked rice. **Yield:** 6 servings.

Butterscotch Oatmeal Bites

You can make these no-bake cookies at a moment's notice for a quick snack or dessert. Plus, they travel well, so you can tuck them into brown-bag lunches for a midday surprise.

2-1/2 cups miniature marshmallows
1 cup butterscotch chips
1/4 cup peanut butter
2 tablespoons butter (no substitutes)
3 cups Cheerios
1/2 cup raisins
1/2 cup flaked coconut

In a heavy saucepan, combine the marshmallows, chips, peanut butter and butter. Cook and stir over medium-low heat until chips and marshmallows are melted. Remove from the heat; stir in Cheerios, raisins and coconut. Drop by 1/4 cupfuls onto waxed paper. Let stand for 10 minutes. **Yield:** 14-16 cookies.

Southwest Selections

DON'T DESERT the kitchen just because the clock's ticking closer to dinner and there's nothing on the menu. Quick-to-fix Beef Quesadillas can be assembled in a snap, while Salsa Rice with Zucchini simmers to perfection in no time. The pretty layers in Summer Melon Parfaits are so appealing.

Beef Quesadillas

Quick-cooking ground beef is the perfect ingredient for on-the-run cooks. Try serving these quesadillas with your favorite taco toppings, such as sour cream, salsa, guacamole, chopped tomatoes, shredded lettuce and sliced olives.

3/4 pound ground beef
1/2 cup refried beans
1 can (4 ounces) chopped green chilies, drained
1/2 teaspoon dried oregano
1/2 teaspoon ground cumin
1/4 teaspoon salt
4 flour tortillas (8 inches)
2 tablespoons butter *or* margarine, melted
1-1/3 cups shredded taco cheese
Paprika

In a skillet, cook the beef over medium heat until no longer pink; drain. Stir in the beans, chilies, oregano, cumin and salt. Cook over medium-low heat for 3-4 minutes or until heated through. Brush one side of each tortilla with butter. Spoon 1/2 cup of the meat mixture over half of the unbuttered side. Sprinkle with 1/3 cup cheese; fold in half. Place on a lightly greased baking sheet. Sprinkle with paprika. Bake at 475° for 10 minutes or until crisp and golden brown. Cut into wedges. **Yield:** 4 servings.

Salsa Rice with Zucchini

You won't create a mess in the kitchen with this recipe. The rice and zucchini are combined in one pan. For added color, toss in some diced yellow squash.

1 cup water
1 tablespoon butter *or* margarine
1 teaspoon beef bouillon granules
1/4 teaspoon ground cumin
1/8 teaspoon salt
1 cup uncooked instant rice
1 medium zucchini, diced
1/4 cup salsa

In a saucepan, bring water, butter, bouillon, cumin and salt to a boil. Remove from the heat; stir in rice,

zucchini and salsa. Cover and let stand for 5-7 minutes or until water is absorbed. **Yield:** 4 servings.

Summer Melon Parfaits

This cool dessert will surely refresh you and your family in the heat of summer. Even kids who don't care for fruit will gobble up this treat.

- **1/4 cup lemonade concentrate**
- **1/4 cup lemon, orange *or* raspberry yogurt**
- **1 carton (8 ounces) frozen whipped topping, thawed**
- **1 cup *each* cubed honeydew and cantaloupe**

In a bowl, combine lemonade concentrate and yogurt; fold in whipped topping. Divide honeydew between four dessert glasses; top with half of the lemon mixture, cantaloupe and remaining lemon mixture. **Yield:** 4 servings.

Great from The Grill

FIRE UP the grill for a sizzling supper! Featuring turkey slices, potatoes and apples, Tangy Turkey Kabobs are a nice change from beef kabobs. Corn 'n' Pepper Packets are grilled in foil packets for quick and easy cleanup. For a refreshing finale, Peanut Butter Sundaes are tops.

Tangy Turkey Kabobs

Unlike traditional kabobs, these call for turkey breast slices, potatoes and apple chunks. The flavorful honey mustard salad dressing shines through in each delicious bite.

1/2 cup honey mustard salad dressing
2 teaspoons dried rosemary, crushed
12 small red potatoes, cut in half
1 pound turkey breast slices, cut into 1-inch strips
2 unpeeled green apples, cut into 1-inch pieces

In a small bowl, combine salad dressing and rosemary; set aside. Place potatoes in a saucepan and cover with water; bring to a boil. Cook for 5 minutes; drain. Fold turkey strips in thirds; thread onto metal or soaked wooden skewers alternately with potatoes and apples. Spoon half of the dressing over kabobs. Grill, uncovered, over medium-hot heat for 6-8 minutes. Turn; brush with remaining dressing. Continue grilling until meat juices run clear. **Yield:** 4 servings.

Corn 'n' Pepper Packets

Grilling foods in foil packets means little mess and cleanup. Plus, the steam cooks the vegetables to perfection. Try experimenting with different seasonings.

4 ears of corn, cut into 2-inch chunks
1 medium green pepper, cut into 2-inch strips
1 medium sweet red pepper, cut into 2-inch strips
2 tablespoons minced fresh parsley
3/4 teaspoon garlic salt
1/4 teaspoon celery seed

1/4 teaspoon pepper
1/4 cup butter *or* margarine, melted

In a bowl, combine vegetables, parsley and seasonings. Place on a piece of heavy-duty foil (about 18 in. x 12 in.). Drizzle with butter. Fold foil around vegetables and seal tightly. Grill, covered, over medium-hot heat for 10-12 minutes. Open foil carefully to allow steam to escape. **Yield:** 4 servings.

Peanut Butter Sundaes

Add a little pizzazz to plain vanilla ice cream with this easy-to-prepare peanut butter sauce. You can even make it ahead and refrigerate it when you know time will be extra tight.

1/2 cup whipping cream
1/2 cup peanut butter chips
2 tablespoons peanut butter
Vanilla ice cream

In a heavy saucepan, combine cream, peanut butter chips and peanut butter. Cook and stir over medium heat for 4-5 minutes or until chips are melted and mixture is smooth. Cool for at least 10 minutes. Serve over ice cream. Refrigerate any leftover sauce. **Yield:** about 3/4 cup sauce.

Paired Up For Flavor

WITH THE combination of fruit and meat, Apple-Mustard Pork Chops taste like fall. Buttery Peas and Carrots may be simple, but the natural sweetness of the vegetables is unbeatable. For a twist on the traditional, make Raspberry Pear Shortcake.

Apple-Mustard Pork Chops

Pairing pork and apples has always meant a surefire recipe. The wonderful aroma of this delightful dish signals the arrival of fall.

4 bone-in pork chops (3/4 inch thick)
1/4 teaspoon salt
1/8 teaspoon pepper
2 tablespoons butter *or* margarine
1/3 cup apple juice
1 tablespoon dried minced onion
1 tablespoon Dijon mustard
Hot cooked rice, optional
Apple slices, optional

Sprinkle pork chops with salt and pepper. In a large skillet, brown pork chops in butter over medium-high heat. Stir in the apple juice; reduce heat to medium. Cover and cook for 10-12 minutes or until meat juices run clear, turning once. Remove to a serving platter and keep warm. Add onion and mustard to skillet. Cook, uncovered, on low for 4-5 minutes. Spoon over chops. Serve with rice and garnish with apples if desired. **Yield:** 4 servings.

Buttery Peas and Carrots

This simple side dish is one you'll rely on often to serve with a variety of main courses.

2-1/2 cups baby carrots, halved lengthwise
2 tablespoons butter *or* margarine
1-1/2 cups frozen peas
2 tablespoons water
1 teaspoon sugar
Salt and pepper to taste

In a skillet, saute carrots in butter for 5 minutes. Stir in the remaining ingredients. Cover and simmer for 10-12 minutes or until the vegetables are tender. **Yield:** 4 servings.

Raspberry Pear Shortcake

This dessert is a nice change of pace from traditional strawberry shortcake. Because the recipe calls for

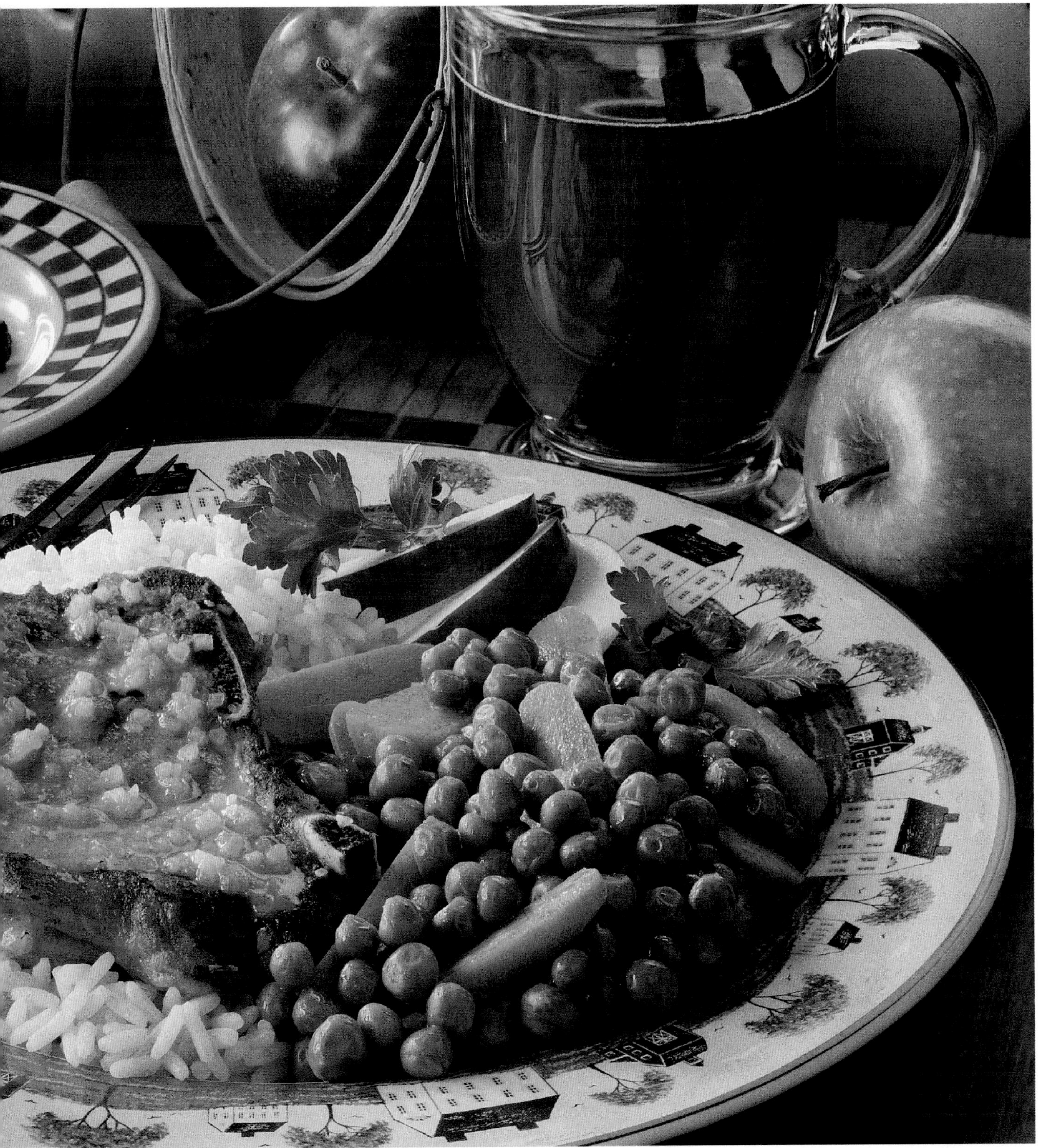

canned pears and either fresh or frozen raspberries, you can make it year-round.

2 cups fresh *or* frozen raspberries, thawed
1 tablespoon sugar
1/4 teaspoon ground cinnamon
1 can (15-1/4 ounces) pear halves, drained
4 individual round sponge cakes
Whipped topping

Place the raspberries in a bowl. In another bowl, combine sugar and cinnamon; sprinkle over raspberries and mash lightly. Let stand for 10 minutes. Place a pear half on each sponge cake. Top with the raspberries and a dollop of whipped topping. **Yield:** 4 servings.

Fabulous Fall Fare

INSTEAD OF picking up fast food, turn over a new leaf and serve your family a homemade meal. It's easy with a tried-and-true recipe like Spicy Flank Steak. As a contrast to the spicy beef, toss together some crunchy Broccoli Coleslaw and slightly sweet Mini Caramel Cheesecakes.

Spicy Flank Steak

The cool and creamy sour cream sauce is a wonderful accompaniment to the slightly spicy steak. If you prefer, you can grill the steak over medium-hot heat rather than broiling.

1/3 cup sour cream
2 tablespoons mayonnaise
1/2 teaspoon garlic powder
1/4 teaspoon celery salt
2 tablespoons chili sauce
1 tablespoon lime juice
1/2 to 1 teaspoon crushed red pepper flakes
1/4 teaspoon salt
1 flank steak (1 to 1-1/2 pounds)

In a bowl, combine the sour cream, mayonnaise, garlic powder and celery salt; refrigerate until serving. Combine the chili sauce, lime juice, pepper flakes and salt; brush half on one side of steak.

Broil 6 in. from the heat for 10 minutes. Turn steak; brush with remaining mixture. Broil 6-10 minutes longer or until meat reaches desired doneness (for rare, a meat thermometer should read 140°; medium, 160°; well-done, 170°). Let stand for 5 minutes. Slice into thin strips across the grain. Serve with the sour cream sauce. **Yield:** 6 servings.

Broccoli Coleslaw

Folks will be pleasantly surprised when they taste this unique coleslaw made with broccoli instead of cabbage. The light vinegar dressing isn't overpowering.

6 cups broccoli coleslaw mix*
1/2 cup chopped green onions
1/3 cup vegetable oil
1/4 cup cider *or* white wine vinegar
2 tablespoons sugar
1 teaspoon seasoned salt
1/2 teaspoon dill weed
1/4 teaspoon celery seed
1/4 teaspoon pepper

In a large bowl, combine coleslaw mix and onions. In a small bowl, combine the remaining ingredients. Pour over coleslaw mix and stir to coat. **Yield:** 6 servings.

***Editor's Note:** Broccoli coleslaw mix may be found in the produce section of most grocery stores.

Mini Caramel Cheesecakes

Using individual graham cracker shells makes it easy to prepare these treats. They taste just like cheesecake without all the hassle.

1 package (8 ounces) cream cheese, softened
2 tablespoons apple juice concentrate
2 tablespoons sugar
1/4 cup caramel ice cream topping
1/2 cup whipped topping
1 package (6 count) individual graham cracker tart shells
Additional caramel ice cream topping, optional
Chopped almonds *or* honey roasted almonds, optional

In a mixing bowl, beat the cream cheese, apple juice concentrate, sugar and ice cream topping until smooth. Fold in whipped topping. Spoon into tart shells. Drizzle with additional ice cream topping and sprinkle with almonds if desired. Refrigerate until serving. **Yield:** 6 servings.

Twists on the Traditional

NEED a break from turkey during the Thanksgiving holiday? Stuffed Ham Rolls feature a savory filling without fuss. A light cream sauce dresses up servings of Pasta with Brussels Sprouts. And Cranberry Peach Crisp combines canned fruit for a fast, filling dessert.

Stuffed Ham Rolls

These savory ham rolls are filled with stuffing and cheese, rolled in a tasty crumb coating and then cooked in a skillet.

- **2 cups seasoned stuffing croutons**
- **1/2 cup boiling water**
- **2 teaspoons plus 2 tablespoons butter *or* margarine, *divided***
- **8 fully cooked ham slices (1/8 inch thick)**
- **8 slices Swiss cheese**
- **1 egg, beaten**
- **1 tablespoon water**
- **1/2 cup dry bread crumbs**

In a bowl, combine stuffing, boiling water and 2 teaspoons butter. Cover and let stand for 5 minutes. Top each ham slice with a cheese slice. Place 1/4 cup stuffing off-center over cheese. Roll up and secure with a toothpick. Combine egg and water. Roll ham rolls in the egg mixture, then in bread crumbs. In a large skillet, saute ham rolls in remaining butter for 4-5 minutes or until golden brown, turning once. Discard toothpicks. **Yield:** 4 servings.

Pasta with Brussels Sprouts

Even family members who don't care for brussels sprouts won't be able to resist them tossed with pasta in a light cream sauce.

- **6 cups water**
- **1/2 teaspoon salt**
- **1 package (10 ounces) frozen brussels sprouts**
- **1 cup uncooked spiral pasta**
- **1/4 cup butter *or* margarine, melted**
- **2 tablespoons whipping cream**
- **2 tablespoons grated onion**
- **1/2 teaspoon salt**
- **1/4 teaspoon ground nutmeg**
- **1/4 teaspoon pepper**

In a large saucepan, bring water and salt to a boil. Add brussels sprouts and pasta. Return to a boil. Reduce heat; simmer, uncovered, for 6-8 minutes or until sprouts and pasta are tender. Drain. Combine the remaining ingredients; pour over pasta mixture and toss to coat. **Yield:** 4 servings.

Cranberry Peach Crisp

This clever recipe simply combines canned peaches and cranberry sauce with a cookie crumb topping for a sweet and crunchy treat.

1 can (15-1/4 ounces) sliced peaches, drained
1 can (16 ounces) whole-berry cranberry sauce
1/2 cup packed brown sugar
1/2 cup all-purpose flour
1/2 cup crumbled oatmeal *or* sugar cookies
1/4 cup chopped walnuts
1/4 cup butter *or* margarine, melted

Arrange peaches in a greased shallow 2-qt. baking dish. Stir cranberry sauce and pour over peaches. Combine brown sugar, flour, cookie crumbs and nuts; sprinkle over fruit. Drizzle with butter. Bake, uncovered, at 400° for 18-20 minutes or until bubbly. **Yield:** 4-6 servings.

Seasonal Specialties

CELEBRATE CHRISTMAS any day of the week with this no-fuss festive dinner. Orange Pork Tenderloin conveniently bakes in the oven, and Savory Broccoli Spears quickly cook on the stovetop. Then dish out generous helpings of Holiday Cappuccino Trifle.

Orange Pork Tenderloin

Dining with flair can be fuss-free when pork tenderloin is featured. Guests will be impressed with tender pork slices and a succulent orange sauce.

1 pork tenderloin (about 1-1/4 pounds), cut into slices
1 tablespoon butter *or* margarine, softened
1/4 teaspoon dried thyme
Dash cayenne pepper
1 cup orange juice, *divided*
1 tablespoon all-purpose flour
1-1/2 teaspoons sugar

Place pork slices in an ungreased 13-in. x 9-in. x 2-in. baking dish. Combine butter, thyme and cayenne. Spread over pork. Pour 3/4 cup orange juice over meat. Bake, uncovered, at 425° for 25-30 minutes or until a meat thermometer reads 160°-170°, basting occasionally.

Transfer pork to a serving platter and keep warm. Pour pan drippings into a measuring cup; add enough remaining orange juice to measure 3/4 cup. Pour into a saucepan. Stir in flour and sugar until smooth. Bring to a boil over medium heat; cook and stir for 2 minutes or until thickened. Serve with pork. **Yield:** 3-4 servings.

Savory Broccoli Spears

Cooking broccoli in broth and soy sauce gives spark to an otherwise ordinary vegetable. The toasted almonds add a pleasant crunch.

2 tablespoons slivered *or* sliced almonds
2 tablespoons butter *or* margarine
1 pound fresh broccoli, cut into spears
1/3 cup chicken broth *or* water
2 teaspoons soy sauce
1/8 teaspoon pepper

In a skillet, saute almonds in butter until golden brown. Remove; set aside. Add remaining ingredients to skillet. Cover; cook over medium heat for 8-10 minutes or until broccoli is crisp-tender. Sprinkle with almonds. **Yield:** 4-6 servings.

Holiday Cappuccino Trifle

This easy yet elegant dessert is so attractive served in

a shallow glass bowl. Garnishing with raspberries, mint and grated chocolate adds the perfect finishing touch. It looks and tastes great.

- **1 can (14 ounces) sweetened condensed milk**
- **3/4 cold water**
- **1 package (3.9 ounces) instant chocolate pudding mix**
- **1 to 2 tablespoons instant coffee granules**
- **2 cups whipped topping**
- **2 packages (3 ounces *each*) ladyfingers**
- **Raspberries, fresh mint and grated chocolate, optional**

In a mixing bowl, beat the milk, water, pudding mix and coffee granules on medium speed for 2 minutes. Fold in whipped topping. Tear ladyfingers into cubes; place half in a 2-qt. glass bowl. Top with half of the pudding mixture. Repeat layers. Garnish with raspberries, mint and chocolate if desired. Store in the refrigerator. **Yield:** 6-8 servings.

Meals on a Budget

These six meals show you how to feed your family well without spending a fortune on groceries.

FRUGAL FARE. Clockwise from upper left: Enchilada Casserole, Skillet Green Beans and Frozen Chocolate Cream Pie (p. 280); Hot Beef Cheddar Subs, Zucchini 'n' Carrot Coins and Fluffy Lemon Dessert (p. 284); Pork Noodle Casserole, Beans with Cherry Tomatoes and Pretzel Dessert (p. 286); Creamy Baked Chicken, Broccoli with Almonds and Chocolate Oatmeal Cake (p. 282).

Feed Your Family for $1.41 a Plate!

EVEN DURING the holidays, when you're trying to squeeze every dime out of your budget, you can put together a flavor-packed brunch to delight friends and family! The frugal menu here is from four terrific cooks, who estimate the total cost at just $1.41 per setting.

Chive-Ham Brunch Bake is a hearty dish that looks as great as it tastes. Edie DeSpain of Logan, Utah shares her recipe, which has a pleasing and colorful mix of tomatoes, onions and cheese.

Scrumptious Eggnog Muffins, suggested by Susan Brown from Northglenn, Colorado, are chock-full of pecans and raisins.

A simple yet special spread for breakfast breads and muffins is Honey Cinnamon Butter. The recipe comes from Sue Seymour of Valatie, New York.

Citrus Fruit Smoothies, from Rose Press of Topeka, Kansas, are truly refreshing. "They combine our favorite juices and fruits in one fabulous drink," she says.

Chive-Ham Brunch Bake

1/2 cup chopped onion
1 tablespoon butter
1 can (5 ounces) chunk ham, drained
1 medium tomato, chopped
2 cups biscuit/baking mix
1/2 cup water
1 cup (4 ounces) shredded Swiss *or* cheddar cheese
2 eggs
1/4 cup milk
1/4 teaspoon dill weed
1/4 teaspoon salt
1/8 teaspoon pepper
3 tablespoons minced chives

In a skillet, saute onion in butter until tender. Stir in ham and tomato; set aside. In a bowl, combine biscuit mix and water; mix well. Press onto the bottom and 1/2 in. up the sides of a greased 13-in. x 9-in. x 2-in. baking dish. Spread ham mixture over crust; sprinkle with cheese.

In a bowl, beat the eggs, milk, dill, salt and pepper; pour over cheese. Sprinkle with chives. Bake, uncovered, at 350° for 25-30 minutes or until a knife inserted near the center comes out clean. **Yield:** 8 servings.

Eggnog Muffins

3 cups all-purpose flour
1/2 cup sugar
3 teaspoons baking powder
1/2 teaspoon salt
1/2 teaspoon ground nutmeg
1 egg
1-3/4 cups eggnog*
1/2 cup vegetable oil
1/2 cup golden raisins
1/2 cup chopped pecans

In a large bowl, combine the first five ingredients. In another bowl, combine the egg, eggnog and oil; stir into dry ingredients just until moistened. Fold in raisins and pecans. Fill greased or paper-lined muffin cups two-thirds full. Bake at 350° for 20-25 minutes or until a toothpick comes out clean. Cool for 5 minutes before removing from pans to a wire rack. **Yield:** 16 muffins.

***Editor's Note:** This recipe was tested with commercially prepared eggnog.

Honey Cinnamon Butter

1 cup butter
1/2 cup honey
1 teaspoon ground cinnamon

Combine all ingredients in a small mixing bowl; beat until smooth. Serve with muffins, toast, bagels, French toast or pancakes. Refrigerate any leftovers. **Yield:** 1-1/3 cups.

Citrus Fruit Smoothies

5 cups grapefruit juice
3 cups orange juice
1 cup water
4 medium firm bananas, cut up and frozen
12 frozen unsweetened whole strawberries

In a blender, place half of each ingredient; cover and process until smooth. Pour into a pitcher. Repeat. Serve immediately. **Yield:** 8 servings.

Feed Your Family for $1.43 a Plate!

IT'S POSSIBLE to save on your grocery bill without scrimping on flavor when feeding your family.

The recipes here are suggested by three budget-minded cooks and combined into a delicious meal you can serve for $1.43 per person.

Enchilada Casserole is a hearty, satisfying entree. Marcia Schmiedt of Anchorage, Alaska shares the zesty recipe.

Skillet Green Beans is a staple side dish in the Columbus, Michigan home of Linda Sugars.

June Brown of Veneta, Oregon recommends rich and smooth Frozen Chocolate Cream Pie.

Enchilada Casserole

1 pound ground turkey
1-1/2 cups chopped onions
2 garlic cloves, minced
1 tablespoon plus 1/3 cup vegetable oil, *divided*
1/3 cup all-purpose flour
2 tablespoons chili powder
3/4 teaspoon seasoned salt
1/8 teaspoon pepper
4 cups water
12 corn tortillas (7 inches)
1-1/2 cups (6 ounces) shredded cheddar cheese
1-1/2 cups salsa

In a skillet over medium heat, cook the turkey, onions and garlic in 1 tablespoon oil until no longer pink; drain. Sprinkle with flour, chili powder, seasoned salt and pepper. Add water and bring to a boil. Reduce heat; cover and cook for 8-10 minutes.

In another skillet, fry tortillas in remaining oil for about 15 seconds, turning once. Drain well. Cut nine tortillas in half. Place cut edge of one tortilla against each short side of a greased 11-in. x 7-in. x 2-in. baking dish. Place cut edge of two tortillas against long sides of dish, overlapping to fit. Place a whole tortilla in center.

Spoon 2 cups of meat mixture over tortillas; sprinkle with 1/2 cup cheese. Repeat layers. Top with remaining tortillas and sauce. Bake, uncovered, at 375° for 20 minutes. Sprinkle with remaining cheese. Bake 5-10 minutes longer or until cheese melts. Serve with salsa. **Yield:** 8 servings.

Skillet Green Beans

1 medium onion, diced
1/4 cup stick margarine
2 packages (16 ounces *each*) frozen cut green beans, thawed
1/4 teaspoon salt
1/4 teaspoon pepper
1/2 cup sour cream
Paprika, optional

In a skillet, saute onion in margarine until tender. Add beans, salt and pepper. Cook until heated through. Serve with sour cream; sprinkle with paprika if desired. **Yield:** 8 servings.

Frozen Chocolate Cream Pie

1-1/2 cups graham cracker crumbs
5 tablespoons sugar, *divided*
1/3 cup stick margarine, melted
1/2 cup plus 4 teaspoons semisweet chocolate chips, *divided*
5 tablespoons milk, *divided*
1 package (3 ounces) cream cheese, softened
3-1/2 cups whipped topping, *divided*

In a bowl, combine cracker crumbs and 3 tablespoons sugar. Stir in margarine. Press onto the bottom and up the sides of an ungreased 9-in. pie plate. Refrigerate for 30 minutes. In a microwave-safe bowl, combine 1/2 cup chocolate chips and 2 tablespoons milk. Microwave, uncovered, on high for 1-2 minutes or until melted. Stir to blend; set aside.

In another bowl, beat cream cheese and remaining sugar. Stir in chocolate mixture and remaining milk; beat until smooth. Set aside 1/2 cup whipped topping. Fold remaining whipped topping into chocolate mixture. Spoon into crust. Freeze 4 hours or until firm. Garnish with the remaining whipped topping and chocolate chips. **Yield:** 8 servings.

Feed Your Family for $1.61 a Plate!

EVEN when your grocery budget is tight, you can still enjoy foods with full flavor and leave the table satisfied.

Three frugal cooks prove it with this company-quality meal. They estimate the cost at $1.61 per setting.

"Creamy Baked Chicken is comforting and easy to prepare," says Barbara Clarke of Punta Gorda, Florida.

Broccoli with Almonds is a tasty, dressed-up side dish from Verna Puntigan of Pasadena, Maryland.

Deborah Sheehan of East Orland, Maine says Chocolate Oatmeal Cake is a treat. "It's so moist, plus it's topped with scrumptious coffee frosting."

Creamy Baked Chicken

1 broiler/fryer chicken (3 pounds), cut up
1 can (10-3/4 ounces) condensed cream of chicken soup, undiluted
1 can (10-3/4 ounces) condensed cream of mushroom soup, undiluted
1 cup (8 ounces) sour cream
1/2 cup water
1 teaspoon snipped chives
Salt and pepper to taste
1/2 teaspoon paprika

Place chicken in a greased 13-in. x 9-in. x 2-in. baking dish. In a bowl, combine the soups, sour cream, water, chives, salt and pepper; spoon over chicken. Sprinkle with paprika. Bake, uncovered, at 350° for 1 hour or until chicken juices run clear. **Yield:** 6 servings.

Broccoli with Almonds

1-1/2 pounds fresh broccoli, cut into spears
1 cup water
1 teaspoon chicken bouillon granules
1/4 cup sliced almonds
3 tablespoons stick margarine
1/2 cup finely chopped onion
1 teaspoon salt

In a large saucepan, bring the broccoli, water and bouillon to a boil. Reduce heat; cover and simmer for 5-8 minutes or until broccoli is crisp-tender. Drain and place in a serving dish; keep warm. In a skillet, saute the almonds in margarine until browned. Add the onion and salt; saute until onion is tender. Pour over broccoli; toss to coat. **Yield:** 6 servings.

Chocolate Oatmeal Cake

1-1/2 cups boiling water
1 cup quick-cooking oats

1 cup (6 ounces) semisweet chocolate chips
1/2 cup stick margarine, softened
3/4 cup sugar
3/4 cup packed brown sugar
2 eggs
1-1/2 cups all-purpose flour
1 teaspoon baking soda
1 teaspoon salt

COFFEE FROSTING:

2 teaspoons instant coffee granules
1/4 cup half-and-half cream, warmed
1/2 cup stick margarine, softened
1 teaspoon vanilla extract
1/8 teaspoon salt
4 cups confectioners' sugar

In a bowl, combine the water and oats. Sprinkle with chocolate chips (do not stir); let stand for 20 minutes. In a mixing bowl, cream margarine and sugars. Add eggs, one at a time, beating well after each addition. Beat in oat mixture. Combine flour, baking soda and salt; add to the creamed mixture and mix well. Pour into a greased 13-in. x 9-in. x 2-in. baking pan. Bake at 350° for 35-40 minutes or until a toothpick inserted near the center comes out clean. Cool on a wire rack.

For frosting, dissolve coffee granules in cream; set aside. In a small mixing bowl, cream margarine; add vanilla and salt. Slowly beat in sugar. Beat in enough of coffee mixture to achieve spreading consistency. Frost the cake. **Yield:** 12 servings.

Feed Your Family for $1.62 a Plate!

IF YOU'RE LOOKING for a great supper or lunch that doesn't require loads of preparation time or lots of money, try this menu.

Our test kitchen staff combined dishes from three budget-conscious cooks to create this super spread. They estimate the total cost at just $1.62 per setting.

Hot Beef Cheddar Subs are like cheesy sloppy joes tucked into hollowed-out crusty rolls.

"My family devours these yummy sandwiches," says Marann Reilly of Lithia Springs, Georgia.

Donna Cline of Pensacola, Florida brightens her table with a big bowl full of fresh veggies.

"We especially enjoy Zucchini 'n' Carrot Coins in summer, when garden-picked vegetables are plentiful and delicious," she says.

Fluffy Lemon Dessert is a fabulous finale from Linda Nilsen of Anoka, Minnesota.

"Each May, I bring this refreshing, melt-in-your-mouth treat to our last church circle meeting of the year," she says. "It's economical and so well-received that I'm not sure they'd let me in without it!"

Hot Beef Cheddar Subs

4 submarine sandwich buns
1 pound ground beef
1 medium green pepper, diced
1 small onion, diced
1 can (10-3/4 ounces) condensed cheddar cheese soup, undiluted
1/4 teaspoon Worcestershire sauce
4 slices American cheese

Cut a thin slice off top of each bun; set tops aside. Carefully hollow out bottoms, leaving a 1/2-in. shell. Set aside 1/2 cup bread. In a skillet, cook beef, pepper and onion over medium heat until meat is no longer pink; drain. Stir in soup, Worcestershire sauce and reserved bread; mix well. Spoon into buns; top each with a cheese slice. Replace tops. Place on an ungreased baking sheet. Bake, uncovered, at 350° for 5-7 minutes or until cheese is melted. **Yield:** 4 servings.

Zucchini 'n' Carrot Coins

1 pound carrots, thinly sliced
2 tablespoons butter *or* margarine
1 small onion, sliced and separated into rings
2 small zucchini, cut into 1/4-inch slices
2 teaspoons dried basil
1/2 teaspoon salt
1/4 teaspoon pepper

In a large skillet, saute sliced carrots in butter for 4-5 minutes. Add the onion; cook for 1 minute. Stir in the remaining ingredients. Cover and cook 4-5

minutes or until the vegetables are crisp-tender. **Yield:** 4 servings.

Fluffy Lemon Dessert

1 can (12 ounces) evaporated milk
1 package (3 ounces) lemon gelatin
1 cup sugar
1-3/4 cups boiling water
1/4 cup lemon juice
3/4 cup whipped topping
1 medium lemon, sliced
10 mint sprigs

Pour milk into a small mixing bowl; place the mixer beaters in the bowl. Cover and refrigerate for at least 2 hours or until chilled. Meanwhile, in a large mixing bowl, dissolve gelatin and sugar in water. Stir in lemon juice. Cover and refrigerate until syrupy, about 1-1/2 hours.

Beat the gelatin until tiny bubbles form. Beat chilled milk until soft peaks form; fold into gelatin. Pour into serving dishes. Refrigerate for at least 3 hours or overnight. Garnish with the whipped topping, lemon and mint. Refrigerate leftovers. **Yield:** 10 servings.

Feed Your Family for $1.69 a Plate!

HEARTY and filling, casseroles are a good choice when you're trying to keep your grocery bills in check and still provide your family with a pleasing, tasty dinner.

The complete meal here is inexpensive yet delicious. The three good cooks who recommend these delightful dishes estimate the total cost at a mere $1.69 per setting.

Pork Noodle Casserole is a savory entree suggested by Bernice Morris of Marshfield, Missouri.

"One of the less expensive cuts of pork becomes tender and tasty in this creamy meal-in-one casserole," Bernice notes.

In Buckley, Washington, Betty Brown's family enjoys Beans with Cherry Tomatoes. "We love this dressed-up version of garden green beans," Betty says. "This skillet dish goes great with any meat."

Delicious Pretzel Dessert saves both time and money. "The recipe makes a big batch of this sweet and salty, creamy and crunchy treat," says Rita Winterberger of Huson, Montana. "That's fine with us because any dessert that's left over is super the next day, too."

Pork Noodle Casserole

2 cups uncooked egg noodles
2 pounds boneless pork, cut into 3/4-inch cubes
2 medium onions, chopped
2 cans (15-1/4 ounces *each*) whole kernel corn, drained
2 cans (10-3/4 ounces *each*) condensed cream of mushroom soup, undiluted
1/2 teaspoon salt
1/2 teaspoon pepper

Cook noodles according to package directions. In a large skillet, cook pork and onions over medium heat until meat is no longer pink. Drain noodles. Stir noodles, corn, soup, salt and pepper into pork mixture. Transfer to a greased 3-qt. baking dish. Cover and bake at 350° for 30 minutes. Uncover; bake 15 minutes longer. **Yield:** 8 servings.

Beans with Cherry Tomatoes

4 bacon strips, diced
1-1/2 pounds fresh green beans, cut into 2-inch pieces
4 garlic cloves, thinly sliced
1-1/2 cups halved cherry tomatoes
1/2 teaspoon salt
1/4 cup slivered almonds, toasted

In a large skillet, cook bacon over medium heat until crisp. Remove to paper towels to drain. In the drippings, saute beans for 12-14 minutes or until crisp-tender. Add garlic; cook 2-3 minutes longer.

Stir in tomatoes and salt; heat through. Sprinkle with bacon and almonds. **Yield:** 8 servings.

Pretzel Dessert

2 cups crushed pretzels
3/4 cup sugar
3/4 cup stick margarine, melted
2 envelopes whipped topping mix
1 cup cold milk
1 teaspoon vanilla extract
1 package (8 ounces) cream cheese, cubed
1 cup confectioners' sugar
1 can (21 ounces) cherry pie filling

In a bowl, combine pretzels, sugar and margarine; set aside 1/2 cup for topping. Press remaining mixture into an ungreased 13-in. x 9-in. x 2-in. dish. In a mixing bowl, beat whipped topping mix, milk and vanilla on high speed for 4 minutes or until soft peaks form. Add cream cheese and confectioners' sugar; beat until smooth. Spread half over crust. Top with the pie filling and remaining cream cheese mixture. Sprinkle with reserved pretzel mixture. Refrigerate overnight. **Yield:** 16 servings.

Feed Your Family for 99¢ a Plate!

YOU CAN be frugal and still prepare a satisfying, full-flavored fall meal for your family. Three budget-conscious cooks prove it with these recipes. They estimate the cost for this meal at 99¢ a serving.

Hearty and wonderfully seasoned Bean Counter Chowder is suggested by Vivian Haen of Menomonee Falls, Wisconsin.

Soft Onion Breadsticks make a yummy, inexpensive addition to any meal. The recipe is from Maryellen Hays of Wolcottville, Indiana.

There's always room for dessert—and there's sure to be room in your budget, too—for Strawberry Sandwich Cookies. "They're crisp and fruity and very pretty," shares Barbara Sessoyeff of Redwood Valley, California. "Folks always ask for the recipe."

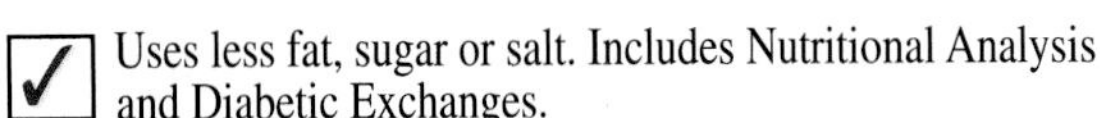

Bean Counter Chowder

✓ Uses less fat, sugar or salt. Includes Nutritional Analysis and Diabetic Exchanges.

1/2 cup chopped onion
2 garlic cloves, minced
1 tablespoon vegetable oil
1 medium tomato, chopped
2 cans (14-1/2 ounces *each*) chicken broth
1-3/4 cups water
1/2 teaspoon *each* dried basil, oregano and celery flakes
1/4 teaspoon pepper
3 cans (15-1/4 ounces *each*) great northern *or* pinto beans, rinsed and drained
1 cup uncooked elbow macaroni
1 tablespoon minced fresh parsley

In a large saucepan, saute onion and garlic in oil until tender. Add tomato; simmer for 5 minutes. Add the broth, water and seasonings. Bring to a boil; cook for 5 minutes. Add beans and macaroni; return to a boil. Reduce heat; simmer, uncovered, for 15 minutes or until macaroni is tender. Sprinkle with parsley. **Yield:** 8 servings (2 quarts).

Nutritional Analysis: One serving (1 cup) equals 285 calories, 3 g fat (1 g saturated fat), 0 cholesterol, 447 mg sodium, 48 g carbohydrate, 9 g fiber, 17 g protein. **Diabetic Exchanges:** 3 starch, 1 meat.

Soft Onion Breadsticks

3/4 cup chopped onion
1 tablespoon vegetable oil
1 package (1/4 ounce) active dry yeast
1/2 cup warm water (110° to 115°)
1/2 cup warm milk (110° to 115°)
2 eggs
1/4 cup butter *or* stick margarine, softened
1 tablespoon sugar
1-1/2 teaspoons salt
3-1/2 to 4 cups all-purpose flour
2 tablespoons cold water
2 tablespoons sesame seeds
1 tablespoon poppy seeds

In a skillet, saute onion in oil until tender; cool. In a mixing bowl, dissolve yeast in warm water. Add milk, 1 egg, butter, sugar, salt and 1 cup flour.

Beat on medium speed for 2 minutes. Stir in the onion and enough remaining flour to form a soft dough. Turn onto a floured surface; knead until smooth and elastic, about 6-8 minutes. Place in a greased bowl, turning once to grease top. Cover and let rise until doubled, about 1 hour.

Punch dough down. Let stand for 10 minutes. Turn onto a lightly floured surface; divide into 32 pieces. Shape each piece into an 8-in. rope. Place 2 in. apart on greased baking sheets. Cover and let rise in a warm place for 15 minutes.

Beat cold water and remaining egg; brush over breadsticks. Sprinkle half with sesame seeds and half with poppy seeds. Bake at 350° for 16-22 minutes or until golden brown. Remove to wire racks. **Yield:** 32 breadsticks.

Strawberry Sandwich Cookies

- **1 cup blanched almonds**
- **3/4 cup stick margarine, softened**
- **1 cup confectioners' sugar, *divided***
- **1 egg**
- **1/2 teaspoon almond extract**
- **1-1/2 cups all-purpose flour**
- **1/8 teaspoon salt**
- **1 tablespoon lemon juice**
- **3 tablespoons strawberry preserves**

In a food processor or blender, process almonds until ground; set aside. In a mixing bowl, cream margarine and 1/2 cup sugar. Beat in egg and extract. Combine flour and salt; gradually add to creamed mixture. Stir in the ground almonds. Divide dough in half; cover and refrigerate for 2 hours or until easy to handle.

On a lightly floured surface, roll out each portion of dough into a 12-in. x 9-in. rectangle. Cut lengthwise into three strips; cut each strip widthwise into six pieces. With a 3/4-in. round cutter, cut out a circle in the center of half of the pieces (discard circles). Place 1 in. apart on ungreased baking sheets. Bake at 375° for 8-10 minutes or until golden brown. Remove to wire racks to cool.

For glaze, combine lemon juice and remaining sugar; thinly spread over whole cookies. Top with cutout cookies; fill center with 1/2 teaspoon preserves. **Yield:** 1-1/2 dozen.

SWEET CORN

Getting in the Theme of Things

Everything you need to plan a memorable event is here: theme-related menus, fabulous recipes and fun decorating ideas.

CELEBRATE GOOD TIMES. Clockwise from upper left: Hungry Pirates Find Tasty Treasures (p. 300), Oranges Color Her Company Menu (p. 294), Cowboy Fare Delights "Pardners" (p. 292) and She Plots a Fresh Garden Party (p. 296).

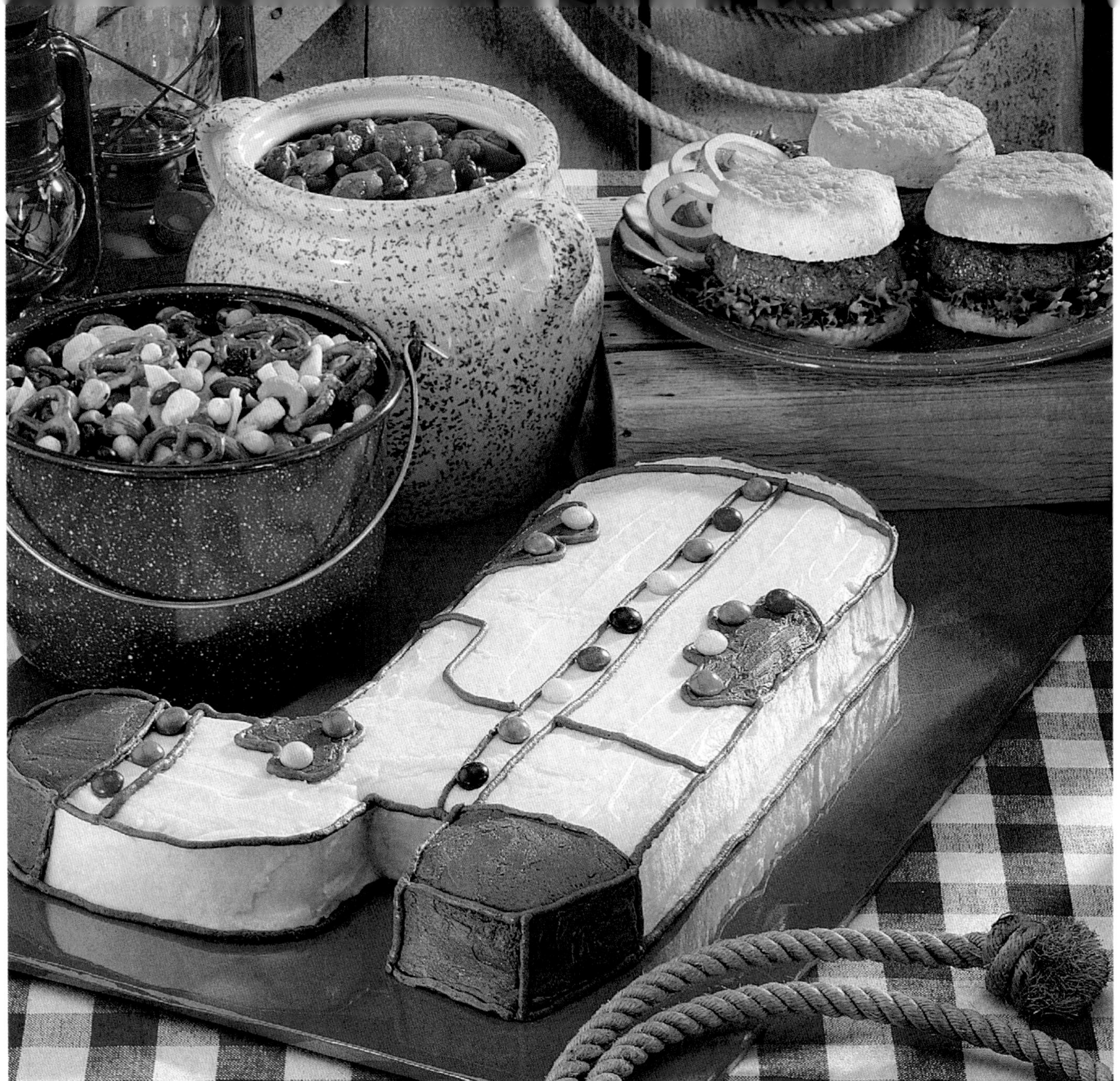

Cowboy Fare Delights 'Pardners'

By Sharon Thompson, Oskaloosa, Iowa

WHEN my son, Isaiah, picked a cowboy theme for his 8th birthday party, my planning took off at a gallop. He wanted a Cowboy Boot Cake, so that was the start of our menu. We created a Western-style meal by adding Chuck Wagon Burgers, Bunkhouse Beans and Happy Trails Snack Mix.

I baked a cake mix in a 9-in. x 13-in. pan and froze the cake overnight before cutting it into pieces to form a boot shape (see diagram on the next page). We iced the boot with white, then I colored some reserved frosting. Using Isaiah's real cowboy boots as a model, I piped on stitches. He added candy accents.

The Chuck Wagon Burgers, which I served on biscuits, looked like they'd been cooked outdoors over an open fire. Bunkhouse Beans are full of spunk and really fit the theme. And the kids absolutely loved Happy Trails Snack Mix, with its contrasting colors.

We transformed our kitchen peninsula into a chuck wagon buffet with cardboard wagon wheels and a wagon roof made from a white sheet. Additional decorations—a nail keg, lanterns, cowboy hats, spurs, ropes and a harmonica—helped set the scene.

Guests in cowboy attire gathered for "grub", piling it high on tin pie plates while listening to *Home on the Range* and other cowboy songs. It was almost like those rustic long-gone days on the prairie!

Chuck Wagon Burgers

In the spirit of true chuck wagon fare, I served burgers on large biscuits rather than traditional buns.

2 pounds ground beef
1 envelope onion soup mix
1/2 cup water
1 tube (16.3 ounces) large refrigerated biscuits
1/8 teaspoon seasoned salt

In a bowl, combine beef, soup mix and water; mix well. Shape into eight 3/4-in.-thick patties. Grill, uncovered, or broil 4 in. from the heat for 5-6 minutes per side or until meat is no longer pink. Meanwhile, place biscuits on an ungreased baking sheet; sprinkle with seasoned salt. Bake at 375° for 12-14 minutes or until golden. Split; top each biscuit with a hamburger. **Yield:** 8 servings.

Happy Trails Snack Mix

Both salty and sweet, this mix has an appealing assortment of pretzels, cereal, dried fruits and candies.

3 cups miniature pretzels
2 cups mixed nuts
1 cup Kix cereal
1 cup chopped dried apple
1 cup raisins
3/4 cup chopped dried pineapple
1 package (2.17 ounces) Skittles bite-size candies
1 package (1.69 ounces) milk chocolate M&M's

Combine all ingredients in a large bowl. Store in an airtight container. **Yield:** 2 quarts.

Bunkhouse Beans

With sliced hot dogs and several types of beans in the mixture, this hearty dish could be a meal in itself.

1 cup salsa
2/3 cup barbecue sauce
2/3 cup packed brown sugar
5 hot dogs, halved lengthwise and sliced
3 tablespoons dried minced onion
2 cans (16 ounces *each*) pork and beans, drained
1 can (15-1/2 ounces) chili beans, undrained
1 can (15 ounces) butter *or* lima beans, rinsed and drained

In a bowl, combine the first five ingredients; mix well. Stir in the beans; pour into an ungreased 2-qt. baking dish. Bake, uncovered, at 375° for 35-40 minutes or until bubbly. **Yield:** 6-8 servings.

Cowboy Boot Cake

This fun boot cake is easily shaped from pieces of a 9-inch x 13-inch cake (see diagram below).

1 package (18-1/4 ounces) cake mix of choice
1 package (8 ounces) cream cheese, softened
2 tablespoons butter *or* margarine, softened
1 tablespoon milk
1 teaspoon vanilla extract
5 cups confectioners' sugar
Food coloring of your choice
Skittles bite-size candies

Line a 13-in. x 9-in. x 2-in. baking pan with waxed paper; grease paper. Prepare and bake cake according to package directions, using prepared pan. Cool 10 minutes; remove from pan to wire rack to cool completely. Wrap and freeze overnight.

Cover a 20-in. x 15-in. board with gift wrap or foil. Level cake top. To make boot, beginning from a short side, cut a 2-in.-wide strip. Cut strip into two pieces, one 5-1/2 in. x 2 in. and one 2-1/2 in. x 2 in. Cut a 10-in. x 2-1/2-in. strip from the large rectangle. To assemble base of boot, center the 10-in. x 2-1/2-in. piece widthwise on board 5 in. from bottom. Place remaining large rectangle on the right side, forming a backward L. Place the 2-1/2-in. x 2-in. piece under the long strip, forming the heel; place remaining strip on the other side, forming the sole. Using a serrated knife, round corners of boot toe, sole, heel and top.

For frosting, in a mixing bowl, beat cream cheese, butter, milk and vanilla until smooth. Gradually beat in sugar. Set aside 1 cup. Spread remaining frosting over top and sides of cake. Tint reserved frosting desired color. Cut a small hole in the corner of a pastry or plastic bag; insert round tip. Fill bag with tinted frosting. Outline boot shape along bottom and top edges of cake. Fill in heel and toe on cake top, smoothing with a metal icing spatula. With remaining frosting and Skittles, decorate boot as desired. **Yield:** 16-20 servings.

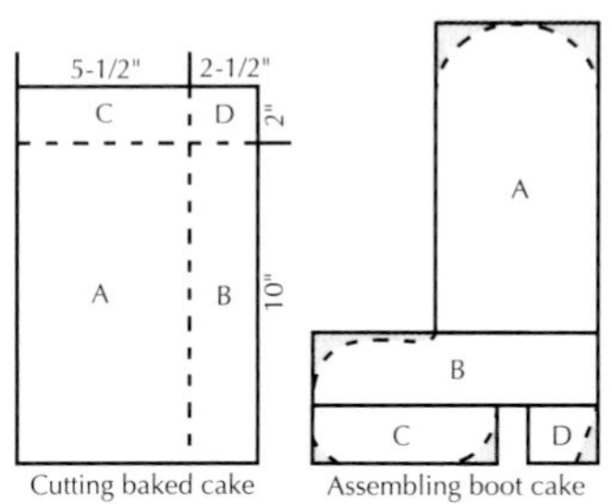

Cutting baked cake
Assembling boot cake

Oranges Color Her Company Menu

By Susan West, North Grafton, Massachusetts

"WHAT an outstanding Orange Day!" my guests exclaimed when I set out my tangy theme buffet. Our colorful gathering was inspired by a visit from my husband Jim's orange-loving grandmother.

Living in Michigan and wintering in Florida, she doesn't get out here to Massachusetts often. When she and Jim's parents *did* visit us, I welcomed them with dishes I concocted using her favorite fruit—from drinks to dessert.

A sweet-tart blend, Citrus Grove Punch teams orange, grapefruit and lime juices. Sparkling bubbles from the ginger ale give each sip a festive tingle.

The entree, Mandarin Chicken, was gobbled up quickly. Sweet orange sections and mushrooms dress up this savory chicken and rice dish.

Everyone loved my Sunny Layered Salad. It features an unusual combination of ingredients in a light, sweet dressing. Another of my creations, Orange Chip Cheesecake, was a hit with its elegant blend of citrus and chocolate. It's quick to make, too.

I gave the table a bright, sunny look with a fruit-print cloth and a homemade centerpiece—a basket filled with oranges and fresh flowers. We all had fun. One other good thing about this orange-theme meal—it won't put a squeeze on your time!

Mandarin Chicken

Even the main dish fit the theme, with mandarin oranges and orange juice in this chicken and rice bake.

✓ Uses less fat, sugar or salt. Includes Nutritional Analysis and Diabetic Exchanges.

1-1/2 cups uncooked long grain rice
4 boneless skinless chicken breast halves (1 pound)
1/2 cup sliced fresh mushrooms
2 cups orange juice
1 cup chicken broth
1/2 teaspoon salt
Pepper to taste
1 can (15 ounces) mandarin oranges, drained
Paprika and minced fresh parsley, optional

Spread rice in a greased shallow 3-qt. baking dish. Top with chicken and mushrooms. Pour orange juice and broth over all. Sprinkle with salt and pepper. Cover and bake at 350° for 45-50 minutes or until chicken juices run clear and rice is tender. Garnish with oranges, paprika and parsley if desired. **Yield:** 4 servings.

Nutritional Analysis: One serving equals 519 calories, 4 g fat (1 g saturated fat), 65 mg cholesterol, 734 mg sodium, 86 g carbohydrate, 1 g fiber, 31 g protein. **Diabetic Exchanges:** 4 starch, 3 very lean meat, 1-1/2 fruit.

Sunny Layered Salad

I topped the colorful layers of this appealing salad with mandarin oranges. Presented in a clear glass bowl, it looks so beautiful on a buffet.

1/4 cup sliced almonds
2 tablespoons sugar
6 cups shredded lettuce
1 can (8 ounces) sliced water chestnuts, drained
1 cup frozen peas, thawed and well drained
1/2 medium cucumber, sliced
2 medium tomatoes, cut into thin wedges
2 cups (8 ounces) shredded mozzarella cheese
1 can (15 ounces) mandarin oranges, drained

DRESSING:
1/4 cup vegetable oil
2 tablespoons sugar
2 tablespoons cider vinegar
1/4 teaspoon salt
1/4 teaspoon pepper

In a skillet, cook and stir almonds and sugar over low heat until sugar is dissolved and almonds are coated. Spread almonds on waxed paper and set aside. In a large glass salad bowl, layer the lettuce, water chestnuts, peas, cucumber, tomatoes, cheese and oranges. Sprinkle with the sugared almonds. Cover and refrigerate for at least 2 hours. In a jar with a tight-fitting lid, combine dressing ingredients; shake well. Pour over salad and serve immediately. **Yield:** 10-12 servings.

Orange Chip Cheesecake

I love to adapt and mix recipes, which led to the creation of this creamy treat years ago. The distinctive citrus flavor is complemented by chocolate!

12 ounces cream cheese, softened
1/2 cup sugar
2 eggs
1/2 teaspoon salt
1/2 teaspoon orange extract
3/4 to 1 cup miniature semisweet chocolate chips
1 chocolate crumb *or* graham cracker crust (9 inches)

TOPPING:
1-1/2 cups (12 ounces) sour cream
2 tablespoons sugar
1/2 teaspoon vanilla extract
1 can (11 ounces) mandarin oranges, drained
Additional chocolate chips

In a mixing bowl, beat cream cheese and sugar until smooth. Add eggs; beat on low speed just until combined. Add salt and orange extract; beat just until blended. Stir in chocolate chips. Pour into crust. Bake at 375° for 20 minutes or until center is almost set. Remove from the oven; increase temperature to 425°.

In a bowl, combine sour cream, sugar and vanilla; spread over cheesecake. Bake 5 minutes longer. Cool on a wire rack for 15 minutes. Refrigerate overnight. Just before serving, garnish with oranges and additional chocolate chips. **Yield:** 8 servings.

Citrus Grove Punch

This pretty, sparkling punch brings in other members of the "citrus family" to blend with orange juice.

3 cups sugar
2 cups water
6 cups orange juice, chilled
6 cups grapefruit juice, chilled
1-1/2 cups lime juice, chilled
1 liter ginger ale, chilled

In a saucepan, bring sugar and water to a boil; cook for 5 minutes. Cover and refrigerate until cool. Combine juices and sugar mixture; mix well. Just before serving, stir in ginger ale. Serve over ice. **Yield:** 6 quarts.

She Plots a Fresh Garden Party

By Sara Laker, Loda, Illinois

WHEN MY TURN came up to host a group of longtime friends for lunch, I planned a Garden Party with food and decorations to highlight a fresh outdoor theme.

My down-to-earth menu included Chilled Strawberry Soup, Creamy Cashew Chicken Salad, Olive-Cucumber Finger Sandwiches and Marinated Garden Tomatoes, along with a slice of pound cake topped with raspberries and whipped cream.

I asked my guests to don gardening hats, and I wore a denim jumper embroidered with flowers, bees and butterflies. Instead of using a cloth, I cut artificial grass carpet to fit the tabletop. The bright green "lawn" got their attention right away and was a great background for my floral dinnerware and garden-inspired decorations.

You don't need a green thumb to copy my centerpiece. I set an ivy plant on my great-grandmother's cake stand and surrounded it with floral moss and tiny flowerpots.

I passed around Olive-Cucumber Finger Sandwiches as appetizers when everyone arrived. They feature crisp cucumber slices with a seasoned cream cheese spread.

Then we sat down to Chilled Strawberry Soup, a smooth treat with a hint of cinnamon. My guests raved!

Creamy Cashew Chicken Salad, served with croissants, has a great-tasting homemade green-goddess dressing. The hearty chicken salad gets its triple crunch from celery, green pepper and cashews.

With it, I served Marinated Garden Tomatoes. They're the ultimate in fresh flavor! Cracked pepper makes the herb-seasoned marinade slightly spicy.

I'd be delighted if I've planted a seed in your mind for a garden-inspired gathering. Using my recipes and ideas, you can let it sprout from there!

Olive-Cucumber Finger Sandwiches

The crisp cucumbers on these easy-to-fix sandwiches get their zip from being marinated for a short time.

1 medium cucumber
1 cup water
1/2 cup cider vinegar
1 package (8 ounces) cream cheese, softened
1/4 cup mayonnaise
1/4 teaspoon garlic powder
1/4 teaspoon onion salt
1/8 teaspoon Worcestershire sauce
36 thin slices bread
Paprika
36 stuffed olives

With a fork, score cucumber lengthwise; cut into thin slices. Place in a bowl; add water and vinegar. Let stand for 30 minutes. Meanwhile, in a small mixing bowl, beat cream cheese, mayonnaise, garlic powder, onion salt and Worcestershire sauce. Cut bread into flower shapes with a 2-1/2-in. cookie cutter. Spread each with cream cheese mixture; sprinkle with paprika and top with a cucumber slice. Remove pimientos from olives; place in center of cucumber. Cut olives into five wedges and arrange around pimiento in a pinwheel pattern. **Yield:** 3 dozen.

Creamy Cashew Chicken Salad

Served on garden greens or a croissant, this all-time favorite salad is loaded with chicken and cashews.

4 cups cubed cooked chicken
1 cup chopped celery
1/2 cup chopped green pepper
1 jar (2 ounces) diced pimientos, drained
1/2 cup mayonnaise
1/3 cup whipping cream
1/4 cup sour cream
3 tablespoons thinly sliced green onions
2 tablespoons minced fresh parsley
1-1/2 teaspoons lemon juice
1-1/2 teaspoons tarragon vinegar *or* cider vinegar
1 garlic clove, minced
1/2 teaspoon salt
1/8 teaspoon pepper
3/4 cup salted cashews
Leaf lettuce and additional cashews, optional

In a large bowl, combine the first four ingredients; set aside. In a blender, combine the next 10 ingredients; cover and process until well blended. Pour over chicken mixture; toss to coat. Cover and refrigerate until serving. Fold in cashews. Serve in a lettuce-lined bowl. Garnish with additional cashews if desired. **Yield:** 6 servings.

Chilled Strawberry Soup

(Not pictured)

Guests loved the flavor of this beautiful fruit soup, calling it elegant, surprising and a real treat!

1 cup apple juice
1 cup water, *divided*
2/3 cup sugar
1/2 teaspoon ground cinnamon
1/8 teaspoon ground cloves
2 cups fresh strawberries
2 cartons (8 ounces *each*) strawberry yogurt
2 drops red food coloring, optional
Additional strawberry halves, optional

In a saucepan, combine apple juice, 3/4 cup water, sugar, cinnamon and cloves; bring to a boil over medium heat. Remove from heat; cool. Place strawberries and remaining water in a blender or food processor; cover and process until smooth. Pour into large bowl. Add apple juice mixture, yogurt and food coloring if desired. Cover; refrigerate until well chilled. Garnish with additional strawberries if desired. **Yield:** 6-8 servings.

Marinated Garden Tomatoes

Tomatoes always come to mind when I think of ripe garden goodness. You can make this a day ahead.

✓ Uses less fat, sugar or salt. Includes Nutritional Analysis and Diabetic Exchanges.

6 large tomatoes, cut into wedges
1/2 cup thinly sliced green onions
1/3 cup olive *or* canola oil
1/4 cup red wine vinegar *or* cider vinegar
1/4 cup minced fresh parsley
2 garlic cloves, minced
1 teaspoon salt
1 tablespoon snipped fresh thyme *or* 1 teaspoon dried thyme
1/4 teaspoon coarsely ground pepper

Place tomatoes and onions in a shallow serving bowl. In a bowl, combine the remaining ingredients; pour over tomatoes. Cover; refrigerate at least 2 hours or overnight. **Yield:** 10 servings.

Nutritional Analysis: One serving (3/4 cup) equals 91 calories, 8 g fat (1 g saturated fat), 0 cholesterol, 244 mg sodium, 6 g carbohydrate, 1 g fiber, 1 g protein. **Diabetic Exchanges:** 1-1/2 fat, 1 vegetable.

Sunflowers Smile on Summer Supper

By Holly Joyce, Jackson, Minnesota

DURING summer vacation from high school, I'm pretty much in charge of the kitchen at our house. My mom's a nurse, Dad's a science teacher, and I have a sister and brother.

One day I was trying to think of a fun meal for my family. The bright sunshine outside made me think of summer gardens and a sunflower theme.

I knew that my dad's garden would provide some of the ingredients for Garden-Fresh Taco Salad. I served it in a big flowerpot with corn chips arranged as petals along the edges. I also served refried beans, Fruit Salad Sunburst, Sunny Citrus Cooler and Sunflower Ice Cream Pie.

Fruit Salad Sunburst shows what can happen when you take time to arrange fruits rather than just tossing them together. Everyone liked refreshing Sunny Citrus Cooler because it has just the right amount of sweetness.

A favorite family dessert got dressed up for the occasion, becoming Sunflower Ice Cream Pie. I decorated the top of the pie to make a bright blossom. It brought smiles to everyone at the table!

My mom helped me find a sunflower print fabric to make napkins for our special dinner. Place cards—with the letters of each person's name on sunflower petals—were set in small terra-cotta saucers filled with sunflower seeds that we could snack on.

I had fun creating this summer theme meal. My family liked it—and I hope you will, too.

Garden-Fresh Taco Salad

I'd made this taco salad before but had never served it "potted" with the chips arranged to look like a flower head! I remembered we had a large flowerpot we used to make a "dirt cake" awhile back. It worked out great.

1 pound ground beef
1 envelope taco seasoning, *divided*
1 large head lettuce, shredded
4 medium tomatoes, seeded and diced
1 medium onion, chopped
2 cups (8 ounces) shredded cheddar cheese
1 cup mayonnaise *or* salad dressing
1 tablespoon salsa
Leaf lettuce
Crushed tortilla chips

In a skillet, cook the beef over medium heat until no longer pink; drain. Stir in half of the taco seasoning. Remove from the heat; stir in shredded lettuce, tomatoes, onion and cheese. In a small bowl, combine the mayonnaise, salsa and remaining taco seasoning. Pour over salad and toss to coat. Line a large bowl or platter with leaf lettuce; top with taco salad. Sprinkle tortilla chips around edge. **Yield:** 4 servings.

Fruit Salad Sunburst

A plate of colorful fruits took on a fresh look for my sunflower theme. This "floral" arrangement has a light pineapple dressing that I like a lot. Even my younger brother said it was "pretty good"! Coming from him, I consider it high praise.

1 tablespoon cornstarch
3/4 cup pineapple juice
2 to 3 kiwifruit
1 pint blueberries
3 medium firm bananas, halved widthwise and lengthwise
1 medium navel orange, sliced and quartered
3 large strawberries, quartered

In a saucepan, combine cornstarch and pineapple juice until smooth. Bring to a boil; cook and stir for 1 minute or until thickened. Cool. Cut the end off one kiwi; place cut side down in the center of a large round platter. Place blueberries evenly around kiwi. Cut remaining kiwi into 1/8-in. slices; place around edge of plate.

Place the bananas in a spoke pattern over the blueberries. Arrange the oranges over bananas and around center kiwi, overlapping slightly. Place the strawberries between the bananas. Drizzle with pineapple dressing. **Yield:** 4-6 servings.

Sunny Citrus Cooler

The sunny color of this refreshing punch matched the bright yellow sunflower decorations for my theme dinner. It's easy to stir up, too, which is good news because a few sips may quench your thirst, but your taste buds are sure to be asking for more.

1 can (46 ounces) pineapple juice
2 cans (12 ounces *each*) frozen orange juice concentrate, thawed
3/4 cup lemonade concentrate
6 cups ginger ale *or* white soda, chilled
Orange slices, optional

In a 1-gal. pitcher, combine pineapple juice, orange juice concentrate and lemonade concentrate. Add ginger ale and mix well. Serve over ice. Garnish with orange slices if desired. Refrigerate leftovers. **Yield:** 1 gallon.

Sunflower Ice Cream Pie

To create this special dessert, I combined all my favorite ice cream toppings—Oreo cookies, chocolate chips, caramel and nuts. The sunflower theme inspired the caramel "petals" on top. This pie's become a new standby at our house. It can be made ahead and stored in the freezer, so it's really convenient.

1-1/2 cups crushed cream-filled chocolate sandwich cookies (about 15), *divided*
3 tablespoons plus 1/2 cup caramel ice cream topping, *divided*
2 tablespoons semisweet chocolate chips, melted
2-1/2 to 3 cups vanilla ice cream, softened
1 tablespoon chopped walnuts
Black decorating gel

Set aside 2 tablespoons crushed cookies for garnish. Combine the remaining crushed cookies, 3 tablespoons caramel topping and the melted chocolate chips; press onto the bottom and up the sides of a greased 9-in. pie plate. Spread ice cream over crust. Freeze.

For sunflower, place reserved cookies in a 2-in. circle in center of pie. Top with walnuts. For the petals, drizzle or spread remaining caramel topping over ice cream. Outline petals with decorating gel. Freeze. Remove from the freezer 10 minutes before cutting. **Yield:** 6-8 servings.

Hungry Pirates Find Tasty Treasures

By Sharon Hanson, Franklin, Tennessee

AFTER our family's dream vacation to Hawaii, we celebrated our son Jordon's 8th birthday with a South Seas flair. I planned a swashbuckling pirate party.

Young buccaneers could opt for mini hot dog boats, dolphin crackers and fruit kabobs. To prevent a mutiny by the older ruffians, "Captain Cook" prepared a buffet with Tropical Island Chicken, Colorful Veggie Coins, cocktail shrimp, a watermelon basket and bread sticks.

We set the mood with pirate map invitations, and when guests arrived, their first stop was at "Captain Hook's Dressing Room", where a trunk overflowed with pirate hats, eye patches, bandannas and sashes (cut from colorful remnants), flowered leis and grass skirts. Once costumed, the children were handed potato sack nets and balloon pirate "swords" along with a pirate's map of hidden treasures in our backyard.

Our guests went wild over Tropical Island Chicken. It grills to a deep golden color and smells terrific while cooking. Slices of carrots, yellow squash and zucchini were right on the money in Colorful Veggie Coins.

My mom's favorite Christmas cookie recipe got an island makeover to become South Seas Sugar Cookies, shaped as palm trees and pineapples. I stacked two 9-in. x 13-in. cakes to make a Treasure Chest Birthday Cake.

Tropical Island Chicken

The marinade makes a savory statement in this chicken recipe. It smelled so good on the grill that guests could hardly wait to try a piece!

- **1/2 cup soy sauce**
- **1/3 cup vegetable oil**
- **1/4 cup water**
- **2 tablespoons dried minced onion**
- **2 tablespoons sesame seeds**
- **1 tablespoon sugar**
- **4 garlic cloves, minced**
- **1 teaspoon ground ginger**
- **3/4 teaspoon salt**
- **1/8 teaspoon cayenne pepper**
- **2 broiler/fryer chickens (3 to 4 pounds *each*), quartered**

In a large resealable plastic bag, combine the first 10 ingredients. Remove 1/3 cup for basting; cover and refrigerate. Add chicken; seal and turn to coat. Refrigerate 8 hours or overnight. Drain; discard marinade. Grill chicken, covered, over medium-hot heat for 45-60 minutes or until juices run clear and a meat thermometer reads 170°, turning and basting often with reserved marinade. **Yield:** 8 servings.

Colorful Veggie Coins

Once you try this medley, you'll serve it time and again.

3 medium carrots, thinly sliced
2 medium yellow summer squash, sliced
2 medium zucchini, sliced
1 small head cauliflower, broken into florets
2 garlic cloves, minced
4 tablespoons butter *or* margarine, *divided*
1 cup chicken broth
1 teaspoon salt
1/2 teaspoon white pepper

Place vegetables in shallow 3-qt. baking dish. In a saucepan, saute garlic in 2 tablespoons butter for 2-3 minutes. Stir in broth, salt and pepper. Pour over vegetables; dot with remaining butter. Cover; bake at 350° for 50 minutes or until vegetables are tender. **Yield:** 12-15 servings.

South Seas Sugar Cookies

Pineapple and palm tree cookie cutters shaped these.

1/3 cup butter-flavored shortening
1/3 cup sugar
2/3 cup honey
1 egg
1 teaspoon lemon extract
2-3/4 cups all-purpose flour
1 teaspoon salt
1 teaspoon baking soda
FROSTING:
1/2 cup butter *or* margarine, softened
1/4 cup butter-flavored shortening
1/2 teaspoon almond *or* lemon extract
1/8 teaspoon salt
3-3/4 cups confectioners' sugar
3 to 4 tablespoons milk
Yellow-gold, brown and green paste food coloring
Yellow and orange colored sugar
Chocolate chips

In a mixing bowl, cream shortening and sugar. Beat in honey, egg and extract. Combine flour, salt and baking soda; gradually add to creamed mixture. Cover; refrigerate 4 hours or until easy to handle. On a lightly floured surface, roll out dough to 1/4-in. thickness; cut with pineapple and palm tree cookie cutters dipped in flour. Place 1 in. apart on greased baking sheets. Bake at 375° for 7-8 minutes or until set. Remove to racks to cool.

For frosting, in a bowl, combine butter, shortening, extract, salt, confectioners' sugar and enough milk to achieve spreading consistency. Tint 1 cup frosting yellow-gold, 1/2 cup brown and 2-1/2 cups green. Frost pineapples yellow-gold and tree trunks brown. With a toothpick, draw lines on pineapples; sprinkle with colored sugar.

Cut a hole in the corner of a pastry or plastic bag; insert #21 star tip. Fill with green frosting; pipe leaves on pineapples and palm trees. Add chocolate chips to trees for coconuts. **Yield:** 2 dozen.

Treasure Chest Birthday Cake

Some guests thought the cake was too cute to cut!

2 packages (18-1/4 ounces *each*) chocolate cake mix
1-1/3 cups butter *or* margarine, softened
8 squares (1 ounce *each*) unsweetened chocolate, melted and cooled
6 teaspoons vanilla extract
7-1/2 to 8 cups confectioners' sugar
1/3 to 1/2 cup milk
5 wooden skewers (three 4 inches, two 7-1/2 inches)
Foil-covered heavy corrugated cardboard (12 inches x 7-1/2 inches)
Candy necklaces, coins *or* candies of your choice
2 pieces berry tie-dye Fruit Roll-Ups

In two batches, prepare and bake cakes according to package directions, using two greased and floured 13-in. x 9-in. x 2-in. baking pans. Cool for 10 minutes; remove from pans to cool on wire racks.

In a large mixing bowl, cream butter; beat in chocolate, vanilla, confectioners' sugar and enough milk to achieve spreading consistency. Center one cake on a 16-in. x 12-in. covered board; frost top. Top with remaining cake; frost top and sides of cake. With a metal spatula, smooth frosting to resemble boards.

For chest lid, insert 4-in. skewers equally spaced 6 in. into one long side of corrugated cardboard lid. Frost top of lid. Cut a small hole in the corner of a pastry or plastic bag; insert star tip #21. Pipe a shell border on edges of lid and for handles on sides of chest.

Place one 7-1/2-in. skewer on each side of cake top, about 3-1/2 in. from back of chest. Position lid over cake; gently insert short skewers into cake about 1 in. from back of chest. Rest lid on long skewers.

Arrange candy in chest. Cut a small keyhole from a fruit roll-up; center on front of cake. Position strips of fruit roll-ups in front and back of chest. **Yield:** 14-16 servings.

Pigskin Party Delights Football Fans

By Sister Judith LaBrozzi, Canton, Ohio

OUR TOWN is home to the Football Hall of Fame and hosts an annual festival to celebrate the game and its finest players. Among the area's enthusiastic fans are many seniors who live at the House of Loreto, a nursing home where I'm head of food service.

Constantly coming up with ways to create "spirit" among our residents and to celebrate at our meals, I quarterbacked a Kickoff Supper to coincide with the festival opening. This theme could be used to cheer on your favorite team at any level—from elementary, high school and college squads to the pros.

For Pigskin Sandwiches, we baked buns in the shape of footballs, then piped on a "seam" and "laces" of softened cream cheese. The sandwiches were stacked with ham, cheese, lettuce and tomato.

Goal-Line Chicken Salad also scored compliments. Chunks of apple and green grapes add nice color. We heard lots of cheers for Pom-Pom Potato Salad. Mashed yolks of hard-cooked eggs add richness to the creamy dressing. The chopped whites are added to the salad.

There was no need to punt when it came to dessert. Buttery Touchdown Cookies rated high scores. Our busy bakers rolled and cut them out with a football-shaped cookie cutter, then frosted them with a chocolate glaze with white icing "seam" and "laces".

Comments like, "I've seen lots of footballs, but this is the first time I've ever *eaten* one—and it was so good!" confirmed that this menu was a winner.

Pigskin Sandwiches

Guests won't need coaching to run for the sandwiches when they're served on football buns.

1 package (1/4 ounce) active dry yeast
1/2 cup sugar, *divided*
2 cups warm water (110° to 115°), *divided*
1/2 cup plus 2 tablespoons butter *or* margarine, softened, *divided*
1-1/2 teaspoons salt

1 egg, beaten
6-1/2 to 7 cups all-purpose flour
Mayonnaise *or* prepared mustard, optional
Lettuce leaves
Sliced tomatoes
18 slices process American cheese
2-1/2 pounds sliced deli ham
4 ounces cream cheese, softened

In a mixing bowl, dissolve yeast and 2 teaspoons sugar in 1/4 cup warm water. Let stand for 5 minutes. Add 1/2 cup butter, salt, egg, and remaining sugar and water. Beat in 4 cups flour until smooth. Stir in enough remaining flour to form a soft dough. Turn onto a floured surface; knead until smooth and elastic, about 6-8 minutes. Place in a greased bowl, turning once to grease top. Cover and let rise in a warm place until doubled, about 1 hour.

Punch dough down. Turn onto a lightly floured surface; divide into 18 pieces. Shape into ovals; place 2 in. apart on greased baking sheets. Cover and let rise until doubled, about 30 minutes.

Bake at 350° for 18-23 minutes or until golden. Melt remaining butter; brush over buns. Remove from pans to wire racks. When cool, split buns. Spread with mayonnaise or mustard if desired. Top with lettuce, tomato, ham and cheese. Replace tops. Place cream cheese in a resealable plastic bag; cut a small hole in the corner of the bag. Pipe laces on football sandwiches. **Yield:** 18 servings.

Goal-Line Chicken Salad

Serve this chunky salad on a bed of lettuce with a sliced tomato on top or mounded inside a ring of melon slices.

4-1/2 cups diced cooked chicken
1-1/2 cups diced apples
3/4 cup halved green grapes
6 tablespoons sweet pickle relish
6 tablespoons mayonnaise
6 tablespoons prepared ranch salad dressing
3/4 teaspoon onion salt
3/4 teaspoon garlic salt
Lettuce leaves

In a large bowl, combine the chicken, apples and grapes. In a small bowl, combine the pickle relish, mayonnaise, ranch dressing, onion salt and garlic salt. Pour over chicken mixture and toss to coat. Serve in a lettuce-lined bowl. **Yield:** 18 servings.

Pom-Pom Potato Salad

The potato salad scored big with home-town football fans. It would be great for a pre-game tailgate party.

3 pounds red potatoes, cooked and cubed
1 cup sweet pickle *or* zucchini relish
1/4 cup chopped celery
3/4 teaspoon onion salt
1/2 teaspoon garlic salt
1/2 teaspoon celery seed
1/2 teaspoon pepper
4 hard-cooked eggs
1 cup (8 ounces) sour cream
1/2 cup mayonnaise
1 tablespoon cider vinegar
1 teaspoon prepared mustard
Additional hard-cooked eggs, cut into wedges

In a large bowl, combine the first seven ingredients. Cut eggs in half and remove the yolks. Chop the whites; add to potato mixture. In another bowl, mash the yolks; stir in sour cream, mayonnaise, vinegar and mustard. Pour over potato mixture and gently toss to coat. Refrigerate until serving. Garnish with egg wedges. **Yield:** 18 servings.

Touchdown Cookies

Even the dessert for our pigskin party got in shape for the occasion! In fact, no one took a "pass" on the opportunity to munch one or two cookies.

1 cup butter (no substitutes), softened
1 cup sugar
2 eggs
1 teaspoon vanilla extract
3 cups all-purpose flour
2 teaspoons cream of tartar
1 teaspoon baking soda
GLAZE:
2 cups confectioners' sugar
4 to 5 tablespoons hot water
3 to 4 teaspoons baking cocoa

In a mixing bowl, cream the butter and sugar. Add eggs, one at a time, beating well after each. Beat in vanilla. Combine flour, cream of tartar and baking soda; gradually add to creamed mixture. Cover; refrigerate for 3 hours or until easy to handle.

On a lightly floured surface, roll out dough to 1/8-in. thickness. Cut with a football-shaped cookie cutter. Place 2 in. apart on ungreased baking sheets. Bake at 350° for 8-10 minutes or until lightly browned. Remove to wire racks to cool.

In a mixing bowl, combine confectioners' sugar and enough hot water to achieve spreading consistency; beat until smooth. Place 3 tablespoons glaze in a small bowl; set aside. Add cocoa to remaining glaze; stir until smooth. Spread brown glaze over cookies. Pipe white glaze onto cookies to form laces. **Yield:** 4-1/2 dozen.

Substitutions & Equivalents

Equivalent Measures

3 teaspoons	= 1 tablespoon		**16 tablespoons**	=	1 cup
4 tablespoons	= 1/4 cup		**2 cups**	=	1 pint
5-1/3 tablespoons	= 1/3 cup		**4 cups**	=	1 quart
8 tablespoons	= 1/2 cup		**4 quarts**	=	1 gallon

Food Equivalents

Grains

Macaroni	1 cup (3-1/2 ounces) uncooked	=	2-1/2 cups cooked
Noodles, Medium	3 cups (4 ounces) uncooked	=	4 cups cooked
Popcorn	1/3 to 1/2 cup unpopped	=	8 cups popped
Rice, Long Grain	1 cup uncooked	=	3 cups cooked
Rice, Quick-Cooking	1 cup uncooked	=	2 cups cooked
Spaghetti	8 ounces uncooked	=	4 cups cooked

Crumbs

Bread	1 slice	=	3/4 cup soft crumbs, 1/4 cup fine dry crumbs
Graham Crackers	7 squares	=	1/2 cup finely crushed
Buttery Round Crackers	12 crackers	=	1/2 cup finely crushed
Saltine Crackers	14 crackers	=	1/2 cup finely crushed

Fruits

Bananas	1 medium	=	1/3 cup mashed
Lemons	1 medium	=	3 tablespoons juice, 2 teaspoons grated peel
Limes	1 medium	=	2 tablespoons juice, 1-1/2 teaspoons grated peel
Oranges	1 medium	=	1/4 to 1/3 cup juice, 4 teaspoons grated peel

Vegetables

Cabbage	1 head	=	5 cups shredded	**Green Pepper**	1 large	=	1 cup chopped
Carrots	1 pound	=	3 cups shredded	**Mushrooms**	1/2 pound	=	3 cups sliced
Celery	1 rib	=	1/2 cup chopped	**Onions**	1 medium	=	1/2 cup chopped
Corn	1 ear fresh	=	2/3 cup kernels	**Potatoes**	3 medium	=	2 cups cubed

Nuts

Almonds	1 pound	=	3 cups chopped	**Pecan Halves**	1 pound	=	4-1/2 cups chopped
Ground Nuts	3-3/4 ounces	=	1 cup	**Walnuts**	1 pound	=	3-3/4 cups chopped

Easy Substitutions

When you need...		*Use...*
Baking Powder	1 teaspoon	1/2 teaspoon cream of tartar + 1/4 teaspoon baking soda
Buttermilk	1 cup	1 tablespoon lemon juice *or* vinegar + enough milk to measure 1 cup (let stand 5 minutes before using)
Cornstarch	1 tablespoon	2 tablespoons all-purpose flour
Honey	1 cup	1-1/4 cups sugar + 1/4 cup water
Half-and-Half Cream	1 cup	1 tablespoon melted butter + enough whole milk to measure 1 cup
Onion	1 small, chopped (1/3 cup)	1 teaspoon onion powder *or* 1 tablespoon dried minced onion
Tomato Juice	1 cup	1/2 cup tomato sauce + 1/2 cup water
Tomato Sauce	2 cups	3/4 cup tomato paste + 1 cup water
Unsweetened Chocolate	1 square (1 ounce)	3 tablespoons baking cocoa + 1 tablespoon shortening *or* oil
Whole Milk	1 cup	1/2 cup evaporated milk + 1/2 cup water

Cooking Terms

HERE'S a quick reference for some of the cooking terms used in *Taste of Home* recipes:

Baste—To moisten food with melted butter, pan drippings, marinades or other liquid to add more flavor and juiciness.

Beat—A rapid movement to combine ingredients using a fork, spoon, wire whisk or electric mixer.

Blend—To combine ingredients until *just* mixed.

Boil—To heat liquids until bubbles form that cannot be "stirred down". In the case of water, the temperature will reach 212°.

Bone—To remove all meat from the bone before cooking.

Cream—To beat ingredients together to a smooth consistency, usually in the case of butter and sugar for baking.

Dash—A small amount of seasoning, less than 1/8 teaspoon. If using a shaker, a dash would comprise a quick flip of the container.

Dredge—To coat foods with flour or other dry ingredients. Most often done with pot roasts and stew meat before browning.

Fold—To incorporate several ingredients by careful and gentle turning with a spatula. Used generally with beaten egg whites or whipped cream when mixing into the rest of the ingredients to keep the batter light.

Julienne—To cut foods into long thin strips much like matchsticks. Used most often for salads and stir-fry dishes.

Mince—To cut into very fine pieces. Used often for garlic or fresh herbs.

Parboil—To cook partially, usually used in the case of chicken, sausages and vegetables.

Partially set—Describes the consistency of gelatin after it has been chilled for a small amount of time. Mixture should resemble the consistency of egg whites.

Puree—To process foods to a smooth mixture. Can be prepared in an electric blender, food processor, food mill or sieve.

Saute—To fry quickly in a small amount of fat, stirring almost constantly. Most often done with onions, mushrooms and other chopped vegetables.

Score—To cut slits partway through the outer surface of foods. Often used with ham or flank steak.

Stir-Fry—To cook meats and/or vegetables with a constant stirring motion in a small amount of oil in a wok or skillet over high heat.

Guide to Cooking with Popular Herbs

HERB	APPETIZERS SALADS	BREADS/EGGS SAUCES/CHEESE	VEGETABLES PASTA	MEAT POULTRY	FISH SHELLFISH
BASIL	Green, Potato & Tomato Salads, Salad Dressings, Stewed Fruit	Breads, Fondue & Egg Dishes, Dips, Marinades, Sauces	Mushrooms, Tomatoes, Squash, Pasta, Bland Vegetables	Broiled, Roast Meat & Poultry Pies, Stews, Stuffing	Baked, Broiled & Poached Fish, Shellfish
BAY LEAF	Seafood Cocktail, Seafood Salad, Tomato Aspic, Stewed Fruit	Egg Dishes, Gravies, Marinades, Sauces	Dried Bean Dishes, Beets, Carrots, Onions, Potatoes, Rice, Squash	Corned Beef, Tongue Meat & Poultry Stews	Poached Fish, Shellfish, Fish Stews
CHIVES	Mixed Vegetable, Green, Potato & Tomato Salads, Salad Dressings	Egg & Cheese Dishes, Cream Cheese, Cottage Cheese, Gravies, Sauces	Hot Vegetables, Potatoes	Broiled Poultry, Poultry & Meat Pies, Stews, Casseroles	Baked Fish, Fish Casseroles, Fish Stews, Shellfish
DILL	Seafood Cocktail, Green, Potato & Tomato Salads, Salad Dressings	Breads, Egg & Cheese Dishes, Cream Cheese, Fish & Meat Sauces	Beans, Beets, Cabbage, Carrots, Cauliflower, Peas, Squash, Tomatoes	Beef, Veal Roasts, Lamb, Steaks, Chops, Stews, Roast & Creamed Poultry	Baked, Broiled, Poached & Stuffed Fish, Shellfish
GARLIC	All Salads, Salad Dressings	Fondue, Poultry Sauces, Fish & Meat Marinades	Beans, Eggplant, Potatoes, Rice, Tomatoes	Roast Meats, Meat & Poultry Pies, Hamburgers, Casseroles, Stews	Broiled Fish, Shellfish, Fish Stews, Casseroles
MARJORAM	Seafood Cocktail, Green, Poultry & Seafood Salads	Breads, Cheese Spreads, Egg & Cheese Dishes, Gravies, Sauces	Carrots, Eggplant, Peas, Onions, Potatoes, Dried Bean Dishes, Spinach	Roast Meats & Poultry, Meat & Poultry Pies, Stews & Casseroles	Baked, Broiled & Stuffed Fish, Shellfish
MUSTARD	Fresh Green Salads, Prepared Meat, Macaroni & Potato Salads, Salad Dressings	Biscuits, Egg & Cheese Dishes, Sauces	Baked Beans, Cabbage, Eggplant, Squash, Dried Beans, Mushrooms, Pasta	Chops, Steaks, Ham, Pork, Poultry, Cold Meats	Shellfish
OREGANO	Green, Poultry & Seafood Salads	Breads, Egg & Cheese Dishes, Meat, Poultry & Vegetable Sauces	Artichokes, Cabbage, Eggplant, Squash, Dried Beans, Mushrooms, Pasta	Broiled, Roast Meats, Meat & Poultry Pies, Stews, Casseroles	Baked, Broiled & Poached Fish, Shellfish
PARSLEY	Green, Potato, Seafood & Vegetable Salads	Biscuits, Breads, Egg & Cheese Dishes, Gravies, Sauces	Asparagus, Beets, Eggplant, Squash, Dried Beans, Mushrooms, Pasta	Meat Loaf, Meat & Poultry Pies, Stews & Casseroles, Stuffing	Fish Stews, Stuffed Fish
ROSEMARY	Fruit Cocktail, Fruit & Green Salads	Biscuits, Egg Dishes, Herb Butter, Cream Cheese, Marinades, Sauces	Beans, Broccoli, Peas, Cauliflower, Mushrooms, Baked Potatoes, Parsnips	Roast Meat, Poultry & Meat Pies, Stews & Casseroles, Stuffing	Stuffed Fish, Shellfish
SAGE		Breads, Fondue, Egg & Cheese Dishes, Spreads, Gravies, Sauces	Beans, Beets, Onions, Peas, Spinach, Squash, Tomatoes	Roast Meat, Poultry, Meat Loaf, Stews, Stuffing	Baked, Poached & Stuffed Fish
TARRAGON	Seafood Cocktail, Avocado Salads, Salad Dressings	Cheese Spreads, Marinades, Sauces, Egg Dishes	Asparagus, Beans, Beets, Carrots, Mushrooms, Peas, Squash, Spinach	Steaks, Poultry, Roast Meats, Casseroles & Stews	Baked, Broiled & Poached Fish, Shellfish
THYME	Seafood Cocktail, Green, Poultry, Seafood & Vegetable Salads	Biscuits, Breads, Egg & Cheese Dishes, Sauces, Spreads	Beets, Carrots, Mushrooms, Onions, Peas, Eggplant, Spinach, Potatoes	Roast Meat, Poultry & Meat Loaf, Meat & Poultry Pies, Stews & Casseroles	Baked, Broiled & Stuffed Fish, Shellfish, Fish Stews

General Recipe Index

This handy index lists every recipe by food category, major ingredient and/or cooking method, so you can easily locate recipes to suit your needs.

✓ Recipe includes Nutritional Analysis and Diabetic Exchanges

✓ *Recipe includes Nutritional Analysis and Diabetic Exchanges*

✓ Recipe includes Nutritional Analysis and Diabetic Exchanges

✓ Recipe includes Nutritional Analysis and Diabetic Exchanges

✓ Recipe includes Nutritional Analysis and Diabetic Exchanges

✓ Recipe includes Nutritional Analysis and Diabetic Exchanges

✓ Recipe includes Nutritional Analysis and Diabetic Exchanges

✓ Recipe includes Nutritional Analysis and Diabetic Exchanges

✓ Recipe includes Nutritional Analysis and Diabetic Exchanges

Alphabetical Recipe Index

This handy index lists every recipe in alphabetical order so you can easily find your favorite recipes.

A

B

C

✓ Recipe includes Nutritional Analysis and Diabetic Exchanges

D

E

F

G

H

I

K

✓ Recipe includes Nutritional Analysis and Diabetic Exchanges

L

M

N

O

P

Q

R

✓ Recipe includes Nutritional Analysis and Diabetic Exchanges

S

T

U

V

W

Y

Z

✓ Recipe includes Nutritional Analysis and Diabetic Exchanges